ROUTLEDGE LIBRARY EDITIONS: SOUTH AFRICA

Volume 8

WHY SOUTH AFRICA WILL SURVIVE

WHY SOUTH AFRICA WILL SURVIVE

A Historical Analysis

L. H. GANN and PETER DUIGNAN

LONDON AND NEW YORK

First published in 1981 by Croom Helm Ltd.

This edition first published in 2023
by Routledge
4 Park Square, Milton Park, Abingdon, Oxon OX14 4RN

and by Routledge
605 Third Avenue, New York, NY 10158

Routledge is an imprint of the Taylor & Francis Group, an informa business

© 1981 L. H. Gann and Peter Duignan

All rights reserved. No part of this book may be reprinted or reproduced or utilised in any form or by any electronic, mechanical, or other means, now known or hereafter invented, including photocopying and recording, or in any information storage or retrieval system, without permission in writing from the publishers.

Trademark notice: Product or corporate names may be trademarks or registered trademarks, and are used only for identification and explanation without intent to infringe.

British Library Cataloguing in Publication Data
A catalogue record for this book is available from the British Library

ISBN: 978-1-032-30347-5 (Set)
ISBN: 978-1-032-31494-5 (Volume 8) (hbk)
ISBN: 978-1-032-31501-0 (Volume 8) (pbk)
ISBN: 978-1-003-31005-1 (Volume 8) (ebk)

DOI: 10.4324/9781003310051

Publisher's Note
The publisher has gone to great lengths to ensure the quality of this reprint but points out that some imperfections in the original copies may be apparent.

Disclaimer
The publisher has made every effort to trace copyright holders and would welcome correspondence from those they have been unable to trace.

This is a reissue of a previously published book. The language is reflective of the time in which this book was published. In reissuing this book, no offence is intended by the Publishers to any reader.

Why South Africa Will Survive
A HISTORICAL ANALYSIS

L.H. GANN AND PETER DUIGNAN

CROOM HELM LONDON

© 1981 L.H. Gann and Peter Duignan
Croom Helm Ltd, 2-10 St John's Road, London SW11

British Library Cataloguing in Publication Data

Gann, Lewis Henry
   Why South Africa will survive.
   1. South Africa — History
   I. Title
   II. Duignan, Peter
   968   DT766
   ISBN 0−7099−0223−9

Typeset by Leaper & Gard Ltd, Bristol
Printed and bound in Great Britain by
Redwood Burn Limited Trowbridge & Esher

CONTENTS

List of Tables
List of Figures
Preface
Map of Southern Africa

Part One: The Peoples of South Africa
Introduction   1
1. The Whites   5
2. The Brown Peoples   33
3. The Africans   44

Part Two: South Africa Yesterday and Today
4. The Politics of South Africa   95
5. The Economics of South Africa   142
6. South Africa: Strategic and Defence Potential   187
7. South Africa: a Revolutionary Situation?   219

Part Three: South Africa and the World
8. South Africa and the West   245
9. The West, the Soviet Union, and South Africa   269
10. Why South Africa will Survive   288

Index   307

LIST OF TABLES

1	Population of South Africa, by Race	2
2	Rate of Natural Increase, 1970	2
3	Projected Population, 1980-2000	3
4	Urban Population, 1904-70	4
1.1	Comparative Output of Some Major South African Industries, 1915-77	18
1.2	Percentage of the Total Vote by Monthly Income Group, 1969	21
1.3	Projected Growth Rate, South Africa, 1975-2005	24
1.4	South Africa: Economically Active Population, 1960 and 1970	30
1.5	South Africa: Estimated Income by Racial Group in Percentages, 1968-77	31
3.1	Size of the Homeland Areas, 1972	62
3.2	African Population Settled in the 'White' and Homeland Areas, 1972	64
3.3	African Urban Population in South Africa, 1970	67
3.4	Population Density of the Homelands, 1972	67
3.5	Investments by the Bantu Investment Corporation and the Xhosa Development Corporation, and by Private Capital, 1971-4	72
3.6	Gross National Income and *per capita* Gross National Income of Transkei	73
3.7	Age and Sex Distribution, Soweto, 1970	86
3.8	Occupations in Soweto, 1968	86
3.9	Major Foci of Discontent among Urban Africans in Durban	88
3.10	People 'Feared and Disliked Most'	88
3.11	Strength of Discontent with Present Conditions	89
4.1	Employment in the Public and Private Sectors, 1974, and Cumulative Growth Rates, 1960-74	101
4.2	Estimated Control of Selected Sectors of the Economy by Afrikaners, 1939 and 1964	109
4.3	Whites' Party Preference according to Language, 1975	109
4.4	South African General Elections, 1910-77	111
4.5	Priorities in the Demands of African Townsmen	132

List of Tables

5.1	Gross Domestic Product by Kind of Economic Activity at Factor Cost, 1911-77	153
5.2	Financing of Gross Domestic Investment, 1946-75	161
5.3	South African Gross Domestic Product, 1965-77	164
5.4	Approximate Work Time Required for Average Manufacturing Employees to Buy Selected Commodities in Retail Stores in Washington, DC and London, at State-fixed Prices in Moscow and Johannesburg during May 1976	166
5.5	Per capita Gross Domestic Product at Market Prices, for Selected Countries; 1974, in US Dollars	168
5.6	Gross Domestic Fixed Investment by Type of Organisation, 1950-76	173
5.7	Population Projections 1970-2000 Broken Down into Population Groups and Regions	176
5.8	Production of and Demand for Minerals, 1974-2000	178
5.9	Availability of and Demand for Water in South Africa: Projections for the Period 1974-2000	181
5.10	Projection of Total Private Consumption Expenditure for Various Racial Groups, 1970-2000	182
5.11	Imports and Exports to and from Major Trading Partners 1969-76	183
5.12	Foreign Investment in South Africa Distinguished by Region	184
6.1	Ships Passing the Cape of Good Hope in One Month (February 1974)	188
6.2	Estimated Demand for Middle Eastern Oil	190
6.3	The Trade of South Africa's Ports, 1977-8	191
6.4	Mineral Potential of the Republic of South Africa	192-3
6.5	Combined South African and USSR Percentages of World's Reserves of Selected Mineral Commodities	195
6.6	South African Navy and Air Force, 1978	203
6.7	South African Defence Expenditures, 1975-8	207
6.8	Deliveries of Weapons Systems Known to be in Service with the South African Defence Forces (by the end of 1976)	209
6.9	Arms Inventory: South African Defence Forces (by the end of 1976)	210
8.1	Total Foreign Liabilities in South Africa, 1975	249
8.2	Exports and Imports to and from Major Trade Partners, 1975	249
8.3	American-South African Trade in the US Context, 1977	250

LIST OF FIGURES

3.1	White Settlement in Southern Africa	49
3.2	Black Settlement in Southern Africa	52
3.3	Black Areas in 1913	61
3.4	Land Claims by the Homelands	75
6.1	Main Oil Movements by Sea, 1973	190
6.2	The Naval Balance, United States-USSR, 1977	200

PREFACE

South Africa is one of the most unpopular countries on the face of the globe; its critics disagree widely among themselves, but they do share certain assumptions. South Africa supposedly is governed by a ruthless white oligarchy that oppresses the blacks; the mass of the people are getting poorer, if not in absolute terms, then at least in comparison with the privileged whites. But the day of reckoning is at hand. Critics claim: the winds of change are irresistible; the tide of revolution cannot be stopped. America and the Western world as a whole should therefore take a tough line against the white minority regime in power at Pretoria — both in the interest of America's legitimate national concerns and of humanity at large.

We disagree with many of these assumptions. We are impressed by the extraordinary social and economic changes that have come over South Africa during the last generation, and by the extent of the progress made in a great variety of spheres. We do not believe that a South African revolution will come during our lifetime; we are convinced that change will rather come from within the ruling white oligarchy rather than by liberation movements. We believe therefore that American support should go to the *verligtes*, the reformers, within the ruling National Party; our slogan is: all power to the moderates!

The present study is a greatly expanded version of a brief policy study, *South Africa: War, Revolution, or Peace?*, which we published in 1978. This book attempts to set South Africa's predicament in a wider setting, and examines the country from the historical, political, economic and strategic standpoint. We are aware that our views concerning South Africa are unpopular within the academic establishment, but we are convinced that an interpretation different from the current 'gloom, guilt and doom' school deserves to be heard.

We should like to express our thanks to Professors Thomas Karis, Edwin S. Munger, Leo Kuper and Paul Seabury, and to John Chettle and Pine Pinaar of the South African Foundation for reading the manuscript. Our appreciation also to the many South African politicians, government and military officials, academics and citizens who talked to us or read portions of this manuscript. Their willingness to give us the benefit of their criticism does not, of course, imply approval of our views.

L.H. Gann
Peter Duignan

Southern Africa

PART ONE:

THE PEOPLES OF SOUTH AFRICA

INTRODUCTION

South Africa is a land of contrasts. The country covers 472,359 square miles, about three times the size of California and five times the size of Great Britain. A traveller going by road from Cape Town to Johannesburg covers 900 miles; if he motors from Cape Town to Durban in the north-east, his route will have exceeded 1,000 miles, the distance from London to Leningrad. South Africa's geographical diversity is as stunning as its size. South Africa has Mediterranean coastland, snow-covered mountains, parkland, forests, steppes and desert — almost every kind of vegetational zone except arctic tundra or tropical rain forest. The peoples of South Africa are equally varied. South Africa is a complex mosaic of differing races and ethnic groups, the world in microcosm. The country's inhabitants include whites, Africans (blacks), Bushmen (San), Asians and Coloureds (people of mixed parentage). The white men's ancestors mostly came from Europe; the Bantu-speaking peoples had their remote origins in the central and north-central parts of Africa; the Asians are of Malay, Indian and Pakistani descent. The earliest aboriginal population is composed of the San, Stone Age hunters who now form but a tiny fragment of the population, and the Khoikhoi (Hottentots), a herding people now largely absorbed into the Coloured people. Each of these four major population groups consists of several different components, whose members often differ considerably from one another.

For all these contrasts, South Africa's population groups have certain demographic features in common. All have benefited from a striking rate of natural increase during the course of the present century (see Table 1). South Africans have continued to increase since 1900. The proportion of whites will decrease somewhat, as the white birth rate has diminished. Africans will improve their numerical position over the remaining population, as African mortality figures have declined and African health has improved (Table 2). South Africa will continue as a multiracial country with a relatively youthful population, a high proportion of which will be of working age (see Table 3).

South Africans today are the most urbanised people in sub-Saharan Africa, though the proportion of townsmen to countrymen differs sharply among the various ethnic segments. Urbanisation is linked to rapid industrialisation. South Africa was the first country on the African

2 Introduction

Table 1: Population of South Africa, by Race

Year	Total	Whites	Blacks	Asiatics	Coloureds
1904	5,174,827	1,117,234	3,490,291	122,311	444,991
1921	6,927,403	1,521,343	4,697,285	163,594	545,181
1936	9,587,863	2,003,334	6,595,597	219,691	769,241
1946	11,415,925	2,372,044	7,830,559	285,260	928,062
1951	12,671,452	2,641,689	8,560,083	366,664	1,103,016
1960	15,902,664	3,008,492	10,907,789	477,125	1,509,258
1970	21,447,230	3,750,716	15,057,559	620,422	2,018,533
1974 (est.)	24,936,000	4,158,000	17,761,000	710,000	2,307,800
1978 (est.)[a]	23,894,000	4,408,000	16,214,000	778,000	2,494,000

Note: a. All statistical material for the earlier history of Africa is subject to inaccuracies. The 1978 figure excludes the population of the Transkei and Bophuthatswana. If these were to be added, the population would amount to 27,400,000.

Source: *Economic, Financial, and Statistical Yearbooks for South Africa* (Da Gama, Johannesburg, various years).

Table 2: Rate of Natural Increase, 1970 (rate per thousand)

Rate	1910	1970
Whites	21.7	14.4
Coloureds	23.2	21.4
Asians	–	25.9
Africans (est.)	–	29.0

Source: *South Africa 1974: Official Yearbook of the Republic of South Africa* (Johannesburg, 1974), p. 71.

continent to experience the Industrial Revolution. The value of South Africa's manufactures is greater than that of all other African countries combined. The Pretoria-Witwatersrand-Vereeniging complex, strategically and economically the heartland of modern South Africa, accounts for about half of the country's industrial output. Set in the southern Transvaal, this small region alone has a manufacturing output more than three times that of Egypt and four times that of Algeria. Qualitatively,

Table 3: Projected Population, 1980-2000 (figures in brackets indicate those economically active)

	1980	1990	2000
Aggregate	29,044,000 (11,327,000)	38,464,000 (15,000,000)	50,288,000 (19,612,320)
Whites	4,767,000 (1,857,200)	5,798,000 (2,261,200)	6,890,000 (2,687,100)
Blacks	20,639,000 (8,049,200)	27,892,000 (10,877,900)	37,293,000 (14,544,270)
Asians	825,000 (321,700)	1,018,000 (397,000)	1,215,000 (473,850)
Coloureds	2,818,000 (1,099,000)	3,756,000 (1,464,800)	4,890,000 (1,907,100)

Source: Figures from J.L. Sadie, cited in W.J. de Villiers, *The Effective Utilisation of Human Resources in the Republic of South Africa* (General Mining and Finance Corporation, Johannesburg, 1974), p. 7.

South Africa's industrial preponderance is equally marked. Within its borders are a variety of backward, black, rural economies alongside a highly industrialised Western economy, the only one in Africa capable of simultaneously turning out merchant ships, sophisticated mining equipment, computers and rockets.

Whites, followed by Coloureds and Asians, have always been the most urbanised people in South Africa. The Africans traditionally lived in their villages or on homesteads scattered throughout the countryside. The proportion of black city folk, however, is increasing rapidly and, taken as a whole, the South African blacks are the most citified African people on the entire continent (see Table 4). Perhaps as many as 9 million blacks now are urbanised or in the modern sector of the economy. With urbanisation has come an increase in wealth, and the spread of new ideas and skills. Urbanisation has also helped to create new social and psychological tensions. South African city-dwellers have a fairly high suicide rate. The incidence of homicide is even higher than that in the USA.[1] Crime, drunkenness and prostitution have all increased greatly as blacks moved from village to town.

Despite the severity of its racial and social problems in the 1960s and early 1970s, South Africa continued to attract a considerable number of immigrants during a time of economic prosperity. Some

4 Introduction

Table 4: Urban Population, 1904-70 (per cent)

Year	Whites	Coloureds	Asians	Africans
1904	53.6	49.2	35.5	10.4
1921	59.7	52.4	60.4	14.0
1936	68.2	58.0	69.5	19.0
1951	79.1	66.2	77.6	27.9
1970	86.7	74.3	86.2	33.6

Source: *South Africa, 1976*, p. 36.

410,512 immigrants, mainly from Western Europe, entered the country between 1960 and 1971, while 118,577 left South Africa. But during the first nine months of 1977 21,026 whites left the country, and new white immigration dropped by half.

This outflow was paralleled by the falling off of new foreign investment — partly as a consequence of an economic slump, partly by reason of investors' fears concerning the country's future. To a minor extent, emigration and 'disinvestment' acted as a political sieve; the most liberal whites (usually drawn from the English-speaking professional upper middle class) were most apt to look for new homes abroad. But the country's white demographic structure as a whole was little altered.

Despite its reputation, South Africa is a country also desirable for black newcomers. Even more blacks than whites have, in Lenin's phrase, 'voted with their feet' to come to South Africa. The total number of blacks born outside South Africa's borders, but now working within the country either as annual labour migrants or as permanent residents with a legal or non-legal status, amounts to well over 0.5 million.

Note

1. According to Fatima Meer, *Race and Suicide in South Africa* (Routledge and Kegan Paul, London, 1976), pp. 233-4, the mean suicide rate for Africans in Durban during the period 1962-71 was 17.3 per 100,000 for Africans and 15.4 for Europeans. This is compared with the following figures during the same period: Denmark, Austria and Sweden — over 20; West Germany — between 15 and 20; the United Kingdom and the USA — between 10 and 12.

1 THE WHITES

Historical Background

South Africa is a country obsessed with its past. No account of that land can be complete without at least a brief sketch of its ethnic origins. The fate of white people, black and brown has been inextricably interwoven. Yet each of these people has retained a separate sense of identity, a sense so strong that there is still no satisfactory national history of South Africa, no account that does equal justice to all segments of its population. At the risk of repetition, we shall therefore try to outline the roots of each major ethnic community.

The first Europeans to settle permanently in South Africa came from Holland. Dutch settlements at the Cape began in 1652, and coincided roughly with the European colonisation of New England. When the Dutch first dropped anchor at the Cape, they merely wanted a stronghold where their ships might refit and obtain food and water on the long trip to the Indies. But the original market garden unintentionally turned into a colony. The settlers began to move inland, and white society gradually split into a number of distinct components. Cape Town grew into a substantial port that provided the inland farmers with a market, an urban community that looked towards both the Atlantic and the Indian oceans. The Cape settlements drew their supplies of grain from European farms in the western Cape, substantial estates, worked by Coloured or 'half-caste' (Eurafrican) labour. The wealthier European farmers built substantial homes for themselves, with whitewashed walls, great verandas and fine portals, simply furnished, but impressive in their dignity.

The sedentary society of the western Cape — linked to Holland by ties of culture, religion and descent — contrasted sharply with the pastoral society of the interior. As the colonists pushed deeper inland, they took to pastoral rather than arable farming. Subdivision of land, accompanied by more intensive cultivation, was not a feasible proposition as long as labour and capital were scarce, markets inadequate, and only land was plentiful. Afrikaans-speaking herdsmen kept trekking in order to avoid competing with their neighbours for pastures and wells. Trekking got rid of boundary quarrels; it also provided opportunities for the poor, who could not afford to buy extensive farmland.

5

6 The Whites

The frontiersmen's methods of cultivation, moreover, were apt to exhaust the soil. 'The veld got tired,' and the trekkers moved on.

The *trekboer* has become a mythological subject. To Afrikaner nationalists, the frontiersman represented all that was noble. The Boers (farmers) of the frontier were the first people in Africa to call themselves 'Africans'. These trekkers supposedly shaped the modern Afrikaner nation, endowing South Africans of a subsequent vintage with the pioneer spirit of independence. British imperialists, on the other hand, commonly looked upon the trekker as a barbarous fellow, offensive to God and man by reason of the Afrikaner's supposed lack of economic enterprise, his assumed hostility to Africans, his reluctance to accept the suzerainty of the British Crown, and his unwillingness to recognise English gentlemen as his social superiors. Many liberal scholars of a more recent vintage took over these stereotypes. According to their mythology, the Afrikaners were a backward, reactionary people, addicted to a peculiarly primitive and bigoted form of Calvinism. The Afrikaners, supposedly, were more racially prejudiced than all other whites, were particularly litigious in the Dutch tradition, and were descended from the lowest class of Dutch emigrants, the kind of people unable to succeed at home. The *trekboer*, the frontier farmer, the most isolated and poverty-stricken of the Afrikaners, was considered to be the prototype of all.[1] According to popular history books written in the liberal vein, the Boer was an eternal anachronism who wandered from one century to the next, with his rifle in one hand and the Bible in the other, a man perpetually behind the times, forever cut off from the progress of humanity.[2]

The realities were nothing like as melodramatic. The *trekboer* was neither a backwoods patriarch, innocent of economic incentives, nor a bloody-minded oppressor. He was shaped by the harsh environment of the frontier. The *trekboer* first supplied the Cape markets with cattle and hides; later the economic centre of gravity shifted more towards new ports that were being opened on the east coast. By this time the trekkers belonged to a new nation, no longer Dutch, speaking a new language — Afrikaans ('African'), a Dutch derivative with great literary potential. The *trekboer* became one of the world's greatest wilderness specialists. He knew how to handle a span of oxen in rough country. He became knowledgeable as a soil prospector, wise in finding the best farming land in the wilderness. He turned into a crack shot and an expert hunter. The wild interior held no terrors for him, as he developed a most effective system of military tactics. The Boer's wagon came to serve both as a mode of transport and as a means of forming mobile pivots in battle. Boer military skill defeated the Khoikhoi and the San.

Later, the Afrikaners met far more warlike opponents, dark-brown or black-skinned people who spoke tongues belonging to the Bantu group of languages, and who were familiar with the use of iron. (The so-called 'Kaffirs' were first encountered in 1704 near what is now Somerset East.) The Bantu were technologically much superior to most of the Indian peoples whom white settlers met on the American frontier. Bantu-speaking people had developed their own systems of arable and pastoral farming which were as extensive as those of the Boers, requiring ever new expanses of woodland and pasture for their sustenance. Not surprisingly, Boers and Africans fought over the land. The blacks fought hard, but the Afrikaners won; they were less numerous, but better armed, mounted and organised than their opponents. The African economies depended solely on the power of human muscles, on rudimentary tools like the hoe, and on simple weapons like shields and spears.

The settlers' relations with their African neighbours were double-edged. The frontiersmen fought bitter battles against the black peoples. But lack of numbers and resources also forced the white pioneers into political — and sometimes even into martial and marital — alliances with African chiefs. The early pioneers might own imported slaves. By and large, however, their herding economy did not require as many servile labourers as were needed in the plantations of the New World. Hence slavery never became an irremovable feature of frontier culture. The Africans proved to be a flexible, adaptive people. Unlike the Indian tribes on the North American and Argentinian frontiers, the Bantu-speaking communities of South Africa were not destroyed.

In addition to war, the frontier witnessed a good deal of trade and other forms of amicable intercourse between black and white. The forms of economic interchange varied. As long as the white man could be kept at arm's length, the various African peoples were satisfied to farm, to engage in commerce with whites, and occasionally even to work for wages in European employment. European contacts were ambiguous in their effects. The colonists created new markets for African cattle and corn. Missionaries began to set up schools. Many African chiefs looked to Europeans for alliances against their local opponents. On the other hand, the whites and blacks competed for arable land, pastures and water in a contest that Europeans were bound to win in the long run.

But the main menace to the settler's existence came not so much from the black man's lance and knobkerrie, but from hunger, thirst and disease, from locusts and cattle sickness, from drought and crop failure, from the very forces of nature that threatened white and black alike in the interior. The frontiersman was shaped by hardship. He was not necessarily a Negrophobe. He was not always ill educated. Indeed, the pioneers placed considerable value on having their children instructed in the Prayer Book and scriptures. They were Bible-reading Calvinists, but South African Calvinism was not excessively intolerant by the standards of small-scale rural communities of the time. The Dutch Reformed Church, moreover, did not originally believe in the racial segregation of whites and non-whites as a matter of religious conviction.[3] The original Dutch Calvinism at the Cape was affected by a variety of theological currents, liberalism in the eighteenth century, pietism and an intense form of evangelicalism in the beginning of the nineteenth century; hence there is nothing to be said in favour of the stereotype according to which the Afrikaners absorbed their racial attitudes at least in part from the undeviating Calvinist orthodoxy professed by their seventeenth- and eighteenth-century ancestors.

By the beginning of the nineteenth century, the white population at the Cape contained about 27,000 men, women and children. Of these, some 6,000 lived in Cape Town, the main city, so that, by contemporary standards, white South Africans were already a relatively urbanised people. This population was further reinforced by immigrants from Great Britain. During the long wars against the armies of the French Revolution and Napoleon, the British seized the strategically vital Cape of Good Hope (permanently, as from 1806). British settlers found homes for themselves on the eastern Cape. Some of them became farmers; others turned frontiersmen like the Afrikaners. The majority, however, became townsmen, so that British influence became dominant in trade and finance. The British also held political power, and tried to reshape Cape society in the British image. In 1833 slavery was outlawed, part of a wider movement to extirpate slavery throughout the British Empire. Guided by missionary and humanitarian influences, they made some attempts to improve the civic condition of 'Hottentots'. Forced labour was abandoned, and the former slaves gradually merged into a wage-earning proletariat. The British also attempted to 'Anglify' the Cape Dutch population — all to no avail.

In order to strengthen their hold on the north-eastern border of the Cape, the British in 1820 induced some 5,000 settlers from Great Britain to settle on the threatened frontier. Many of the newcomers were not suited to farming under African frontier conditions. They came from cities like London and Edinburgh. Others had been brought up in partly industrialised counties such as Middlesex and Lancashire. These pioneers were not paupers. Even a short perusal of the emigrants' list shows that the newcomers included a large number of well educated people — schoolmasters, surgeons, ministers of religion and master mariners. Blacksmiths, wheelwrights, carpenters and such were also among the colonists. There were market gardeners and farmers. These pioneers encountered harsh conditions in a harsh country. As Kipling later wrote in 'South Africa':

> Half her land was dead with drought,
> Half was red with battle;
> She was fenced with fire and sword,
> Plague on pestilence outpoured,
> Locusts on the greening sward
> And murrain on the cattle.

The newcomers' difficulties often exceeded those of the old-timers. Englishmen who had done well on a holding, say, in Devon, with its lush meadows and manicured countryside, were not necessarily suited to making a living on the Cape or in Natal, where much of their previous experience at times was worse than useless. Some colonists stuck it out on the land, and acquired much in common with their Boer neighbours. Many more made their way to the towns, where they provided considerable stimulus to economic development, and where they — and subsequent immigrants — helped to give a curiously English imprint to much of South Africa's urban life. English-speaking South Africans also developed an accent of their own, a blend of Afrikaans, Scottish and Cockney sounds, as distinctive as the speech of Australia.

The Afrikaners did not necessarily dislike their new neighbours. Many accommodated themselves to British rule. But the more uncompromising elements decided to get rid of British influence, with its real or supposed snobberies, its foreign ways, its missionary and 'negrophilist' notions, by trekking to the interior. 'We complain', wrote Piet Retief, one of the most prominent trek leaders, in words that were to echo again in later years from Cape Town to Salisbury,

> of the unjustified odium that has been cast upon us by interested and dishonest persons under the name of religion, whose testimony is believed in England to the exclusion of all evidence in our favour,

and we can foresee as the result of their prejudice nothing but the total ruin of our country.⁴

The so-called Great Trek has been evaluated in many different ways. Some historians explain it as the frontiersmen's declaration of independence. But not all Afrikaners trekked. (Only about 6,000 people, about one-fifth of the white population of the eastern Cape, participated in the movement.) Most slave-owners stayed at home, whereas a good many ex-slaves took part in the trek.

Afrikaners regard the Great Trek as a milestone in the building of Afrikaner national consciousness. But there is evidence that Afrikaans at the time was still regarded overwhelmingly as a class badge, the idiom of the uneducated, rather than as a symbol of national distinctiveness. Cultivated Afrikaners during the period preferred to speak and write in Dutch. Many of the first South Africans to use Afrikaans as a written language were not of Afrikaner parentage, including the Frenchman C.E. Boniface, the Scot A.G. Bain and L.H. Meurant. Modern Afrikaner nationalism is of more recent vintage; it derives from the 1860s and the 1870s; its progress was marked above all by the creation of national-minded bodies such as the Genootskap van Regte Afrikaners (1877). The Great Trek can therefore best be interpreted as a local solution for local frontier problems.

Its impact, none the less, was far-reaching. By the end of 1837, some 6,000 men, women and children had crossed the northern boundary of the Cape Colony. Trek wagons rolled further and further inland. The trekkers fought bitter wars against the Bantu-speaking people of the interior; they suffered great hardships. In the end they founded two independent states, the Orange Free State and the Transvaal, where Afrikaans-speaking farmers held sway over the indigenous peoples.

As the Afrikaners conquered more land, their racial attitudes seem to have hardened, threatened as they felt themselves by the fury of their enemies and the immensity and the natural perils of the new-won land. During the first two centuries of Dutch settlement at the Cape, the church had insisted on common church membership and common worship for whites and blacks alike. Many Coloureds, some of them 'respectable' craftsmen of good social standing, became converts to the church. Cultural assimilation, however, was not an easy matter. Towards the end of the eighteenth century, the clerical authorities began to hold separate weekday services in simplified language to enable Coloureds to follow the ordinary Sunday service held in High Dutch. Afrikaner congregations widely resisted the principle of common church services. The church generally withstood all attempts of frontier congregations to segregate white and non-white members. In 1859 the church at last gave way to popular pressure. The new policy was based on the assumption that the church could not afford to alienate too many white church members. Separation, moreover, would benefit the Coloureds, who would feel more comfortable in their own congregation and who would have a better chance of participating in church government.

Separation was also encouraged by the missionary strategy of Andrew Murray and other clergymen recruited in Scotland and Holland, who considered that separate congregations would facilitate the work of evangelisation. Clerical separation also found defenders among influential scholars like Gustav Warneck, a nineteenth-century theologian strongly influenced by German romantic thought. Warneck taught that the Gospel should be proclaimed, not to mankind in the abstract, but to particular nations who should practise Christianity in ways appropriate to their own particular cultures and build up independent *Volkskirchen*. The ecclesiastical picture was further complicated by the rigid neo-Calvinism of Abraham Kuyper, a Dutch theologian whose adherents in late-nineteenth-century South Africa set up their own organisation, the Gereformeerde Kerk, whose rigid Calvinism came to be widely, though mistakenly, attributed to the Dutch Reformed Church as a whole.

But whatever the clergymen's theories, the gulf between whites and Coloureds became wider. The liberal and 'enlightened' Calvinism that had held sway in Holland during the eighteenth century disappeared. Many of the newcomers from Europe brought to their land of adoption a harsher and more uncompromising form of orthodoxy, populist and inclined to political action. This orthodoxy was later mistakenly attributed to frontier provenance. The frontiersmen's religion, moreover, seemed to make them even more outlandish to many British Anglicans and sceptics, to men and women commonly contemptuous of their own Nonconformist sects at home, with their real or supposed lower-middle-class affiliation.

Politically, the new farmer republics were not left to their own devices for long. In 1867 diamonds were discovered near the Orange River. Prospectors of many nationalities, most of them English-speaking, came to the Cape. Kimberley became a tough frontier town attracting newcomers, white and black, from many parts of the world to work the wealth in gems.

Economically, the new discoveries meant that for the first time in

South African history a substantial amount of capital flowed into a region hitherto dependent on a few agricultural exports like merino wool and hides. The precious stones were first secured by small entrepreneurs practising open quarrying, but the old methods soon became inadequate. Control over the industry passed into the hands of a few large companies who worked the mines with modern methods, companies headed by great mining magnates such as Cecil John Rhodes, a British empire-builder. The diamond industry was sufficiently profitable to generate more investment within South Africa. The change for additional expansion came in 1886, when gold was discovered at the Witwatersrand in the Transvaal. In time, South Africa became the world's greatest producer of gold

The advance of the miners' frontier had far-reaching consequences. Mining encouraged the construction of railways and created a need for a broad range of new secondary industries. Mining compounds provided markets for agriculture. Johannesburg developed from a backwoods community to become the centre of Africa's greatest industrial complex. The mining industry also attracted immigrants, migrant labourers from tribal areas in the countryside, to do the bulk of the unskilled work. In addition, ten thousand new immigrants came to Johannesburg from Europe, mainly from Great Britain. They were a mixed lot — miners, artisans, merchants, pimps, whores, physicians, engineers — mainly urban people who imposed the English language and English ways on the Witwatersrand. Johannesburg became a bustling city set within a relatively backward rural economy, a stronghold of Englishry within Afrikanerdom. English-speaking South Africans — and British imperialists like Lord Milner — anticipated that English-speaking South Africans would one day become the most numerous section of the white population. English predominance in the mining industry was paralleled by British supremacy in banking, commerce, and in the country's scientific and technological institutions.

By the turn of the present century, the population of South Africa had vastly grown. No one knows exactly the number of people who inhabited the area now comprised within the Republic of South Africa at the end of the eighteenth century — probably something between 1 and 2 million. In the early 1900s their numbers had increased to about 5 million (some 1 million whites, less than half a million Coloureds, just over 100,000 newcomers from India, and 3.5 million Africans speaking various languages). A demographic revolution began. This country gained a substantial number of new immigrants — white, Asian and African. Death rates dropped. Improved medical and transport facilities and increased supplies of food helped to shift the demographic balance. Above all, the well-being of all races increased, albeit at a vastly different pace, by reason of unromantic innovations such as brick houses in place of simple huts, sewage, piped water, the increased availability of soap, iron bedsteads, cheap underwear and other little-mentioned aids to hygiene and personal comfort.

Demographically, the Bantu-speaking and Coloured peoples of South Africa fully held their own with the white immigrants, who remained a minority within the area, unlike other countries of European settlement like the United States, New Zealand, Australia, Chile or Argentina. Politically, however, the dark-skinned races were unable to exert much power. The warring Bantu kingdoms were conquered; in 1879 British Redcoats, for instance, finally destroyed the Zulu kingdom, a warlike raider state founded upon the technology of the Early Iron Age. Mission-trained Africans acquired a certain measure of education, but the military and technological balance of power remained with the whites. The whites themselves, however, were sharply divided into townsmen and countrymen, employers and employees, immigrants and old-timers and, above all, English-speakers (many of them with an urban background) and Afrikaans-speakers (primarily of rural origin).

The Impact of the Boer War

Anglo-Afrikaners rivalry came to a head during the South African War of 1899-1902. Great Britain, with strong local support in the Cape Colony and Natal, went to war against the Orange Free State and the Transvaal, the goal — South African supremacy. The struggle began against a foe whom many British officers considered hardly superior to warlike Indian mountaineers; it ended as the greatest military venture ever undertaken by a European power overseas. Nearly 450,000 men — including English-speaking South Africans and volunteers from countries as far afield as Australia and Canada — served under the Union Jack, against about 87,000 on the Afrikaner side. To the Boers it was a war of national defence, known in Afrikaans history books as the 'Second Freedom War'. To the British South Africans in the Transvaal, it was a war for equal rights with their Afrikaans-speaking burghers. Socialists mistakenly regarded the war as a struggle for South Africa's gold. (The so-called 'Rand Lords' were, in fact, divided.) It was a white civil war, with Afrikaners, Jews, Irishmen and even Englishmen arrayed on opposite sides. Above all, it was a war of territorial unification, comparable, in a certain sense, to the US Civil War. Our own interpretation runs counter to that of scholars like Peter Richardson and especially Shula Marks. According to their view, the British went to war for economic motives, though not in the crude sense of 'stealing' the Transvaal gold, as suggested by contemporary opponents of Britain in Africa. As they see it, the mining magnates — men like Rhodes and Beit — looked to British conquest of the Transvaal in order to smash a regime run by backward rural notables, and set up instead an administration capable of dealing with the needs of a modern mining economy. The Transvaal administration supposedly offended the mine-owners by being expensive, inefficient, corrupt and incapable of providing the vast range of administrative services required by a modern mining economy depending on vast capital investments. The mine-owners wanted an end to oppressive monopolies and wasteful taxes; they desired cheap communications, efficient police services, a modern agricultural system capable of supplying the cities with cheap food, and a stable immigrant population of managers and technicians, capable of supplying the country with a great range of new skills. The South African mining capitalists, according to Shula Marks, were particularly influential within the context of British capitalism because South African gold sustained the world's main currencies linked to the gold standard. The British victory in 1902 cemented an alliance between the British mine industry and the well-to-do Afrikaner farmers, men like Louis Botha, the Union's first Prime Minister, who was himself linked to the new market economy.

Marks's interpretation runs counter to the evidence adduced by scholars like Robert V. Kubicek, a modern American historian. Kubicek points out that an empire-builder like Rhodes was quite untypical among the Rand Lords. No other magnate shared his political preconceptions or his boldness. Most of the Rand capitalists were interested, above all, in speculation; much less capital was actually invested than had been raised by skilful promoters. Huge amounts went into safe government securities. Some mines were enormously profitable; but others incurred great loss. By the middle of the 1890s even the greatest groups, Corner House and Gold Fields, were attempting to take money out of South Africa, and invest outside the Empire. The financiers were divided among themselves; politically feeble; absentee, non-British, or internationally oriented interests tended to predominate; the last thing they wanted was a South African war. We ourselves are also impressed by the relatively small part played by South African trade and investment within the context of British capitalism as a whole. We believe that British propaganda during the Boer War and before grossly underestimated the Afrikaners' 'modernity'. The pressure of taxation on mining entrepreneurs was higher in Rhodes's Southern Rhodesian fief than in the Transvaal. Kruger never challenged the mine-owners' property rights, not even during the war. The Union of South Africa was in no wise an unqualified victory for the 'high mining school'. Much to the disgust of Unionist and imperial-minded politicians like Sir Francis Chaplin, a senior mining manager and later Administrator of Southern Rhodesia, the Unionist Party failed to attain dominance. The 'poor whites' were largely enfranchised; Afrikaner rural radicalism remained a powerful force, Southern Rhodesia failed to join the Union. On the other hand, Anglo-Afrikaner rivalry had been a powerful factor in South African politics long before the discovery of gold in the Transvaal; the First Boer War had broken out at a time when the very existence of auriferous deposits in the Transvaal was still unknown.

After long and bitter fighting, the British won a military victory and, in 1906, restored self-government to the defeated Orange Free State and Transvaal. Four years later, the four South African colonies joined in the Union of South Africa, a fully self-governing dominion, as independent of British political control as was Canada. Within the emergent dominion, the franchise remained almost entirely confined to whites; within the European-descended population, the Afrikaners remained a majority. Afrikaans remained the most widely spoken language in South Africa. The whites remained the dominant group in the new union.

The formation of the Union of South Africa marked the first step in British decolonisation of Africa. Victorious in war, the British abandoned the leadership for which they had fought. The political balance of power increasingly inclined towards the Afrikaners. For more than half a century, former Boer generals played leading parts in South African politics (James Barry Munnik Hertzog became a leader of the National Party; Louis Botha and Jan Christian Smuts rose to head the pro-British South African Party, later known as the United Party; all three served at one time or another as Prime Minister). Afrikaner nationalism, profoundly shaped by the experience of war and recovery, hardened into a civic religion, firmer and more rigid than any of the ideologies adopted by British South Africans.

The years that followed the Boer War also saw an astonishing development of Afrikaans literature. Poets like Totius, Celliers and Leipoldt — the so-called *Driemanskap* (triumvirate) — were equal to

16   *The Whites*

the best of their colleagues overseas. All South African Prime Ministers since 1910 have sprung from the Afrikaners. Most of the country's bankers, mining magnates and factory-owners were English-speaking South Africans; English-speakers dominated the professions, the administration, the armed services and the universities. English-speakers at first provided most of the supervisors, foremen and skilled workers in the mines and on the railways. But as the economy expanded and diversified, Afrikaners slowly managed to rise, followed in turn, at an even more hesitant pace, by Coloureds and Africans. Indeed, the socioeconomic history of South Africa might be written almost entirely in terms of ethnic succession, a term familiar in American sociology.

In 1870 the Boers were precisely what the name indicated — farmers. Even the village schoolmaster and the Dutch Reformed *predikant* was apt to be a foreigner, a Hollander, or sometimes a Scotsman. Afrikaners, however, began to move into the cities. They gradually replaced English-speaking South Africans as foremen and skilled workers on the mines, on the railways, and as artisans and supervisors in private business, especially in construction work. Ethnic succession, however, was accompanied by bitter social tensions. The Afrikaners looked askance at the mine magnates (later lampooned as *Hoggenheimers*). Their anger increased as the mine-owners tried to replace white workers with African labourers content with lower wages than those paid to Europeans. In 1922 the white workers of Johannesburg, most of them Afrikaners, rose in revolt. Militarily, the rising was suppressed. Politically and socially, however, the workers made some gains, and entrenched their position by an industrial colour bar designed to protect white wages at the expense of black competitors. South Africa's colour system had solidified.

The Whites in Modern Times

During the first third of the present century, up to the outbreak of World War Two, South Africa generally remained a country beset by poverty, dependent mainly on the export of raw materials and the import of foreign capital. More than half of the white population in the 1930s, mostly Afrikaners, were officially classed as 'poor white', and some of the Afrikaners' best prose literature hinged on the misery and sense of social disorientation experienced by the first generation of poverty-stricken Afrikaner townsmen. Then came an economic transformation. The most distinguished academicians of the 1930s and

1940s had predicted that South Africa's industrial progress was bound to be slow. Colour-bar legislation designed to protect white men against black, said the experts, together with other obstacles like lack of capital, would prevent the country from embarking on a rapid course of industrialisation. The union was supposedly locked in a vicious cycle of poverty from which it could not speedily emerge.

As happened so often in South African history, the experts turned out to be wrong. The Industrial Revolution on the African continent began in South Africa. Manufacturing started to expand in World War One, and South Africa began to turn out steel in the 1930s, thus laying the foundations of its huge industrial complex. During World War Two industrialisation increased at a phenomenal pace. Manufactures became increasingly diversified and complex. By the 1950s South Africa was the first African country to have attained industrial parity with the developed nations of the world.

The social effects of industrialisation were far-reaching. The process of ethnic succession continued, and was vastly speeded up by the coming to power of the Afrikaner National government in 1948. Government-favoured Afrikaners began to make their mark in business, banking, insurance and, especially, public corporations. Coloureds and Africans slowly moved into the more skilled jobs in mining and industry that were abandoned by the Afrikaners. Afrikaner intellectuals moved from the parson's house and the schoolroom into the universities. The 'poor whites', who had accounted for about half the European population during the 1930s, disappeared. At the same time, the European community came to be composed largely of wage- and salary-earners. Today, only about 18 per cent of the 'economically active' whites are classed as entrepreneurs — that is to say, as members of the bourgeoisie in the classical sense employed by Karl Marx. The whites, however, supplied the bulk of the country's managers, technicians and specialists. Today's proportion of whites in primary industries such as agriculture is declining.

The share of Europeans in manufacturing, and particularly in the service sectors of the economy, keeps growing, so that white incomes have greatly increased. By the 1970s, the white South Africans' *per capita* income ranked among the leading half dozen nations in the world. A larger proportion of white South Africans were receiving a university education than in any other nation outside the USA. Of the male white population between 25 and 64 years of age, nearly 30 per cent had obtained an educational level of twelve years, and approximately 7 per cent had university degrees, including doctorates. A higher

Table 1.1: Comparative Output of Some Major South African Industries, 1915-77 (million rand, at factor cost)

Period	Agriculture, Forestry and Fishing	Mining and Quarrying	Manufacturing	Total
1915	56	67	17	304
1920	124	102	41	562
1930	78	86	52	555
1940	125	185	123	990
1950	454	338	470	2,549
1960	601	684	1,023	4,965
1970	1,032	1,237	2,820	11,839
1977	2,502	3,991	7,051	31,453

Note: The above figures refer to some, not all, industries.

Source: *South Africa, 1974: Official Yearbook of the Republic of South Africa* (Johannesburg, 1974), p. 402; *South Africa, 1978: Official Yearbook of the Republic of South Africa* (Johannesburg, 1978), p. 402.

proportion of European women had entered the labour market than in any other community in Africa. Over 30 per cent of women aged between 15 and 64 were in gainful employment. White South African women were in this sense the most emancipated on the continent.

Industrialisation caused equally important changes in inter-white relationships. There was a new form of ethnic succession. The Afrikaners became essentially an urban people. In 1900, only about 10 per cent of the Afrikaners had lived in towns and cities. By 1970, the proportion had almost exactly reversed, with only 12 per cent of the Afrikaners still resident in the countryside. The shift to the towns went with an educational revolution. By 1945, the total number of white university students in South Africa did not exceed 14,000 — the majority of them English-speaking. By 1977, the total number of white students had grown to 111,000 (47,000 of them at Afrikaans-speaking universities, and 35,000 — mostly Afrikaners — at the University of South Africa). The Afrikaners found new jobs in government, management and highly skilled occupations. Their place in the lower ranks of industry, as semi-skilled workers and foremen, was increasingly taken by Coloureds, and even more by Africans who moved into the cities and occupied posts previously held by poorly paid whites, commonly Afrikaners. Afrikaners, once the butt of ethnic jokes told at Afrikaner expense by English-speaking South Africans – the 'van der Merwe' stories – began to make fortunes in industry, banking, commerce and publishing, where English-speakers had once been supreme. Afrikaners' political predominance solidified when the National Party, largely an Afrikaans-speaking body, secured supremacy at the polls in 1948, a position it has held ever since.

The Dominance of the Afrikaners

Afrikaners remain South Africa's dominant ethnic group, and make up the most numerous segment of the European population. Afrikaans is the most widely spoken language in South Africa. According to the 1970 census, 47.6 per cent of the Europeans stated that Afrikaans was their home language; 18.1 per cent indicated that they spoke both Afrikaans and English at home; 29.7 per cent spoke English. The corresponding figures for the Coloureds were 78.9 per cent, 14.8 per cent and 6 per cent. To a considerable extent, the political history of present-day South Africa is the history of the Afrikaner people. The Afrikaners like to see themselves today as a white African tribe. They consider that they have as much right to South Africa as do the blacks. They also argue that they have lived in Africa for three centuries, a longer time than most whites have lived in the New World, and longer than the Australians or New Zealanders have lived in their countries. Afrikanerdom rests on three pillars: the Dutch Reformed Churches, the National Party and the Afrikaans language.

The Dutch Reformed Church is not a rigidly centralised body. Today there are three main groups.* But, by tradition, the church has been one of the principal means of cementing the Afrikaners as a people. (The church has also played an important part in the history of the Coloureds.) In the past, the Bible – especially the Old Testament, with its grim tales of wars against the unbelievers, of treks, of droughts, plagues and other natural calamities – was much nearer to the trekkers' experience than to that of any Western European people. In the wilderness, the church preserved both a rigid standard of morality and the written word.

* The most important is the Nederduitse Gereformeerde Kerk which commands the allegiance of 42.9 per cent of all whites, followed by the Nederduitsch Hervormde Kerk and the Gereformeerde Kerk, with 6.6 and 3.3 per cent respectively.

Afrikaner Calvinists today have lost some of their dogmatic fervour. Some clergymen of the Dutch Reformed persuasion — for example the Reverend Beyers Naude — have become prominent critics of apartheid. This is not surprising, for the Dutch Reformed Church is not merely the religion of the Afrikaners, but also commands the allegiance of many Coloureds and some Africans. Though not an 'Established Church' like the Anglican Church in England, the Dutch Reformed churches are more powerful than any Christian community in Western Europe. Their importance can be compared only with that of other national churches, such as the position of the Catholic Church in present-day Poland or the Greek Orthodox Church in Cyprus. Some 90 per cent of the Afrikaner people, or about 48 per cent of the white population, are Dutch Reformed, as against 12.6 per cent who are Anglicans, 8.7 per cent who are Methodists and 6.2 per cent who are Catholics. Disdainfully referred to by English-speaking critics as the 'National Party at Prayer', the Dutch Reformed churches will continue to yield considerable, though diminishing, power in the life of white South Africa.

Earlier, as secularisation continued to make steady inroads on Afrikaner life, nationalism increasingly became an urban movement. At the same time, the National Party to some extent began to take the place of the churches as the focus of Afrikaner national life. The party was formed in 1914 to defend both the cultural heritage and the economic interests of the Boer. The educated sons of backwoods farmers became pastors, teachers and professors. Many of them moved into the cities, where educated Afrikaners built up a network of interlocking institutions — cultural bodies, trade unions, sports and social clubs, charitable organisations and such. A nationalist-minded Afrikaner was able to move from the nursery to the home for the aged while remaining within the charmed circle of Afrikaner organisations — schools, sports, Boy Scouts, Chamber of Commerce or trade union, glee club and many other institutions of this kind. According to the image widely accepted among English-speaking South Africans, the most important of these bodies is the Broederbond, said to be a semi-secret body of intellectuals, politicians and businessmen that in reality runs the country.[5] The real power of the Broederbond, however, in no wise corresponds to its conspiratorial reputation.

Generalisations with regard to the National Party today are hard to make. Its power varies considerably. So does its local composition. The Afrikaners, above all, are neither a regimented nor a *gleichgeschaltet* people. The United Party and its predecessor were traditionally supported by a substantial minority of Afrikaners. Generals Louis Botha and Jan Christian Smuts, two of South Africa's most distinguished prime ministers, both made their reputations by leading coalitions that comprised a majority of English-speaking and a minority of Afrikaans-speaking white voters; Botha led South Africa into World War One on the British side, and Smuts was responsible for aligning South Africa with Great Britain in World War Two.

The majority of Afrikaans voters, on the other hand, vote for the National Party, not because they necessarily approve of all its policies, but because they widely consider the party to be the political embodiment of the Afrikaner *volk*. The party's political evolution reflects the Afrikaners' changing social composition. During the 1930s, the National Party in many ways resembled an Eastern European peasant party led by country-born intellectuals, anti-urban in orientation, anti-Semitic in outlook. A generation later, the National Party had changed into a party comprising both businessmen and skilled workers, reconciled to industry, wedded to a mixed economy. Its appeal has remained more populist than that of the United Party, and its influence is much more powerful among the poorer whites (see Table 1.2).

The National Party attained power in 1948 under D.F. Malan, a former clergyman of the Dutch Reformed Church, later a Cabinet Minister under General Hertzog. Malan's succession to the premiership marked a new chapter in the political life of South Africa. The 'age of the generals' came to an end. At the same time, the Nationalists made a determined effort to strengthen the Afrikaners' position in the administration, the armed services and the economy; to a very considerable extent, they succeeded in their design. They made no attempt to nationalise mines and factories for the purpose of 'Afrikanerising' the economy. But the army, the diplomatic corps and the police — once English-speaking preserves — came to be mainly controlled by Afrikaners.

Table 1.2: Percentage of the Total Vote by Monthly Income Group, 1969

	Under R 300	R 300-499	R 500 and over
National Party	63.8	56.6	48.1
United Party	19.3	23.4	27.6

Source: David Welsh, 'The Politics of White Supremacy' in Leonard Thompson and Jeffrey Butler (eds.), *Change in Contemporary South Africa* (University of California Press, Berkeley, 1975), p. 76.

Afrikaners occupied the leading positions in state-run enterprises like the South African Iron and Steel Corporation (ISCOR). They also acquired a major position in the learned professions and the sciences, and in the state corporations that now employ an important part of the South African economy. Seventy-one per cent of the whites employed by the state are Afrikaners.[6] The bureaucratic element now plays so important a part in the life of the Afrikaners that their opponents have begun to mutter about 'ethnic socialism'. But the stereotype of the ill-educated, stupid Afrikaner has less validity than ever before.

The National Party came to power to 'solve' the 'native problem'. English-speaking South Africans have believed in social segregation with the same conviction as their Afrikaans-speaking neighbours. The colour bar in industry originally owed more to British workers (especially to British miners) than to the Afrikaners. The British, however, also had a contrary tradition — one widespread among missionaries, intellectuals and civil servants — that called for the gradual assimilation of the non-European elites into a wider English-speaking community. The Afrikaners, in the past, have likewise absorbed a variety of other Europeans — Scotsmen, Englishmen, Germans, French Huguenots, some Jews. In the more remote past the Afrikaner nation also absorbed some Khoikhoi and Bantu-speaking people. But Afrikaner tradition has never approved of such racial assimilation. The Afrikaners have tended to regard themselves as an endangered people — imperilled first of all by a harsh environment and by hostile tribes along the frontier, later by the threat of biological absorption, then also by the force exerted through British predominance in the political and cultural sphere. The Afrikaners were determined to resist 'Anglification'; they meant to survive as a white island in a black sea; they meant to remain as a separate nation.

Once in power, the National Party embarked on a vast scheme of human engineering designed to reconstruct South Africa on the basis of separate nations — Afrikaners, Zulu, Xhosa and so forth. South Africa, the National Party believed, must be reconstituted on the basis of apartheid; separate development for the various races was to give each of these nations its proper place in a homeland. But as industrialisation proceeded, the 'white' areas themselves grew increasingly 'black'. Above all, the social composition of the Afrikaner nation itself began to change. Afrikaner society became socially more differentiated; the Afrikaners produced a substantial bourgeoisie and substantial intelligentsia of their own.

For many of these 'new men' the old verities ceased to be sacred.

Even conservative members of the Establishment have begun to proclaim that apartheid must become a 'dynamic' concept whose content may as yet change in a future as yet uncharted. The conservative (*verkrampte*) wing of the party remains as yet the most powerful. It is entrenched in the civil service, the police, the party caucus and the Afrikaner cultural organisations; it derives support from white workers and employees, from the smaller farmers and the rural clergy. The reformist (*verligte*) wing of the party, on the other hand, is strong among Afrikaner businessmen and professional people, among technicians, in both the private and public sectors, and also among senior members of the defence establishment who are anxious to create a wider social consensus and who want to strengthen the country's industrial potential.

At the same time, there seems to be a significant change in the Afrikaners' sense of self-identification. An investigation of national attitudes among Afrikaans-speaking students, traditionally one of the most nationalist segments in Afrikaner society, indicated that most of them regard themselves primarily as South Africans and only secondarily as Afrikaners. Of the 92.4 per cent who described themselves as Afrikaners, 73.5 per cent indicated that they primarily thought of themselves as South Africans, 23.5 identified themselves as Afrikaner, and 2.9 per cent called themselves English-speaking South Africans. Some 73.7 per cent of the respondents stated that being a South African meant 'a great deal' to them; nobody said that it meant 'nothing'. Interestingly enough, the student-respondents assumed that South Africans of all colours had a great deal in common; the difference between the rich and the poor was held to be more significant than between races. Individual samples of the kind cited above have, of course, only limited significance. But taken in conjunction with wider evidence from political speeches, literary works, personal attitudes at work and at play, they serve as straws that blow in the wind.* And the wind may be blowing away from ethnic separatism towards a more all-embracing sense of South African nationality. But the growing sense of the Afrikaner *volk*, under siege before the threat of black consciousness and the attacks on world opinion, continues to operate against such a development. Ethnic self-consciousness and demography pose grave problems to the formation of a South African nationalism (see Table 1.3).

For all practical purposes, however, the Afrikaners today still

---

* Representatives of 50,000 white Afrikaans university students voted solidly against the government's apartheid policy in July of 1979.

Table 1.3: Projected Growth Rate, South Africa, 1975-2005 (exclusive of immigration)

Ethnic Group	Numbers, 1975 (millions)	Annual Growth Rate (per cent)	Numbers, 2005 (millions)	Annual Growth Rate (per cent)
Whites	4.125	1.54	6.067	1.16
Asians	0.734	2.34	1.317	1.62
Coloureds	2.432	2.99	5.530	2.47
Africans	17.823	2.87	42.809	2.78
Total	25.114	—	55.723	—

Source: J.L. Sadie, *Projections of the South African Population* (Industrial Development Corporation, Johannesburg, 1972).

constitute the South African *Staatsvolk*, the dominant ethnic group, whose power corresponds roughly to that of the Kikuyu in post-independence Kenya, the Tutsi in Burundi, or the Austrians and Hungarians in the defunct Habsburg Empire. But the Afrikaners are far from all-powerful. Their influence in South Africa has to be shared with that of English-speaking South Africans, who make up about 37 per cent of the white population.

The Position of English-speaking South Africans

During the nineteenth century, immigrants from Great Britain supplied the bulk of the administrative and military elite. They provided most of the country's skilled white labour force and most of its intellectuals. Scottish (and Dutch) clergymen preached to Afrikaner congregations on the frontier. Miners and engineers from England and America played a major part in pioneering the gold and diamond industries. English-speaking people came as physicians and engineers. They opened the country's first banks; they founded the first universities. English-speaking South Africans also made an important, though not advertised, contribution to scientific farming and to the transport industry, including railway construction and the shipbuilding industry.

The stream of British immigration continued into the twentieth century, increasing after World War Two. More Britons chose to find new homes for themselves in South Africa than did Europeans of any other nationality.[7] But even the Continental-born Europeans were apt to join the English-speaking rather than the Afrikaans-speaking community. The Afrikaners' attitude towards immigration thus remained ambivalent. On the one hand, they wished to strengthen white numbers. On the other, they feared to be swamped by Continental Europeans and Englishmen. Despite calls for a 'white South Africa', white South Africans never encouraged mass immigration of the Australian kind, and thereby contributed to that imbalance between white numbers and black that they professed to fear.

English-speakers still hold many advantages. They are, on average, better educated than their Afrikaans-speaking neighbours. The percentage of English-speaking matriculants in the early 1970s was nearly twice that of Afrikaans-speaking matriculants. In proportion to the population, twice as many English-speakers as Afrikaans-speakers graduated from universities, 3.0 per cent as against 1.5 per cent of the total population. English-speaking South Africans remained strongly entrenched in the leading positions in industry, commerce and banking, even though the Afrikaners' share had shown a significant increase. In 1939 Afrikaners supposedly had a controlling share of only 8 per cent of the country's commerce, and 3 per cent in industry; by 1965 their share had risen to 29 per cent and 11 per cent respectively. The English-language press predominates in South Africa. It continues to be almost universally hostile to the government, and provides the world with most of its news concerning South Africa. English-speaking universities remain centres of academic opposition to the Afrikaner Establishment, as do the English-speaking churches.

South Africans of British descent also enjoy intangible assets. The educated black and brown people of South Africa apparently look with greater favour on British-descended South Africans than on Afrikaners or Jews. The British, to some extent, have preserved their position as a social reference group, a privilege not accorded to any other European community. According to a series of 'social distance' tests worked out by M.L. Edelstein and other South African scholars, Indians in South Africa, for instance, preferred British South Africans to tribal Africans, Afrikaners, Jews, city-born Africans and Coloureds — in that order. Educated Africans (that is, African matriculants in Soweto) likewise preferred British-descended people to Afrikaners, Jews and Indians — in that order.[8] Educated Coloureds responded to these social distance tests in a similar fashion. Edelstein's findings will surprise those who believe that Afrikaners, being more 'honest' in their racial attitudes, will therefore be more popular than Englishmen, or that Jews, the most liberal section of the white community, will be rewarded for their liberal standpoint by being accorded lower social distance ratings than Gentiles. These statistics will also shock those who believe that a great non-European unity front, held together by a common hatred of all whites, is in the making among educated 'non-Europeans'.

No account of the English-speaking community would be complete without reference to Jewish South Africans, who form a subgroup among the whites. Numerically, the Jews do not account for much. There are only about 120,000 Jews in South Africa and their political impact is slight. A few South African Jews have made their names as liberal-minded parliamentarians such as Harry Schwarz and Helen Suzman. Some have played a part in left-wing politics. But Jews in South Africa have never risen to the positions accorded to them in the former days of white-dominated Rhodesia where Sir Roy Welensky became Prime Minister of the erstwhile Federation of Rhodesia and Nyasaland, and where Max Danziger guided Southern Rhodesia's economy through the troubled days of World War Two. In the economic, cultural and academic spheres, on the other hand, South African Jews have always played a major part.

South African Jews are as heterogeneous in their composition as the remainder of the English-speaking community. This was not always the case. The earliest Dutch pioneers included a small number of Jews of Spanish descent who were absorbed within the Afrikaner people. During the nineteenth century the Afrikaner nation continued to be enriched by some Jewish newcomers, men like Lion Cachet, a Dutch convert to Calvinism, a theological conservative, and a founder of the Afrikaans language movement. In the last part of the century the small congregations of British, German and Dutch Jews in South Africa became heavily outnumbered by newcomers from Eastern Europe, especially from Lithuania, a region in maritime contact with Great Britain and the British Empire. The newcomers imposed their religious orthodoxy on South African Jewry. They also occupied a lowlier place on the socio-economic ladders than their co-religionists who had previously come to South Africa from Holland and Germany. The pioneers often made their living as petty traders, hawkers, prospectors and artisans. Many South African Jews rose into prominence in the gold and diamond industries, in commerce, banking, later in manufacturing, and finally in academia, the arts and the sciences. By 1960 most South African Jews were native-born. Most were city-dwellers, heavily concentrated on the Witwatersrand and, to a lesser extent, in the Cape Town region. Most South African Jews know Afrikaans, but the great majority use English as their native tongue. Yiddish and German are no longer spoken among the descendants of immigrants.

No political party today puts forward an anti-Semitic programme. By 1951, the National Party had dropped its anti-Semitic stance. Much to the surprise of both left-wingers and right-wingers in Great Britain, anti-Semitic publications legally sold in Great Britain may not be distributed in South Africa on the grounds that they violate the South African Publications Act in being 'harmful to the relations between any sections of the inhabitants of the Republic'. But Jews have traditionally met with a good deal of social discrimination. They reacted by lending their support to the more liberal parties, especially the Progressive Party. Some intellectuals turned to Communism. But in a country where every community turned to some form of ethnic nationalism, the Jews were no exception. Overwhelmingly, and perhaps to a greater extent than in any other Western country, South African Jews threw their support behind the Zionist movement. The South African Zionist Federation enjoys a considerable degree of power within the Jewish community, comparable to that of the South African Jewish Board of Deputies, the central representative institution with which most of the country's Jewish congregations and Jewish societies are affiliated.

There is, indeed, a curious psychological link between Jews and Afrikaners. Both regard themselves as members of a minority nation, peoples of the Covenant whose very existence was threatened in the past and might be threatened in the future. Israel and South Africa are both menaced from without; both have been reviled in the United Nations by what passes as progressive world opinion. Despite the many differences between them, the two countries have imperceptibly drawn together, with consequences that cannot as yet be easily assessed. Israel and South Africa have extensive trade and financial relations. The government of South Africa liberalised its foreign exchange relations to allow South African Jews to invest in Israel, and the Israelis provide South Africa with military hardware.

To conclude, the standing of the English-speaking community — Gentile and Jewish alike — in the country's economic and intellectual life is in no wise reflected in its political power. English-speaking South Africans no longer look to Great Britain for their imperial inspiration; they are badly divided over the question of apartheid. They lack the sense of national cohesion evinced by both Afrikaner Nationalists and by the Zionists. As we shall show in the section on politics, the 'English' parties have not been able to make much headway since

1948, and the influence of liberals — whether English- or Afrikaans-speaking — does not much extend beyond the wealthy suburbs.

Contrary to established orthodoxies, however, English-speaking South Africans are not without power in South African politics. They exert influence both on the provincial and on the national levels. Natal's provincial government is dominated by English-speaking South Africans. Natal wants greater powers and autonomy for the provinces. British Natalians have considered the possibility of a constitutional convention of the kind that set up the so-called 'Turnhalle' constitution in Namibia. (The Turnhalle convention stood for group representation on the part of each ethnic community, a form of group veto, and the dismantling of apartheid.) Other schemes, favoured by some English-speaking as well as Afrikaans-speaking South Africans, concern some kind of cantonal arrangement with decentralised powers, or a new territorial realignment leaving the whites with a reduced *Vrystaat* (free state) of their own, joined in a confederal constitution with its black neighbours.

By 1978 the South African government was committed to even more far-reaching changes. Connie Mulder, then the South African Minister for Plural Relations (formerly called Bantu Affairs), issued a statement cast in an anticolonial vein reminiscent of the Boer War period. According to Mulder, the imperial powers had 'artificially' amalgamated South Africa during the latter part of the nineteenth century. A 'resubdivision' of the subcontinent had become essential; once the process was completed, there would be no more South African citizens, black or white.

We shall return to these projects in the section dealing with the politics of South Africa. But whatever happens, the English-speaking South Africans are too divided and numerically weak to act on their own. They criticise Afrikaner predominance, just as the Luo (Kenya's second-largest ethnic community) look with apprehension on the ethnic supremacy of the Kikuyu. Above all, the English-speaking South Africans suffer from a collective loss of national confidence. In the heyday of the British Empire the English-speakers had proudly regarded themselves as an imperial vanguard. The disruption of the British Empire, the widening political gap between Great Britain and the 'white dominions', on the one hand, and South Africa on the other, have weakened the British South Africans' sense of British identity, as did South Africa's departure from the Commonwealth. English-speaking South Africans thereafter briefly attempted to look upon the United States as a new 'imperial' power, capable of sustaining the cause of

Englishry in South Africa. But the flirtation with America was destined to be brief, and President Carter's policy of restrained hostility to South Africa finally put an end to South Africa's brief venture into phil-Americanism.

Some English-speaking South Africans have ceased to be Britons and have turned into 'Anglokaners'. Others have suggested schemes for an Anglo-African alliance, but this idea belongs in the realm of political fantasy. The ultimate fate of South Africa is more likely to be decided by some kind of accommodation between the Afrikaners and the Zulu, numerically the two most powerful communities in South Africa. Even in the intellectual sphere, English-speaking culture in South Africa has distinct weaknesses. English-speaking academicians have made a major contribution to South Africa's cultural life. There is, for example, a South African variant of English literature. During the nineteenth century, British South Africa produced some fine writers like Olive Schreiner. Her *Story of an African Farm* depicted life in the backveld without the sugary romanticism that overlaid so much Victorian writing on the Empire. British South African authors in the twentieth century include artists like Nadine Gordimer and Alan Paton, concerned with what they regard as the whites' failure to take up South Africa's challenge of racism and poverty. With the exception of Sarah Gertrude Millin, a proud, embittered Jewish woman, almost every English-speaking writer of note in Southern Africa has been an abolitionist. English-speaking intellectuals have found the touchstone of their literary integrity in opposition to South Africa's or Rhodesia's racial institutions. Much of their writing — for instance Doris Lessing's novels — have a curiously anaemic quality — guilt-ridden and introspective — quite out of touch with South African society at large.

Some of these literary men and women became exiles, along with liberal or leftist journalists, politicians, agitators, academicians and professional men (especially practitioners of the social sciences and physicians, a substantial number of them Jewish). These exiles enriched British literary and academic life; they provided numerous specialists in African studies; they also added a peculiarly South African tincture to liberal and left-wing protest in British society. But they did not create a truly South African literature, much less a characteristically South African school of painting, sculpture or architecture. The derivative nature of British South African culture and the British South Africans' failure to provide political leadership were hardly unrelated. Descendants of British imperial pioneers have become resigned to playing a secondary role in politics.

Table 1.4: South Africa: Economically Active Population, 1960 and 1970 (thousands)

Type of Activity	1960							1970			
	White	Coloured Total	Male	Asians	Africans	Total	White	Coloured Total	Male	Asian	African	Total
Agriculture, forestry and fishing	119	120	115	11	1,439	1,689	99	119	107	7	2,014	2,239
Mining	62	4	4	1	548	615	63	7	7	1	605	676
Manufacturing	211	93	58	32	309	645	280	169	97	63	512	1,024
Electricity, gas and water	10	3	3	–	26	39	14	3	3	–	32	49
Construction	72	40	40	2	161	275	96	77	77	10	264	447
Trade, catering and accommodation	195	41	35	28	166	430	273	78	53	51	314	716
Transport, storage and communication	116	17	17	4	69	206	164	28	27	8	140	340
Finance, insurance and property	61	3	3	1	22	87	146	7	5	3	35	191
Community, welfare and personal services	260	145	42	23	821	1,249	325	161	50	23	1,064	1,573
Unspecified and unemployed	45	88	58	24	329	486	37	55	29	14	625	731
Total	1,151	554	375	126	3,890	5,721	1,497	704	455	180	5,605	7,986

Source: Department of Statistics, *Population Census 1960 and 1970*, Table 5.3 (Government Printer, Pretoria, 1970), p. 80.
Note: The real number of black unemployed was much higher than these figures would indicate.

Table 1.5: South Africa: Estimated Income by Racial Group in Percentages, 1968-77

Group	1968	1977
Whites	73.4	64
Coloureds	5.4	7
Asians	2.4	3
Africans	19.8	26

Source: Heribert Adam, *Modernizing Racial Domination: the Dynamics of South African Politics* (University of California Press, Berkeley, 1977), p. 7, and *Survey of Race Relations in South Africa* (Institute of Race Relations, Pretoria, 1978), p. 102.

Ethnicity, to a considerable extent, is linked to social status. The whites provide most of the independent middle class, the managers and the technicians; blacks furnish the greater part of the semi-skilled and unskilled working class, and of the poorest tillers of the land; the Coloureds and Indians are in the more intermediate positions (see Table 1.4). Europeans, in consequence, have by far the highest incomes, followed by Asians, then Coloureds, with Africans at the bottom (see Table 1.5). But colour, class and income are no longer invariably linked. There are now wealthy black and brown people whose incomes may considerably exceed that of a white man; the skills and purchasing power of the so-called 'non-European' communities have continued to grow, probably with far-reaching results for the future of South Africans' race-caste structure.

Notes

1. See Harrison M. Wright, *The Burden of the Present: Liberal-radical Controversy over South African History* (Rex Collings, London, 1977), p. 40. Also L.H. Gann, 'Liberal Interpretations of South African History', *Rhodes-Livingstone Journal*, vol. 25 (1959), pp. 40-58.
2. See, for instance, Leo Marquard, *The Story of South Africa* (Faber and Faber, London, 1955), pp. 69, 153.
3. See Susan Rennie Ritner, 'The Dutch Reformed Church and Apartheid', *Journal of Contemporary History*, vol. 2, no. 4 (1967), pp. 22-37.
4. Cited in L.H. Gann and Peter Duignan, *White Settlers in Tropical Africa* (Penguin Books, London, 1962), p. 31. The present account recapitulates L.H. Gann, 'The White Experience in South Africa', *The Wilson Quarterly* (Spring 1977), pp. 39-50.

5. The Afrikaner-Broederbond was formed in 1918 as a cultural organisation, open only to Afrikaans-speaking Protestant men over the age of 25. See J.H.P. Serfontein, *Brotherhood of Power: an Exposé of the Secret Afrikaner Broederbond* (Rex Collings, London, 1979).

6. F. van Zyl Slabbert, 'Afrikaner Nationalism, White Politics, and Political Change in South Africa' in Leonard Thompson and Jeffrey Butler (eds.), *Change in Contemporary South Africa* (University of California Press, Berkeley, 1975), p. 11.

7. About 12 per cent of the white population in 1970 was foreign-born, compared with 20 per cent in 1911. Between 1967 and 1971 alone, some 200,000 Europeans settled in South Africa. The percentage distribution between the various nationalities between 1963 and 1968 was as follows: United Kingdom, 37.1; Portugal, 10.4; Germany, 7.6; Greece, 4.1; Italy, 3.6; Netherlands, 3.4.

8. Melville Leonard Edelstein, *What do Young Africans Think?* (Labour and Community Consultants, Johannesburg, 1974), *passim*.

2 THE BROWN PEOPLES

The Coloureds

South Africa's racial problems differ greatly from those of the United States. But there are some striking similarities in the respective positions of South African Coloureds and of American blacks. The Coloureds, like many black Americans, are of mixed origin. Like Afro-Americans, there are wide differences in physical appearance, culture and social status — so much so that many Coloureds deny the very existence of a separate Coloured people. Their ancestors include members of every ethnic strain that ever came to the country — Khoikhoi, San, Malays, Indians, Afrikaners, Englishmen and Africans. No ethnic memories tie the Coloureds to any land other than South Africa. In many ways, the Coloured is indeed the archetypal South African.

The Coloureds have traditionally been the stepchildren of South African society. Their ancestors comprise Malay slaves, Khoikhoi labourers, San forcibly 'apprenticed' to white farmers, or children born of illegitimate unions between whites and African or Khoikhoi women. Some of them managed to rise in the social sphere. Coloureds, especially those descended from Malay parentage, once made up a substantial section of the skilled working class at the Old Cape. Others threw in their lot with runaway slaves, with African tribesmen, and with white pioneers and outcasts on the frontiers of white settlements. Some Coloured frontiersmen became cattle-keepers, skilled on horseback, wise in the ways of the wilderness where they led a roving existence. Some groups — for instance the so-called Basters — lived very much like white trekkers, familiar with the High Dutch Bible, skilled in the use of horse, ox wagon and guns, prized as allies and feared as foes.

But, in the long run, Coloured frontiersmen could not hold their own against the much more numerous whites. The greatest number of Coloured people lacked a stake in the land; they made their living as farmhands, wagoners, overseers, and in other lowly occupations. They became South Africa's first fully fledged proletariat. The development of mining, and later of the manufacturing industries, created new jobs for them. They drifted into the cities. Some of them improved their social position as clergymen, teachers and, in more recent years, as businessmen. But the Coloureds essentially remain a community of wage-earners, without much land of their own, and without a stake in urban means of production except as workers.[1]

The Coloureds now comprise something like 2.5 million people, just under 10 per cent of South Africa's population. In demographic terms, they occupy about the same position as the blacks in North America. Like Afro-Americans, they are a relatively youthful group; nearly 45 per cent are under the age of fifteen. In recent years, their death rate has declined, while their birth rate remains high, so that the Coloured population continues to grow at a rapid rate. Their demographic position thus remains assured.

In economic terms, the Coloured dependency rate — that between the very young and the very old with the wage-earners — is high; 60 for the whites, as against 91.9 for the Coloureds. Coloured families thus carry a considerable burden in having to care for children and old people. The Coloured rate of capital accumulation remains small. On average, they save only about 5 per cent of their disposable income. Coloured entrepreneurs have to struggle with a host of social and legal difficulties. Their bourgeoisie remains weak, and consists largely of shopkeepers, craftsmen and professional people. Only 3.6 per cent of the 'economically active' Coloureds rank as entrepreneurs, compared with 18 per cent of whites. The greater part of the Coloureds are employed in industry and construction work, but there is now a substantial class of white-collar workers with jobs in community, welfare, personal services and trade (see Table 1.4, p. 30). The number of Coloured employed on the farms remains considerable, but is declining.[2] The burden of unemployment is much higher on the Coloureds than on the whites. (In 1978, the number of registered Coloured unemployed workers amounted to 1.7 per cent of the economically active population. Corresponding figures for whites and Indians were 0.66 and 2.21 per cent respectively. In terms of unemployment, however, all these three groups did better by comparison than black Americans during the same period.)

Overall, the Coloureds during the 1970s in some ways still resembled the 'poor whites' of the 1930s — mostly country-bred Afrikaners trying to adjust to an unaccustomed life in the cities without the requisite skills. This is not to say that poverty in the countryside is preferable to misery in the cities; the reverse is true. Romantic verbiage about the beauties of country life notwithstanding, an unskilled labourer in a modern South African town is infinitely better off materially than a hired hand on an old-time farm or a traditional African tiller who worked the land with axe and hoe. In terms of accommodation, in terms of services provided by schools, clinics, cinemas, hospitals and shops, in terms of heating and of piped water supplies, a slum-dweller has a better life than the men and women who used to crowd into dilapidated, vermin-ridden hovels of the kind that once housed the farm labourer in South Africa (and, for that matter, in England, Ireland and Poland).

With all these reservations, and with due allowance for improvements made in Coloured standards of living and skill over the last decades, most of the Coloureds continue to have a hard time. According to the Theron Commission that investigated their condition between 1973 and 1976, some 1 million Coloureds were members of households whose income was rated below the poverty line. The Coloured poor were beset by inadequate housing, by unemployment and underdevelopment, by a considerable degree of illiteracy, and by a variety of health problems. Witnesses called to give evidence before the Commission pointed to widespread alcoholism and poor work morale. Coloured people have a high crime rate. Their illegitimacy rate is the country's largest, as many Coloured couples disdain marriage and prefer to set up temporary unions unrecognised by the law; their illegitimacy rate reached 43.1 per cent in 1970, against a white illegitimacy rate of 3.0 per cent.

The psychological problems of the Coloured people rival their material difficulties. Material difficulties are intensified by a sense of inner division and anomalies. About 90 per cent of the Coloureds speak Afrikaans. Theirs is an Afrikaner working-class culture, albeit a culture in which the Dutch Reformed Church does not play as important a part as it does among white Afrikaners.[3] To all intents and purposes, the Coloureds are disinherited Afrikaners — without being recognised as such by the parent group. They are split into a bewildering array of small groups, held together by ties of kinship, and distinguished by similar levels of income and by similarities in their physical appearance. The Coloureds were stripped of their right to elect members to the white Parliament; they are not a powerful political lobby.

In consequence, they are much divided as to their true ethnic identity, a problem that does not trouble any other ethnic community in South Africa. According to the Theron Commission, the Coloureds who possess the strongest sense of forming a distinctive people are rural folk who speak Afrikaans as their native tongue and who belong to the middle or lower middle class — those who, in fact, have most in common with their Afrikaner neighbours. Those who do *not* want to identify themselves as members of the Coloured people fall into three categories. The largest group wishes to be known simply as South Africans; its members derive mainly from lower-middle- or middle-class and urban backgrounds, especially from Cape Town. A lesser segment looks to association with the whites. By far the smallest section tends toward the doctrine of Black Consciousness; its members wish to throw in their lot with the Africans, and consider that all oppressed people of colour should unite against white domination. Advocates of Black Consciousness usually belong to the middle income groups; many of them are intellectuals, and their strength likewise centres on Cape Town.

Coloured politics have traditionally been linked to white politics. Coloured men in the Cape Province and Natal had been entitled to the vote since 1853 under the traditional Cape franchise. Their right to vote was entrenched in the Act of Union of 1910. The National government, however, reduced Coloured representation in Parliament to a symbolic status by placing the Coloureds on a separate voters' roll in 1956. The government then limited their vote in 1969 to only electing a Coloured Parliament with limited powers of internal self-government. This council can legislate on matters such as finance, local government, social welfare, pensions, etc.; its acts, however, have to be ratified by the State President, and its powers are circumscribed in a wider sense by financial and bureaucratic considerations. The Coloured community, divided as it is, has supported a variety of political parties, including the moderate Federal Coloured Peoples' Party of South Africa. This party is willing, on the whole, to co-operate with the government. But the Labour Party of South Africa, a more militant organisation, explicitly rejects any form of racial discrimination, and has now gained the bulk of Coloured support.

Such politics reflect the Coloureds' ambiguous position in society. There is electoral apathy; there are deliberate abstentions. By 1969 the number of Coloureds who cast their vote had dropped to just over half of those actually entitled to the franchise. There is widespread bitterness. Thus, according to field studies used by the Theron Commission, only 27.4 per cent of the urban Coloureds were content with the manner in which they were represented in the governmental system, 26.2 per cent were uncertain, and fully 46.4 per cent were dissatisfied. There is overwhelming opposition to the idea of instituting separate homelands for the Coloured people; 67.3 per cent oppose the notion, while only 20.5 per cent approve it. The South African Coloureds overwhelmingly reject the National Party's policy of apartheid, and the legislative machinery in which that policy is embodied — the Population Registration Act, the Mixed Marriages Act, the Immorality Act, the

The Brown Peoples

Group Areas Act, the Separate Amenities Act, the Separate Representation of Voters Act and such measures.

Nevertheless, the Coloureds have made more progress in the economic and educational spheres during thirty years of the National government than had been achieved during the three decades preceding 1948. The Coloureds had long been reserved a portion of the jobs in the railway system and in other government agencies. They have served in the South African Army. In the two world wars the Cape Corps were mostly used in service units, but they did some fighting as well. In World War Two, 45,000 Coloureds enlisted in the army, and 3,012 were wounded or killed. There were signs in 1978 that the government planned to use more Coloured people in the armed services. This will have great social and political consequences in the future.

South African Coloureds, as a group, probably compare favourably in their condition with black Americans at the time of World War Two. The National government has set up a Coloured university, the University of Western Cape. Its academic standards have vastly improved. Enrolment of Coloured students has increased from 800 in 1959 to 3,142 in 1974, and university graduates now find few problems in getting jobs. The number of Coloured children at school has increased strikingly, as compulsory education for Coloured pupils of school age has been gradually introduced, starting in 1974. The proportion of secondary students increased. The records of 1974 show 473,114 Coloured children in primary schools and 108,730 students enrolled in secondary schools — a somewhat higher proportion than in the People's Republic of China, where about 20 per cent of all teenagers were estimated as attending high schools.

The National government and the municipalities have attempted to improve Coloured housing, and more than 90 per cent of urban Coloureds live in dwelling units erected by public authorities. Living conditions vary from deplorable to good. The best Coloured housing schemes — such as Mitchell Plain, a new town being built by the Cape Town Council on the False Bay Coast — form models of urban development. The government also set up in 1962 the Coloured Development Corporation in order to encourage the emergence of a Coloured bourgeoisie by providing prospective entrepeneurs with capital and skilled advice.[4] At the same time, the Coloured Affairs Administration provided a new range of civil service jobs, with the result that the Coloureds are becoming ever more enmeshed in that complex bureaucratic network that increasingly envelops every ethnic group in South Africa.

But the ultimate problem of political and social inequality remains.

As Coloured education improves and Coloured living standards go up, Coloured discontent has increased. Coloureds bitterly resent — among other things — the disparity in educational expenditure for white children on the one hand and 'non-Europeans' on the other. Whites argue that they pay the bulk of the nation's taxes and therefore deserve a greater return in government services; Coloureds reply that the Coloured contribution to the country's labour force is inadequately rewarded. The Coloureds detest the social colour bar, as well as the difference in salaries often paid to whites and Coloureds respectively for the same job. Coloureds were deeply offended by a government slum clearance scheme that entailed the forcible removal from their long-time urban home in District Six, a part of Cape Town. Miserable and crime-ridden as it was, District Six was a permanent residence where Coloureds had a sense of community. The removal was, at least, a political mistake. Coloured school boycotts and the recent dissolution of the Coloured Representative Council, a bitter government critic, have added fuel to the fire. The Coloured issue may in the long run well be the weakest link in the structure of apartheid, a fact brought home to white South Africans in 1980 by P.W. Botha, the first South African Prime Minister publicly to acknowledge the injustice entailed by the disparities in educational expenditure for whites and Coloureds respectively. Most of the ruling Afrikaner people have no guilt complex with regard to the Africans, whom they regard as tribal people who were fairly conquered in battle. The Afrikaners are, however, well aware that the Coloureds, unlike Indians and Africans, are linked to the Afrikaner nation by ties of blood, history and language. Many Afrikaners thus have a nagging sense of guilt about the Coloureds' fate. The Coloureds are, after all, the only Afrikaans-speaking people in the whole world, with the exception of the Afrikaners themselves, and many of them may justly be looked upon as brown Afrikaners. The Coloureds are modern men, not tribal. They live in towns or on farms, and they work for wages. To most Afrikaner intellectuals, there is no moral justification for treating the Coloureds as inferior, or for denying them full civic rights. In the future, white Afrikaners and brown might well draw together; but if they do, South Africa's accustomed race-caste system must disintegrate.

The Indians

The Indian people of South Africa are ethnically one of the most diversified groups on the entire continent. Comprising about 800,000 people, they are split into several linguistic segments. The older generation speaks Tamil, Telegu, Hindi, Gujerati and Urdu; younger people have widely become Anglicised. The Indians follow many different religions. There are Hindu (about 70 per cent), Muslims (about 20 per cent), Zoroastrians, Christians of various denominations and agnostics.

In their origins, Indians are equally distinct. They first arrived in Natal in 1860 as indentured workmen on sugar plantations whose owners preferred permanent wage labourers to African migrants. The newcomers, mainly Hindu, had the option of either being repatriated at the end of their contract or of accepting a piece of Crown land equal in value to the cost of their return passage. The majority chose to take up land; some remained as farmers; others became workmen or petty traders. The indentured labourers were followed by 'passengers', more prosperous Indians who were able to pay for their own passage — most of them Muslims from the northern and western parts of India. When gold was discovered on the Witwatersrand, they made their way into the Transvaal (they were not admitted into the Orange Free State). About 85 per cent of the Indian population today lives in Natal, most of them in Durban or in a 150-mile radius of Durban; the remainder have largely settled on the Witwatersrand and Pretoria. Present-day Indians are, like most of the Coloureds, essentially an urban people.

Within the South African race-caste structure, the Indians occupy a position that in many ways resembles that of the Coloureds. Indians, like Coloureds, are excluded from the central organs of the government. (The South Africans, at the time of writing, are considering steps to upgrade the political status of Indians and Coloureds by means of a new system of racial Parliaments and Cabinet government, but the full impact of these proposed reforms could not as yet be assessed.) Indians in general have to cope with social discrimination and various political and legal disabilities in the same way as Coloureds.

But the example of Indians in South Africa — and also of Chinese in South-east Asia, Lebanese in West Africa and Jews in diverse parts of the world — shows that social or legal discrimination may play only a minor part in determining the economic fortunes of any given ethnic community.[5] Indians have a considerably higher average income than Coloureds, as indicated in preceding statistics. Like the Jews, they have a low rate of alcoholism and a low rate of crime. In particular, Indians do not go in for violence; they do not often come into conflict with the law (one in every 1,250 Asians is in prison at any one day in the year, as opposed to one in every 126 Coloureds). Indians have a higher life expectancy than Coloureds (59.3 years for Asian men, as opposed to 48.8 years for the Coloured). Indians, on the whole, are better educated than Coloureds and, as we have seen before, they have attained much more success in business and the professions than their Coloured fellow citizens.[6]

There are many sociological explanations for the Indians' relative success in comparison with that of the Coloureds. The Coloured people were burdened historically with the stigma of illegitimacy. The bonds of kinship are weak among the Coloured poor. Indian families, on the other hand, are tightly knit. The extended family system is, however, growing weaker among the Indians, as sons gain increasing economic independence, and as daughters begin to get jobs in industry and the professions. Nevertheless, family ties remain powerful. Indians, unlike many Coloureds, have a strong sense of cultural pride; Kogila Moodley, an expert on Indian sociology, goes so far as to speak of 'cultural narcissism'.

According to the ignorant stereotype widely prevalent among white and black South Africans alike, all Indians are traders who can 'live on the smell of an oil rag'. Factually, the majority of Indians are employed in manufacturing industries, followed by construction; trade now ranks only third among their occupations. The modern community of Indians has been shaped by industry rather than by commerce. Industrialisation brought enormous occupational changes among South Africa's Indian people. During the early 1920s some 35 per cent of the Indian labour force was still engaged in agriculture. But Indians, like Europeans, Coloureds and, later, Africans, increasingly moved into the cities. By the early 1970s the share of Indians employed on the land had dropped to about 7 per cent; more than 22 per cent of the total made their living in manufacturing, especially in light industries like clothing and furniture; 18 per cent derived their income from services of various kinds. The Indian community now comprises a substantial number of industrial entrepreneurs. Between 1961 and 1973 the number of Indian-owned industrial undertakings went up from 181 to nearly 700.[7] South Africa likewise draws on the skills of numerous Indian professional men — physicians, lawyers, accountants and such. Accordingly, South African Indians find themselves in a much more secure economic position than their compatriots in independent Third World countries like Ceylon and Kenya, where their activities have been substantially circumscribed, or Burma and Uganda, whence they were expelled.

Politically, however, they remain in a cleft stick. Indians of all political leanings bitterly resent their political inferiority *vis-à-vis* the whites. The Indian community, in fact, has a long history of opposition to white rule. Gandhi, the pioneer of Indian independence, first developed his technique of non-violent resistance to the British in South Africa, where he helped to found the Natal Indian Congress before World War One. But Indians, especially those who are well established businessmen, also have a stake in the established order. The Nationalists originally wanted to solve South Africa's Indian problem by repatriating the Indians. Few elected to go. In 1961, however, the National government reversed its traditional policy, and agreed to accept the Indians as a permanent part of the population. The government set up a partially elected Indian Council, an Indian Affairs Department with numerous new openings for bureaucratic appointments and an Indian university. Indian housing conditions have considerably improved over the last thirty years; so have Indian social services. However much Indians may dislike the National government, they know that Indians are better off under white rule in South Africa than under black rule in Tanzania, Uganda or Mozambique. Indians are equally aware of how widely the Africans resent them as employers, middlemen or competitors in skilled jobs.[8]

Not surprisingly, Indian politics in South Africa reflect this ambivalence. Indian bodies such as the Natal Indian Congress, reconstituted in 1971 on an anti-apartheid programme, have a curiously anaemic quality that reflects the Indians' lack of real power. The Black Consciousness movement finds some support among Indian students and young professionals, but cannot easily gain mass support. In 1978 the Indian Reform Party, the Coloured Labour Party and the Zulu Inkatha movement decided to form an alliance designed to create a new constitution for a 'non-racial' society. But given the numerical weakness of the Indian community, existing tensions between Indians and Zulu, and the Indians' fear of losing their stake in the event of an African take-over, the Indians are most likely, in the long run, to side with the whites.

Notes

1. See, for instance, J.S. Marais, *The Cape Coloured People, 1652-1937* (Witwatersrand University Press, Johannesburg, 1957), and W.P. Carstens, *The Social Structure of a Cape Coloured Reserve* (Oxford University Press, Cape Town, 1966), for two standard works.

2.

Employment Classification	Male (per cent)	Female (per cent)
Managerial, professional, technical	2.2	6.2
Skilled and semi-skilled white-collar	10.8	9.1
Artisans	7.8	–
Skilled and semi-skilled blue-collar	17.3	33.2
Unskilled urban labour	22.4	41.8
Agricultural labour	20.2	3.2
Unidentified, unemployed	19.3	6.5

The statistics in this chapter are derived from the so-called Theron Commission Report, as summarised in *The Theron Commission Report: a Summary of the Findings and Recommendations of the Commission of Enquiry into Matters Relating to the Coloured Population Group* (South African Institute of Race Relations, Johannesburg, 1976).

3. A small minority, the so-called Cape Malays, adhere to the Islamic religion. The overwhelming majority of Coloureds are Christian, though Calvinism does not occupy as important a position among the Coloureds as it does among the Afrikaners. In 1970, Coloureds accounted for 28.4 per cent of the Dutch Reformed Church membership, followed by 18.8 per cent of the 'Apostolic', or dissident evangelical churches, 16.5 per cent of the Anglican Church, followed by various other Christian denominations.

4. The Coloured Development Corporation was set up in 1962, with the state as its only shareholder. By 1977 some R 34 million had been invested. The Corporation lends money at less than ordinary market rates, and takes greater risks than private firms would be willing to accept. It invests in a wide variety of business, including shops and light industries like carpentry and welding. Coloured businessmen are obliged to contribute tools, some capital, or other assets to the businesses in which they receive Corporation assistance. The Corporation specifically aims at the creation of a Coloured middle class, which thereby becomes directly linked to the state. It considers that Coloured businessmen face peculiar difficulties, and need special facilities until they can be fully integrated into the economy, but the Corporation should ultimately work towards its own extinction. This will not be an easy task, as an estimated 70 per cent of Coloured purchasing power is spent in the 'white' areas where shopping facilities are more pleasant than in the Coloured townships, and where most Coloureds earn their living. Coloured shops do much of their business over the weekend, between 5 p.m. on Friday until Saturday afternoon, which does not ease the task of the Coloured shopkeeper.

5. See, for instance, Floyd and Lillian O. Dotson, 'The Economic Role of Non-indigenous Ethnic Minorities in Colonial Africa', in Peter Duignan and L.H. Gann (eds.), *The Economics of Colonialism* (Cambridge University Press, Cambridge, 1975), pp. 565-631.

6. See Kogila A. Moodley, 'South African Indians: the Wavering Minority', in Leonard Thompson and Jeffrey Butler (eds.), *Change in Contemporary South Africa* (University of California Press, Berkeley, 1975), pp. 250-79. An older standard book is Fatima Meer, *Portrait of Indian South Africans* (Avon House, Durban, 1966).

7. Figures from *South Africa 1976: Official Yearbook of the Republic of South Africa* (Johannesburg, 1976), p. 215.

8. For details concerning ethnic stereotypes with regard to Indians, see Melville Leonard Edelstein, *What do Young Africans Think?* (Labour and Community Consultants, Johannesburg, 1974), in particular the table on p. 107.

3 THE AFRICANS

Communities in multi-ethnic societies are commonly preoccupied with their real or supposed roots in history and their respective priorities of residence. Arabs in Palestine say they have a better right to the land than the Jews, because the Jews were late-comers. Jews argue, on the other hand, that great Jewish monarchs had ruled in the Land of Promise over a millennium before the birth of Mohammed. American Indians and their defenders in the United States insist that the Indians be called 'Native Americans' on the grounds that the Indians are somehow more 'native' to the soil of America than second-generation Irish or German Americans.

South Africa resounds with similar controversies. Afrikaners take pride in showing that Dutch settlers had come to the Cape long before the arrival of Bantu-speaking peoples to the province. African nationalists and their friends reply that Bantu-speaking communities had already begun to enter present-day South Africa in the early Middle Ages. These arguments are concerned less with history than with establishing historical title deeds in support of present-day claims. We shall waste little effort in adjudging their respective merits. We prefer to look at the African past in terms of clashing frontiers of settlement, an endeavour that will necessarily lead to some repetition, as history — unlike peace — is indivisible.

The Structure of Traditional Society

The Bantu settlements in Southern Africa are of ancient origin. Sometime during the fourth and fifth centuries AD, Bantu-speaking peoples began to penetrate south of the Limpopo River. Their ancestors had come from the African heartland in and around the Congo forests; their descendants gradually colonised South Africa. As early as 1554, European seafarers wrecked off the coast of Natal encountered 'Kaffirs, very black in colour, with woolly hair'. These villagers, members of the Nguni people, belonged to an Iron Age culture that displaced those of the Stone Age developed by the San (Bushmen), who were gradually pushed into the least hospitable parts of Southern Africa.

The black settlers differed widely among themselves in social composition and technological achievements, and in the motives that impelled them to look for new land. Metaphors such as 'waves of migration' merely conceal our ignorance of Africa's early past. They obscure the daring of early pioneers, the ingenuity of early inventors, the heroic deeds of early conquerors. Unfortunately, however, the details of these migrations can no longer be fully reconstructed from the scanty evidence offered by archaeological remains and myths, legends, and even genealogical tables made available to scholarship through the work of ethnohistorians.

We do know, however, that the early immigrants spoke a group of related idioms belonging to the Bantu groups of languages. The newcomers knew how to clear the bush with axes and with fire; they tilled the land with hoes; they lived in small round huts of wood and mud; they were familiar with the arts of working iron, copper and gold; they were skilled in the arts of carving wood and bone, fashioning pots, and weaving baskets and mats. They had worked out a variety of agricultural systems that were based on shifting cultivation, and that combined husbandry and pastoral farming in varying degrees.

They lived in small village communities; they depended, above all, on help from their kinsmen and neighbours. The land — the basis of all wealth — did not belong to any particular individual. Each recognised member of a village was allowed to work the land, in accordance with local custom; his right derived from his membership in the group. This is not to say that traditional society was communistic. Each family worked its own gardens and kept its crops, subject to certain social obligations. Kinship groups had cattle of their own. Hoes and axes, fishing nets and bows — important means of production in their own right — belonged to individual people, though they might be bequeathed to others as part of a well defined system of mutual obligation.

An African Aristotle, anxious to study the different political constitutions among the Bantu, would have found great variety and constant change. The scale of political organisation varied from small-scale, stateless societies, dependent on ties of kinship and neighbourhood, to larger, well organised kingdoms marked by striking disparities of power. But, in general, chiefs, elders and headmen controlled the allocation of land and fishing sites. Chiefs, helped by councillors, arbitrated disputes. They organised the defence of the community against attacks from outside; they frequently had ritual functions. Above all, the chief was expected to be a generous lord. To the Bantu-speaking peoples, as to the Saxons of old, the king was a 'loaf-ward' or bread-giver who rewarded his followers and fed the hungry when the crops failed. In a society that had no means of storing food over long periods, generosity was indeed the best policy. The road to power lay through a man's ability to secure the loyalty of his relatives and the allegiance of strangers by judicious presents. There was also an element of economic compulsion. A chief was usually able to enforce a short period of compulsory labour which enabled him to build up a small surplus of food against bad times. A powerful ruler, moreover, collected tribute in kind; but this was ultimately redistributed amongst his followers in the form of gifts.

Commoners also believed in the virtues of co-operation, and of securing the help of others by generosity. Niggardliness, on the other hand, was the mark of a bad citizen. The man who took all and gave nothing, and whose crops flourished when everybody else's failed, was likely to be killed as a witch. Most aspects of life were ruled by custom, approved by the ancestral spirits, while individual enterprise was discouraged for fear of wrecking that tribal cohesion on which survival itself depended.

In the technological sense, Iron Age herdsmen and farmers were vastly superior to the Stone Age hunters whom they supplanted. They were professional smiths; there were specialists in ritual, in healing or divining. There was also a clear-cut division of labour between the sexes. The men went out hunting, deliberated on public affairs, and fought as members of tribal levies. In agricultural societies it was normally the men who were expected to perform tasks requiring great physical strength, like lopping off big branches to make ash beds for planting. In pastoral societies, men or boys herded the cattle. The women did the domestic chores, looked after small children, and performed many jobs such as hoeing and weeding. Men associated with men in their work, and women with women. Children were looked after not merely by their mothers, but by a host of aunts, cousins and other relatives. The tribesmen felt themselves members of a close-knit community that supported its members in sickness and in health, in peace or war, through a complicated network of kinship and other obligations. The ideal villager was as far from the tom-tom-beating 'pre-logical' primitive of legend as could possibly be imagined. Traditional Africans valued courtesy, self-control and good manners. (Black villagers today are still apt to look down on whites for being uncouth and ill-bred.) Respect was accorded to the man who was balanced, capable, hard-working, a good neighbour and a good citizen. Prestige went to the chief capable of holding his own in court, in council and in war, a man of insight, reason and judgement. Their achievement, the colonisation of Southern Africa, was immense, and their social organisation offered many advantages to their members.

Nevertheless, tribal life also knew much unhappiness.* Polygamy, while it may relieve some psychological or even physiological stresses, creates new tensions of its own, especially between wives who competed for the favours of the same husband. The Bantu-speakers, for instance, had to devise codes of family duties which were much more onerous and elaborate than any that exist in European families. They also faced vast natural forces they could neither understand nor control. Drought and famine were ever-present dangers, and so were the supposed machinations of witches and wizards.

There were few labour-saving devices — neither wagons, wheels nor ploughs. No tribal community possessed sufficient resources to tide itself over prolonged periods of want, and yet want always lurked around the corner. The rains might not fall; locusts might destroy the crops; cattle plagues might strike down the herds; hostile war parties might carry off the women and empty the granaries. Life, accordingly, was much more precarious than among modern men who can accumulate capital reserves, partially control their natural environment, and ensure economic co-operation on an intercontinental scale.

The Bantu-speaking peoples were immeasurably inferior, materially and technically, to Western societies — even to those that flourished in England or France a millennium ago. The indigenous Africans did not know how to build a sailing ship or a wheel, or how to sink a deep-level mine. They could neither read nor write. Hence knowledge was hard to store, dependent as it was on human memory. There was no scientific knowledge in the modern sense — no germ theory of disease; there was no knowledge of plant breeding or of veterinary science; there were no cattle dips and dams, no fences, no agricultural machinery.

---

* The words 'tribe' and 'tribal' have fallen out of favour with modern Africanists on the grounds that their use slights traditional African institutions, that the words are offensive to Africans, that many modern 'tribes' are of colonial provenance, and that their use is 'unscientific'. We do not share these assumptions. We do not consider that a common descent from the tribes of Judah and Benjamin should be offensive to modern Jews, or that the Germans should feel insulted by the fact that Bavarians and Saxons are referred to as *Stämme*. We are impressed by the way in which African 'progressives' like Nkrumah and Neto have consistently attacked what they considered to be the evils of 'tribalism'. We ourselves use the word 'tribe' in a very specific sense. We refer to a community of peoples in which there is no private ownership of land, where every citizen in good standing has an inalienable right to use available land by virtue of membership to the community.

Bantu monarchs may have tried to distribute regional surpluses through gifts; but they could not easily stockpile food to tide their subjects over bad seasons. Even had they solved the problem of constructing and administering a network of warehouses, and of preventing their contents from being spoiled or eaten by insects, they could not have conveyed large quantities of corn or cassava from one part of their vast kingdoms to another. Salt could be traded fairly easily; but cattle comprised the only mobile source of food that could be easily shifted in bulk.

The economic surplus at the disposal of any African society was limited. Even the most advanced Bantu kingdoms may have suffered from a perennial manpower shortage: there were simply not enough people to complete all the jobs that needed doing. For jobs as varied as paddling a canoe, hurling a spear, hoeing the soil or bearing burdens, the indigenous African peoples had to rely entirely on the power of a man's back, arms and legs — on the power of human muscles. There were some exceptions. The Sotho of South Africa, for instance, learned how to ride ponies. But few African communities south of the Sahara managed to harness draught animals to pull ploughs and wagons until the nineteenth and twentieth centuries, when European newcomers introduced these methods of traction. African technology, unlike European medieval technology, could neither convert the force of wind into rotary motion for the purpose of grinding grain nor utilise water to run a mill. The Bantu-speaking peoples had no means of defending their children against infectious disease or their herds against cattle plagues. Sickness and hunger were ever-present threats, whenever the rains failed, or when the herds were struck down by epidemics, or when enemy raiders rustled the livestock, ravaged the crops, or abducted men and women whose labour power could not easily be replaced. Southern Africa's precolonial population therefore remained small. The Africans' astonishing demographic increase only occurred during the last century of white governance.[1]

In coping with the Western onslaught, the indigenous peoples faced a difficult problem at a time when the Industrial Revolution placed an ever-growing array of new military, industrial and administrative techniques into Western hands. Some Africans attempted to meet the new challenges by reshaping their armes and their states. They tried armed resistance and political accommodation; they sought to learn from their conquerors and to establish listening posts in Western society; they embarked on rebellions, and they compromised. Whatever road they took, however, led to some measure of Westernisation.

The Africans

Figure 3.1: White Settlement in Southern Africa

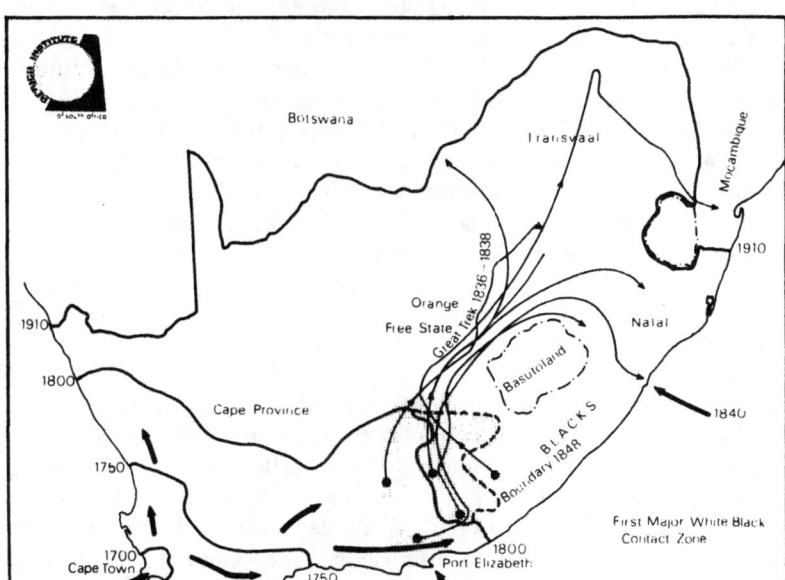

Source: T.S. Malan and P.S. Hattingh, *Black Homelands in South Africa* (Africa Institute, Pretoria, 1976), p. 2.

Reactions to Conquest

The first serious clashes between whites and blacks occurred on the eastern frontier of the Cape, at a time when the scientific and technological gap between the peoples of Western Europe and those of black Africa was increasing in an immeasurable fashion. The colonists had ploughs and wagons, muskets, horses, a host of mechanical tools and weapons that tribal societies could not produce. The newcomers were familiar with Western military and political organisation; they were in touch, however tenuously, with the latest currents of Western thought. The colonists pushed inland along two main axes (see Figure 3.1). The *voortrekkers* (Boer frontiersmen) settled in the relatively dry but healthy upland regions of the northern interior. Other colonists preferred to seek new land near the east coast along the line of greater rainfall. The high veld was thinly populated, but the coastal land contained a much larger indigenous population. From the later part of the eighteenth century, the two competing groups of pioneers, black and white, began to collide. The year 1779 stands out in conventional South African history books as the first of many 'Kaffir wars'.

The struggle between whites and blacks extended over a century. The battle lines during this protracted period were never clearly drawn, as black men looked for alliances with whites against local opponents, and as the whites were equally disunited — Britons against Boers. We can therefore give only a few examples.

Black-White Contact

The greatest warriors in South African history were the Zulu, whose nation was composed originally of a congeries of small, peaceful kingdoms which traded with white merchants settled in various east coast ports. The Nguni ancestors of the Zulu, like the *trekboers* of the interior, seem to have become more dependent on imports from abroad. The struggle for local commercial monopolies may have put a premium on military efficiency. Whatever the explanation, traditional organisation underwent profound change. By the beginning of the nineteenth century, soldiering had become a highly skilled occupation. The Zulu regiments were armed with long-handled throwing spears, short stabbing spears and great oxhide shields. Shaka, greatest of Zulu kings, trained his forces to fight in close order, to advance in crescent-shaped formations behind the cover of their shields and to charge home, while keeping a tactical reserve for the decisive thrust. Prisoners were incorporated into the Zulu regiments. War thus served to strengthen both Zulu numbers and Zulu fighting power. The Zulu kingdom became what John Barnes, a modern British anthropologist, has called a 'snowball state'.

The Zulu state was probably not the first of its kind in African history. Presumably the constitution of the Zimba and of other ancient conquerors had a good many parallels with that of the Zulu and kindred peoples. (Not only the Zulu, but the ancient Hebrews, another cattle-keeping warrior people, took captured women for their spoils; the code of Moses as employed against the vanquished Midianites was indeed even harsher than the practice of Shaka.) Nevertheless, Zulu warfare was extremely destructive, and the Zulu turned out to be peculiarly efficient in the art of winning battles. The regiments were stationed in military towns where they drilled and danced together under the authority of officers appointed by the king. During their period of service the men were not allowed to marry. They fed on the produce of the royal herds; they drank the king's beer; they received their weapons from the royal stores. They came to think of themselves first and foremost as followers of the king, and the monarch acquired far greater power than had been held by the Nguni kings of old.

Shaka took care to keep on good terms with the British. He traded with the whites, and under Shaka's reign (1820-8) the Zulu never tried to fight the redcoats. But military specialisation made the Zulu irresistible to their immediate neighbours, and Shaka made full use of his superiority. A bloodthirsty tyrant, he nevertheless proved as able an organiser as he was a tactical innovator and field commander. When he was assassinated in 1828 his kingdom did not disintegrate. Instead, the Zulu state continued to play an important part in South African history until the Zulu host was overwhelmed by the British in 1879. The last of the great military South African Bantu kingdoms perished. But the Zulu survive to this day as a people with a strong sense of pride and nationhood, potentially the most powerful of South Africa's African peoples.

Outside Zululand proper, the effects of Shaka's campaigns were equally far-reaching. The Zulu raids not only caused a great deal of immediate destruction; they also forced other tribes to flee from the Zulu reach, and thereby carried terror far beyond the original centre of disturbance. When Shaka perished, much of the country now comprised within the modern Orange Free State, the Transvaal and Natal had been devastated, or at least thrown into confusion. This disaster occurred at the very time when the Boer immigrants were looking for new homes further north. Hence, the Zulu raids had the unintended effect of facilitating in some respects subsequent Afrikaner expansion beyond the Orange River.

Zulu militarism also forced other tribes to strengthen their state organisation for the sake of survival. In 1840 Mswazi, one of the great rulers of his time, became king of Swaziland; he further expanded his territory, assimilated numerous petty Sotho clans into his people, stengthened his military forces, and consolidated the Swazi state with its highly stratified society (see Figure 3.2). Swaziland later came under direct British protection (1902), and thereby avoided being absorbed into what became the Union of South Africa (now the Republic of South Africa).

The Sotho, another Bantu-speaking people, were mixed farmers;

52 The Africans

Figure 3.2: Black Settlement in Southern Africa

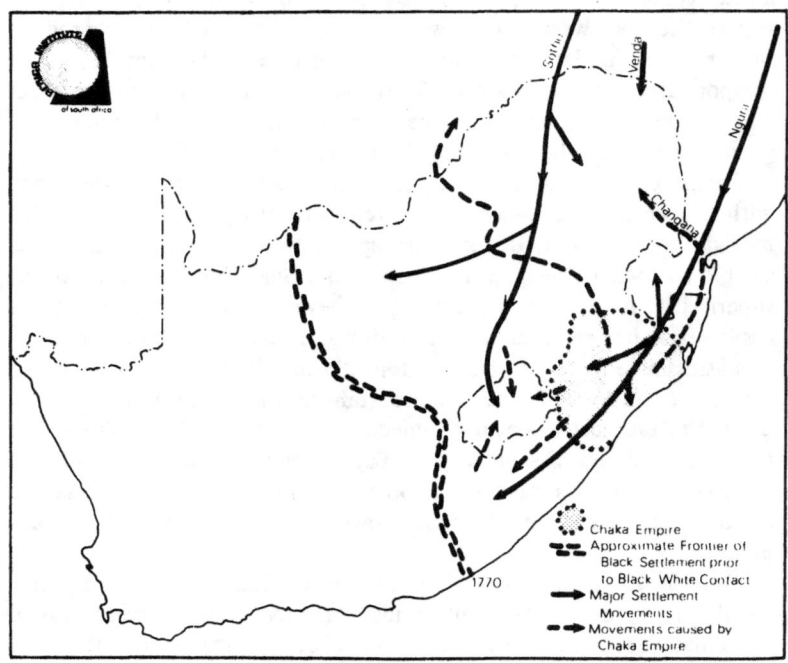

Source: Malan and Hattingh, *Black Homelands in South Africa*, p. 20.

they, too, learned how to play off the British against the Boers. The Sotho at one time occupied an extensive region, including the northern and western fringes of Basutoland, where land was more plentiful than on the narrow coastal belt. Perhaps for this reason, the problem of land shortage did not become as acute among the Sotho as it did in Zululand, and the Sotho were not forced into building a powerful military monarchy. Whatever the reason, the Sotho could not at first compete with the Nguni, and suffered terribly from Nguni attacks. Their fortunes began to improve only after Mosheshwe (Moshesh), one of the greatest nation-builders of South African history, led his people into the rugged mountains of central Basutoland. Here Mosheshwe settled on Thaba Bosiu, a natural stronghold with easily defended slopes, with a top large enough to accommodate many people and their horned beasts, and surrounded by fertile pastures in the valley where the people could graze their animals in peacetime. The king successfully rallied the remnants of many broken tribes and welded them into the Sotho (Basuto) nation.

Having to deal with so many disparate elements, Mosheshwe was in no position to impose the Zulu military system upon his people. Instead, his kingdom grew rather by peaceful attraction, diplomacy and conciliation. The Sotho, moreover, were ready to learn from others. When mounted Griqua freebooters swooped down upon Sotho cattle, Mosheshwe encouraged his people to acquire guns and horses. Within a brief period of time, the Sotho became a nation of mounted warriors with their own tough breed of ponies, one of the few Bantu tribes capable of raising irregular cavalry like the Boers. Mosheshwe also called in French Protestant missionaries. Thus Sotho converts learned how to read and write, so that the Sotho had a relatively early start in the subsequent race for literacy.

Sotho evangelists participated in European mission work in many parts of Southern Africa. The white clergymen provided the Sotho with diplomatic advisers familiar with European ways, and with a lobby capable of rousing philanthropic opinion in Europe on the king's behalf. Mosheshwe sought to gain British backing against the Boers, but this policy proved difficult to implement when the British recognised the independence of the two Boer republics. The Sotho had to prove their mettle, not only against the Orange Free State burghers, but also against the British. In the end, the Sotho lost a good deal of their most fertile acres to the Orange Free State; like the Swazi, however, they survived as a nation, and retained a viable territorial base. In 1868 the Sotho secured formal British protection, a considerable diplomatic victory for Basutoland at the time, and the Sotho thus prevented their country from being wholly absorbed by the white settlers' frontier.

The patterns of black and white land occupation differed in many respects. The blacks, for the most part, did not take possession of the land as private property, but established a variety of communal systems. They did not exploit the resources of the land on a scale comparable with that of the whites. Black tillers and herdsmen emphasised subsistence production to a much greater extent than white farmers; they built neither towns nor harbours and roads. But there was never any rigid segregation. The white and black streams of settlement flowed into one another, as many blacks found work on European farms, and later in the townships and cities established by white colonists. Many Africans made a determined attempt to benefit as individuals from the new economic and intellectual opportunities brought about by European penetration, the creation of new markets, the development of new skills, the establishment of missions and the ending of inter-tribal warfare.

In 1841, for instance, Protestant missionaries, supported financially by the Free Church of Scotland, set up a training institution at Lovedale which served both black and white pupils. It provided instruction not only in reading and writing, but also in trades urgently needed on the frontier, such as wagon-making, blacksmithing, masonry, printing and bookbinding. The students included Africans from many different ethnic groups. In addition, girls began to attend. Institutions like Lovedale received support from the local British administration, which was anxious to spread saleable skills and expand commercial opportunities. Hence, Lovedale and other mission stations began to train a new kind of African: teachers, evangelists and craftsmen, who made a major contribution to the economy of the Cape. Missionaries and administrators also encouraged settled farming by Africans. Ploughing and irrigation furrows first made their appearance on mission stations; subsequently the authorities encouraged their adoption among African farmers. Official initiative helped to diversify the indigenous economy, as did the efforts of missionaries and the example of white farmers. The European impact was therefore double-edged in its effect, destructive and constructive at the same time.

By the end of the nineteenth century, the Cape Colony provided a substantial African elite schooled by the missions – teachers, clergymen, traders, craftsmen, interpreters, clerks, even journalists and newspaper editors. More than a hundred thousand African children were at school. Vernacular newspapers such as *Isigdimi Sama Xosa* (*Xhosa Messenger*) had a wide circulation. A substantial number of educated Africans made use of their right to vote under the 'colour-blind' franchise regulations of the Cape Province. The 'new African' was represented by men like Tengu Jabavu, a mission-trained newspaperman, scholar and politician. Jabavu looked to humanitarian opinion in Great Britain and the Cape as a counterweight to settler power. In addition, Cape Africans began to be influenced to some degree by the black Americans' struggle for equality.

During the South African War (1899-1902) most educated Africans looked to a British victory, hoping that the British might extend the Cape franchise to the Boer republics of the north. The Cape franchise was dependent on property qualifications, rather than on racial affiliation; only a minority of Africans were able to make use of the suffrage, but the vote at least appeared to be a token of future equality. The treaty of Vereeniging (1902), which ended the Boer War, however, proved to be a disappointment to the African elite. Reluctant to offend their own settlers in South Africa, fearful of creating a new 'Ireland in the Antipodes', the victorious British abstained from extending the Cape franchise to the conquered Boer states. The British therefore lost their opportunity of creating a new political counterweight to the Boers; the Union of South Africa, founded in 1910, was essentially a white South African state in which the imperial factor no longer played an effective part.

Educated Africans responded by founding the African National Congress (1912), an ultraloyalist body representing the emergent African bourgeoisie. The congressional leaders comprised men of remarkable ability; they received support from influential South African liberals like W.P. Schreiner. But as a political factor, the congress turned out to be remarkably ineffective, as did like-minded bodies in the trade union field. The African organisations suffered from internal dissensions, from rivalries of a personal and an ethnic kind within the leadership, and also, in some cases, from financial irregularities. African organisations, in a more general sense, were impeded by the migrant nature of the African labour force. Above all, the political weakness of the African National Congress reflected the economic deficiencies of an African bourgeoisie composed mainly of professional men, traders and contractors, without a major stake in the means of production. Africans continued to make progress in the field of education; many improved their individual fortunes in the economic field. But effective political power seemed beyond their grasp, and South Africa remained a 'white man's country' in the political sense.

The Roots of Segregation

The Europeans did not wholly expropriate the indigenous African peoples. The blacks in South Africa were never stripped of their land in as thoroughgoing a fashion as the North American Indians, the Maori in New Zealand, or the indigenous Americo-Indian population of Brazil, the Argentine and Chile. Unlike any of these countries, South Africa retained a substantial number of native reserves. In Natal, for instance, the system was established by Sir Theophilius Shepstone, Secretary for Native Affairs from 1853 to 1857. He had a major share in creating native 'locations' to preserve such lands as had not been pre-empted by white settlers. Systems of governance within the reserves varied a great deal. By and large, however, the conquerors governed through indigenous chiefs and councils possessing a greater or lesser extent of legitimacy in African eyes. African customary laws continued to operate, subject to such modifications as the conquerors thought fit in the interests of 'natural law and justice'. Differing systems of communal tenure continued, permitting the indigenous people to retain a stake in the land by virtue of their clan and kinship ties.

Areas devoted to African use in Southern Africa extended far beyond the homelands. The present-day Republic of South Africa includes but a portion of the lands known as British South Africa before the formation of the Union of South Africa in 1910. What was once known as British South Africa also comprised the so-called High Commission Territories that achieved independence during the 1960s under the respective names of Botswana, Swaziland and Lesotho. Their people, the Tswana, Swazi and Sotho, remained linked to their neighbours in the Republic. Their home countries became economic dependencies of South Africa, as much as the homelands. Had the former High Commission Territories been included in the original Union of South Africa, the area available to blacks in South Africa would amount to about 353,000 out of 765,000 square miles, that is to say about 46 per cent of the country's surface.

The very existence of these territories greatly modified the shape of South African capitalism. Whereas no provision of a territorial kind was made for the aboriginal population of European-settled countries like the Argentine, New Zealand or Brazil, South Africa maintained large native reserves which, in effect, became huge labour reservoirs. Generations of African villagers became used to leaving their homes in places like Zululand or Swaziland to work in Durban or Johannesburg. On the expiration of their contracts, they returned home. The system assumed that black migrant workers were perpetual transients without a permanent stake in the cities. A substantial part of the Africans' wages became payable in kind. Employers such as the big mining companies provided food, housing, medical attention, even entertainment. The system did not prevent real wages from rising. From the turn of this century to the present, there was a striking improvement in, say, the quality of food, housing and health care made available to black workmen.[2] But Africans were reduced to the status of eternal minors, non-economic men, supposedly incapable of understanding their own best economic interest, dependants to whom cash wages were only a kind of pocket money writ large.

The system could not have endured had a free land market been permitted to operate across racial lines. By the end of the last century, circumstances seemed propitious for the creation of an independent African peasantry at the Cape. In various parts of the Cape and the Transvaal, Africans had bought surveyed holdings, often through syndicates. But few black farmers managed to survive the vicissitudes that struck the cash economy during the 1890s — fluctuating prices, the great rinderpest epidemic during 1896-7, difficulties over succession to title over syndicate purchases, and unequal competition from white farmers who enjoyed access to bank loans, as well as marketing advantages through being located more closely to the lines of rail than their black neighbours.

In addition, missionaries and administrators, as well as many white farmers, had strong ideological and political objections to the operation of a free market economy. Until 1913 Europeans were indeed able to purchase 'native' lands in the Cape and in Natal (though not in the Transvaal and the Orange Free State), subject to certain restrictions. Africans had reciprocal rights in the 'white' areas. The operation of a free land market, however, naturally benefited the wealthier whites; had Europeans been granted full freedom of purchase, the 'native' areas would largely have disappeared, and the blacks would have been reduced to a landless proletariat, a grim prospect for white conservatives.

Revolutionary capitalism, with its corollary of a free land market and free social mobility, did not therefore prevail in South Africa. Outright proletarianisation ran counter to the views of missionaries, humanitarians, African administrators and more enlightened white politicians such as Jacobus Wilhelmus Sauer. The Native Land Act of 1913, introduced by Sauer with support from missionary opinion — and even from African bodies like Tengo Javabu's South African Races Congress — put an end to the erosion of native land holdings. Under the new act, Europeans and Africans were alike forbidden to acquire land in each other's areas. Just over 7 per cent of the South African territory (later enlarged to about 13 per cent) became 'Scheduled Areas' reserved for African occupation alone. Africans, on the other hand, could no longer acquire land outside the reserves. Even the African National Congress initially accepted the principles of separation. As the Reverend John Dube, President of the Congress, put it in a letter to the South African Prime Minister, Louis Botha, in 1914, 'we make no protest against the principle of segregation insofar as it can be fairly and practically carried out.'[3]

Latter-day critics have interpreted the system in a variety of ways. According to radical critiques of South African society, the system was engineered by capitalists in search of cheap labour and superprofits. Labour migrancy, the argument goes, relieved white industrialists and mine-owners of the burden entailed in paying old-age pensions or family allowances. Black workmen retained a spurious degree of security through their tribal affiliation. Chiefs continued to exercise a measure of control that would have disintegrated with the disruption of traditional modes of land ownership. The black proletariat was slow in developing a proper sense of class consciousness. Skilled labour migrants failed to obtain the remuneration that would have been their normal due. Black family life was disorganised — all for the sake of swelling the capitalists' bank balances.

In fact, late Victorian and Edwardian capitalists disliked the system. Employers in Rhodesia and South Africa alike had little love for the migrant worker. In the beginning of the twentieth century, mining companies on both sides of the Limpopo scoured the world for what Chambers of Mines called 'non-spasmodic' or 'reliable' labour — that is, for wage workers wholly dependent on wages. Employers tried to import Chinese and Indian workermen; but the poorer Europeans resented such attempts, and the economies of Southern Africa became dependent, to a considerable extent, on labour from the reserves. Full-blooded representatives of Southern African capitalism like Henry Wilson Fox, manager of the British South Africa Company at the beginning of the century, would have liked to eradicate these reserves. Prosperity, Fox explained in a confidential memorandum to his directors, would only come if the communal system of tenure went by the board, and if tribesmen were turned into proletarians. Fox, in fact, resented the way Native Commissioners talked of their Africans, and acquired a professional vested interest in the Africans' 'retrograde' way of life.[4]

But revolutionary capitalists like Fox could not prevail against the 'humanitarian' views of missionaries, civil servants and 'Negrophilist' politicians. South Africa became habituated to an intensely *étatiste* (state-centred) system, paternalistic and oppressive alike, with an enormous superstructure of labour regulations, pass laws, 'influx control' laws, and other instruments of misplaced social planning. The system worked quite well from the employers' standpoint as long as South Africa depended mainly on unskilled black labour employed in primary industries like farming and mining. The system only became grossly inefficient when new manufacturing industries and more mechanised forms of mining and farming required a labour force with skills of a kind than a labour migrant could not easily acquire.

The system greatly impeded, though it could not prevent, a 'normal' class formation among blacks. African businessmen found positions for themselves in the interstices of the South African economy; successful entrepreneurs opened shops and started to make money as contractors or as small builders. But successful Africans could not invest their money in the more valuable 'white' areas or in the towns. Tenants on white farms could never become landowners on their account. At the same time, the state acquired an immense degree of power through its responsibility for administering the reserves, enforcing pass laws, and a host of related restrictions that interfered with the operation of a free wage and market economy.

Skilled African labourers encountered similar difficulties. The effect of industrialisation was again double-edged. Africans acquired a great variety of new skills unknown to tribal economies. Indeed, the very white artisans who denounced African competition often turned out to be the most successful teachers of industrial skills which they passed on to their African trainees and assistants. But at the same time, white workers in highly unionised industries, such as the mines and railways, desperately feared African competition in skilled and supervisory jobs. The Europeans' attitude seemed reasonable enough at a time when white jobless workers enjoyed no unemployment compensation and few other social benefits that might shield them from the effects of a slump. But white interests competed with those of African workmen willing to work at wages lower than those acceptable to Europeans. The whites alone had sufficient power to make their influence felt both through the ballot and the bullet. Whites pioneered the first labour organisations in South Africa and Rhodesia. White workers had considerable influence in South African politics through the exercise of the vote. The Mines and Works Act of 1911, for instance, permitted the Governor-General to promulgate regulations that governed employment in particular occupations. White capitalists saw nothing wrong in employing black miners at wage rates inferior to those paid to whites. But in 1922 the European miners on the Rand took to arms, and succeeded in enforcing their will on the mining industry. The Apprentice Act of 1922, the Industrial Conciliation Act of 1924 and the Wages Act of 1925 further entrenched the colour bar in industry. The Europeans could not prevent the emergence of a skilled African labour force; indeed, many of the African labour migrants acquired quite an elaborate industrial training. But segregation remained firmly entrenched, affecting every aspect of life in South Africa.

Despite superficial similarities, the pattern of race relations in South Africa and in the American South differed sharply. The American

South had been built on slavery and slave-run plantations. The system was eliminated only after a bitter civil war. Slavery in South Africa was never as important as in the United States; in 1833 the British peacefully abolished the system throughout their Empire, including the Cape. The *trekboers* of the interior did not require great armies of slave workers to herd Boer cattle; the mining capitalists wanted hired hands, not servile labour. They came to depend for much of their unskilled work on villagers from the reserves who took up employment to pay their taxes, or to accumulate enough cash to pay bridewealth for wives, or to acquire European-made manufactured articles.

American blacks, like white immigrants from Europe, had no separate territorial homelands in America where their ancestral languages and customs might have survived, as French survived in Quebec. Black Americans were assimilated to a great extent into the life of the United States, and established ties of language, culture and religion within the country itself. In South Africa, on the other hand, cultural assimilation was much less thorough. Tswana, Zulu, Sotho and other Bantu-speaking peoples were neither Anglicised nor Afrikanised. They remain distinct ethnic groups, even in the cities where English has become a lingua franca, and where African writers have developed a vigorous branch of English literature. South Africa, in other words, is not a melting pot; it is an ethnic and racial mosaic, comparable in certain aspects to such multi-ethnic communities as the old Austro-Hungarian Empire, but with the added difference that nearly half the population remains in tribal societies.

The Development of the Homelands

In theory, the reserves could have been turned into economic assets. Given their geographical extent and location, their systematic development should not have occasioned insuperable problems. Many native areas are situated in well watered areas, superior to those in European ownership (see Figure 3.3). Three-quarters of the Transkei enjoys a rainfall of more than 30 inches per annum, and could – in theory – be turned into a South African breadbasket. By 1978 the total area comprised within the homelands (formerly the native reserves) was equal to that of England and Wales. Lebowa is the size of Israel; the Transkei is considerably larger than Belgium (14,718 as against 11,778 square miles; see Table 3.1). World opinion, or what passes as such, has frequently asserted that the South African homelands are not

The Africans

Figure 3.3: Black Areas in 1913

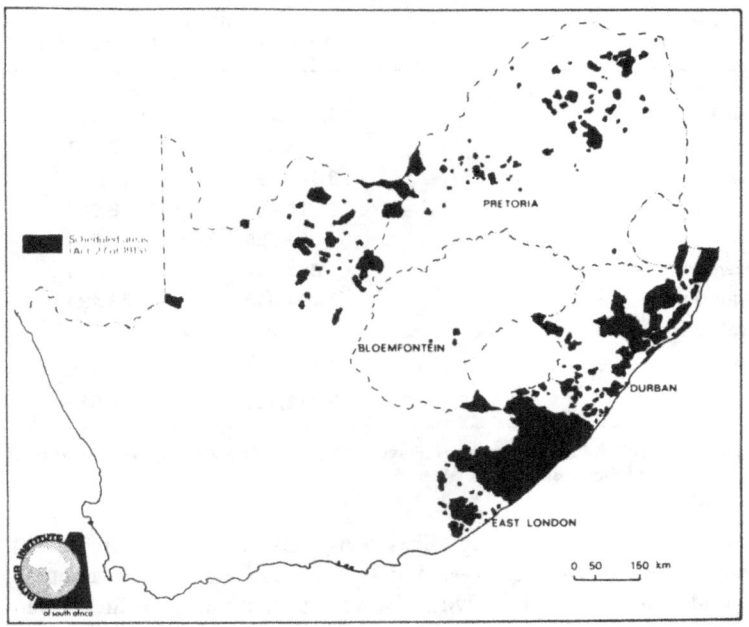

Source: Malan and Hattingh, *Black Homelands in South Africa*, p. 25.

viable in a territorial sense; yet the Transkei is larger than 30 other member states of the United Nations. It has a *per capita* income greater than that enjoyed by 20 other members of the United Nations. It is much more extensive than the West Bank which progressive opinion wishes to be turned into a homeland for the Palestinians. The population density of the homelands, for the most part, remains relatively low, a mere fraction of the population densities in Western Europe or India. Neither is it true to say that all mining areas are excluded from the homelands; mining is the first source of employment within the homelands after subsistence agriculture.

Nevertheless, the homelands on their own could never solve the problems of South Africa. The most enlightened homeland policy could provide no more than a palliative, unless the homelands were to be enormously enlarged. Traditionally, the reserves have all suffered

Table 3.1: Size of the Homeland Areas, 1972

Homeland	Total Area	
	Hectares	Square Miles
Transkei	3,672,212	14,178
Ciskei	918,547	3,547
KwaZulu	3,144,421	12,141
Lebowa	2,214,086	8,549
Venda	604,355	2,333
Gazankulu	667,292	2,576
BophuthaTswana	3,754,018	14,494
Basotho Qwaqwa	45,742	177
Swazi	211,807	818
	15,232,480	58,813

Source: South African Institute of Race Relations, *The African Homelands of South Africa* (Johannesburg, 1973), p. 5.

from major disabilities. Capitalists were unable or unwilling to risk their funds in the reserves. Social services remained inadequate, especially by comparison with the towns; marketing facilities were insufficient. The reserves were generally ill provided with roads, not to speak of ports and railways. They remained backwaters — all too often rural slums. Soil erosion had reached serious proportions. For all the theories advanced by segregationists, the greater part of the country's black population came to settle in the 'white' areas in a process of migration that has continued to accelerate to the present day.

> The Black man ... is also a human being created by God, just as we are ... one thing you have no right to do, and that is touch the right to human dignity of anybody, be he black or white. And if he comes to you and says, I want political rights, then I say to him you may have political rights but not in my territory. I have stated my view to the Black leaders very clearly ... and I have never hesitated to say to them: Look, we are different to you, we have our land and you may have your land, you will have no say whatever over my land and my children ... I am not prepared to integrate with them on any basis whatever. ... We in South Africa are actually very fortunate that we do not suffer from the colour complexes from which the rest of the world suffers. [B.J. Vorster] [5]

The Africans

Ever since the Nationalist Party came to power in 1948, the homeland concept has dominated Nationalist thinking concerning the future. It is only recently, during the late 1970s, that a substantial number of Nationalist supporters have begun to question the future of apartheid. For most of the National Party's era of predominance, the territorial separation concept has served as a guide to action, and also as a justification for existing power relationships, just as the remote vision of a classless society in centuries to come serves Communists as an explanation of present ills and as a key to history. The Nationalists defend their policy of ethnic grouping and territorial separation between the races on a number of grounds: white self-interest, Nationalist mystiques regarding the land, and humanitarian concern for the blacks. As the Afrikaners see it, the national or ethnic principle is essential to the survival of all South Africa's racial groups. In addition, the Nationalists rely on economic arguments. Homeland development, in their view, goes with economic decentralisation and the planned development of backward rural areas made possible through the emergence of light industries, the expansion of transport and the increasing importance of hydro-electric power and other resources of recent industrial technology.

At the time of writing, the homelands have a long way to go, even in terms of the Nationalists' declared policies. The majority of South Africa's black population lives more or less permanently in the 'white' areas. The drift to the 'white' cities has accelerated rather than diminished. Industrialists are reluctant to invest money in the homelands, in areas where services are scanty, and where skilled workmen and managers from the cities are reluctant to settle. Urban development in the homelands as yet remains limited. Though a beginning has been made (see Table 3.2), the majority of blacks continue to reside in the 'white' areas.

In demographic terms, about half the African population is still rural. African villages have a culture and language of their own. Their ideal of a worthy man has nothing in common with the stereotype of the lusty, tom-tom beating savage or the stern rebel clutching his tommy-gun. The ideal of the good man is surprisingly like the image of a southern Italian peasant concerning a *uomo ben educato*: courteous, reliable, respectful, judicious, measured, familiar with the rules of etiquette and good conduct — not a townee full of book learning and ill mannered (*mal educato*), who may be well educated (*ben istruito*) in a purely formal sense, but who does not make a good citizen.

The Bantu homelands have certain features in common with southern

Table 3.2: African Population Settled in the 'White' and Homeland Areas, 1972

Homeland	In the Homelands	In White Areas	Total	Percentage of the Total African Population
Xhosa	2,206,182	1,723,905	3,930,087	26.1
Zulu	2,134,951	1,891,107	4,026,058	26.7
Pedi	1,001,188	602,666	1,603,854	10.7
N. Ndebele	70,008	111,740	181,748	1.2
Venda	251,235	106,684	357,919	2.4
Shangaan	392,910	344,259	737,169	4.9
Tswana	610,529	1,108,838	1,719,367	11.4
S. Ndebele	55,249	177,772	233,021	1.5
Shoeshoe (S. Sotho)	144,005	1,307,785	1,451,790	9.7
Swazi	112,020	386,696	498,716	3.3
Other	18,902	299,321	318,223	2.1
Totals	6,997,179	8,060,773	15,057,952	100.0

Source: South African Institute of Race Relations, *The African Homelands*, p. 37.

Italy — backward rural areas embedded within a more highly industrialised state. And like southern Italy, the homelands do not subsist in isolation. Villagers are in touch with the cities through work, through education, through ties of trade, through the radio, and through a hundred other bonds. The so-called 'tribal' traditions that appeal to visitors are in decay. 'Tribal' costumes, strongly influenced by the fashions once imported by missionaries and white trekkers, are rarely worn. Tribal customs and beliefs are in a state of flux. Ironically, many Africans now look to the past investigations of academic anthropologists to enlighten blacks concerning vanished customs and beliefs. The Zulu language, for instance, survives, and so do certain Zulu customs; but the system of governance and the religious beliefs that once sustained traditional Zulu society have gone beyond recall.[6]

Agricultural development, the key to prosperity in the homelands, as yet leaves much to be desired. Even the potentially rich Transkei must actually import food from South Africa proper. There are many reasons for this state of affairs. Capital and skilled manpower are scarce, marketing facilities inadequate. Most homeland farmers prefer city wages to the uncertain returns from farming. A large percentage of able-bodied men are away from the villages working in the towns, as they are in many other parts of black Africa. Anthropologists, missionaries and local employers are in the habit of denouncing labour migration, either on the grounds that innocent villagers are corrupted by the big city, or that labour migration disrupts family life and interferes with the local economy by denuding the villages of labour, or by causing local wage rates to rise. Advocates of the system argue that labour migrants can earn much more cash in the towns than they can do at home, that skills and money acquired in the cities will also benefit the reserves, and that the evidence for the supposedly ill effects of labour migration on kinship is far from clear-cut, and the skills, goods and cash acquired in the cities will also benefit the countryside. A great deal of course depends on local conditions.* Demographic orthodoxies notwithstanding, the homelands, in all probability, may at present perhaps have too few people to do all the jobs that need to be done and too few customers to support local industries. Some of the homelands might actually benefit from a broader demographic base.

Development is also held back by the problem of land tenure. Traditional systems of African land tenure were complex. But, by and large, they were based on the right of individual male members of a community, on reaching maturity or on marriage, to use land for cropping and grazing. Consequently, land was not regarded as a commercial asset. In the past, the system allowed every married man to hold a piece of land. But as living standards rise and as the population grows, the farming unit becomes too small; the situation is aggravated by lack of formal titles, by the farmers' inability to raise capital, and by inadequate marketing facilities. Some argue that labour migration is by no means confined to South Africa, that young men leave their villages

---

* In the Lebanon, the labour migrants who seek their fortunes abroad mainly come from Christian villages. Yet the Christian villages tend to be more prosperous than the Muslim villages. In Zambia, the Mambwe supposedly benefit from labour migration in the economic sense. Mambwe agriculture, depending on a system of intensive mound farming, is of a kind that gives employment to women and old men; the farmers do not need a great deal of physical strength. The Bemba system of agriculture, on the other hand, was disrupted by labour migration. The Bemba used to practise a system of extensive farming in which cultivators lopped branches off the trees, and burned the branches so as to fertilise the soil. This kind of farming required a great number of strong, agile men, and decayed when the men left for the city.

in search of jobs in lands as far afield as Lebanon, Cyprus and Tanzania, that all these migrants can earn more cash in towns than they can in the villages, that the labour migrants are better judges of their own interest than the well-meaning missionaries or sociologists who presume to speak for them. The black Bantu villager is a good farmer; given the opportunity, he likes to make money. But lacking incentives in the form of individual tenure and an effective demand for his produce, he naturally prefers to grow crops for domestic use only. Not surprisingly, agriculture in the homelands is backward, far inferior in methods and output to white farming in South Africa. Even a casual traveller in the Transkei is struck by the extent of soil erosion, and distressed by the sight of abandoned contour farming schemes. Poverty continues to stalk the land. The migrant labour system goes on. In 1975, 1,181,700 workmen were away from the homelands, as against 1,007,220 in 1970. About a hundred thousand new workers come to the South African labour market every year, in addition to the 1.8 million black workers at present employed in the 'white' economy (see Tables 3.2 and 3.3).

The homelands have other deficiencies. Many homelands consist of widely scattered pieces of land. The homelands leaders themselves bitterly censor the system; far from being the licensed puppets of government, they have become determined critics, all the more influential by reason of their ability to wok from within the system. Financial aid to the homelands is extensive but unpopular among white voters, especially at a time of creeping inflation and recession. The South African bureaucracy, moreover, continues to expand — a subject to which we shall return. The South African white civil service is being paralleled by burgeoning bureaucracies within the homelands, often inefficient and corrupt. South Africa, in short, continues to be torn by vast regional disparities that, in certain respects, reproduce the differences between the 'First' and the 'Third' worlds on a local scale.

Nevertheless, the Nationalists have achieved greater success since 1948 than their critics ever imagined. They have enjoyed certain advantages. Compared with the countries of South-East Asia or Western Europe, the homelands, for the most part, are not overpopulated, even assuming that all labour migrants were to return to their real or assumed place of origin (see Table 3.4).

The homelands have a considerable agricultural potential. At present, about 70 per cent of their farming potential is said to be wasted. Considerable mineral resources remain to be exploited; Bophutha-Tswana, for instance, contains vast deposits of platinum. The Nationalist

Table 3.3: African Urban Population in South Africa, 1970

	Homeland Townships	Urban Townships	Total	Percentage of Group Concerned
Xhosa	159,041	1,048,002	1,207,043	30.7
Zulu	230,662	1,013,291	1,243,953	30.9
Pedi	58,286	319,355	377,641	23.5
N. Ndebele	6,633	41,337	47,970	26.4
Venda	2,797	62,640	65,437	18.3
Shangaan	21,936	204,278	226,214	30.7
Tswana	79,981	597,287	677,268	39.4
S. Ndebele	5,122	75,082	80,204	34.4
Shoeshoe	8,045	638,798	646,843	44.6
Swazi	7,845	169,362	177,207	35.6
Other	2,008	237,583	239,591	75.3
Totals	582,356	4,407,015	4,989,371	33.1

Source: South African Institute of Race Relations, *The African Homelands*, p. 37.

Table 3.4: Population Density in the Homelands, 1972

Homeland	Density of Population per Square Mile	
	De facto Population	De jure Population
Transkei	122	212
Ciskei	148	261
KwaZulu	173	332
Lebowa	127	236
Venda	113	153
Gazankulu	104	252
BophuthaTswana	61	114
Basotho Qwaqwa	136	7,085
Swazi	144	562

Source: South African Institute of Race Relations, *The African Homelands*, p. 39.

government, unlike its predecessors, has induced the South African taxpayer to provide substantial funds to the homelands, much greater in relation to South Africa's resources than the foreign aid made available by the West to the Third World nations. Between 1975 and 1976, government expenditure on the homelands exceeded 400 million rand; the true expenditure figures may well be larger, but are probably being concealed from the white electorate by a complicated and perhaps deceptive system of book-keeping. The work done by South Africa's public corporations in the homelands has been more effective than most similar programmes mounted in Africa from Western Europe or the United States. Homeland development has also provided a career and a sense of mission to idealistic young Afrikaners, more constructive than the narrow nationalism of old.

Economic development of the homelands rests on certain assumptions. The Nationalists traditionally distrusted both the free enterprise system and the 'Hoggenheimers' who supposedly ran it. Even after the party's theoretical conversion to a system of capitalist competition, the Nationalists looked to public enterprise both as a means of ethnic advancement and as an instrument for enhancing South Africa's power and prosperity. Nationalist policy-makers took these attitudes to the development of the homelands. Economic progress, in their view, should be planned. The homelands must avoid the lackadaisical do-nothing spirit that, in their view, had characterised a territory like Basutoland under British rule. Public bodies should have a major share in financing and directing development, financed to a considerable extent at the taxpayer's expense. Growth, according to South African theoreticians, must be accomplished by the creation of an export economy in the homelands; revenue from exports will bring about a 'domestic multiplier' effect: the homelands will build up local industries and improve their farming; the homelands will come to sell merchandise rather than manpower; new townships will spring up, complete with factories, schools and social services, thereby restoring South Africa's social and economic equilibrium.

Critics of the homelands are many. African nationalists denounce the system as a crude device for perpetuating white rule, and for creating a docile black bourgeoisie of black politicians, administrators, traders and entrepreneurs in petty industries that will serve the wider objects of South African monopoly capitalism. While the white majority favours the present policy of the homelands, the bulk of urban blacks oppose it. African blacks want a unitary state (80 per cent) while 90 per cent of whites reject the concept.

Perhaps the most pointed attacks on the system come from advocates of unfettered private enterprise. Adherents of free trade are concerned with the rapid growth of the public sector in the homelands, which now accounts for nearly 30 per cent of the so-called market economy. (There are now over 100,000 civil servants in the homelands.) Partisans of free enterprise argue that state corporations are ill suited for the purpose of economic pioneering, that civil servants are not inclined to take risks, that state corporations tend to be expensively run and overstaffed, that the use of public money entails hidden costs in that the taxpayers might have been able to use these funds to better effect on their own account. Free-enterprise economists also argue that there is little point in artificially promoting industries in areas ill favoured by communications, distant from markets and existing pools of skilled labour; they believe that scarce capital is being diverted into what may be unprofitable pursuits. They also point to the civil servants' notorious proclivity for running potentially profitable enterprises at a loss. The Bantu Mining Corporation, for instance, has consistently run up deficits of a kind that would not be tolerated in private industry.

According to Nationalist planners, however, the needs of the free market must take second place to the requirements of nation-building. The key to nation-building is agriculture, by far the most important pursuit in the homelands. Some 14 per cent of the homeland area is arable, as against 8.2 per cent in South Africa proper, and 98 per cent of the homeland area is suitable for grazing in some form or other. In fact, the homelands could probably produce enough food for 30 to 35 million people, if only homeland resources were fully utilised.

Agricultural planning has made some progress. Traditional systems of shifting cultivation have been largely eliminated. Land is being subdivided into separate residential, cultivated and pastoral areas. As the land is subdivided, fences go up, boreholes are sunk, dams and cattle dips are constructed, anti-erosion works get under way, and reclamation projects are completed. Farmers are taught new methods, including the practice of rotational grazing. The South Africans have paid special attention to the development of cash crops such as sugar-cane and fibre plants, products that will serve as raw material for new industrial enterprises. Agricultural experts have tried to deal with overstocking by teaching more selective methods of animal breeding, by providing a more acceptable marketing organisation, and by pushing agricultural education.

Given the miserable state of most homelands in the past, progress since the early 1960s has been impressive. Between 1969 and 1974 the gross domestic product derived from agriculture, forestry and fishing in the homelands has gone up from 78,134,000 to 123,898,000 rand. There have been some improvements in farming methods, and in individual incomes of farmers. These more than doubled between 1951 and 1973, going from 46.3 rand to 98.8 rand per annum. Nevertheless, agriculture in the homelands remains relatively unproductive, and still hinges mainly on subsistence production. On the average, only about 10 per cent of homeland production is for the market, as opposed to more than 60 per cent in the Republic of South Africa proper.

Separate development, moreover, presents the Nationalists with a number of apparently insoluble ideological problems. The Nationalist Party keeps reiterating its faith in private enterprise. But the doctrine of separate development in many ways conflicts with the requirements of private enterprise. Homeland development, as explained before, rests to a large extent on the public sector, rather than on South African agrobusiness and commerce. Agriculture has always been one of the first functions transferred from the South African administration to the homeland governments. These governments, in turn, have built new bureaucracies — expensive, inflexible, sometimes corrupt, less efficient than private firms, and perhaps less suited to providing economic incentives to peasant farmers than to private entrepreneurs.

More seriously, agricultural modernisation conflicts with the Nationalists' declared political objectives. Traditional systems of governance through chiefs went with traditional systems of agriculture based on shifting cultivation; the two could not easily be separated. Nationalist planners now hope to create African agricultural settlements similar to Israel's *moshavim*, independent smallholders' co-operatives. Whatever the merits of the Israeli model for Africans, smallholders skilled in the arts of agricultural co-operation cannot govern themselves through traditional chiefs and traditional customs.

Industrialisation poses similar questions. The Nationalists have achieved very real advances in promoting homeland manufactures. Even a casual visitor to, say, a match-making factory in Umtata is struck by the efficiency of operations and the quality of the machinery used. Industrialisation has proceeded at a faster pace than farming; factories look to outside markets and outside sources of capital; they are more easily subject to control than thousands of scattered farmers. Housing provided for factory workers is equally impressive, and so are the new schools and hospitals. Factory workers, however, are even less likely to submit to traditional forms of governance. An industrial proletariat in the homelands will not be satisfied with the rule of chiefs.

The faster the rate of industrialisation, the more political discontent may accelerate.

Industrialisation at present depends on a blend of public and private enterprise, promoted through bodies like the Bantu Investment Corporation (BIC, set up in 1959), South Africa's Industrial Development Corporation, and local bodies like the Transkei Development Corporation (TDC, formerly the Xhosa Development Corporation, established in 1966), and the Bantu Mining Corporation (created in 1969). The corporations seek to encourage white entrepreneurs to set up factories on an agency basis at selected 'growth points', at townships like Umtata and Butterworth in the Transkei. Industrialists have been traditionally reluctant to put money into the homelands; they now receive many inducements to risk their investors' savings in places like the Transkei. Investors receive loans at low interest rates, tax incentives, transport rebates, preferential treatment in government contracts; factory buildings and workers' housing are supplied at low charges or cost-free. Private investment in the homelands has increased from 2.5 million rand in 1971 to 53.879 million rand in 1976. Private investment tends to gain an increasingly powerful role after an initial period of state investment (see Table 3.5).

In terms of South Africa's general investment statistics, the figures in Table 3.5 are minute. But within the context of poverty-stricken rural areas these sums are impressive, and the money spent in the homelands is of considerable local significance. The balance sheet clearly contains a large debit account. As indicated before, the Transkei, like the other homelands and like independent African countries such as Swaziland, still relies mainly on migrant labour and subsistence agriculture for its income. The homelands remain heavily dependent on South African assistance; of the 1976-7 budget's total of 138.8 million rand, 95 million came from South Africa. The total number of job-seekers rises faster than the number of locally created jobs; the majority of the *de facto* population has as yet received little or no education. While competitive industries have grown up in 'growth points' like Umtata and Butterworth, most of the Transkei has seen but little development. The homelands, moreover, owe a heavy debt to state enterprise. This means that every economic decision inevitably becomes a political decision. The struggle for political control grows fiercer, because the rewards of victory are great and the cost of defeat is disastrous.

These weaknesses, however, contrast with some solid achievements. Between 1968 and 1976 the assets of the Transkei Development

72 The Africans

Table 3.5: Investments by the Bantu Investment Corporation and the Xhosa Development Corporation, and by Private Capital, 1971-4 (cumulative)

Year ended on	BIC and XDC Investment			Estimated Private Investment	Investment by the BIC, XDC and Private Enterprise
	Infra-structure	Buildings and Loans	Sub-total		
	R (1,000)	R (1,000)	R (1,000)	R (1,000)	R (1,000)
1970-1	1,756	1,260	3,016	2,500	5,516
1971-2	3,878	6,560	10,438	12,801	23,239
1972-3	5,942	13,616	19,558	23,193	42,751
1973-4	6,931	21,780	28,780	30,500	59,280

Source: Figures supplied by the Bantu Investment Corporation.

Corporation (TDC), for example, have risen from 3.1 million to 93,077,602 rand; its operating profits increased from 13,905 to 1,324,360 rand; the number of jobs created by the TDC went up from 489 to 17,236. Development has centred on light industries such as the production of matches, textiles, spare parts for automobiles and such. In addition, the TDC has attempted to build up a class of indigenous entrepreneurs in subsidiary industries — garage-owners, butchers, storekeepers, transport operators, building contractors — who receive assistance through loans, training and other means.

For all their respective deficiencies, the homelands have done well in comparison with independent Africa. There has been a striking rise in the national income of the Transkei, for instance (see Table 3.6), which has a higher national income per head of population than well established states like Tanzania and Zaire, not to speak of poverty-stricken states like Guinea and Burundi. The evils that strike critics in the homelands are not unique to South Africa. All countries in sub-Saharan Africa must cope with rural poverty, with the strains brought about by decaying tribalism, labour migration and rapid urbanisation. South Africa is unique in a very different sense; it is one of the few countries that, in effect, has deliberately attempted to push industrial development of backward rural regions remote from the main cities. The homelands, moreover, contain substantial mineral wealth. (Lebowa has vast reserves of vanadium, platinum and andalusite, as well as about half the estimated chromium reserves of South Africa; KwaZulu

The Africans

Table 3.6: Gross National Income and *per capita* Gross National Income of Transkei (million rand)

	1960	1973
Gross national income[a]	92.0	407.3
Income of *de facto* black residents[b] and migrant workers	84.6	392.1
Gross domestic product[c]	40.2	105.8
Commuters[d]	–	2.8
Migrant workers[e]	44.4	283.5
Non-blacks[f]	7.4	15.2
Income *per capita*		
Gross domestic product (blacks)	29.0	55.0
Gross national income (blacks)	54.0	169.0
Gross national income	58.0	175.0
Income of continually absent Transkeian citizens	98.1	273.1

Notes:
 a. In the calculation of the gross national income, persons are considered as 'inhabitants' of Transkei if they normally or permanently live or work there, or if their interests are mainly situated there.
 b. Foreign blacks excluded.
 c. The share of the blacks in gross domestic product.
 d. Income earned by persons who work on a daily basis in white areas.
 e. Income earned by persons from the homelands who work on a contract basis for fixed periods of time in white areas.
 f. The income of non-blacks is calculated according to the compensation per employee.

Source: Bureau for Economic Research re Bantu Development, *Africa Institute Bulletin*, vol. xiv, nos. 7 and 8 (1976).

contains great bauxite reserves; BophuthaTswana has iron, platinum and other metals.) Given time, some of the homelands will become major mineral producers.

Whatever economic successes the Nationalists have achieved in the homelands, they have failed in the political sense. Urban Africans in the 'white' cities bitterly object to the government's policy of forcing upon them an unwanted homeland citizenship. There is little political democracy in the so-called Bantustans. Afrikaner Nationalism does not favour social distinctions. But social stratification in the homelands has become rigid; its gradations are expressed in the very topography of a homeland capital like Umtata. Ministerial houses and a Holiday Inn — frequented by African politicians, European businessmen and tourists — stand on high ground. The middle class, white and black, live further down the hillside; the 'Native Township' lies at the bottom of the valley. Homeland government, for all its ills, is not tyrannical in the Ugandan or Guinean sense; nevertheless, well documented tales of corruption, misappropriation of funds and governmental inefficiency make the rounds. Too many village chiefs are old, illiterate, or addicted to the bottle. The new, younger chiefs tend to be townsmen who do not know traditional ways and beliefs. They are commonly more interested in making money than in perpetuating ancient beliefs. Certainly, the Transkei's incipient industrial and agricultural development could hardly survive if South Africa were to withdraw its experts and its cash.

But even if the chiefs were all brilliant men, they would face an almost impossible task, given the social variety of the homelands. Few men can move in several worlds quite comfortably; there is no hard and fast distinction between 'tribal' and 'modern' sectors. A polygamist can be a successful bus operator; a 'traditional' witch doctor may successfully modernise his operations by installing a card index for his patients and donning a white coat instead of the accustomed garb; on the other hand, a highly educated man may well turn out to be a failure in the so-called 'modern' world. Nevertheless, there are differences between those who look to the world of Johannesburg as their ideal and those who prefer the accustomed ways. Perhaps half the Africans in the homelands put their trust in the old ways more than the new; they pay bride-price for their spouses; they believe in witchcraft, and call on medicine men for help. The other half have cut their links with traditional customs; many of them are Christians; many more have some fomal education (though even high-school graduates do not necessarily shed their belief in the spirit world and the supposed machinations of wizards and witches). Even the traditionalists do not necessarily like the homeland system, since homeland government has little to do with the olden-day laws now in decay. The homeland system rests on a narrow social basis, the new bourgeoisie of local officials and businessmen who derive distinctive advantages from local autonomy. But the vast majority of Africans reject the 'homeland' concept.

The homelands have other weaknesses. The Transkei (independent in 1976), and BoputhaTswana (independent in 1977) have both failed to achieve international recognition. Far from becoming more conciliatory, the homeland governments have stepped up their demands on South Africa. The homeland leaders, to some extent, wish to undo

Figure 3.4: Land Claims by the Homelands

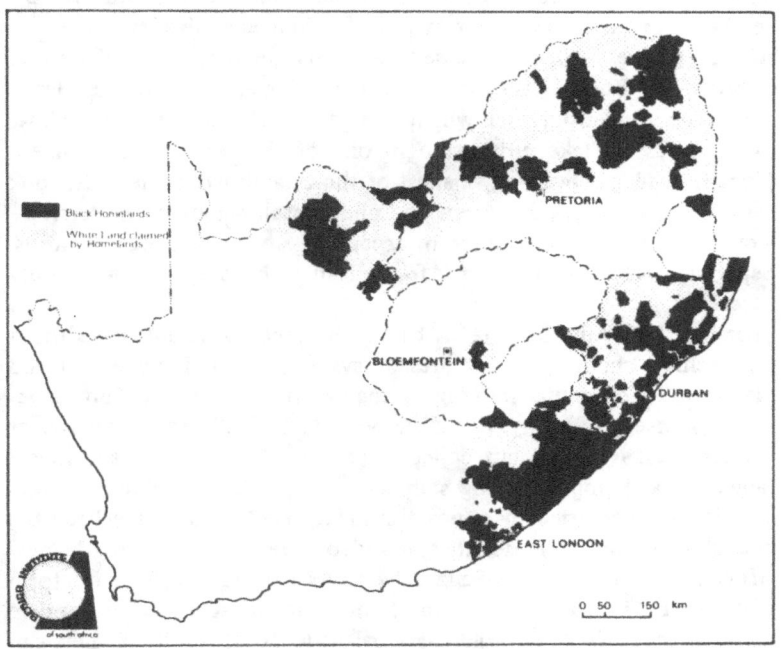

Source: African Institute (Pretoria).

the effects of white conquests made in the last century; they claim considerable areas of 'white' South Africa (see Figure 3.4).

Having failed to obtain territorial concessions from South Africa, Chief Kaiser D. Matanzima, the Transkei's Prime Minister, broke off diplomatic relations with South Africa in 1978 — a desperate step, given the Transkei's total dependence on South Africa for skilled manpower and capital. In cutting his links with the Republic, Matanzima predicted a bloody struggle between black and white South Africans unless Pretoria would mend its ways and submit to African majority rule. Chief Gatsha Buthelezi, head of the not yet independent KwaZulu, was no less critical of the South African establishment. According to

Buthelezi, the homelands' present position is intolerable; they exist as 'labour reservoirs' and 'economic buffer zones' for South Africa's central economy. (The part played by homeland leaders in South African politics will be discussed in a subsequent section.) The Chief Minister of BophuthaTswana, Lucas Mangope, rejected the Bantu Homeland Citizenship Act which compelled Africans living in 'white' urban areas to take citizenship in one of the homelands. Kenneth Mopeli, head of Qwaqwa, smallest of the established homelands, took a similar line. Over-population and underdevelopment in the territory would prevent his country from accepting any more urban Africans. Separate development, most African leaders believe, cannot possibly succeed.

In our view, the homelands cannot become viable entities without far-reaching changes in the present systems of land ownership and more land. Communal farming of the traditional kind can no longer meet the needs of today. Socialists point to the collectivised villages of Tanzania as a model; but collectivised agriculture has conspicuously failed to raise popular living standards or figures of production wherever it has been tried in Africa. Its main beneficiaries have been the new class of party functionaries and ideologues, the Wabenze, the new African elite of Mercedes-Benz drivers. As we see it, effective reform requires the individual farm, for farmers are most likely to improve their methods if they hold personal title to the soil, if they can personally benefit from new improvements, and if they can borrow money on the security of their own land. Communal tenure must go, part of the gradual but purposeful process. Not all migrant workers can become peasant farmers; those who become wage-earners must, however, find a new form of security in the towns, one that can take the place of the security provided in days gone by through the traditional stake in the land. African workmen, in other words, require the same benefits gradually acquired by white workers – pension schemes, sickness and disability insurance, and also the right to invest their savings in urban houses, businesses and land.

The homelands cannot solve these problems on their own. Even politically, the homelands, up to now, have failed from the Afrikaners' standpoint. Yesterday's puppets, in fact, have turned into the critics of today; unless well managed, they may become the enemies of tomorrow. The key to homelands, oddly enough, will be found in the towns. Moreover, the homelands can only succeed if they increase their territorial size to an extent few white South Africans as yet envisage, although Prime Minister Botha is now talking about more land for the blacks. If the whites want separate development of an effective kind, they will have to make political and territorial adjustments never previously considered in their country's history.

The future remains uncertain. At the time when this manuscript went to press, an international commission appointed by the Ciskei government suggested that South Africa should not grant independence to the remaining homelands. The commissioners found that urban and rural Africans alike were opposed to local independence for the Ciskei on the grounds that the country was ill endowed; that the Transkei, BophuthaTswana and Venda had not secured international recognition, and that independence would cut off the Ciskei from the political and economic benefits that would in future accrue to the peoples of South Africa. The commission proposed that the port of East London and the adjoining white farming area of equal size should be joined into a multiracial condominium, governed by whites and blacks, and supported economically by new industries and a free port. The Ciskei would remain part of South Africa for the purpose of foreign affairs, defence and the provision of national services like railways. Given the failure of past multiracial 'partnership' policies in Rhodesia, such an arrangement will not be easy to carry out. The project, however, merits serious discussion and might turn out to be a modest contribution to South Africa's future.

The Urban African

The cities of South Africa, like many medieval towns in Eastern Europe, were created by immigrants. Cape Town and Johannesburg, Pretoria and Durban all owe their existence to colonial enterprise. Whites, and to a lesser extent Indians and Coloureds, were the country's first town-dwellers; the Africans were slower in taking the road to the city.

The African trek to the town went through five stages. The first phase (about 1887 to about 1923) was marked by the discovery of minerals and their initial exploration. Black men migrated to the towns in search of seasonal jobs; most of their womenfolk stayed at home in the villages. The African demographic structure in certain respects paralleled the demographic composition of white pioneers. The earliest immigrants who flocked to townships like Kimberley, Johannesburg and Bulawayo had consisted mainly of unmarried young men. But whereas white women met no influx restrictions, European officials, missionaries and African chiefs and clan heads were all equally opposed to the migration of black women to the cities lest the women should become 'corrupted', lest tribal life should 'decay', and lest Africans should acquire a permanent stake in the cities.

Housing conditions differed vastly. The mines provided compounds for unmarried men. In addition, migrants settled in a haphazard fashion on vacant land near the white cities, making do with such housing as they could provide for themselves, fashioned from sheets of corrugated iron, sun-baked brick, and such. These slum-dwellers were mostly hired hands; but there was also a small component of men and women who furnished services of all kinds — bicycle repairers, hairdressers, hawkers and prostitutes, as well as more respectable women who lived with migrants for limited periods, providing a measure of affection and doing household chores in return for financial help. In general demographic terms, South Africa's urban population as yet remained small; by the beginning of the present century more than 75 per cent of the black population lived in what are now called the homelands, and only 10 per cent in the 'white' urban centres.

For all their deficiencies, the towns exerted an irresistible pull on the countryside. There was misery, crime and degradation. But the towns also offered a release from tribal bonds; immigrants found new friends, interests, ideas, jobs. Overcrowded as the slums might be, there were facilities for sewage; running water came out of taps — a tremendous improvement for housewives. Miserable as the urban shanty or the mineworkers' hostel might be, they were commonly superior to the dark, overcrowded, vermin-filled, pole and dagga huts in the disease-ridden villages. City pay might be low and rations poor, but there were no famines when the rains failed, and even the poor did not actually starve.

The second stage in African urban history was marked by the Native (Urban Areas) Act of 1923, which provided for legal segregation between whites and blacks, accompanied by attempts to clear the native slums. White legislators continued to operate on the assumption of black 'impermanence' in the urban areas. South Africa continued as a backward economy, dependent mainly on the export of primary products like gold, diamonds, wool and such. White unemployment was high; the cities were supposedly 'white' reservations; whereas 'poor whites' were regarded as unemployed for reasons beyond their control, jobless black townsmen continued to be regarded as 'wastrels' and 'idlers'.

Yet from about 1933 onward, increasing numbers of blacks moved into the cities. Between 1900 and 1939 the black population of Johannesburg increased from 60,000 to 244,000, reaching about 1 million in the mid-1970s. Urban development went on apace, despite strict measures at 'influx control', reinforced by elaborate pass laws of a most repressive kind. At the same time, the black city population began to experience a natural increase of its own, as babies were born in the towns, and as a new group of blacks came into being city folk born and bred, men and women who had never known any other life than the kind led in urban streets.

The third phase was marked by the Group Areas Act of 1950, followed by the Native Services Act of 1952. Again, official policy lagged far behind the realities of the city. During World War Two, South Africa had entered into a new industrial revolution. Manufacturers accounted for an increasing share of the national wealth; the 'poor white' was largely absorbed in industry; there was an increasing demand for skilled black workmen, permanently settled in the cities. The Group Areas Act and the Native Services Act continued to operate essentially in terms of the old 'impermanency' doctrine. But having gained office on an uncompromising programme of apartheid, the Nationalists — ironically enough — did infinitely more than all their predecessors combined to improve conditions in the urban areas. Between 1960 and 1978, the number of black primary students nearly doubled, the number of blacks in institutions of higher learning quadrupled; the number of African secondary school students went up nine times. Compared with white and brown people, Africans still remained at a considerable educational disadvantage. Nevertheless, the black labour force became better educated, and Africans began to move up the educational ladder, just as the Afrikaners had done a generation or two before. At the same time, the government inaugurated vast urban renewal schemes. The new town of Soweto, near Johannesburg, was an improvement over traditional *bidonvilles* like Sophiatown (Johannesburg), Lady Selborne (Pretoria) and Cato Manor (Durban), where the majority of the country's black urban population had lived before.

Under the new dispensation, the large numbers of scattered slums were consolidated into major townships. Their inhabitants were grouped on an ethnic basis, in accordance with the Nationalists' political notions. But government policy to the contrary, the proportion of black town-dwellers to countrymen continued to increase. By 1960 the ratio reached 38 per cent to 62 per cent, roughly similar to the proportion of city-dwellers to peasants in Tsarist Russia at the beginning of the present century. Above all, the proportion between men and women equalised; in Johannesburg, the ratio between African men and women changed from 12 to 1 to 1 to 1 between 1900 and 1969. The urban blacks ceased to be immigrants; they increasingly became a settled urban population. Labour became increasingly stabilised. Urban skills increased, and occupations once considered 'white' increasingly turned 'black'. (For example, the garment industry, the railroads, the post office, the mining and building industries and the motor repair business have now become predominantly staffed by Africans.)

To meet its apparent dilemma, the government, during the 1960s, tried to develop urban centres in the previously discussed homelands. Blacks could only rent houses in the so-called 'white' urban areas, but black townsmen could buy houses in the homelands. At the same time, the South Africans attempted to resettle 'non-productive' blacks in the homelands, and to limit the number of blacks that could be employed in certain industries.

Urban development made genuine progress. Anti-South African films like 'Last Grave to Dimbaza' might lampoon the new Ciskei township of Dimbaza as a sort of concentration camp where the last African was about to be buried. But the real Dimbaza grew up as a proper city, complete with factories, medical facilities, schools, cinemas and a long waiting list of Africans anxious to settle there.

Nevertheless, the homeland townships were no answer to South Africa's urban problems. Only a small proportion of African town-dwellers lived in the homelands; manufacturing and mining continued to centre mainly on the great cities of 'white' South Africa. Within 'white' South Africa, the black urban population acquired an increasing degree of purchasing power. Standards of dress, personal hygiene and self-assurance increased in a remarkable fashion. African city-dwellers increasingly became a stable part of the population.

Official South African notions of apartheid to the contrary, blacks, by 1975, already owned 132,992 — or 29.7 per cent — of the 447,733 houses in black urban residential areas outside the homelands.[7] In 1976 the Department of Bantu Administration at last accepted the principle of home ownership for blacks in urban areas. In 1977, in an extraordinary doctrinal reversal, the government at last recognised that industrial black workers would no longer be regarded as 'temporary sojourners'. The Community Councils Act, 1977, made provision for transferring a variety of administrative powers to elected councils. After the Soweto riots, moreover, an Urban Foundation came into being to improve living conditions in the black townships. White South Africa had at last accepted black urbanisation. By 1977 the proportion of urban Africans in South Africa was higher than in any other country in sub-Saharan Africa. There were about 4.5 million urban blacks; they still included, however, more than 1 million migrant workers.

Despite these advances statutory restrictions on movement and on residence continued in force, enmeshing urban Africans in a network of detested regulations.[8] These restrictions, disliked by many white businessmen as well as by black workers, were enforced through an elaborate array of pass laws. Their violations form a fruitful source of legal offences. (Between 1975 and 1976 a total of 381,858 cases were investigated by the police.)

Physical Conditions in the African Townships

All black townships in South Africa in no wise resemble the hell-holes depicted in anti-South African propaganda. The townships vary widely, from detestable to good. The *Official Yearbook of the Republic of South Africa, 1976*, has an accurate description:

> The inhabitants [of Soweto] are served by, and have access to, a vast complex of infrastructural services equalled in no other Black city in Africa. Recently as many as 10,000 houses were erected in a single year. Accommodation for the families of unskilled workers is provided at a nominal fee, whereas the more affluent citizens build or buy their own houses which compare favourably with those of their White neighbours in nearby Johannesburg. The rental for the average house is less than R10 a month. Soweto is served by more than 130 schools with a combined enrollment exceeding 100,000. There are about 12 clinics, 48 creches and close on 70 clubs for men, women and children, 6 libraries, more than 1,500 shops, 167 churches of 70 religious denominations, 3 big sports stadiums, 102 sports fields, 3 athletics tracks, 42 tennis courts, 2 golf courses and 39 playgrounds. There are few cities in the entire Third World which can boast such a range of facilities.[9]

Soweto has other advantages. There are no high-rise apartment blocks. Each little house has its own piece of ground where children can play and where gardens can be laid out. Soweto has a bourgeoisie of its own, men able to live in substantial houses. By 1977, 50,000 motor cars were registered in Soweto.

Informed critics of the government do not challenge these assertions;

but they argue that such statistics as have been cited above do not tell the whole truth. Soweto has educational facilities, children's playgrounds, club houses, even golf courses. But there are not enough informal gathering facilities. The little houses in Soweto are arranged like brick boxes in unending rows; they lack front porches or stoops, those essential gathering places for the family that are increasingly being eliminated in suburbs all over the world, and that once served an essential role in watching the neighbourhood. There are not enough places where young people can hang out — candy stores, drug stores, pool halls, taverns, basements in the rectories of sympathetic priests, those informal facilities that can turn slums into neighbourhoods.[10] Not surprisingly, adolescents are apt to drift into trouble. The crime rate is high; it is not likely to decline as long as high-ranking police officials do not actually live in the community they are supposed to protect. There are wealthy Sowetans able to live in fine houses and purchase Mercedes Benz cars; but even they are forced to live in the immediate vicinity of poor quarters, without being able to move out into a more attractive suburb. Soweto, in an economic sense, is an artificial community. It has no industries of its own except on the most rudimentary level — filling-stations, bakeries, bicycle repair shops, but no major factories. The city depends on the export of labour, just like the rural homelands. Soweto may become a flourishing city one day, but only if it can become a manufacturing centre in its own right.

The physical condition of the African townships still leaves much to be desired. There is a great housing shortage. According to a Ministerial statement made in 1977, the housing shortfall in the major cities amounted to 50,000, but it is, in fact, much greater. There are all too many examples of overcrowding, of poor ventilation, inadequate toilet, kitchen and washing facilities. A study of housing provided to migrant workmen in the Cape Peninsula, for example, especially castigated the accommodation provided by many private employers in hostels and barracks. Researchers found that forty men were put in double bunks within the space of 120 feet; sixty men, on the average, had to make do with two toilets, two cold-water taps and no showers[11] — conditions that remind one of conditions in Maryhill Barracks, a condemned military barrack still in use in Glasgow, Scotland, for British soldiers during World War Two.

There can be no doubt concerning Soweto's superiority over traditional shanty towns like Sophiatown; or over the *bidonvilles* that surround cities like Lusaka, Nairobi, Algiers, in the rest of Africa, or over the *barrios* that disfigure Lima and other great cities in Latin America. A Russian unskilled worker in Moscow or Kiev, an Asian immigrant in contemporary London, not to speak of a slum-dweller in Delhi, would admire a city like Soweto, in which the average house accommodates less than six persons. Black housing may be acceptable by the standards of Latin American *barrios* or Algerian *bidonvilles*, but they compare poorly with those available to South African whites. In 1970 the average Soweto house had four rooms and was rented at an average rental of R5.80 per month by the council, which also provided water and electricity. Overcrowding, with its attendant ills, remains rife in the older townships, and the vast improvements made over the last thirty years have failed to diminish black discontent.

What kind of people live in such houses? There is a widespread notion, oddly shared in South Africa by many white racists and Marxists alike, of an undifferentiated black mass, homogenous, impoverished, without distinctions of ethnicity, skills or class — fierce, angry revolutionaries lusting for the white man's blood. A related stereotype, drawn ultimately from early-nineteenth-century romanticism in Germany, represents the city dwellers as deracinated men and women, without social bonds, devoid of tradition, irreligious, irreverent, atoms in a cold and impersonal universe, bereft of all the comforts associated with a village society deeply rooted in the soil and the land.

These misconceptions are reinforced by literary images current in modern black writing. The late 1960s saw the emergence of a new school of African prose represented by artists like Nat Nakassa. In the 1970s they were succeeded by a new school of African poets, including Oswald Mtshali, Wally Serote and Sipho Sempala, products of the segregated townships around Johannesburg. The new African writers introduced the African townsman to literature. They were bitter, astringent, harsh and uncompromising. As Sempala put it in his poem 'Measure for Measure':

> go measure the distance from cape town to pretoria
> and tell me the prescribed area I can work in
> count the number of days in a year
> and say how many of them I can be contracted around
> calculate the size of the house you think good for me
> and ensure the shape suits tribal tastes
> measure the amount of light into the window
> known to guarantee my traditional ways

count me enough wages to make certain that i
grovel in the mud for more food
teach me just so much of the world that i
can fit into certain types of labour
show me only those kinds of love
which will make me aware of my place at all times
and when all that is done
let me tell you this
you'll never know how far i stand from you[12]

The literary image of the militant black worker has since gained added force from the Soweto riots and the Black Consciousness movement, to be discussed later. The theoreticians of Black Conciousness look to an anti-white unity front of all oppressed, be they brown or black, who — one day soon — will avenge their wrongs suffered at the hands of white tyrants.

The imagery is powerful. But the social facts do not sustain the assumptions on which the images are built. There is indeed much poverty in Soweto. But there is no misery of the kind found, say, in Addis Ababa, Kinshasa or Karachi. Black wages in South Africa, on an average, are low by comparison with white salaries, a subject to which we shall return. This wage gap, to some extent, reflects the vast disparity between skilled and unskilled labour, a disparity characteristic of all Third World countries, including independent African states such as Zambia and Ghana.[13] Black South African wages, on the whole, are higher than those paid in independent African countries for the same jobs.

Experts disagree on the question of how much these wages can buy, a hard problem to work out in a country where a substantial proportion of unskilled and semi-skilled wages are paid in kind, in terms of subsidised housing, subsidised hospital fees and such. South African economists have worked out the so-called poverty datum line (PDL), the theoretical minimum needed without malnutrition or physical distress. Critics, however, have attacked previous conclusions based on the PDL on the grounds that the PDL is based on unrealistic assumptions. According to the University of South Africa's Bureau of Market Research, calculations based on the PDL in the past have tended to assume that an African urban family depends on a single wage-earner. Sometimes this is the case, and the income is grossly inadequate. But usually the average number of wage-earners per black African family ranges from about 1.6 to 2 persons. The average black male worker living alone in Johannesburg may earn anything from one and a half to four times the minimum subsistence level (MSL). A considerable proportion of black families, as well as single workers, live well above the PDL, a fact reflected in the Africans' growing purchasing power and the increased importance of the African domestic market.

African workmen, in other words, do not all live in a state of indigence or degradation. Neither do they all subsist in a state of perpetual anomie. Despite widespread stereotypes, most African townsmen continue to recognise numerous ties of family and friendship; these ties often involve a substantial outlay in terms of goods and services that never figure in a statistician's table. This urban network of obligations is in some ways quite different from the network of obligations recognised in the villages. The network is now geographically dispersed, and less visible to the outside observer than the obligations delineated by social anthropologists in African villages. But the bonds of society continue to operate in the village and town. In fact, they become enlarged, as city folk form new groups, burial societies, welfare societies, sport clubs, trade unions and churches, orthodox or dissident.

Black urban society is thus variegated and complex. Nevertheless, sociologists can arrive at certain generalisations. Overall, the black townsman, like the white pioneers on the Southern African mines two generations ago, is a youthful person. Nearly half of Soweto's people are under the age of twenty. Grandparents are few (see Table 3.7). The age distribution of the townships, in turn, affects the crime rate, crime being primarily a young man's failing.

Second, the black townships are varied in an ethnic sense. Ethnic distinctions among Africans are real; they are not quickly wiped out by urbanisation, but persist in many different fashions, shaping personal conduct — witchcraft beliefs, marriage customs and political attitudes (including attitudes towards other tribes) — in a variety of ways. In Soweto the dominant people, in terms of numbers, are the Zulu, South Africa's most powerful black ethnic component, followed by a variety of lesser groups.

The majority of Soweto workmen are, indeed, unskilled. By 1969 Soweto's social profile was in many ways remarkably like that of an Irish community in a large American city during the 1870s, or of a Polish community half a century later. Nevertheless, skills were on the increase; in 1969 nearly a quarter of Sowetans laboured in semi-skilled jobs; just under 12 per cent made their living in clerical, administrative, managerial or professional occupations, or they ran stores and workshops on their own account (see Table 3.8).

The Africans

Table 3.7: Age and Sex Distribution, Soweto, 1970

Age	Male	Female	Total
0–4	4.14	4.34	8.48
5–9	5.73	5.93	11.66
10–14	6.70	6.81	13.51
15–19	6.21	6.27	12.48
20–24	4.75	4.94	9.69
25–29	3.36	4.08	7.44
30–34	2.91	4.07	6.98
35–39	2.66	3.60	6.26
40–44	2.90	3.27	6.17
45–49	2.59	2.56	5.15
50–54	2.30	2.20	4.50
55–59	1.72	1.35	3.07
60–64	1.06	0.94	2.00
65 +	1.13	1.48	2.61
Totals	48.16	51.84	100.00

Source: Melville Leonard Edelstein, *What do Young Africans Think?* (Labour and Community Consultants, Johannesburg, 1974), p. 56.

Table 3.8: Occupations in Soweto, 1968

Occupation	Percentage
Professional	1.8
Proprietor and managerial	4.7
Skilled labour	1.1
Semi-skilled labour	22.2
Unskilled labour	56.8
Administrative and clerical	3.9
Pensioner	1.9
Housewife	2.5
Unemployed	3.4
Unemployable	1.6
All occupations	100.0

Source: Edelstein, *What do Young Africans Think?*, p. 59.

Regarding collective attitudes, there is evidence of wide discontent. African townsmen, like their brothers on the land, are caught in a vast network of racial discrimination. Its structure and effects will be discussed at greater length in the sections on economics and politics. Suffice it to say at this point that discrimination affects every area of society, that it is based on the notion of social planning, that it is enforced by a vast and expensive bureaucracy, and that the objectives of social planning consistently diverge from social facts.

Discrimination is pervasive and is a profound source of hostility. But contrary to liberal and left-wing stereotypes, Africans — like poverty-stricken American townsmen — are far more afraid of criminals than of the government, or even of the police. Crime is pervasive, much more so than in Latin American *barrios* where physical living conditions are much worse. The South African townsman in certain respects is the beneficiary of a welfare state. His rents are subsidised by public bodies; there is, in effect, a national health insurance scheme for blacks which provides subsidised hospital services. But black townsmen in South Africa are subject to stringent regulations in every department of life. Their personal freedom is much more circumscribed than the freedom of *barrio* dwellers who can move freely, who can use their own resources to put up their own shanties, and who have a greater personal stake in the quality of their neighbourhood than South African blacks.

Black townsmen mostly deplore the system under which they live (see Table 3.11). But in certain ways they have also been co-opted into a structure of government that provides a variety of welfare services. According to a social survey made of African townsmen in Durban in 1975, the authorities ranked astonishingly low on the list of people 'hated or feared'. Only a minority looked to organised political action; an insignificantly small group placed their hope in political violence. The fear of witches and wizards, once widespread, has largely died out. Urban Africans, on the other hand, expressed a surprising degree of resentment against parsons, social workers, teachers, doctors and other members of the service professions. These were even more unpopular than chiefs or informers (see Tables 3.9, 3.10 and 3.11).

Despite the attempts of politicians and literary men to bring about an anti-white alliance, there is, in fact, little evidence of the growth of a collective anti-white consciousness among brown and black men. According to social distance tests carried out by the late M.L. Edelstein, a South African sociologist, educated Coloureds identify more readily with English-speaking South African whites than with Afrikaners, Jews or Africans. Indians also identify more with English-speaking white

Table 3.9: Major Foci of Discontent among Urban Africans in Durban (per cent)[a]

	Less than Standard 8	Standard 8 or above
Discontent with economic conditions	62	62
Discontent about general race discrimination	54	56
Resentment directed against whites	44	34
Resentment of government or administration	18	21
Discontent with housing, community conditions	10	16
No discontent manifest	6	6

Note: a. Since more than one response could be given, percentages exceed 100.

Source: Lawrence Schlemmer, *Black Attitudes: Reaction and Adaptation* (University of Natal, Institute for Social Research, Durban, 1975), p. 9.

Table 3.10: People 'Feared and Disliked Most' (per cent)[a]

	Less than Standard 8	Standard 8 or above
Criminals (gangsters, 'tsotsis')	49	46
Police, law enforcers	25	37
Whites	11	10
Ministers of religion, teachers, social workers, doctors	4	15
Other Africans (chiefs, informers, etc.)	9	4
Authorities, government	2	1
Wizards and witches	1	1

Note: a. Since more than one response could be given, percentages exceed 100.

Source: Schlemmer, *Black Attitudes*, p. 11.

Table 3.11: Strength of Discontent with Present Conditions (per cent)[a]

	Less than Standard 8	Standard 8 or above
Emphatic rejection of apartheid, expressed preference for majority rule	71	77
Political-action oriented, unspecified	17	16
Political-action oriented, non-confrontational or non-violent	13	23
No discontent manifest	6	6
Political-action oriented, violent	2	1

Note: a. Since more than one response could be given, percentages exceed 100.

Source: Schlemmer, *Black Attitudes*, p. 12.

South Africans than with Coloureds, city Africans, Jews, Afrikaners and tribal Africans, in that order of reversed preference. Africans — that is to say, African matriculants from Soweto — felt about the same degree of social distance toward English-speaking South African whites as they felt towards Coloureds, followed by Jews, Afrikaners and Indians in that order of respective dislike. Parental occupation made little difference in the scale of prejudice; the sons of unskilled workers were slightly less hostile to Afrikaners and Jews than the sons of professional men and clerks, and were somewhat more contemptuous of Coloured than upper-class African students. Otherwise the differences were minute. At the same time, black inter-ethnic antipathies continued; in Zulu eyes, the Venda were hardly more desirable than English-speaking whites.[14]

We shall return to these issues in a later section. At this point, we shall assert that South African cities are not powder kegs about to explode, cauldrons about to boil over, or boilers about to burst. Like cities elsewhere in the world, they are beset by unromantic problems like crime, pollution, inadequate transportation, unemployment and such. The ever-difficult task of making a living dominates the life of the people, rather than the spectre of the barricades.

Notes

1. The first census for all provinces of South Africa was taken in 1904. The population of the country as a whole was assessed as follows:

Whites	1,117,234
Africans	3,490,291
Asians	122,311
Coloureds	444,991
Total, all races	5,174,827

2. For a contrary interpretation, quite unconvincing in our view, see Francis Wilson, *Labour in South African Gold Mines, 1911-1969* (Cambridge University Press, Cambridge, 1972).
3. Cited in Peter Walshe, *The Rise of African Nationalism in South Africa: the African National Congress, 1912-1952* (University of California Press, Berkeley, 1971), p. 47.
4. See L.H. Gann, *A History of Southern Rhodesia: Early Days to 1934* (Chatto and Windus, London, 1965), p. 187.
5. From a speech by B.J. Vorster, 17 June 1971, at Naboomspruit, reprinted in O. Geyser, *B.J. Vorster: Selected Speeches* (Institute for Contemporary History, Bloemfontein, 1977), pp. 142-3.
6. For a critical account of the homelands, see, for instance, Muriel Horrell, *The African Homelands of South Africa* (South African Institute of Race Relations, Johannesburg, 1973). For a sympathetic and well documented account see Axel J. Halback, *Die südafrinkanischen Bantu-Homelands* (Weltforum Verlag, Munich, 1976).
7. See P. Smit and J.J. Mooysen, *Urbanisation in the Homelands* (University of Pretoria, Institute for Plural Societies, Pretoria, 1977), *passim*, especially p. 15.
8. The most general restrictions on place of residence derive from the Group Areas Act, No. 36 of 1966, as amended. This Act, consolidating previous measures, stipulates that only members of a particular racial group may occupy premises in an area designated for occupation by members of that group. Any disqualified person must obtain a special permit to live in a Group Area designated for another race. Even more restrictive measures apply to Africans in terms of the Urban Bantu Areas Act, No. 25 of 1945, as amended. Under this law, an African who does not qualify to live in an urban area must return to his homeland, unless he was born in an urban area and continues to live there, unless he has legally lived in the area for ten years for one employer. There are also statutory restrictions on freedom of movement. Movement from one area to another is widely controlled by permits. Sexual relations across the race barrier are rendered illegal; all social services are racially segregated; there were racial restrictions on certain kinds of employment — the entire structure of discrimination being supported by an all-pervasive bureaucracy and a deeply held belief in the superior virtues of social planning.
9. *Official Yearbook of the Republic of South Africa, 1976* (Johannesburg, 1976), p. 233.
10. See the account in Andrew M. Greely's brilliant study, *The American Catholic: a Social Profile* (Basic Books, New York, 1977), especially p. 229.
11. Institute for Race Relations, *A Survey of Race Relations in South Africa* (Institute of Race Relations, Johannesburg, 1977), p. 414.
12. Sipho Sempala, *The Soweto I Love* (Rex Collings, London, 1977).
13. In the United States in 1961, unskilled earnings accounted for about 64 per cent of skilled earnings; in South Africa in 1961, unskilled earnings amounted to 20 per cent of skilled earnings. In Ghana the proportion was even

less. International comparisons are extremely hard to make, as conditions differ, and as the statistical material available for differing countries differs widely in coverage and quality. Attempts have been made to compare the wage differential between whites and blacks in South Africa on the one hand, and in independent countries on the other. They have not been unfavourable to South Africa. In 1976 the ratio of white to black wages in South Africa was 4.7 to 1 in manufacturing, 3.8 to 1 in commerce, and 3.6 to 1 in central government. In Zambia in 1972, the ratio was 5.6 to 1, and in Kenya in 1973 the ratio was 12 to 1.

14. See Melville L. Edelstein, *What do Young Africans Think?* (Labour and Community Consultants, Johannesburg, 1974), especially p. 105, Table B, and p. 104, Table A. See also Theodor Hanf, Heribert Weiland and Gerda Vierdag, *Südafrika: Friedlicher Wandel Möglichkeiten demokratischer Konfliktregelung — Eine empirische Untersuchung* (Mathias Grunewald Verlag, Mainz, 1974), *passim*, especially pp. 365, 374, 379.

PART TWO:

SOUTH AFRICA YESTERDAY AND TODAY

4 THE POLITICS OF SOUTH AFRICA

On a sweltering summer day in 1908, delegates from the four South African colonies met to discuss the unification of South Africa, and to put the final touches to reconciliation between Briton and Boer. The various colonial representatives had several constitutional models before them. Among the self-governing white states within the British Empire, the Dominion of New Zealand was organised along unitary lines, as was the United Kingdom. Australia and Canada, on the other hand, were federations. The South Africans would have acted wisely had they opted for a federal constitution. But the tide rushed the other way. The President of the convention, Sir Henry de Villiers, had been impressed during a visit abroad by the weaknesses of the Canadian constitution; the British Natalian delegates were left to fight the cause of federalism which, to all intents and purposes, went by default. South Africa's inner divisions followed a curious system of apportioning the main functions of government between the country's principal cities. Parliament met in Cape Town; the executive branch centred on Pretoria; the Supreme Court of South Africa sat at Bloemfontein. But the Union of South Africa (now the Republic of South Africa) was set up essentially as a unitary state.

The Formal Structure of Government

The country's formal head is the State President, elected for seven years by an electoral college consisting of both houses of Parliament. His office is essentially honorific; he is supposedly above party politics — like the British Queen whom, in effect, he replaced when South Africa became a republic in 1961. The State President's executive council comprises all members of the Cabinet (discussed below); but again, its functions are essentially formal.

Real power rests with Parliament, built in the main on the British Westminster model. Until its recent abolition in 1980, the Senate served mainly as a revising chamber, able to delay Bills introduced into the lower house. The lower house, or House of Assembly, is made up by 165 members elected by the white voters — one member returned for each constituency by a simple majority. Like the British model, the South African Parliament has unrestricted legislative powers to make laws for 'the peace, order, and good government of the republic'. The Supreme Court of South Africa, unlike the US Supreme Court, cannot invalidate Acts of Parliament except those that conflict with the 'entrenched' clauses of the constitution; the court therefore is much inferior in power to that of its American namesake, an arrangement often regretted by liberal critics of the South African regime.

Under the South African dispensation, moreover, individual Members of Parliament as a rule count for less than legislators in Washington, DC. There is nothing comparable to the congressional staffs which provide American senators and representatives with counsel based on detailed research. Neither are there great, privately financed 'think tanks' — such as the Brookings Institution — able to produce facts and figures as well as analytical critiques equal or superior to the information furnished to individual Ministers by their respective department personnel. The nearest approach to such think tanks are the South African Institute of Race Relations, a liberal body, and the South African Bureau of Racial Affairs, a Nationalist organisation.

The State President of South Africa, like the British sovereign, appoints his Ministers from such Members of Parliament as have the confidence of a majority in the House of Assembly. Together, the Ministers form the Cabinet, headed by the Prime Minister. Traditionally the most influential man in South Africa — head of his party, head of the executive, head of his faction in Parliament — the Prime Minister bears enormous responsibility and, in effect, wields more power than an American President. The Prime Minister not only runs the government; he also heads the party and controls it in a manner available to no US president. A Prime Minister proven in office also becomes, in an intangible sense, a leader of the Afrikaner nation, with powers that transcend his purely political role.

Technically, the Prime Minister can be ousted by a defeat in the assembly or by desertion of his followers. In practice, South African prime ministers — men as different as Botha, Smuts, Verwoerd and Vorster — have dominated the country's affairs and enjoyed an extraordinary degree of personal ascendancy. The Prime Minister presides over the Cabinet, a Ministerial council that meets at least once a week (perhaps several times a week during a busy session). The Ministers submit their proposals, chiefly in so far as they relate to their own Ministries, and discuss general issues of policy. Final decisions rest with the Prime Minister, whose power is hard to defy.

The Prime Minister's position is strengthened through the bureaucracy within the Prime Minister's department which, in effect, serves as an executive secretariat with far-reaching functions. The secretary of the Prime Minister's department chairs a subordinate committee of departmental secretaries, and holds individual responsibility for policy implementation. In addition, there are six ongoing committees, each entrusted with authority over some broader area like state security. These have taken the place of overlapping and ineffective Cabinet committees formerly set up on an *ad hoc* basis; each of them is chaired by a close political associate of the Prime Minister. The Prime Minister thus serves as the linchpin of government. At the same time individual Ministers enjoy a great deal of autonomy within their respective departments. Their policies may well diverge from one another over some major issues. In the last instance, the Prime Minister can always enforce his will, but he may not always choose to do so, or he may not always be aware of all the issues involved.

B.J. Vorster, the country's late Prime Minister, once enjoyed unrivalled personal authority, a point to which we shall return. He formulated South Africa's grand strategy with the help of a small number of Ministers and high-ranking civil servants, all of whom are Afrikaners and all of whom had long tenure in office. They included General Hendrick J. van den Bergh, head of the Bureau of State Security, R.F. Botha, Minister for Foreign Affairs, C.P. Mulder, P.W. Botha, Hilgard Muller; among the senior civil servants, Brand Fourie; and among the soldiers, General Magnus Malan.

At the end of 1978 Vorster retired from the premiership, to be replaced by Pieter Willem Botha, then Minister of Defence. Botha was a new phenomenon in Afrikaner politics, a party functionary who had made his career within the National Party as an organiser. He was a tough-minded believer in law and order and military strength — not for nothing was he known within his party as 'Piet Wapen' (Piet the Weapon). But Botha, a lawyer by training, previously leader of the National Party at the Cape, also was in many ways a *verligte* (reformist); he stood for limited reforms and for co-operation with the Coloureds, a policy more congenial to the Cape than to the Transvaal branch of the party. In 1961 he had entered the Cabinet as Minister of Coloured Affairs, Community Development and Housing; in this capacity he had worked to improve Coloured living conditions. In 1965 he became Minister of Defence, and proceeded to turn the South African Defence Force into a formidable military establishment. A pragmatist anxious to strengthen the country's military power base, he established the

Cape Corps — a Coloured unit — and introduced voluntary military service for women, South African Indians and blacks. He likewise favoured plans for a revised constitution that would give some say to Indians and Coloureds in the country's central government. Botha's cautious reformism found further expression in a Cabinet reshuffle, occasioned at the end of 1978 by the 'Muldergate' scandal involving the illegitimate use of Information Department funds. Instead of picking Dr Andries Treurnicht, a convinced believer in apartheid, Botha selected Pieter W. Koornhof, a *verligte*, to replace another pragmatist, Mulder, as his Minister of Plural Relations and Developments.

Vorster, on his retirement from the Prime Minister's office, stepped into the presidency, only to retire in 1979 as the result of 'Muldergate'. The information scandal was symptomatic of wider internecine arguments within the National Party; it also contributed to worsening relations between the Afrikaans-speaking and English-speaking sections of the South African Establishment. The information scandal moreover did away with plans to set up a presidential republic along American or French Gaullist models. (In 1976 the Cabinet had appointed a committee to consider constitutional changes in the direction of an executive presidency. Such a constitutional revision would have concentrated more power into the hands of the leadership; revision would also have enabled the government to introduce a more effective system of consultation with 'non-white' groups.) The government also published a new constitutional plan in 1977, providing for a so-called Indian Parliament, as well as a Coloured Parliament. Each of these would have enjoyed certain limited powers to make laws for its own community; the three legislatures between them — white, Indian and Coloured — would elect a joint Cabinet Council in which the whites would have a majority and choose an executive President. The future shape of South Africa's constitution cannot as yet be clearly discerned, but the British-imported Westminster model will probably not survive in South Africa any more than in any other part of the continent.

The armed forces are much less important in South African politics than in African countries like Zaire or Nigeria. The bureaucracy plays a much greater role, given the extent of Ministerial independence within the Cabinet structure, the bureaucrats' prestige, and their real or assumed expertise on all matters of government. The South African civil administration centres on 14 Ministries. Some of these deal with functions like labour, foreign affairs or defence. Others cope with housekeeping tasks such as finance or the public service. A third group of departments looks after the subordinate ethnic groups, such as the Department of Plural Relations (formerly Bantu administration).

The public service staff is grouped into eight main horizontal divisions that reflect, in some sense, the social divisions of white society as well as the administrative functions of public servants. The administrative division consists of departmental heads and other supervisors; they form the managerial element in government. The professional division includes specialists like engineers, physicians and lawyers; the technical division is composed of artisans, foremen and technicians. In the clerical division are clerks, typists and other subordinate employees, while the so-called unclassified divisions account for a vast body of semi-skilled and unskilled employees.* Each division has a vertical structure consisting of a series of grades marking seniority and appropriate remuneration, depending on responsibility.

South Africa's white society resembles society in Australia and other settler countries, in that status groups are not rigidly separated from one another. An able private soldier in the army can rise to be a general. An ambitious clerk can work his way up to become an administrative control officer, or even an Under-Secretary. The bureaucracy does not form a social caste. Hence, a civil servant may move from one department of state to another, or indeed to any part of the public sector; but in general most spend their respective careers in one particular department, making for a considerable degree of administrative conservatism and stability.

We have dealt with the politics of the civil service in other chapters. While the Afrikaners hold a dominant position within the civil service, the service is not politicised as it is in a one-party state, and it does not regard itself — and is not regarded by the dominant National Party — as the ruling party's executive organ.† The public services are by no means

* In 1977 the Administrative Division — the power elite — comprised 5,985 officers, as against 8,897 in the Professional Division, 14,063 in the Clerical Division, and 8,125 in the Technical Division. The managers, specialists, clerks and skilled workers were supported by a great army of semi-skilled and unskilled employees, including 2,008 in the General A Division, 28,083 in the General B Division, and — the largest body of all — 27,558 unclassified workers. Positions in the Administrative Division in South Africa, unlike the Administrative Division in the traditional British civil service, are normally filled by promotion from posts in the Clerical Division. Incumbents are required to hold at least a matriculation certificate; usually, however, they possess a university degree. See J.N. Cloete, 'The Bureaucracy' in Anthony de Crespigny and Robert Schrire (eds.), *The Government and Politics of South Africa* (Juta, Cape Town, 1978), p. 60.

† Recruitment, promotion and general conditions of service are controlled by the Public Services Commission, a department of its own. The Commission, however, does not supervise the public services as a whole; departments such as the

homogeneous in the political sense; they are affected by the ideological divisions that affect white society as a whole. By and large, the technical departments, the administrations of large municipalities, the armed services and the departments concerned with economic development tend to be reformist on the all-pervading issue of black/white relations. Conservative sentiments are more powerful in the police, and in the strictly administrative departments. Despite these divisions, the public service is cohesive; it enjoys wide respect; it is reasonably efficient, and does not suffer from widespread corruption, thereby giving South Africa a tremendous advantage not enjoyed by the bulk of black African states. The civil service, moreover, has to operate in a country where white society is in the minority, and where the Europeans do not show the respect traditionally given to the bureaucracy as, for example, in Central and Eastern Europe.

Nevertheless, the central executive remains extraordinarily powerful. To a certain extent, inter-bureaucratic dissensions indeed still take the part of 'normal' politics, especially in the field of race relations. The central state administration looks after African, Coloured and Indian affairs; the Department of Plural Relations and Development forms a powerful fief of its own, complete with a broad range of administrative services and economic functions.*

The central administration also plays a key role in the country's economic affairs; in a certain sense, South Africa is a semi-socialist country. (We shall deal with the role of the public sector in the chapter on economics.) By 1974 the public sector, even exclusive of public corporations like the South African Iron and Steel Corporation (ISCOR) or the Industrial Development Corporation, employed as many persons as mining and commerce (see Table 4.1). Overall, the

Bureau of State Security, the Department of Defence, the South African Police, the prison service and the provincial administrations are excluded from its supervision.

* The Department contains three main subdivisions, known as directorates. The Directorate of African Affairs Administration administers labour, housing, identification and related matters, and promotes the settlement of Africans in the homelands. The Directorate of Homeland Affairs operates a research division, a homeland territories branch, an agricultural advisory services branch, a political development branch, a community affairs branch (concerned with welfare services) and an ethnological services branch. The Directorate of Management Services contains a legal affairs division, a finance directorate, a homeland training division (concerned with training African officials) and other specialist services. In addition to these directorates, the department operates a number of major statutory bodies, including the Bantu Investment Corporation and the Bantu Mining Corporation.

Table 4.1: Employment in the Public and Private Sectors, 1974, and Cumulative Growth Rates, 1960-74

	Persons Employed 1974[a] (thousands)	Cumulative Annual Rate of Growth 1960-74[b] (per cent)
Private Sector		
Agriculture	1,505	nil
Mining	664	0.50
Industry	1,316	5.33
Construction	405	8.83
Commerce	494	3.64
Banks and building societies	70	5.80
Total: private sector	4,454	2.36
Public Sector		
Electricity	52	4.11
South African railways	232	0.47
Communications	64	3.22
Central government	371	5.39
Provincial administration	209	2.97
Local governments	203	2.13
Universities	22	7.60
Total: public sector[c]	1,153	2.99

Notes:
a. Given to provide relative weights.
b. Growth rate in number of persons employed.
c. Not all categories of public servants are included in the table and the totals should not, therefore, be accepted as comprehensive; but the annual rates of growth are nevertheless representative for the purposes of comparison.

Source: A.D. Wassenaar, *Assault on Private Enterprise* (Tafelberg Publishers, Cape Town, 1977), p. 73.

annual growth rate of the public sector was larger than that of the private sector. The public sector, by 1975, accounted for 48 per cent of the total gross domestic fixed investment in South Africa; total expenditure of the public sector in 1975 amounted to more than 33 per cent of the gross national product.[1]

The movement towards public enterprise began with the formation of the South African Railways and Harbours (1910), now one of the largest commercial enterprises in the southern hemisphere. The trend has continued ever since. There are state-owned diamond diggings (at Alexander Bay) administered by the Department of Mines; there is a government guano island under the Department of Industry; there are 22 public corporations, most of them fully state-owned, some with minority private share holdings. These bodies include the Reserve Bank of South Africa, the National Finance Corporation, the Industrial Development Corporation of South Africa, the Electricity Supply Commission, ISCOR, the South African Coal, Oil and Gas Corporation (SASOL), and others. South Africa has a nationalised central bank, a nationalised iron and steel industry (coexisting with a private iron and steel sector) and a nationalised oil industry. Many of its investment corporations are nationalised, as is the Land and Agricultural Bank of South Africa, responsible for making loans to farmers, and the Southern Oil Exploration Company, which is entrusted with South Africa's vital search for oil. The government supports a great network of agricultural and industrial research institutes. It exercises tight control over agricultural production through a variety of pricing mechanisms. At the time of writing, South Africa experienced a reaction comparable to the conservative drift in the USA and Great Britain. The South African Establishment began to speak increasingly in favour of encouraging the private sector and rationalising the public services. Nevertheless, South Africa continued to stand out as a classic example of a semi-bureaucratised economy, and in this respect resembled most other African countries.

The operations of the central executive are, however, subject to a variety of restrictions. We will point to the press, the churches and the universities below. Equally important is the role of judicature, proud of its integrity built on the tradition of Roman-Dutch law. The system of justice and administration embodies a costly, elaborate and oppressive system of racial discrimination that interferes both with the personal freedom of South Africans and with the freedom of the market. There are statutory restrictions on the place of a person's residence, his ability to buy land or open offices in the place of his choice, his ability to associate with others for social purposes or gain, and — at the time of writing — even on his right to marry or to have sex with a person of another race.* On the other hand, the courts are

---

* A full description of this restrictive legislation would require a handbook of its own. Specially noteworthy are the Group Areas Act, No. 36 of 1966, as subsequently amended; the Bantu Urban Areas Consolidation Act, No. 25 of 1945, as

known for their lack of corruption. Justice is generally administered more speedily and at less expense to the litigant than in the United States, where judicial formalism is carried to much greater lengths. The judicial structure is reasonably simple, and the country's judicial tradition may as yet play a major part in promoting domestic reforms.*

Below the central government there is a second layer of provincial governments. To this day, the four provinces — Cape, Natal, Transvaal, Orange Free State — retain a certain degree of autonomy reflecting regional differences within the European (though not the African or Indian) population. The central government's supremacy is mirrored in the position of the administrator, the chief executive officer within each province. He is virtually a governor, appointed by the State President for a five-year term. The administrator is assisted by a quasi-Cabinet, styled the executive council; its members are chosen by the provincial councils, elected bodies empowered to enact local ordinances.

The provinces are responsible for a variety of functions, including white education (excluding universities and technical colleges under the central government), the bulk of hospital services for all races, provincial road services, nature conservation, the supervision of urban administration and others. The functional division between the central and the provincial governments involves many inconsistencies. For example, the provinces run hospitals for maternity, orthopaedic and convalescent patients of whatever race, whereas the central government looks after hospitals for infectious diseases and institutions for the mentally disordered. Despite these absurdities and despite the limits on provincial power, provincial loyalties survive and, to a minor extent, they even cut across white ethnic ties, as Cape Afrikaners are apt to pride themselves on a greater degree of liberalism than Transvaalers, or

subsequently amended; the Prohibition of Political Interference Act, No. 51 of 1968, which makes it an offence to belong to a racially open political party; the Shops and Offices Act, No. 75 of 1964; the Physical Planning and Utilisation of Resources Act, No. 88 of 1967, and many more.

* The Supreme Court is the highest court of appeal. Below it there are seven divisions at the provincial level, each with a presiding judge president and 'puisne' judges appointed by the state-president-in-council. In addition there are local divisions as well as magistrates' courts, each in charge of a magistrate who performs both judicial and administrative functions. Parallel to the 'white' courts, there is a series of 'Bantu' courts with a limited jurisdiction. These comprise chiefs' courts concerned with civil cases arising from Bantu law and custom, courts of Bantu affairs, commissions staffed by officers of the Department of Plural Relations Administration and Development, Bantu appeal courts and special courts.

as Natalian English-speakers somehow claim a greater sense of Englishry than their Anglophone compatriots in, say, the Orange Free State. (Some Natalians even speak of gaining independence from South Africa.)

Local authorities form the third level of white government. Municipal councils vary in composition and powers, ranging from city councils, town councils, down to village councils, local boards and health councils. The city and municipal councils are elected by the white voters; they are empowered to make by-laws. They deal with the wide range of local subjects, including the construction and maintenance of streets, traffic control, the provision of water, sewerage and electricity, town planning, housing, parks, recreational services, a variety of health services, fire-fighting, public libraries and other such services. In the past, the muncipalities also provided services for the black urban areas. In 1973, however, the Department of Bantu Administration and Development took over the administration of all African urban areas outside the homelands, a major addition to its power. The Republic is now divided into 22 administrative areas with a board for each. Each area comprises a number of black residential areas previously administered by white town councils. The Urban Bantu Councils Act of 1961 permitted the setting up of elected black town councils in African residential sections, and the drift toward self-governing black townships now seems irresistible.

White Party Politics, 1910–77

Politics is a South African obsession. Professors talk politics; society hostesses talk politics; truck drivers talk politics. Yet few people are ever converted to their interlocutor's viewpoint in these interminable discussions. The character of South Africa's political debate is influenced strongly by the ethnic roots of South African politics. The Union of South Africa, formed in 1910, was in certain respects a compromise between English-speaking mine-owners, merchants and businessmen and solid, respectable Afrikaner and British farmers who had a stake in the cash economy. The Union, however, disappointed the 'poor whites' — white urban workers and poverty-stricken Afrikaner countrymen, including the most backward farmers (some of these joined a short-lived rebellion against the Pretoria government when South Africa, in 1914, entered the war against Germany).

The British remained a minority, despite early-twentieth-century

British hopes — and Afrikaner fears — to the contrary. But the British — self-confident, optimistic, victorious in war, predominant in business, convinced that the British system of government offered a workable model to the whole Empire — felt no need to entrench British group rights against the Afrikaans-speaking majority. The founding fathers of the South African Union made no attempt to apportion parliamentary or civil service jobs in terms of British or Afrikaner quotas. Let individual competition prevail and all would come out as well.

In terms of political organisation, the white electorate, at the time of Union, was split into three groups. The Unionist Party represented, above all, the mining industry; it was overwhelmingly British in composition, urban in origin, and proud to wave the Union Jack. There was a small Labour Party, representing the foremen and skilled workers — especially the white labour elite in the mines. The principal party was the South African Party, a moderate Anglo-Afrikaner coalition. The party was led at first by Louis Botha, a well-to-do farmer and an ex-Boer commander, one of the most prominent representatives of the 'age of the generals', an era when South Africa was led by politicians who had made a military reputation in the citizen armies of the Transvaal and the Orange Free State during the Boer War. Botha was determined to reconcile Briton and Afrikaner within the confines of a new dominion that would respect the mine-owners' property and remain tied to Great Britain by bonds of trade and diplomacy. In 1914 South Africa joined the war against the Kaiser's Germany, much to the disgust of the militant Afrikaner nationalists, and South African troops occupied South-West Africa.

Jan Christiaan Smuts, Botha's chief lieutenant, accepted a seat in the British war Cabinet, and in 1919 helped to found the League of Nations. He succeeded Botha as Prime Minister in that year, and resolved to continue Botha's pro-imperial and pro-business policy. Smuts, having been weakened in an election, sought an alliance between the Unionist Party with the South African Party. The British hold on politics weakened, but Smuts's economic views essentially paralleled those of the mine-owners. In 1922 Smuts smashed an armed rising on the part of white, mainly Afrikaan-speaking, miners on the Witwatersrand; white rural and urban radicals never forgave Smuts, whom they derided as an 'Imperial Cossack'. Smuts succeeded in securing effective South African control over the former German South-West Africa in the form of a 'C Mandate', but he failed in his attempt to secure Southern Rhodesia's adherence to the Union of South Africa. He thereby lost the potential votes of a considerable English-speaking bloc north of the Limpopo River, and his dreams of a Greater South Africa came to naught.

In the meantime, the Afrikaner nationalists had regrouped their forces. In 1914 James Barry Munnik Hertzog, a leading Afrikaner politician, had broken away from Botha. Hertzog, like Smuts, was an Afrikaner by origin, a lawyer who had gained a high position in the Boer forces during the South African war. He founded the National Party (popularly known as the Nationalist Party), dedicated to the slogan 'South Africa first' on the international plane, and to the so-called 'two-stream policy', envisaging separate development of Britons and Afrikaners within South Africa.

The National Party began its career as a rural organisation, led by teachers, clergymen and lawyers, representing, above all, the Afrikaans-speaking farming community as against urban interests. During and after World War One, however, an increasing number of Afrikaners left the farms in order to look for jobs in the mines and on the railways. The white mine workers' rising at Johannesburg in 1922 led to co-operation between the Nationalists and the Labour Party, since both sought to protect white workmen against the great British capitalists on the one hand, and against competition from Africans on the other. The South African Defence Force had actually experienced difficulties in putting down the Witwatersrand rising in 1922, since Afrikaner reservists — poverty-stricken backwoodsmen, many of them — had sympathised with their kinsmen employed on the mines and respected the strike leaders. 'Who is that General Strike?' In 1924 the Labour Party and the Nationalists formed a coalition government — the 'pact government' headed by Hertzog — and the 'high-mining school' was displaced from power.

Under the new dispensation, white workers attained protection through colour-bar legislation; Afrikaans supplanted Dutch as the country's official language, side by side with English. The Union acquired a national flag of its own, a change bitterly resented by English-speaking South Africans and symbolic of the profound shift within the white power balance. The pact government pushed a vigorous protectionist policy, designed to safeguard the country's infant secondary industries against foreign imports. The pact was also responsible for extending the scope of nationalised enterprise by creating, in 1928, the state-owned ISCOR.

The pact government fell victim to the world-wide economic slump of the early 1930s. South Africa was forced to go off the gold standard, but Hertzog was so shaken that in 1933 he consented to the formation of a fusion government with Smuts. In 1934 the main body of the Nationalists and the South African Party merged into the United South African National Party, known for short as the United Party. The United Party had the backing of big business — especially the mining companies — and of the English-speaking universities, the Anglican (Episcopalian) Church, and the English-language press; it enjoyed support from most English-speaking voters and from a number of Afrikaners who looked upon Smuts, *die oubaas*, with a strong sense of loyalty.

In its hey-day the United Party stood for a policy of racial segregation scarcely distinguishable from that advocated by the Nationalists. In 1936, for instance, the Representation of Natives Act removed the remaining African voters from the voters' roll at the Cape; the Native Trust and Land Act extended territorial apartheid as solidified through the Natives' Land Act of 1913. Smuts introduced legislation in 1934 making interracial property transfers illegal in Durban. In the face of stiff Indian opposition, Smuts later brought in a more comprehensive measure that went on the statute book as the Asiatics Land Tenure and Indian Representation Act, 1946.

Smuts's foreign policy was outward-looking, however, very different from the isolationism advocated by the Nationalists. Smuts sympathised with the League of Nations; he supported the cause of Zionism; he took pride in the British connection, and in 1939 joined Great Britain in the war against Nazi Germany, a decision that provoked Hertzog's resignation from the government. South Africa mobilised its military and economic resources. The South Africans sent a substantial white volunteer army abroad, and South Africans distinguished themselves in East Africa, North Africa and Italy. South African economic aid, command of the major share in Western gold production and control over the Cape route all proved to be major assets for the embattled British Empire.

On the domestic front, the United Party veered mildly in a populist direction, and extended the scope of South Africa's mixed economy. As examples, the United Party initiated large-scale public housing schemes in South Africa, and pioneered the state marketing boards that came to play a vital part in marketing the country's agricultural produce. Unlike his successors, moreover, Smuts continued to enjoy a good press overseas. As a Cambridge man, a philosopher of 'Holism', he was in good standing with the academic intelligentsia; he stood out as a statesman of international stature, and he took an important part in the formation of the United Nations.

In the meantime, the National Party was shaken by a bitter struggle between nationalists of the traditional kind, men and women who supported a parliamentary system of government, and admirers of Nazi Germany. The most powerful of these groups were the 'New Order', led by Oswald Pirow, and the Oseewa-Brandwag (OB), under Dr J.F.J. van Rensburg. The Afrikaner dissidents were, on the whole, more anti-British and neutralist than pro-Nazi; few of them had any direct contacts with the Germans whom they supported. Initially, the OB and the National Party co-operated; but, from 1940 onward, the Nationalists became increasingly suspicious of the OB, with its anti-parliamentary and pro-German leanings. Dr François Daniel Malan, the National Party's leader, refused to have any more truck with the OB. The Smuts government interned a number of leading OB members, including B.J. Vorster, the country's late Prime Minister, and the OB disintegrated for lack of public support.

The National Party's relatively pro-moderate and pro-parliamentary course paid off. Smuts, like Churchill before him, failed to carry his wartime prestige into the years of peace. Many returning veterans, the majority of them Afrikaans-speaking, were discontented with conditions in South Africa. The country suffered from an acute housing shortage and from inflation. The Smuts government seemed administratively inept. Above all, Smuts could not maintain his position among the Afrikaans-speaking South Africans, and the general election of 1948 put the National Party into power with a small majority; the Nationalists won 70 seats and its ally, the moderate Afrikaner Party, gained 9, as against the United Party's 65 and the Labour Party's 6. For English-speaking South Africans of the traditional kind, the shock was tremendous; the very laws of nature seemed to have been put into reverse.

Beyond the Limpopo River, the Nationalist victory led to the formation of the Federation of Rhodesia and Nyasaland (1953-63), a short-lived state resting on a precarious alliance between British Rhodesian settlers and traditional British colonialism, designed to create a counter-weight to Afrikaner nationalism in the south and African nationalism in the north. In South Africa, however, the English-speaking groups were unable to rebuild their power, and the Nationalists steadily consolidated their strength. The Nationalists absorbed the moderate Afrikaner Party in 1951; the Labour Party ceased to be represented in Parliament after 1953, as most white workers threw in their lot with the Nationalists. Between 1953 and 1977 the National Party increased its representation from 94 to 134 seats; the United Party that had once

Table 4.2: Estimated Control of Selected Sectors of the Economy by Afrikaners, 1939 and 1964 (per cent)

	1939	1964
Commerce	8	28
Mining	1	10
Finance	5	14
Industry	3	10

Source: Howard Brotz, *The Politics of South Africa: Democracy and Racial Diversity* (Oxford University Press, Oxford, 1977), p. 42.

Table 4.3: Whites' Party Preference according to Language, 1975 (per cent)

	Afrikaans-speakers	English-speakers	Total Sample
National Party	83.3	23.4	60.4
Progressive Reform Party	1.0	36.2	14.5
United Party	4.7	24.1	12.2
Herstigte Nasionale Party	3.3	0.5	2.2
Democratic Party	1.3	3.5	2.1
Abstain, no information	6.5	12.3	8.7

Source: Brotz, *The Politics of South Africa*, p. 41.

commanded 57 seats disappeared from the political arena.

The Nationalists effectively used political power to advance Afrikaners in the civil service, the defence forces and the public corporations. Nationalists benefited even more from the entrance of Afrikaners into private business (see Table 4.2). Contrary to the expectations of white liberals, the Nationalists made a genuine effort to develop the homelands, inducing reluctant white voters to devote much more money to Africans development than the electorate had been willing to spend in the past. Nevertheless, the National Party managed to hold on to the bulk of the Afrikaans-speaking white vote, while gaining a sizeable contingent of English-speaking converts (see Table 4.3).

The United Party was unable to escape from its ethnic limitations. Many of the new immigrants who might have voted in favour of the United Party failed to take out South African citizenship (of 400,000 immigrants who came to South Africa between 1961 and 1974, only about one-tenth acquired South African nationality). The proclamation of a republic in South Africa and its enforced withdrawal from the Commonwealth was a heavy blow to the party; so was Vorster's policy of emphasising a common white South African nationalism in place of a restrictive *volk* loyalty. The United Party was also beset by structural weaknesses. It was a loose coalition joining English-speakers and businessmen, farmers, technicians and professional people. Its membership was informal; its ideology ill defined. The party advocated a federal system of government, moderate social reforms and the preservation of the *status quo*. This approach invited attacks from the Nationalists on the right and the Progressive Reform Party on the left.

The Progressive Reform Party was strong in the well-to-do suburbs of Johannesburg and Cape Town; it attracted much support from professional men, academics, liberal bankers and mining magnates like Harry Oppenheimer, a determined opponent of apartheid. The United Party, indifferently led by Sir de Villiers Graaf, was unable to contain its dissensions, and in 1977 the party disintegrated. The New Republic Party (NRP) was left as the rump of the United Party, with the South African Party on the right and the Progressive Federal Party on the left.

The National Party, accordingly, made tremendous gains. The elections of 1977 gave the party an electoral victory without parallel in the country's history since 1910 (see Table 4.4). The National Party — the point bears repeating — was not a homogeneous group. The *verkramptes*, the conservatives, continued to have strong support among the white trade unions, the smaller farmers, the police, the churches, the civil service, the cultural associations and the white-collar workers. The *verligtes*, the moderate reformers, were influential in the universities, in a section of the church, and in the world of Afrikaner journalism, industry and commerce. The *verligtes* also held a strong position within the Bureau of State Security (BOSS), whose directorate was realistic with regard to South Africa's future relations with its neighbours, and to the need to pre-empt revolutionary unrest by measured reform. The army was divided, with the colonels and generals tending to be *verligte*, and the lower ranks, from sergeant to major, apt to be *verkrampte* — a striking reversal of the revolutionary pattern within the Portuguese army at the time of the 1974 *coup*. The *verligtes*, above all, were not an organised movement; they lacked force of

Table 4.4: South African General Elections, 1910-77

	1910	1915	1920	1921	1924	1929	1933	1938	1943	1948	1953	1958	1961	1966	1970	1974	1977
National Party	–	27	44	45	63	78	75	27	–	–	94	103	105	126	117	120	134
Herstigte Nasionale Party	–	–	–	–	–	–	–	–	–	–	–	–	–	–	–	–	3
South African Party	67	54	41	79	53	–	61	–	–	–	–	–	–	–	–	–	0
United Party	–	–	–	–	–	–	–	111	89	65	57	53	49	39	47	44	0
Unionist Party	39	39	25	–	–	–	–	–	–	–	–	–	–	–	–	–	0
Labour Party	4	4	21	9	18	8	2	3	9	6	5	–	–	–	–	–	0
Dominion Party	–	–	–	–	–	–	–	8	7	–	–	–	–	–	–	–	0
Socialist Party	–	–	–	–	–	–	–	1	–	–	–	–	–	–	–	–	0
Afrikaner Party	–	–	–	–	–	–	–	–	–	9	–	–	–	–	–	–	0
Progressive Party	–	–	–	–	–	–	–	–	–	–	–	–	1	1	1	7	0
National Union	–	–	–	–	–	–	–	–	–	–	–	–	1	–	–	–	0
Independents and others	11	6	3	1	1	1	12	–	2	–	–	–	–	–	–	–	0
New Republic	–	–	–	–	–	–	–	–	–	–	–	–	–	–	–	–	10
Progressive Federal Party	–	–	–	–	–	–	–	–	–	–	–	–	–	–	–	–	17
Vacancies	–	–	–	–	–	–	–	–	–	–	–	–	–	–	–	–	1
Total seats	121	130	134	134	135	148	150	150	150	150	156	156	156	166	165	171	165

Source: *Official Yearbook of the Republic of South Africa, 1976* (Johannesburg, 1976), p. 184; *Africa Research Bulletin* (London, 1977), p. 4699 C.

numbers; while they were unable to exercise some influence within the National Party, they were unlikely to break away and split the ranks of Afrikanerdom.* The *verkramptes*, on the other hand, might conceivably one day leave the party and join the right-wing Herstigte Nasionale Party (HNP).

By 1979, the Prime Minister was resolved to accept − if necessary − losses both on the left and on the right. The Nationalists, in 1979, suffered a narrow defeat in a Johannesburg by-election. The party had been somewhat weakened through abstentions occasioned by the 'Muldergate' scandal, through confusion resulting from conflicting statements by individual Cabinet members, from defections to the extreme right, and from dissensions between Botha and Dr Andries Treurnicht, the conservative leader of the party's Transvaal wing.

The struggle between reformers and conservatives also had a foreign policy dimension. The *verligtes* and their allies looked to a form of *détente* with black independent governments; reformers − including Vorster − supported political change favouring moderate black over white government in neighbouring Namibia and Rhodesia. Even South African intervention in Angola, following the breakdown of the Portuguese empire, became a matter of controversy. South African intervention derived support from the advocates of *détente* who intended to back UNITA, a black nationalist organisation, as against the MPLA, and who expected applause from President Kaunda of Zambia as well as from the United States. The opponents of *détente*, including defence experts like Admiral Biermann, had opposed the Angolan venture. Western unwillingness to lend support to South Africa over this issue stengthened their position and contributed to Vorster's resignation. Botha's ability to control his party's rank and file − essential in a country where lobbies and interest groups play a much smaller role in politics than in Great Britain and the United States − remained of crucial importance. Despite the rifts in his party, he continued to control the membership and maintained his parliamentary ascendancy.

At the time of writing, the splintered opposition still commanded much economic strength. But the English-speaking parties could not convert wealth into political power. British decolonisation had deprived

---

* A third group, hard to classify either as *verligtes* or *verkramptes*, are the partitionists, who are strong within the South African Bureau of Racial Affairs, a Nationalist association dedicated to the study of interracial problems. The partitionists wish to divide South Africa into three states − one white, two black. The white state would be vastly smaller than South Africa at present; the black states would come to comprise much of the country's English-speaking areas. In practice, white South Africans will never agree to such a scheme, except after a crushing military defeat.

British conservatives of their accustomed bearings. English-speaking South African liberals remained optimists. They assumed, like the Marxists, that, in the last instance, class loyalties would transcend ethnic loyalties. The British liberal assumption derived from the experience of Great Britain in the nineteenth century. Great Britain, ethnically a fairly homogeneous country, gradually enfranchised first the middle classes, and then the working classes, thereby co-opting the entire people into the parliamentary system. The British model, unfortunately, had no applicability to multi-ethnic societies of the kind common in many parts of Africa or the Middle East, and even in advanced, industrialised Eastern European countries like Czechoslovakia and Poland. After World War Two, for instance, the Czechs expelled some 3 million Germans from the Sudetenland, irrespective of class affiliation; the Poles did the same to about 9 million Germans east of the Oder-Neisse line. The Russians, despite their Marxist convictions, applied the same policy to the Germans in the eastern part of East Prussia and to the Poles east of the Curzon line.

British liberals took little note of the experiences of Eastern and Central Europe, experiences that they commonly regarded as quite irrelevant to their own society. The liberals welcomed decolonisation in Africa, but they were soon thrown on the defensive when the newly independent black states largely repudiated the liberal legacy. 'Multiracialism', a firmly held liberal ideal during the 1940s and early 1950s, proved a failure in Tanzania and Kenya. Idealists were disappointed by the unforeseen emergence of black tyrannies in countries like Uganda, by bloody ethnic slaughters in lands as far afield as Nigeria and Burundi, and by the white exodus from Algeria, Mozambique and Angola. The liberals had consistently taken an optimistic line regarding the future of independent black Africa; but in South African terms, their commitment failed to pay political dividends.

The Nationalists, on the other hand, had no ideological 'investment' in liberalism. Unlike their opponents, they were reasonably united and self-confident, well able to deal with their opponents on both sides of the political spectrum. In the election of 1977 the Nationalists won 134 out of 166 seats and wiped out the right-wing Herstigte Nasionale Party, the splinter group that had fought the election under the Nationalists' traditional slogan of *blanke baaskap* (white supremacy). The traditional conservatives within the English-speaking camp suffered a disaster of almost equal severity. The South Africa Party obtained only 3 seats, and the New Republic Party got 10. The Progressive Federal Party (PFP) became the official opposition with 17 seats. Its support derived mainly from well-to-do and well educated South Africans of British or Jewish descent, the PFP called for a qualified but non-racial franchise — now a difficult position to maintain in a world that had rejected the 'color-blind' but property-weighted franchise of Rhodesia with as much hostility as the Afrikaners' notions of apartheid.

The 1977 elections marked a cautious shift to reformism, and to an Anglo-Afrikaner *rapprochement*. The HNP represented the original principles of the National Party, but had gained no more than 3.21 per cent of the vote. The HNP's defeat indicated a striking shift in Afrikaner opinion; by the end of 1977 public opinion polls showed that 70 per cent of the Nationalist supporters were ready for changes in official race politics. The 'poor white' had ceased to count in Parliament. The bulk of the white workers no longer needed job reservation, and the industrial colour bar — long since attenuated in practice — was officially ended. At the same time, the National Party had gained a number of English-speaking converts, including conservative-minded British Natalians, English-speaking workers, clerks and technicians from the Rand, and some orthodox Jews loyal to the synagogue. On the other hand, many of the new British immigrants had failed to register for citizenship and could not, therefore, give effective support to the traditional 'British' parties, even had they wanted to do so.

White politics in South Africa, then, has continued to be determined by the Anglo-Afrikaner split, and the ethnic alignment of South African politics did not change a great deal. The National Party gained 64.78 per cent of the vote, and the HNP 3.21 per cent, giving the Afrikaner parties a total of 67.99 per cent; the Progressive Federal Party obtained 16.71 per cent, the New Republic Party 11.59 per cent, and the South African Party 1.68 per cent of the vote respectively, leaving the primarily English-speaking parties with 29.98 per cent, roughly corresponding to the country's white ethnic composition.

Vorster nevertheless regarded the election as a mandate for white unity. In his post-election speeches, he declared that foreigners would now 'think twice' before acting against the Republic, that South Africans would now stand united in defence of their country, and that urban terrorism would be controlled by drastic measures. At the same time, Vorster was willing to make changes of a kind that went further than anything Smuts would ever have considered feasible or even desirable. Black property rights in black areas were somewhat extended; black workers attained greater bargaining rights in industrial disputes; job reservation virtually disappeared; professional men and women of all races achieved equal pay for equal work in government; black and brown South Africans gained greater access to common facilities.

Above all, Vorster began to take cautious steps to incorporate Indians and Coloureds into the political community. As mentioned earlier, a new constitutional plan provided for three separate Parliaments, responsible respectively for whites, Indians and Coloureds, each empowered to make laws for its own population group. Legislation affecting all groups would be considered by a Council of Cabinets drawn from each of the 'ethnic' Cabinets. Vorster's plan bore some similarity to the South African design for Namibia (South-West Africa), based on independence through separate ethnic representation for each major population group.

Vorster failed to obtain Indian and Coloured agreement for his design. Moreover, his change of policy was little known abroad. Vorster lacked an international propaganda machine comparable to the interlocking networks available to the South African opposition through the UN, the Communist nations, and the Western prestige media and academic bodies. South Africa's official propaganda agency (as distinct from private bodies like the South Africa Foundation) was beset by scandals that diminished the impact of South Africa's case. The National Party was unable to persuade a doubting world that South Africa was about to change. Within the National Party, the *verligtes* suffered through guilt by association, as *verligtes* had been implicated in the scandal.

Nevertheless there was change in South Africa. The average Nationalist voter, vintage 1948, would probably have looked upon the Nationalist Party of 1978 as a collection of negrophilists and trimmers. If public opinion in South Africa and the world at large might be likened to two railway trains going along parallel tracks, the South African train and the world opinion train were both travelling in the same direction — but at vastly different speeds. An observer sitting in the world opinion train would experience the optical illusion that the slow-moving South African train was not merely stationary, but actually going backwards. An observer in the South African train, on the other hand, would be conscious of the distance that his country had gone since the 1950s.

The Ruling Party Today

Conventional academic interpretations of South African politics divide into two main categories — Marxist and liberal. Marxists regard the National Party as the willing creature of international and local South African capitalists. According to interpretations put forward in such journals as the *African Communist*, great multinational corporations, abetted by South African mining magnates, pay the piper and call the tune. Apartheid reflects the interests of South African capitalism by providing mines and factories with cheap labour. This interpretation, however, fails to explain why the Progressive Party — backed by wealthy men like Harry Oppenheimer, one of South Africa's great mining magnates — should always have been politically powerless. The theory also failed to account for the demise of Smuts and the United Party, a group that championed the British connection in both the political and the financial sense.

Oddly enough, the conventional Marxist interpretation is not sufficiently Marxist. The main opposition to apartheid in South Africa comes from the ranks of business men. Merchants and factory-owners have sound economic reasons for their preference. Apartheid is costly in financial and administrative terms; apartheid interferes with the free flow of labour and with its most profitable use; businessmen, moreover, have become increasingly conscious of the fact that the capitalists' prosperity must increasingly depend on the prosperity of an ever-growing number of African customers.

Liberals, on the other hand, are more inclined to interpret South African politics in terms of morality and constitutional reform. Liberals often regard the Nationalist Party as a quasi-totalitarian body, enormously powerful, sustained by a ruthlessly centralised hierarchy, an all-embracing ideology, iron discipline and an extensive network of associated organisations held together overall by a secret freemasonry known as the Broederbond. Such interpretations confuse the Afrikaners of today with the Germans of a generation earlier. These assessments take little account of South African realities. All totalitarian parties, Fascist or Communist, share certain characteristics. The party, the leader or the party's ruling elite pretends, for all practical purposes, to be all-good, all-wise and all-powerful, endowed, in some measure, with the three attributes of God. The party operates on strictly hierarchical and unitary lines; it tolerates no criticism from below. It claims to be the demiurge of history, resolved to create a new man. Totalitarians are universally optimistic; they see themselves as the wave of the future; they see their own society as a model for the world at large.

The National Party stands for none of these things. The Nationalist world outlook has a strong tinge of pessimism. There is a strong Calvinist sense of human inadequacy and sin, shared even by a non-believer like Hendrik Frensch Verwoerd, a Hollander by origin and Prime Minister from 1958 to 1966. The National Party cannot easily be stereotyped. It now has a substantial number of English-speaking sympathisers. It is more an urban party than a rural party. It represents a rising bourgeoisie, skilled workmen, managers and supervisors; the 'poor white' voter has almost disappeared. Yet the Afrikaner Nationalists still share something of their ancestors' traditional pessimism, far removed from the self-confidence of British liberals. Nationalists are still apt to look upon the Afrikaners' past as a tale of woe in which the Afrikaners' very existence was menaced by Britons and blacks, by the perils of the long treks into the interior; later by defeat in the Boer War, then by the trek to the towns, and by proletarianisation.

The sense of physical insecurity often went with a sense of social resentment. The Afrikaner countryman was widely treated with contempt by the old Anglo-Dutch establishment in Cape Town, later by the Hollander-Afrikaner administrative and professional hierarchy in Pretoria and Bloemfontein, and then by the Anglo-Jewish oligarchy of Kimberley and Johannesburg. Hollanders commonly looked down upon Afrikaans as an uncultured *patois*. British imperial propaganda of the late Victorian and Edwardian eras, curiously echoed by British liberal propaganda of a later era and by radical films shown on American campuses during the 1970s, commonly stereotyped the Boers as unprogressive, pious, prejudiced, brutal rednecks — 'lower than the kaffirs', in the phraseology of Kipling's contemporaries. The sense of social resentment (one oddly shared in certain respects by Afrikaners and Africans alike) sharpened the edge of Afrikaner nationalism in the past. Traces of it continue to this day.

At present, the old perils have gone; but new dangers seem to have taken their place. The Afrikaners now feel themselves menaced by African nationalists at home — threatening to turn South Africa into another Congo or Angola — and by world opinion abroad, hypocritical, sanctimonious and uncomprehending, just like British missionary opinion in the past. This philosophy — defensive, parochial and pessimistic — makes no claim to world leadership. The Afrikaners, unlike German Nazis or Russian Communists, never felt that they were marching in the vanguard of history; they never idolised their leaders as supermen; their ideology was — and remains — unsuited for a totalitarian party.

The party's future evolution is hard to predict. During the 1930s the Afrikaners had mainly been a rural people. The average Nationalist voter was an indigent farmer, a teacher, a rural clergyman or a white worker, often out of a job. In certain respects the National Party resembled a pre-World War Two peasant party in Eastern Europe, anticapitalist, anti-urban, anti-Semitic and ethnocentric. By the 1970s the majority of the Nationalist voters were townsmen; their level of skills had greatly improved; their fear of being reduced to the status of 'poor whites' by dint of African competition had much diminished. The churches, as well as the traditional cultural organisations and youth leagues, shaped by small-town culture more than by the big city, had lost some of their former influence; as a group, even the Nationalist politicians no longer commanded the same authority that they had held in the past, and even the old certainties regarding apartheid began to weaken.

In certain respects, the National Party had become like the old United Party, a coalition containing bankers, factory-owners and professional men, as well as white workers and farmers. The conservative wing remained strong in the caucus, the cultural organisations, the civil service and the police; it derived support from white workers and employees, and from the small farmers. But there was now a substantial reformist group made up of businessmen, professional people, technicians and specialists in both the public and private sector, clergymen and members of the defence establishment anxious to strengthen the country's industrial power and determined to create a wider social consensus. The Nationalist Party no longer spoke of combating the Jews or repatriating the Indians. Among young Afrikaners engaged in rural development schemes there was a genuine spirit of idealism and a degree of technical competence that, but for the missionaries, would, in an earlier generation, have been put in the service of the white poor rather than the blacks.

In organisational terms, the National Party remains a federation — not a unitary party, like the old United Party. It consists of four provincial parties, each with its provincial congress and its own provincial leader.[2] The party's affairs are co-ordinated by a federal council composed of the leader of the parliamentary caucus, seven delegates from each provincial congress and a youth representative. According to the party's constitution, all federal council decisions have to be approved by the provincial congresses in order to be binding on the provincial national parties. The provincial parties wield a considerable degree of autonomy. Provincial party congresses, for instance, have to approve changes in the party's programme; decentralisation is also evident in the selection of the party's parliamentary candidates, a choice mainly left to individual constituencies. The party's relatively loose structure, in other words, is reminiscent more of the commando (militia) system of the defunct Boer republics than of a modern mass party.

According to South African liberal orthodoxy, the National Party is secretly governed by the Broederbond. The Broederbond's membership is indeed confidential; entry is solely by invitation. Members are supposed to display the highest 'moral and religious standards', to seek no honours, expect no rewards, to help to promote harmony among the Afrikaner people, and to foster Afrikaans traditions and culture. Members are supposedly drawn from every occupation in which Afrikaners are to be found, but clergymen, parliamentarians, teachers, academics and civil servants are heavily represented in the organisation. The Broederbond supposedly has some ten thousand members organised into about four hundred cells. It is an influential group. Over recent years it has become increasingly *verligt* in its compositions, as have the learned professions in general. The Broederbond is important as a forum of opinion, but it is in no sense a secret power elite able to impose its policy on the entire National Party.[3]

National Party leadership traditionally derived, not from disciplined *apparatchiks* — from a permanent staff of party functionaries — but from political men trained in the church (Malan), in the academic professions (Verwoerd), in the law (Hertzog, Strijdom, Vorster); some of these have had additional experience in journalism (Malan, Verwoerd). Botha, the present Prime Minister, is South Africa's first leader who has risen through the ranks of the party bureaucracy, but he does not as yet represent a permanent pattern. Traditionally, the party's principal personalities have come from small towns; their professional backgrounds reflected the prestige enjoyed by learning, culture and professional attainments in the provincial society that has — up to now — predominantly shaped the party's leadership.

The National Party has associated movements of its own, including the Jeugbond, the party's youth league. In addition, it is linked informally to a wide assemblage of voluntary bodies of philanthropic, cultural, professional, educational or athletic types. All of them stress the Afrikaner heritage; all of them are of relatively recent origin, having grown up at a time when the Afrikaners began to move into the cities, and when the traditional organisations of Afrikaner society — the extended family, the church and the commando — could no longer cope with the demands of a new society. Their influence is extensive; their powers have traditionally been exerted *vir kerk, volk en taal* (for church, nation and [Afrikaans] language, the motto of the Afrikaans Christian League of Women).

Other bodies include, for instance, the Voortrekkers, an Afrikaans scout movement (about 35,000 members in 1972), and the Afrikaanse Studentebond (about 50,000 members). Even more powerful is the Federasie van Afrikaanse Kultuurvereniginge (FAK) set up in 1929. The FAK contains representatives from Afrikaans churches, women's groups, youth groups and such. The FAK has traditionally performed a great variety of tasks, ranging from the promotion of Afrikaans culture — literature, art, films — from the compilation of a national songbook to the erection of the great Voortrekker Monument. In 1939 the FAK's economic conference decided to set up a number of organisations designed to promote Afrikaans enterprise in industry, commerce and finance. One of the most prominent was the Reddingsdaadbond, designed to encourage Afrikaners to save capital, set up their own firms, acquire technical and business training, and so forth. By 1957 the Afrikaners had developed a much wider range of economic organisations; the Reddingsdaadbond was dissolved, its functions being taken over by the Ekonomiese Instituut of the FAK and the Afrikaanse Handelsinstituut, representative of Afrikaans businessmen. The Afrikaans-language publishing houses play an equally significant role; so does the Afrikaans press, especially *Die Burger*, the leading Afrikaner newspaper, well known for its sober style and objective reportage.

The National Party aside, the Dutch Reformed churches between them form the most important national institutions of the Afrikaner people. The most numerous by far is the Nederduitse Gereformeerede Kerk; the Hervormde Kerk and the Gereformeerde Kerk are smaller groups. They are Calvinist in doctrine, but divided by considerable differences of opinion, both regarding theology and politics. Widespread misconceptions to the contrary, a conservative theology does not necessarily entail a conservative approach to politics; liberal theologians, on the other hand, do not necessarily oppose apartheid. The Dutch Reformed Church has been called 'the National Party at prayer'; Nationalist politicians are fond of equating church, *volk* and party as one. But in fact the churches are no longer homogeneous bodies. The critics of apartheid now comprise a substantial number of Dutch Reformed clergymen.

The Nationalist Party, like the Dutch Reformed Church, is not a monolithic group. There is a reformist wing (*verligtes*) and a conservative wing (*verkramptes*), though the average MP is likely to describe himself as *behoudend* or conservative, rather than as *verligt* or *verkrampt*. There are secularists and religious enthusiasts. There are critics of the regime in the party, in academia and in business. While R.F. 'Pik' Botha, the Foreign Minister, is prepared to dismantle apartheid, ex-Nationalist Party member Dr Albert Herzog, now leader of the Herstigte Nasionale Party, calls for more rigorous enforcement of apartheid and for making no concessions to the blacks. The labour leader Arrie Paulus claims he is willing to die for apartheid, but the former rector of the Rand Afrikaans University and member of the Broederbond Dr Gerrit Viljoen believes the Mixed Marriages and Immorality Act will be repealed in a few years, and foresees Africans getting a qualified franchise. The National Party can permit itself to be led by a lapsed Calvinist who has turned to atheism, but the appointment of a Jewish, Catholic or Greek Orthodox – or even an Anglican – party leader would, for the moment, be hardly conceivable.[4]

What of the future? According to the conventional image, grim-faced Afrikaners will never negotiate, but will withdraw for a last stand into the *laager*. White South Africans will certainly fight if they believe that they have no alternative. But there is greater willingness to compromise than many critics assume. By 1974, 40 per cent of the Afrikaners and 76 per cent of the English-speaking South Africans were willing to concede a qualified franchise to Africans, as against the one-man/one-vote formula. More important, a large proportion of Afrikaners had become willing, by 1977, to accept major concessions and sacrifices if the Prime Minister were to announce that a new course had become essential to the white community's own interests.* By the late 1970s, the split within the party was open for all to see. At the 1979 conference of the FAK, for instance, Professors H.B. Thom and Gerrit Viljoen, both prominent Broederbonders, argued that the National Party could no longer serve as a vehicle of Afrikaner exclusiveness. Even more alarming to conservatives within the party were the reformist views expressed by Afrikaner churchmen at the South African Christian Leadership Conference and the resolutions passed by the Afrikaanse

---

* According to the findings of Theodor Hanf, Heribert Weiland and Gerda Vierdag, *Südafrika, friedlicher Wandel. Möglichkeiten der demokratischen Konfliktregelung – Eine empirische Untersuchung* (Kaiser, Grunewald, Mainz, 1977), 47.2 per cent of the Afrikaans-speaking members of the National Party were willing, in 1977, to support the Prime Minister unconditionally if he were to announce that major concessions and sacrifices had become necessary in the interests of the white community. Only 3.5 per cent of all Afrikaner Nationalists were totally unwilling to support any such policy. The remainder were willing to accept a policy of qualified concessions. The Prime Minister would have gained unconditional support from about one-third of the United Party, and between 10 and 15 per cent of Progressive voters.

Studentebond conference at Stellenbosh asserting that apartheid and the 'homelands' policy had failed. The new course found support from the current Broederbond leadership, the Nationalist newspapers and many Afrikaner intellectuals. The conservatives, on the other hand, continued to enjoy strong support from the rank and file of party members — especially in the Transvaal — from men and women who could not imagine their party as the instrument for dismantling apartheid.

Only the future can show how the party will deal with the new challenges. Too much should not, of course, be made of public opinion surveys, however well conducted. Nevertheless, white South Africa, by the late 1970s, was no longer embedded in rigid *immobilisme*. At the time of writing, the threat to the Afrikaners' dominant position in South African politics did not derive from an unreasoning conservatism, much less from opposition on the part of English-speaking or black South Africans. The National Party was threatened by dissensions from within, tensions of the kind exemplified in the Muldergate scandal that had cost Vorster the presidency and that threatened to discredit the *verligtes*, leaving the party a prey to disagreements. One cannot ignore the possibility that white leadership will split in South Africa just as did the Portuguese leadership in Africa. The chance seems to us remote, however. Only the future will show how far the rift can be closed.

Black African Political Organisations

White South Africans pioneered the creation of political parties in South Africa, parallel to the country's modern government and press. Educated Africans, however, soon learned from the example of their white neighbours; during the latter part of the nineteenth century they began to take an active interest in the politics of the Cape and founded a variety of bodies to represent their interests.

African nationalism was slow to grow. There could be no African nationalism before 1910, because there was no united South Africa (the African National Congress was not founded until 1912). There is no tribal or ethnic nationalism as such, although the Zulus and Xhosas may be nascent nationalist groups. African nationalism could only develop as urbanisation and industrialisation created a large number of Africans who had a common experience of urban living and wage labour. Western education and Christianity were two other elements necessary for national consciousness.[5] Educated Christians and urban workers became the 'main carriers of African nationalism', but that nationalism was weak and badly divided until structural changes in the economy created a sufficient number of modern men.

African nationalists never quite agreed on the question of how far they should co-operate with the white sympathisers. Roughly speaking, the African politicians divided into those who looked to a multiracial South Africa, to be established in co-operation with white allies, and into advocates of an African South Africa, where whites and Indians would merely be tolerated as minorities.

The 'Multiracial' and 'Black' Opposition

South Africa's oldest existing political organisation today is the African National Congress (ANC). The ANC was founded in 1912 as the South African Native National Congress – two years before the formation of the Afrikaners' National Party. The two bodies had certain features in common. Each of them initially served a predominantly rural constituency; each was led by educated men – clergymen, teachers, civil servants – a salaried, diploma-bearing elite drawn mainly from a rural background. Each had a strongly pedagogic streak. The first president of the ANC was the Reverend John Dube, a clergyman who had resided in the United States and who created the Zulu Christian Industrial School, founded on the principles of Booker T. Washington's Tuskeegee. Both the ANC and the National Party looked to an ethnic constituency – Africans and Afrikaners respectively. The National Party hoped to consolidate the Afrikaner people into a nation. The ANC was determined to fuse into 'one political people all tribes and clans of various tribes and races'. The Nationalists had high regard for the traditional virtues preached by the church; so did the ANC, whose constitution vowed to 'encourage inculcation and practice of habits of industry, thrift and cleanliness among the people, and propagate the gospel of the dignity of labour', as well as to 'uplift the standard of the race morally and spiritually, mentally and materially; socially and politically'.[6]

The formal organisations of the Nationalist Party and the ANC also ran along parallel lines. The ANC was intended to be run through a hierarchy of local branches, district branches, provincial congresses and a national congress. Afrikaners and African politicians alike wrote copiously and wrote well. Their views even coincided with regard to certain specific issues. Few Afrikaners would have quarrelled with the editorialist of *Imvo Zabantsundu* who, in 1909, explained to his readers that the rumoured appointment of Winston Churchill as Governor-General for South Africa would be rejected by all South Africans who wanted 'a man of fixed and steady principle, not a political mountebank however clever'.[7]

But this is where the parallel between Afrikaners and Africans came to an end. The Afrikaners did not much rely on outside support. In so far as they looked abroad, they turned to Holland and Germany rather than to Great Britain. The ANC, on the other hand, hoped for help from educated, English-speaking well-wishers; in its early years the ANC, indeed, had much in common with the Aborigines Protection Society, supported by middle-class and upper-middle-class humanitarians in Great Britain.

The Afrikaners, above all, had the vote; they had real power, whereas the Africans lacked the franchise, except for a small number of well-to-do blacks at the Cape. The Africans were divided socially between educated men, brought up in mission schools, and chiefs of the traditional kind. The 'new' Africans wished to transcend tribalism. Nevertheless, they could not at first do without the chiefs who, under the terms of the original constitution, were *ex officio* members of the congress and had the right to reject any branch motions 'hostile to the interests of the Chiefs'.

The ANC depended on a fluctuating membership. Its financial resources were scanty; its material poverty was sometimes made worse by speculation. African political organisations and independent African churches were infinitely more divisive than the secular and religious bodies set up by the Afrikaners. The never-ending dissensions and splits within the African churches, trade unions and political movements reflected to some extent the migrant nature of South Africa's labour force. The constant formation of new bodies, moreover, allowed a relatively large number of ambitious Africans to hold secretaryships, presidencies and vice-presidencies — positions of ritual importance, psychologically satisfying to a people who were excluded from posts entailing the exercise of real power.

The ANC's political programme, for most of its history, was extremely moderate, calling for the elimination of the colour bar in schools, mines and factories, and for 'equitable representation of Natives' in Parliament. The whites' unwillingness to make even a minimum of concessions stands out as a tragedy in their country's history. Moderates such as Dube would have managed to co-operate quite successfully with a man such as Botha. Failing to make headway of any kind, the ANC gradually stepped up its demands with regard to land, labour and related questions. Even so, the Congress for long did not go much beyond the goals acceptable to the civil rights movement in the United States. The moderate stand was represented by men like Chief Albert Lutuli, an American-educated mission teacher, president of the ANC from 1952 to 1967, and recipient of the Nobel Peace Prize. Lutuli called for a 'common South African multiracial society', and for a strategy of passive resistance rather than violence.

The moderates, however, increasingly came under fire from members of the more radical Youth League that was created in 1944. In 1949 a number of Youth League members — including Nelson Mandela and Oliver Tambo, both young attorneys and partners in a law firm — were elected to the executive in place of more moderate members. The ANC began to call for an end to white domination, and during the 1950s it embarked on passive resistance campaigns against the pass laws, the Group Areas Act, the Suppression of Communism Act and other features of apartheid. In addition, the ANC became increasingly sympathetic to the South African Communist Party (SACP, further discussed in the section on defence).

The SACP began its career among South African intellectuals of British and Jewish ancestry who, in 1921, founded the Communist Party of South Africa (CPSA), South Africa's first multiracial party and the first Marxist-Leninist party on the African continent. The party was Stalinised in the late 1920s, and it submitted to the Moscow-backed policy of creating a 'South African native [black] republic as a stage toward a workers' and peasants' government with full protection and equal rights for all national minorities', thereby giving up hope for white working-class support. In 1935 the CPSA abided by Moscow's turn to a popular front, and softened its domestic line. The CPSA turned in 1939 to 'revolutionary defeatism', in line with Moscow's pro-German stand. After the German invasion of the Soviet Union, the CPSA backed South Africa's war effort. The party was banned in 1950, and its operations effectively disrupted. Three years later, in 1953, the party was re-founded as the South African Communist Party (SACP), dedicated to a 'democratic revolution' to be achieved in alliance with 'progressives' of all races and social classes, a step on the way to a socialist society. The SACP attempted to work through a series of front organisations set up on ethnic lines, including the Congress of Democrats (COD, white), and the South African Indian Congress (SAIC, Asian). In addition, Communists worked their way into leading positions within the ANC. The SACP, unlike the other South African parties, allotted some leading positions to black men and Indians.

In 1955 the ANC and the various other congresses united in the South African Congress Alliance, and the Congress of the People issued the so-called 'Freedom Charter', a milestone in the history of South Africa's opposition. The Freedom Charter went beyond the ANC's traditional demands for constitutional reforms, and called for public ownership of 'the mineral wealth . . . the banks and monopoly industry', as well as for a share-out of the land among the tillers. The language of socialism had replaced the ANC's traditionally moderate and democratic idiom. The party called for solidarity with all oppressed races, but nations under Soviet domination were excluded from the ranks of the downtrodden.[8]

The signatories of the Freedom Charter expected rapid results. So did many Western academicians, government officials and intelligence experts, who assumed that the South African revolution was imminent. On the face of it, South Africa's situation was a textbook example of a revolutionary situation (a subject discussed in further detail in the section of defence). The ANC claimed to speak for the immense majority of the African people; the Africans enjoyed the approval of world opinion, just as Afrikaners had enjoyed it half a century before. The decolonisation of Africa was going on apace, and the ANC believed that the overthrow of white power in Southern Africa was merely a chapter in the greater story of Africa's liberation. The ANC had other advantages. Internationally, it later came to enjoy the support of the Organization of African Unity (OAU), the UN and the Soviet bloc and its allies. It was able to rely on the services of able and dedicated Communist cadres drawn from all races. Moses Kotane, General Secretary of the Communist Party of South Africa and a member of the ANC's executive committee, was an African; Dr Yusuf Dadoo, Vice-Chairman of the ANC's revolutionary council and later Chairman of the South African Communist Party, was an Indian; Ruth First (Slovo), an executive member of the Congress of Democrats and one of the SACP's leading intellectuals, was of Lithuanian-Jewish origin; Abraham Fischer, head of the SACP's underground organisation in South Africa during the early 1960s, came from one of the country's most distinguished Afrikaner families.

The government responded to the growth of opposition by supressing all militant opposition groups. The rule of law weakened, and non-whites lost what small power they held in parliamentary government. The ANC proved a broken reed, because it mistakenly believed that the strategy used by anticolonialists against the British in countries like Zambia and Malawi — boycotts, non-co-operation, intimidation of unco-operative Africans — would work against white South Africans, that passive resistance would, somehow or other, produce a chain reaction leading to a series of accelerating concessions from the government and result in its overthrow. This strategy, however, took no account of the country's military and organisational realities. The whites were competently led, technically efficient and self-confident. The ANC was divided between the so-called 'moderates', who advocated an interracial class alliance, and the 'radicals', who saw the coming struggle in terms of a purely black revolution. The ANC was short of money and short of numbers. At the height of its influence, in 1955, the membership amounted to less than 30,000, with only a handful of 'hard' cadres. The ANC's branches were poorly co-ordinated, poorly disciplined and ill controlled from the centre, often preoccupied with petty local squabbles. Above all, the leadership suffered from a kind of Jericho complex which assumed that the enemy walls must fall, if only the ANC trumpets blew loud enough.

In 1959 the African National Congress split into two wings: the Pan Africanist Congress and the ANC itself. The interracial alliance and ideology of the white leadership in the congress and the ANC caused an Africanist reaction. The parent body became, to all intents and purposes, a mass organisation of the South African Communist Party and in 1960 was banned, like the SACP before it. In 1961 the ANC founded a guerrilla organisation known as Umkhonto we Sizwe (spear of the nation), but attempts at sabotage ended in failure. Communist cadres continued to operate within the framework of the ANC. *The African Communist* indeed bitterly complained at the unwillingness of liberal Western intellectuals to give Communists due credit for their work in the South African resistance movement.* The ANC established all manner of contacts with what might be called the *guerrilla internationale*, a well financed growth industry with interlocking contacts, receiving help from a variety of sovereign states. An alliance was formed with ZAPU (Zimbabwe African Peoples' Union) in Rhodesia (Zimbabwe), SWAPO (South-West African Peoples' Organisation) in Namibia, FRELIMO in Mozambique, and MPLA in Angola — by now ruling parties in sovereign Marxist-Leninist states. But the ANC failed to set up an effective underground organisation within South Africa itself.

Dissensions continued within the party's ranks, leading to numerous expulsions. The government arrested the leaders left behind in South

---

* See, for instance, the anonymous review of *Challenge and Violence*, ed. Karis and Gerhart, in *The African Communist*, no. 72 (first quarter 1978), pp. 113-15. The reviewer complained of the 'screening or of deliberate selection to exclude Communist documentation' and downplay Communist participation in the liberation movement.

Africa, including Fischer, Govan Mbeki and many others. The ANC, like the SACP, became large an exile organisation.[9] In return for political and financial support from the Soviet bloc, the ANC-SACP alliance followed every twist and turn of Soviet policy. On issues as varied as Zionism, Maoism or American neocolonialism, *Sechaba* (organ of the ANC) or *The African Communist* in no wise differed from *Neues Deutschland* or *Pravda*. Enmeshed in the complex network of pro-Soviet front organisations, the ANC and SACP became important for their publicity value abroad, rather than for their involvement in the internal South African revolution.*

Africanist Movements

The majority of 'non-European' movements have certain features in common. The stress ethnicity more than social class; they look upon the Africans as a proletarian people, collectively oppressed by an alien white minority. They look with pride upon the African heritage and try to make the African past relevant for the future — not an easy task in a country where Sotho, Venda or Zulu notions of the past do not necessarily coincide. They tend to idealise workmen and peasants, but they are led by teachers, lecturers, journalists and attorneys, rather than by poor people. Their leaders have no direct stake in the industrial revolution: engineers, managers, industrial chemists are conspicuous by their absence, not surprising in a country where most of the industrial and managerial key positions continue to be held by whites. They stress black power, but their ideological arsenal owes little to African traditional thought. Notions derived from Chairman Mao may sometimes blend with ideas derived from Richard Wright, Frantz Fanon,

---

* Moses Mabhida, an ANC executive member and a Vice-President of the South African Congress of Trade Unions (SACTU), a small, Communist-dominated body, thus served as deputy member of the Communist-dominated World Federation of Trade Unions (WFTU). Mark Williams-Shope, Secretary-General of SACTU, was a full member of the WFTU. Brian Bunting, a member of the SACP's central committee, was a member of the Communist-dominated International Organization of Journalists (IOJ) and a Tass correspondent in London. Ruth Mompati, leader of the ANC's women's section, was a member of the pro-Soviet Women's International Democratic Federation (WIDF); Josiah Jele, member of the ANC executive, worked for the secretariat of the Soviet-dominated World Peace Council (WPC). Oliver Reginald Tambo, President-General of the ANC, also served as President-General of the WPC. Vella Pillay, a member of the SACP, served as Vice-Chairman of the Anti-Apartheid movement in London. The ANC sent out broadcasts through the Zambian, Tanzanian and Angolan radio corporations. It published a number of journals, including *Secheba*, printed in East Germany, ideologically aligned to *The African Communist*, which was published in London.

George Padmore, Leon Trotsky and militant black Americans like Robert F. Williams. In addition, there are more pacific strains coming from the African ecclesiastical opposition. The various opposition groups are divided as bitterly as the dissident African churches; their impact — at present — depends more on their foreign connections and their propagandist power than on their ability to threaten the government in military or political terms.

The Pan-Africanist Congress of Azania (PAC) came into being in 1959 when African dissidents walked out of the ANC. Robert Sobukwe, a university lecturer from Witwatersrand known to his followers as 'the Prof', joined with Potlako Kitchener Leballo, a teacher from Lesotho, to form a new organisation that would put African interests first, without being subordinate to the white ruling clique of the SACP. PAC stood for a policy of uncompromising black nationalism. The party's programme is summed up in the title of its militant wing: POQO ('we alone', reminiscent of the Irish Sinn Fein) symbolises the party's programme. The PAC looks for assistance to Peking, and proclaims a doctrine of unrelenting guerrilla war, to be started in the cities. According to Leballo, the towns must belong by night to the black masses, who must harass the white enemy by bombs, sniper fire and arson. Urban unrest will spread to the countryside, and the white regime must collapse after a protracted struggle. In support of these principles, the PAC has obtained arms, cash and a certain amount of training from the People's Republic of China, as well as money from Libya, and — for good measure — from the World Council of Churches.

In 1960 PAC was banned, and the South African security forces made short shrift of POQO. After Sobukwe's death in 1978 the party was reorganised under Leballo's leadership. The PAC resolved to strengthen underground organisations in South Africa, to liquidate 'white settler colonialism' and 'its economic base, which is the capitalist mode of production'.* This objective was to be achieved by emphasising armed insurrection in the countryside. At the time of writing, however, PAC's published programme bore little resemblance to the realities of the South African situation, and its military impact on South Africa remained negligible. Leballo was ousted; PAC was in disarray.

* *Azania News* (Consultative Conference Special), vol. 13, nos. 7-8 (July-August 1978), p. 1. PAC was organised on the basis of 'democratic centralism' under the chairmanship of Potlako K. Leballo, who headed both PAC and its central committee. The central committee's military work was directed to a special military committee. Policy-making powers were formally entrusted to the Consultative Conference, whose ordinary meetings were scheduled, however, to take place only once every three years.

The Unity Movement of South Africa (UMSA), led by Dr Isaac Tabata, proceeds on somewhat different lines. UMSA is a Trotskyite organisation, not formally banned in South Africa at this time, influential mainly among Coloured intellectuals. The movement aims at uniting Africans, Coloureds and Asians into a united front. Unlike the ANC and PAC, UMSA failed to receive support from the Organization of African Unity (OAU), and at present its organisation remains weak.

Another opposition movement is centred on those very black universities set up by Afrikaner nationalists to 'contain' discontent among Africans. The African students took the Afrikaners at their word. In 1969 a black group broke away from the 'multiracial', English-dominated, English-speaking National Union of South African Students (NUSAS). The dissidents formed an organisation of their own known as the South African Students' Organization (SASO), containing about 6,000 members. SASO bitterly opposed apartheid and the South African government's system of Bantu education. SASO advocated a new form of black awareness, entailing the liberation from psychological oppression brought on blacks by their own feelings of inferiority, and from physical oppression brought about by a racist system of government. In 1972 SASO helped to establish the Black Peoples' Convention (BPC) as a political movement for all non-whites.

The various conferences had assembled in 1971 to form such a convention as part of a wider Black Consciousness movement, supported by men as different as Chief Gatsha Buthelezi of the KwaZulu Homeland and Steve Biko of the SASO. Most delegates were united in the general principle of black self-assertion, and agreed to define the word 'black' in such a manner as to include Coloureds and Indians. Biko indeed went far beyond PAC in favouring a broad black front against the whites. The Black Renaissance Convention, held in 1974, was more moderate in character. It was organised by black Catholic and Protestant church leaders, including clergymen of the Dutch Reformed Church. It brought together African, Coloured and Indian participants — businessmen, trade unionists and professional people. The conference rejected separate development; it called for a democratic South Africa governed on the principle of 'one man, one vote'. The BPC, like SASO, rejected participation in all political bodies set up for non-whites, such as the Coloured Representative Council and the homeland legislative assemblies.

SASO was blamed for unrest at university campuses and was banned from several colleges. In 1976 the government arrested the entire SASO executive committee, including Mongezi Stofile, its President. A year later Steve Biko, a medical student, Honorary President of the Black Peoples' Convention, who had been banned in 1972, was beaten to death while in police custody. The notions of the BPC had wide appeal among schoolboys and students in Soweto and other black townships where popular discontent led to widespread disturbances in 1977. The Black Consciousness movement was reconstituted in 1978 through the formation of the Azania Peoples Organization (AZAPO), led by Ishmael Mhabela, leader of the Soweto Action Committee. AZAPO was closed to whites, but open to Indians and Coloureds as well as to Africans; the movement stood for peaceful opposition to apartheid, and was determined to unite all non-Europeans in a final struggle to wrest control from the whites. Led by Curtis Nkondo, a former school principal, AZAPO is committed neither to violence nor to any specific social system. But according to AZAPO, South Africa faces a new peril, the creation of a black middle class that threatens the future of the black masses by providing the whites with a new ally. Pretoria's policy, designed to replace racial by economic discrimination, will make liberation harder to achieve than before — a standpoint that oddly parallels that of Afrikaner *verligtes*. AZAPO looks to spreading its views through schools, universities and trade unions, but only the future can show whether AZAPO can overcome its existing weaknesses.

Movements of Moderate Reform

South Africans, white and black, are bitterly divided in their assessment concerning the legal black opposition. Militant revolutionaries and *verkrampte* nationalists have one notion in common. They believe that compromise is out of the question, that power is indivisible, that the choice lies between being anvil or hammer, subjects or overlords. At the time of writing, the great mass of Africans do not, however, envisage the country's future in such stark terms. The overwhelming majority, even of urban Africans, do not belong to political organisations of any kind. There is as yet little racism in reverse. Most blacks would be willing to concede full civic rights to whites if the boot were on the other foot, and if blacks were to run the country.[10] Only a minority — less than 40 per cent of urban Africans — identify themselves in tribal terms; only about 10 per cent consider the abolition of social discrimination between white and black as a matter of major importance. But blacks overwhelmingly demand an improvement in their economic condition, with political advancement, improved education and better social relations as subordinate priorities (see

Table 4.5: Priorities in the Demands of African Townsmen (per cent)

	Economic Priorities	Education	Better Social Relations	Political Demands
Soweto	48.9	13.8	15.8	24.6
Durban	49.2	14.2	11.1	25.5
Pretoria	65.7	17.7	5.0	11.6

Source: Theodor Hanf, Heribert Weiland, Gerda Vierdag, *Südafrika: Friedlicher Wandel. Möglichkeiten der demokratischen Konfliktregelung — Eine empirische Untersuchung* (Kaiser, Grunewald, Mainz, 1977), p. 381.

Table 4.5).

These attitudes may change in the future. They reflect the situation in a country where militant African opposition has to cope with rigid pass laws, an efficient government intelligence network and powerful armed forces. Africans, for the time being, overwhelmingly backed moderate bodies willing to co-operate within the legal framework.

Many moderates derive their inspiration from religious sources. But generalisations concerning the impact of religion on South African politics are hard to make. South Africa is a divided land in the religious as well as the ethnic and cultural sense. The dissensions between South Africa's ethnic communities are replicated to some extent within the churches; these are split both on denominational, ethnic and theological lines, and cannot therefore speak with one voice. Yet their collective force is considerable. Ironically enough, the most numerous group of South African Christians now comprises members of African Independent Churches (about 3,500,000) who profess a variety of orthodox, unorthodox and sometimes bizarre doctrines, and who are split into numerous organisations of varying size and cohesion. Next in order of importance come the members (white, Coloured and African) of the Dutch Reformed Churches (about 3,300,000), Methodists (just under 2,000,000), Catholics (1,800,000), Anglicans and Episcopalians (1,700,000), and other smaller groups.

The churches are divided politically as well as theologically. On the one end of the theological spectrum are conservative Afrikaners whose beliefs have been shaped by the typology of Israel, the exodus and the promised land; theirs is a theology of liberation that sees the working of God's will exemplified in Afrikaner history. At the other end of the spectrum is to be found the theology of liberation elaborated by black churchmen, some of them influenced by Latin American divines who look to a 'strategic' alliance with Marxism. The centre is occupied by liberal Afrikaners and by the bulk of the English-speaking churches in South Africa who look to a policy of peaceful accommodation; their clergymen almost universally tend to be more liberal than the congregations who pay the pastors' salaries.

The most powerful of these movements is the Inkatha Yen-kululeko Yesiwe (national cultural liberation movement), a Zulu nationalist organisation headed by Chief Gatsha Buthelezi. Inkatha took its present form in 1975 when it was launched in the KwaZulu legislative assembly. According to its critics, Inkatha is an elitist organisation, dominated by Zulu chiefs who are resolved to exclude the masses from all real power, and who use the movement as a means of perpetuating the Bantustan policy and entrenching Buthelezi's position in KwaZulu. But, in fact, Buthelezi has bitterly opposed apartheid, and uses his power as head of the Zulu homeland to fight against apartheid from within the system. The excision of the Transkei from South Africa has turned the Zulu into South Africa's largest and most powerful black community, but Buthelezi is determined to be more than a mere homeland leader. Inkatha's objectives have broadened, and its leaders speak of creating a national organisation geared to the emancipation of South Africa's black community as a whole. On their own, Chief Buthelezi argues, the homelands are in no position to cut their links with South Africa. Buthelezi instead makes a bid for the centre — moderate blacks and white liberals — so as to change the power equation.

In 1978 Buthelezi formed an alliance with the Indian Reform Party, an Asian group, and with the more substantial Coloured Labour Party, then led by Sonny Leon. The new grouping, styled the South African Black Alliance (SABA), also obtained support from various other groups, including the ruling party of the Qwa-Qwa homeland. The party's provisional constitution, drawn up in Cape Town in 1978, looks to the creation of a just society, the formulation of a common strategy against apartheid, the unification of all black organisations striving for political, economic and social change, and a national convention that will draw up a constitution for a non-racial South African society. The new alliance faced a variety of tactical problems. Buthelezi and Inkatha were opposed to the application of economic sanctions against South Africa, while the Coloured Labour Party was in favour of an embargo. SABA, according to its critics, was an alliance of leaders that failed to involve the mass of the people. The alliance put its trust in peaceful means, and was therefore incapable of reaching its own goal. But SABA also had distinct advantages. Unlike most other opposition movements, SABA was able to speak from government-created platforms, thereby giving its leaders a certain measure of security and official respect.

The public support for SABA is hard to assess. Inkatha, with a signed-up membership of 150,000, is perhaps the largest black body in South African history and dominates the KwaZulu legislative assembly. The Coloured Labour Party is the most powerful of the Coloured parties and ran the Coloured Representative Council. The Indian Reform Party and the Qwa-Qwa Dikanwetla Party are smaller groups. Zulu predominance within SABA is likely to deter the alliance from gaining nation-wide black support, and the organisation's pacific approach arouses the contempt of militant intellectuals. Opinions differ with regard to Inkatha's influence. The public mood is apt to fluctuate, and interviewers do not always elicit their informants' true beliefs. Nevertheless, a German team recently managed to secure some surprising results (1977). It found that among urban Africans, the most popular African leader at the time was Gatsha Buthelezi, who was rated first by 43.8 per cent of all informants; his support went far beyond members of the Zulu people; he stood out as the dominant political personality. The ANC leadership ranked second, with 18.3 per cent. The most popular ANC personage within the group was Nelson Mandela, with 18.6 per cent, whereas men such as Oliver Tambo, Walter Sisulu and Albert Luthuli secured less than 1 per cent. The leaders of other homelands ranked in third place, with 21.7 per cent. The PAC secured only 7.4 per cent; the Black Consciousness leaders 5.6 per cent – a surprisingly high figure in view of the fact that Black Consciousness only had a few years in which to organise.[11]

At the present time, the various African opposition movements remain splintered and relatively powerless. But for all their dissensions, they have a good deal in common. They draw on a mixture of personal apprehension and frustration, but also on a widespread sense of long-term optimism. According to the investigation carried out by the German team mentioned above, only about half of all South Africans – white or black – describe their personal condition as 'happy'. But whereas about a quarter of all whites, especially Afrikaner Nationalists, fear that their condition will change for the worse during the next decade, Africans are much more optimistic. According to the findings of Hanf, Weiland and Vierdag, more than 60 per cent of all blacks expect to be 'happy' in the next ten years.[12]

The various African opposition movements also have certain resemblances in a structural sense. They depend heavily for their leadership on intellectuals. The old 'imperial' elite had not relied on politics for a livelihood. Cecil John Rhodes, Prime Minister of the Cape (1890-6), had been a mining magnate; Sir Godfrey Huggins, later Lord Malvern, Prime Minister of Rhodesia and then of the Federation of Rhodesia and Nyasaland (1933-56), had been one of his country's most successful surgeons; Louis Botha had been a prosperous farmer. The new African elite, on the other hand, look to politics both as a vocation and as a professional career, as does an Afrikaner like P.W. Botha. The African elite is apt to place its trust in the revolutionary state rather than in private enterprise, both as a means of righting public wrongs and as an instrument for private advancement. The leading representatives of the new elite tend to see themselves as future members of a post-revolutionary ruling stratum of party functionaries, politicians and ideologues. They share the social prejudice, widespread also in white academia and the white public services, that a tenured position financed at the taxpayer's expense is somehow more honourable or socially useful than income derived from private enterprise. The new elite, at the same time, suffers bitterly from the social and economic disabilities inflicted upon educated Africans. This sense of resentment sometimes mingles with a sense of technological and organisational inferiority vis-à-vis the dominant whites, a sense quite different in quality from, say, the dislike felt by a Dutchman or a Dane for the German occupiers in World War Two, or by a Jewish Zionist for the British in Mandatory Palestine.

The black movements that we have outlined above all suffer from a variety of organisational weaknesses that mirror the social characteristics of the leadership. (See Chapter 7 for an analysis of the weaknesses in the black opposition.) For all their radical terminology, those movements have been unable to create that indispensable instrument for effective underground warfare, a revolutionary 'counter state', complete with schools, law courts, police and other services capable of competing with or replacing the services provided by the occupying power. In World War Two the Polish underground had run its own underground schools and universities; in the Anglo-Irish War the Irish Republican Army had operated secret law courts where Protestants as well as Catholics might seek justice. At the present time the South African underground has not even begun to set up parallel organisations of government comparable to those evolved during the Algerian revolution. However much the people of Soweto, for instance, might dislike the government, they do not at present look to the underground for protection against thieves, for the settlement of disputes, or for help with unemployment. Until the various underground organisations transform themselves into mass movements with their own civilian and military state organs, they will not turn rhetoric into a revolution.

Political opposition in South Africa has until now been easily suppressed.[13] Every black, white, Coloured or Indian group which has emerged to resist apartheid has been defeated by the government. Yet the numbers of political prisoners and 'banned' people are quite small when measured against the standards of Communist or right-wing regimes. Political opponents are restricted to four forms.

(1) Convicted political prisoners in state prisons, such as Robben Island, number 440 (54 are Namibians).

(2) Political detainees — those held without charge or trial — are of three types: those held for interrogation purposes under Section 6 of the Terrorism Act, those detained as political state witnesses under the Internal Security Act, and those held in preventive detention under the Internal Security Act. It is difficult to fix the number of political detainees, since the authorities do not publish their names nor inform their families. The Christian Institute and the South African Institute of Race Relations estimated 700 people were detained after the Soweto riots. From 1974 to 1976, 217 people were detained.

(3) Banned people, at present numbering about 160 people. In all more than 1,300 people have been under banning orders since the Suppression of Communism Act was passed in 1950. Forty people were banned in 1976.

(4) The category of banished people is no longer used. More than 140 were banished to internal exile in the 1940s and 1960s.

Coloureds and Indians in Politics

South African Coloureds and Indians differ greatly in income, status and social composition. But they have certain features in common. Both groups are at present politically powerless; both occupy intermediate positions between the whites and the blacks; both have serious identity problems, a feature to which we refer at greater length in the section on the peoples of South Africa. Neither group has developed a sense of ethnic nationalism to rival that of the Afrikaners; neither possesses a territory of its own capable of fitting into the official apartheid scheme. The Coloureds are more divided than the Indians, and suffer from high rates of criminality, alcoholism, illegitimacy and unemployment.

The Coloureds, in a certain sense, now hold a place similar to that of black Americans a generation ago. The Coloureds are mainly an urban people, primarily working-class in composition, linked to the dominant Europeans by ties of language and culture. Whites are more likely to feel guilty about the past treatment meted out to the Coloureds than about the subjugation of the Africans. Opinion polls show that more than 70 per cent of the whites are prepared to modify apartheid in favour of the Coloureds. The government has formulated plans for a Coloured parliament; public transportation in Cape Town has been desegregated; Coloured education has significantly improved, as have opportunities for educated Coloureds in business, the civil service and the professions. The 2.5 million Coloureds represent a significant manpower reserve for the economy, the military and the police. Coloureds are likely to improve their position; they might as yet play a major part in determining South Africa's future.

Coloured politics began as moderate politics. A minority of Coloureds had been enfranchised under the property-weighted but 'colour-blind' franchise of the Cape. These voters consisted mainly of professional men and traders who had little in common with the mass of Coloured farm labourers or urban poor. The African People's Organization – in fact, though not in name, a Coloured body – was led from 1905 to 1940 by Dr Abdullah Abdurahman, a surgeon and a Cape Town city councillor, originally a supporter of the pro-imperial Unionist Party. In 1943 the Smuts government set up a Coloured Advisory Council; its unintended effect was to polarise Coloured opinion in the political sense. The Coloured National People's Union agreed to collaborate with the government. The National Anti-Coloured Advisory Council Committee, later a part of the so-called Non-European Unity Movement, refused to co-operate with the working of the council, which was seen as an instrument of segregation. Coloured militants, mainly recruited from students and schoolteachers, were strongly influenced by Trotskyite thought; but they were too divided among themselves, and too remote from the rank and file of the Coloured people, to create a mass Coloured movement. The minority of relatively well-to-do Coloureds on the Cape voters' roll tended to support Smuts and his United Party.

In 1956 the Nationalist government removed the Coloureds from the common voters' roll, but, as a *quid pro quo*, created in 1969 the Coloured Representative Council. Five different parties initially put up candidates; the most important of these were the moderate Federal Coloured People's Party (FCPP) and the Coloured Labour Party (CLP). The FCPP and the CLP both looked to eventual emancipation of the Coloureds; but while the FCPP tried to attain this objective by a policy of moderation, the CLP refused to collaborate in the government's apartheid policy. The FCPP stood for a sense of Coloured group identity, but the CLP rejected this concept. Instead, the CLP increasingly began to adopt the language of Black Consciousness, and called for a united non-white front. The CLP became the most powerful elected group on the Coloured Representative Council, but was in turn opposed by those militants who considered all who participated in the council's deliberations as 'Quislings'.[14]

The South African Indians, as we have pointed out earlier, are not a united group. They profess differing religions — Hinduism, Islam, Christianity and Zoroastrianism. They speak different languages — Tamil, Telugu, Hindi, Gujerati. But the Indians are better off materially than the Coloureds; they have a greater sense of group cohesion than the Coloureds. India and, to a lesser extent, Pakistan are powers of consequence, whereas the Coloureds have no homeland but South Africa.[15]

Mahatma Gandhi's political career began in South Africa, where he pioneered his technique of civil disobedience in 1907. So successful was his campaign of non-violent resistance that he secured, in 1914, an agreement from the South African government promising that anti-Hindu discrimination would be alleviated. Historically, the Indian elite consisted of merchants and entrepreneurs. Their leaders concentrated on specifically Indian grievances; they relied on negotiations, deputations, petitions and discussions to gain limited concessions from the white governments. The expansion of the country's educational system produced a new elite of professional men and intellectuals whose demands became more radical than those of their predecessors. The new elite has sought to work with all groups, not just Indians; they called for direct action and human rights. A radical wing inside the Natal Indian Council (NIC), which called for union with Africans and direct resistance, caused a split within the council. In 1947 the older group founded the Natal Indian Organization (NIO); the rump NIC was pro-Communist, and alienated the whites and conservative Indians.

The radical Indian group sought links with white and black organisations, such as the African National Congress. In 1952 the radicals concluded a formal alliance with the ANC, and launched a passive resistance campaign against the Group Areas Act. Indians joined the

Congress of Peoples in 1955 in issuing the Freedom Charter. Many arrests were made; the ANC was banned in 1960, and so were many Indian radicals.

A year later, however, in 1961, the Nationalists modified their anti-Indian position to the extent of recognising Indians as a permanent part of the South African people. The Department of Indian Affairs, set up in 1961, provided the Indians with an official channel to express their needs; so did the South African Indian Council (SAIC), set up as a consultative body in 1964. Today the South African Indians are divided into four main groups:

(1) the SAIC adherents, broadly speaking, accept the present position. They fear an African take-over, fearful of what has happened to Indians in Uganda, Kenya and Tanzania since those countries achieved independence under black governance;
(2) pragmatists who accept existing government policies, but only for the sake of expediency;
(3) abstainers who distrust the government, but who do not want to be involved in politics;
(4) radicals who look to an alliance with SASO and the Black Peoples' Convention.

The advocates of co-operation with the government point to a number of successes obtained by negotiation. By 1979, for instance, Indians had secured more than 460 jobs within the bureaucracy of the Indian Affairs Department alone. Indian businessmen and entrepreneurs fear lest their property be seized in a black take-over. They argue that Indians are much more vulnerable than whites, and should therefore pursue a policy of caution, however objectionable the white government may be. The Natal Indian Congress (NIC), set up in 1971, looks upon the Black Consciousness as a racial movement. The NIC limits its membership to Indians, but has remained weak and divided. Young radical Indians, most of them intellectuals, support SASO.

But, generally speaking, the BPC has not won over many Indians. The BPC seems too militant, and it preaches black domination. Memories survive from the Durban riots, when over a hundred Indians were killed by Africans. Africans are apt to look upon Indians as 'cheeky traders' out to exploit their customers; African intellectuals often censure the Indians for their 'cultural arrogance', and their proclivity for self-segregation. Coloureds frequently hold unfavourable stereotypes concerning Indians; Indians all too often hold similar prejudices concerning the Coloureds. Generally speaking, Indians fear to commit themselves to the other camp, and as a community they will probably continue to work for limited concessions rather than root-and-branch reforms.

Notes

1. See A.D. Wassenaar, *Assault on Private Enterprise* (Tafelberg Publishers, Cape Town, 1977), p. 74. For a brief outline of the public corporations, see Anthony Hocking, *South African Government* (MacDonald, Cape Town, c. 1976), p. 46, a popular account.
2. For a detailed account of the party written in English, see W. Kleynhans, 'White Political Parties' in Anthony de Crespigny and Robert Schrire (eds.), *The Government and Politics of South Africa* (Juta, Cape Town, 1978), pp. 94-116. The standard account in Afrikaans is O. Geyser and A.H. Marais (eds.), *Die Nasionale Party* (Academia, Pretoria, 1975), part 1.
3. For contrasting accounts of the Broederbond see Adriaan Nicolaas Pelzer, *Die Afrikaner-Broederbond: Eerste 50 Jaar* (Tafelberg, Cape Town, 1979) and J.H.P. Serfontein, *Brotherhood of Power: an Exposé of the Secret Afrikaner Broederbond* (Rex Collings, London, 1979).
4. René de Villiers, 'Afrikaner Nationalism', in Monica Wilson and Leonard Thompson (eds.), *The Oxford History of South Africa* (Oxford University Press, Oxford, 1971), Vol. 2, Chapter 2.
5. See Leo Kuper, 'African Nationalism in South Africa, 1910-1964', in *Oxford History of South Africa*, Vol. 2, Chapter 9.
6. 'Constitution of the South African Native National Congress, September 1919' in Sheridan Johns (ed.), *Protest and Hope, 1882-1934*, Vol. 1 of Thomas Karis and Gwendolen M. Carter (eds.), *From Protest to Challenge: a Documentary History of African Politics in South Africa, 1882-1964* (Hoover Institution, Stanford, 1972), pp. 76-82. Other studies include Gail M. Gerhart, *Black Power in South Africa: the Evolution of an Ideology* (University of California Press, Berkeley, 1978), and D.A. Kotze, *African Politics in South Africa: 1964-1974; Parties and Issues* (St Martin's Press, New York, 1975).
7. *Imvo Zabantsundu* (31 August 1909), cited in Johns, *Protest and Hope*, pp. 56-7.
8. The Freedom Charter, 26 June 1955, is reprinted in Thomas Karis and Gail M. Gerhart (eds.), *Challenge and Violence, 1953-1964* (Hoover Institution, Stanford, 1977), Vol. 3 of *From Protest to Challenge*, pp. 205-7.
9. By 1978 the ANC had offices or representatives in London, New York, Rome, Amsterdam, East Berlin, Lagos, Cairo, Luanda, Algeria, New Delhi, Stockholm, Lusaka, Dar es Salaam, Mogorogoro, Dakar and Toronto.
10. See Theodor Hanf, Heribert Weiland and Gerda Vierdag, *Südafrika: Friedlicher Wandel, Möglichkeiten der demokratischen Konfliktregelung – Eine empirische Untersuchung* (Kaiser, Grunewald, Mainz, 1977), especially pp. 353 ff. According to the authors' findings, only 5.5 per cent of African urban informants belong to any organisation: 1.1 per cent are members of trade unions; 2.7 per cent back the Inkatha movement; 1.7 per cent support various Black Consciousness organisations.
11. Hanf *et al.*, *Südafrika: Friedlicher Wandel*, pp. 371-2.
12. Ibid., pp. 441-2.

13. See *Political Imprisonment in South Africa: an Amnesty International Report, 1978* (Amnesty International, London, 1978).
14. See Pierre Hugo, *Quislings or Realists: a Documentary Study of Coloured Politics in South Africa* (Raven Press, Johannesburg, 1978).
15. See Kogila H. Moodley, 'South African Indians: the Wavering Minority', in Leonard Thompson and Jeffrey Butler (eds.), *Change in Contemporary South Africa* (University of California Press, Berkeley, 1975), Chapter 1; Fatima Meer, *Portrait of Indian South Africans* (Durban, 1969); idem, *The Ghetto People* (Africa Publication Trust, London, 1976); Frene Ginwala, *Indian South Africans*, Minority Rights Group Report No. 34 (Minority Rights Group, London, 1977). The literature on race relations in general is too vast to be cited even selectively. For a comprehensive guide see Pieter J.S. Potgieter, *Index to the Literature on Race Relations in South Africa, 1910-1975* (G.K. Hall, Boston, 1979). For the historical background see the following two standard histories, each of which is provided with an extensive bibliography: Eric A. Walker, *A History of Southern Africa* (Longman, London, 1962), and Wilson and Thompson, *Oxford History of South Africa*.

5 THE ECONOMICS OF SOUTH AFRICA

The Beginnings of a Modern Economy: 1652-1914

From the early days of Dutch settlement, South Africa's economic history has hinged upon foreign trade. When the Dutch colonists first arrived at the Cape, they were fortunate in having a foreign market for fresh meat, butter, milk, wine, fruit and vegetables at their very doorsteps. The crews and passengers of the ships that rounded the Cape on their way to the East Indies clamoured for fresh food. The Cape farmers thus had an export market in the harbour of Cape Town, a market that expanded with the development of new ports and the extension of coastal shipping along the eastern Cape. The growth of new coastal markets stimulated colonisation in the interior as mariner, merchant and *trekboer* became partners in a common enterprise.[1] African herdsmen and hunters also became enmeshed to some extent in the growing network of trade, as subsistence farmers increasingly grew used to selling part of their crops in order to purchase knives, hatchets, clothes, tea, coffee, salt and other commodities alien to the village.

The immigrants at the Cape developed what, by the standards of contemporary Africa south of the equator, was a relatively complex economy. The newcomers depended upon the power of the wind; they also knew how to harness draught animals for pulling carts, ploughs and wagons. There were no great plantations requiring slavery for such work. The Europeans, right from the start, required servile labour, but their economy had no need for great masses of African slaves — carriers, or armies of plantation workers equipped only with primitive tools. The colonists developed industries such as viticulture in the Western Cape, but there were no huge landed estates such as those of Mauritius, Zanzibar or the New World, producing tropical crops for export. Hence slavery at the Cape was not overly harsh by the standards of Brazil or Louisiana. Masters were apt to know their slaves personally; a good deal of skilled work was done by servile workmen (especially Malays from the East).

The Dutch also provided for manumitting slaves, and during the seventeenth century some freed slaves were absorbed into white society — including enterprising women like Angela from Bengal, who was freed by her master, become a communicant in the Dutch Reformed

Church, married a free burgher, and ended as a prosperous and independent widow.[2] White South African race attitudes, in other words, were shaped by the experience of the frontier rather than by slavery. Slavery was abolished under British auspices in 1833, a generation earlier than in the United States, two generations before the disappearance of slavery in Brazil and Cuba. The demise of slavery occasioned infinitely less disruption in South Africa than in the USA, and South Africa passed into the era of wage labour with comparative ease.

During the first part of the nineteenth century there were some inroads into traditional methods of white farming. Newcomers from Europe, including settlers from Great Britain and Germany, introduced a variety of new techniques and new crops. The iron British plough replaced the old-fashioned boards nailed together and armed with a clumsy share. Lord Charles Somerset, an early British Governor, introduced the first threshing machine in 1821; in the following decade a variety of implements of American origin began to reach the colony. A Stellenbosch wheelwright, Joseph Simpson, perfected a reaping machine. Other pioneers included men like Maximilian Thalwitzer (a German-Jewish merchant converted to Calvinism), who played an important part in creating the South African merino wool industry. Merino wool, for a time, became South Africa's most important article of foreign trade, amounting to 76 per cent of all Cape exports in 1863, in addition to luxury products like mohair, ostrich feathers, hides and skins, articles of relatively small bulk and great value that would bear the heavy cost of transport by ox wagon from the interior.

The modernisation of the Cape, in other words, began long before the discovery of minerals. The Cape, as well as Natal, the Orange Free State and the Transvaal, owed its original economic impetus to farming for the market to small-scale agricultural processing industries and craftsmen – millers, smiths, coopers, chandlers, wagon-builders, brewers, tanners, foundrymen, whalers, wheelwrights and such. Progress speeded up as local banks and credit institutions came into being, followed by the establishment of some great London banks. These included the Standard Bank of South Africa which opened its doors in 1862, one of the first institutions to register in London on the new principle of limited rather than unlimited liability for its shareholders.

By the 1860s the Cape was economically by far the most developed part of sub-Saharan Africa; its trade was the largest, its infrastructure the most elaborate to be found between Cape Point and the Sahara. The colonists constructed roads, bridges and ferries; they built a network of schools, including an infant college (South Africa College, founded in 1829, and established as the University of Cape Town in 1918); they were in touch with scientific and medical endeavours in Europe; they enjoyed the rudiments of an urban existence. A traveller passing through Cape Town in the 1840s would be able to admire a variety of great public buildings, visit clubs, coffee houses and restaurants, take a leisurely stroll through the public gardens, walk at night through streets illuminated by gas light. He would find that water was piped to the wealthier private houses, and that the less prosperous would be able to use public taps placed in the streets at convenient intervals. He would be able to mix with professional men in touch with the scientific endeavours of Europe; he would be as remote from the 'Darkest Africa' of legends and storybooks as a New Englander would be from the Indian cultures of North America's remote interior.

By the standards of Lesotho, or even of Zanzibar, Lagos or Bornu, the Cape economy was complex. By comparison with Western or Central Europe, on the other hand, the Cape was but a backward and remote outpost. Few emigrants from Europe thought of making a new home for themselves in Africa; the immense majority of settlers preferred the journey across the Atlantic to North and South America. Yields from taxation remained so small in the South African colonies that they had to take frequent recourse to depreciating their respective currencies. In economic terms, the Cape resembled a Balkan kingdom like Serbia. The bulk of the Cape population, white and black, depended on agriculture. In 1865, to be exact, South Africa's white population amounted to no more than 180,000 people; 75 per cent of the employed population was engaged in farming; only about one-eighth pursued crafts of various kinds, and less than one-sixteenth was engaged in trade. The infant export economy was subject to sharp price fluctuations, sudden gluts and extended periods of depression. There was no scope for mass immigration; the Cape would never become another New Zealand or another Australia, much less a new California in the South Atlantic.

The last three decades of the nineteenth century brought about dramatic change. In 1867 Schalk van Niekerk, an Afrikaner farmer, called on his friend Jacob near the Orange River. The children were playing marbles with a brilliant stone, and Van Niekerk pocketed it as a curiosity. The stone turned out to be a diamond, the first sold commercially in South Africa. There were further finds. In 1870 the so-called 'dry diggings' were discovered at Kimberley, and the diamond fields soon attracted a great migrant population of white prospectors, diggers, merchants and craftsmen, as well as African labourers anxious to earn enough money to buy a musket, clothes or other imported merchandise. News of the discovery spread rapidly; Africans made their way to Kimberley from as far afield as Barotseland in what is now Zambia, and from Matabeleland in what is now Zimbabwe, from kingdoms still outside the realm of white political control. The migration was the first large-scale initiation of Africans into a wage labour economy.

The discovery of diamonds – and later, of gold – in South Africa has sometimes been described as a lucky accident helping to propel South Africa into the modern world. But a truly primitive economy would not, in fact, have been able to exploit such discoveries. South Africa, by the second part of the last century, had already been linked to the markets of Europe. It contained a substantial class of white entrepreneurs, and, by comparison with the rest of Africa, a substantial infrastructure. The growth of the diamond industry gave a new impetus to South Africa's economy. Cape farmers ceased to be dependent on a small and fluctuating export trade and on shipping; white farmers found a growing market for meat, sugar, grain, wine and other commodities. Black cultivators also benefitted to some extent. There is evidence that Africans supplied corn, leaf tobacco, cattle and other commodities in increasing quantities to the diamond fields and to other towns. Growing revenue from the diamond industry enabled the government to construct railways. Profits made in diamond mining were invested in other forms of enterprise, and by the 1880s South Africa had the makings of a coal-mining industry and a modern system of transport. There were substantial port facilities, for example the great Albert Dock operating in Cape Town. South Africa, especially the Cape, also pioneered in the provision of experimental farms and technical education on the soil of Africa. In 1885, for instance, a viticultural station opened its doors at Groot Constantia, and four years later an agricultural school started at Stellenbosch.

The Cape Colony was thus the first territory in sub-Saharan Africa to acquire a modern economic infrastructure, as the value of the diamonds shipped abroad from the Cape in 1882 exceeded that of all other merchandise sent overseas from the rest of Africa. The diamond industry had begun as a small man's enterprise. Technical and financial considerations led to a process of amalgamation, and the industry came to be run by great magnates, men like Cecil Rhodes, whose power was such that the industry could provide out of its own surplus for most of its growth. Capital accumulated in diamond mining also found its way into gold mining, which became a major industry after the discovery of gold on the Witwatersrand in 1886.

The gold industry soon passed into the hands of great companies such as Rhodes Gold Fields of South Africa, Ltd, formed in 1887, which raised foreign and domestic capital, provided expert advice, and centralised purchasing, technical and other services. The 'small worker' never stood a chance, for deep-level mining required a high degree of skill and capital, while the MacArthur-Forrest process of extraction, used from 1890 onward, was uneconomic unless applied to large quantities of ore. Gold mining soon became South Africa's greatest industry. By the time the four South African colonies united into the Union of South Africa (1910), the gold mines already employed 225,000 workers, paid £18 million in wages a year, and produced gold worth £32 million a year. About a quarter of South Africa's income derived from the production of gold, which increased at a stupendous rate. Between 1897 and 1937 production rose from 2,744,000 ounces to 11,735,000 ounces. The gold industry became the country's largest single employer.

According to a widespread academic assumption concerning 'underdevelopment', extractive industries promoted by expatriate capitalists in underdeveloped countries are noxious in their effects. Foreign entrepreneurs are supposed to make superprofits by dint of exploiting cheap labour. They create nothing more lasting than big holes in the ground, it is claimed. Once the precious ores have been extracted, the colony is left impoverished, for mining does not promote significant changes in other sectors of the economy. The economic history of South Africa lends no support to such generalisations.

Mining development was indeed bought at a heavy price. The mining capitalists, as we have pointed out elsewhere, were anxious to secure a 'non-spasmodic supply of labour'; they would have preferred a permanent unskilled work-force made up of Chinese and other Asian immigrants, wholly dependent on wages. Opposition from white workers and British liberals prevented the mine-owners from employing Chinese workers and thereby adding yet another major ethnic group to South African society. At the same time, the owners were strong enough to prevent the creation of a white unskilled labour force on the mines, a labour force endowed with the vote and therefore politically dangerous. According to the owners, white labour would have been too expensive. The evidence, however, is by no means conclusive. After the end of the Boer War, Frederick Hugh Page Creswell, a British engineer, recruited white farmers ruined by the war for unskilled work on the Village Main Reef on the Rand. With the help of machinery and good management,

Creswell obtained greater production with white unskilled workers than with unskilled Africans. On this basis, he formulated the theory that South African industry should be developed with white labour alone. Creswell (later leader of the (white) Labour Party) could not, however, convince the mine-owners. White workmen asked for higher wages than Africans; they were familiar with trade union organisation; they were politically vocal; they had the vote; and they were too scanty in number to satisfy the never-ending demand for labour.

Reluctantly, the mining companies became increasingly dependent on African migrant workers. The pattern of migrancy was by no means universal. Coal-mines in Natal and the Transvaal provided 'locations' where Africans might bring their families; hence these mines were able to employ African workmen on an almost permanent basis. This system, however, was little employed on the gold-mines, and not at all on the diamond fields.[3] The Rand Lords depended for their unskilled work-force on African migrants, and of these migrants there never seemed to be enough. The advent of mining had occasioned a considerable rise in wages. As a British official source put it:

> In the olden days labour was cheap and plentiful, the remuneration being the privilege of squatting [settling] upon the [white] farms and possibly a certain amount of mealie meal for food and other small perquisites. But since the introduction of mining, the growth of towns, and the general opening of the Colony, a great change has come over the native. His rate of pay has increased enormously, and he now receives £2 to £3 or even more per month, in the towns or in the mines, in addition to food and sleeping accommodation.[4]

Labour migration was equated with the real or imagined evils of town life which supposedly corroded the peasant-bred virtues of old. The literature of rural migration to the cities, including Eastern European migration to the United States, is replete with such accounts that glorify the village:

> It was a thoroughly known place where one's ancestors lay buried, it did not loom up to terrifying heights before one's eyes, it required no special knowledge of machines in shops or on trolleys, and it seldom had much to do with the rigors of the clock ... [It] encouraged that indifference to time which a true religious existence demands and a life of pauperdom enables. To many of the immigrants, when they first arrived, ... the sheer noise of the streets, the

bulk of the buildings, the constant pushing and elbowing and rushing of daily existence, was terrifying.[5]

The passage refers to the Eastern European *shtetel*, as against New York's East Side during the late Victorian era. It might, with a few alterations, be inserted into many an account of labour migration in colonial Africa. The passage contains an element of truth, but it also embodies the assumption widely accepted among so many littérateurs, theologians and social scientists — that modern cities are unusually wicked, that culture shock or 'future shock' is a dread disease to be strictly avoided, that the 'wanderer between two worlds' is more miserable than the stay-at-home, because the migrant lacks the emotional security available at home.

Labour migration has accordingly found many censors in colonial Africa. Critics of the system argued that labour migration depleted the villages of its young men, that the migrants were 'spoiled' by the white man's immoral ways (a conclusion popular among Victorian civil servants and missionaries), that labour migration helped to disrupt indigenous agriculture, wiped out indigenous crafts, and upset the natural equilibrium of society. Migrant labour, according to the critics, was coerced labour; the migrants were compelled to work through the pressure of taxation that could only be paid in cash, and through contrived land shortages that prevented Africans from expanding commercialised agriculture. The social imbalance brought about by labour migration mirrored in microcosm the global imbalance occasioned by the dependence of the colonial periphery on the capitalist West.

We ourselves hold a somewhat different position. We agree that the imposition of taxes helped to 'mobilise' labour. But the migrants' motives were complex. Lozi and Ndebele villagers travelled to Kimberley and, later, to Johannesburg long before the British had begun to enforce the payment of taxes in what later became Southern and Northern Rhodesia. Labour migration drained the villages of manpower, but it also enabled underemployed rural people to sell their labour power for prices much higher than those available at home. Labour migrants went abroad to acquire knives, muskets, pots and pans, clothes, commodities that rural economies could not supply at all — or only at high cost. Many migrants were driven also by a sense of adventure; they brought back cash and new ideas.

As regards the cultural disruption brought about by labour migration, we are impressed by the toughness and resilience displayed by ordinary men and women in adapting their lives to new and contradictory ideas. We do not regard culture shock as a supreme evil. The cities, in addition to bringing miseries, represent new opportunities, new challenges, and often a sense of personal liberation. It is true that labour migration often disrupted traditional village ways. Yet it was precisely those Africans who had experienced the greatest cultural and political disorientation through European contacts — the Mfengu, the Thembu, the Xhosa — who responded in the most positive fashion to the new market economy. The decline in traditional ways was influenced by many other factors: the villagers' demand for new implements (wagons, ploughs, hatchets), new foods (sugar, cheap salt, coffee, tea), new service agencies (schools, clinics, churches), all of which played their part in changing the tenor of life.

The African mine-worker certainly had a hard life. Higher wages in a place like Kimberley or Johannesburg had to be balanced against the perils of working on the mines, where the comforts of home were missing and where life was filled with danger. The black mine-workers suffered from disease and overcrowding even more than the white pioneers; they had accidents; they suffered considerable loss of life. Yet it may be doubted whether conditions in the South African goldmines were ever quite as bad as those encountered, say, by Irish immigrants in Boston during the 1850s,[6] or by Jewish workers in the New York garment industry during the 1880s and 1890s. These European immigrants to the United States were able to bring their families, yet their living — or dying — standards seem incredibly grim in retrospect. The mine-workers' conditions, moreover, improved with better medical care, improved safety measures and a more adequate diet, so that mining gradually became a more favoured form of employment than working on white farms. Nevertheless, there was a difference between the South African mines at their best and the New York slums at their worst. However miserable the newcomers to the East Side might be, they were, at any rate, accepted by their compatriots as part of America's permanent labour force. They were left to their own devices. Their lives, however miserable at first, were their own. The African migrant workers were not accorded this recognition. The wages paid by the mining industry were regarded as a mere supplement to the income drawn by migrant labourers from the land. The mine-workers' treatment did improve, but such improvements mainly depended on payment in kind — housing, food, medical services. These were provided by the mining companies, and also by many other employers, to a labour force consisting of a dependent clientele whose dependence on the employer increased rather than diminished.

The 'cheapness' of African labour was occasioned by the same causes that occasioned its supposed 'shortage'. These included an inefficient use of easily available manpower, the availability of land to the mass of Africans at a time when the country's black population was less than one-third of its present size, the relative inefficiency of a fluctuating labour supply, the whites' reluctance to permit Africans to break away from traditional forms of tenure through the operation of a free land market in the 'white areas', and the unwillingness of skilled white workmen to be underbid by African labourers. South Africa, in other words, helped to perpetuate its tribal institutions, and restricted the size of its internal market through a policy that regarded black men as unskilled producers of primary products rather than as customers. The process of draining men from tribal lands also retarded the development of those lands.

The country's progress was astounding, nevertheless. Mortality in the mines diminished as the managements gradually introduced improved medical care, better food and more humane recruitment systems. The development of the Witwatersrand gave a boost to railway-building; the construction boom and new transport facilities had far-reaching effects on whites and blacks alike. By 1896, just ten years after the first gold discoveries, Johannesburg had been linked by rail to all the main ports at the Cape and in Natal. By 1913 the South African railways comprised 8,281 miles, by far the greatest system in Africa. The new lines permitted the mine-owners to import heavy machinery and to export ores in large quantities; they also enabled farmers to send maize (corn) and beef to the Rand at relatively low cost. Intensive cash-crop production became a profitable business in parts of South Africa; the cultivation of maize on the high veld received additional encouragement from low railway rates, designed to encourage a return traffic. Some maize farmers improved the quality of their crops; cattle farmers turned out more beef. There was an incipient agricultural processing industry, as money was to be made in canning fruit, processing cheese, bacon and tobacco, and other products. Agricultural colleges were opened in various parts of South Africa and, from 1916, agricultural faculties at various South African universities began to train advanced students.

Deep-level mining is, of itself, a complex process requiring a host of ancillary enterprises — facilities for the treatment and processing of ores, power plants, waterworks, cement plants, repair shops and such installations. Mining both required and created a great variety of managerial, technical and scientific skills. Gold-mining created new forms of enterprise. Coal-mines were opened to supply the railways and electricity plants with fuel. The new cities required an elaborate network of roads, telegraphic communications and other conveniences. The vast agglomeration of people in Johannesburg and elsewhere called for permanent housing to take the place of the pioneers' miserable shacks. Townsmen, white and black, required a vast array of new services — shops, post offices, banks, public utilities; the city-dwellers needed food, furniture, clothing and a host of other merchandise. The basis was laid for a 'multiplier-accelerator' process of economic growth that changed the face of South Africa. The formation of the Union of South Africa in 1910 had speeded progress by creating a unified free trade area and eliminating the economic squabbles between the four colonies. In terms of economic production and diversity, the Union of South Africa, by 1914, was the giant of the continent.[7]

Looked at in another way, South Africa was as yet an underdeveloped country, dependent on the export of a few primary products, especially gold and diamonds. In 1912 gold and diamonds accounted for £38,342,000 and £9,153,000 respectively, out of the country's total exports of £62,974,219. Mining accounted for a larger share of the national production than did agriculture, not to speak of manufacturers (see Table 1.1, page 18). South Africa depended heavily on commerce with Britain, a great industrialised state which in 1912 supplied 58.1 per cent of its exports. South Africa's economic production had grown enormously, but the country as yet largely relied on Great Britain for its manufactured imports, most of them consumption goods such as haberdashery, cotton goods and hardware, with machinery accounting for no more than £2,689,000 out of a total import bill of £62,974,421. To make matters worse, the country was not even self-sufficient in food — more than one-tenth of its imports, the largest single item, consisted of victuals. If modern development economists were to be believed, South Africa had experienced 'growth without development', supposedly an unhappy state preventing 'real' economic expansion linked to structural change.

Contrary to a widespread stereotype, South Africa was far from being an investor's paradise. Some South African entrepreneurs, men like Cecil Rhodes and Alfred Beit, certainly made a great deal of money — so much so that the legendary 'Rand Lord', complete with potbelly, hooked nose, top hat, cigar and a huge diamond ring, had come to be many a cartoonist's embodiment of capitalism at its most unsavoury. But in fact a great deal of mining capital was also lost in South Africa.

152 The Economics of South Africa

The mining firms moreover had to pay substantial fees and taxes; hence, the rate of return secured on gold-mining stock was substantially smaller than was indicated either by the promotional literature put out by the advocates of imperial expansion or the condemnatory tracts published by radicals and socialists. Between 1887 and 1911 the rate of return on the large mines amounted to no more than 3.3 per cent, as against a rate of return of 5.2 per cent for the period 1887-1965.[8] South Africa, in other words, was very much like most of the newly independent states in Africa today. The country had gained political independence from Great Britain, but it depended on economic ties with Great Britain, which supplied most of its foreign capital and dominated its foreign trade. According to present-day development economics, South Africa was in a state of neocolonial vassalage, locked in a cycle of poverty from which it could not escape. But, as happened so often, South Africa defied all the theorists.

The Road to Maturity: 1914–65

When, in 1914, General Botha's government decided to go to war against the Kaiser's Germany, his country was in a parlous economic condition. South Africa, as we have seen, depended for its livelihood mainly on mining and farming; its manufacturing potential was negligible. Most of the black population and many of the white people were devoid of industrial skills; the majority of the African tillers relied on subsistence farming requiring a minimum of physical capital or technological knowledge; many of the country's white farmers were scarcely in a better situation. But, from World War One onward, South Africa underwent a series of accelerating economic changes, and by the early 1960s it had changed beyond recognition. Its gross domestic product had expanded – and continued to grow – in a manner that in 1914 would have appeared Utopian to the most ardent optimist (see Table 5.1).

The Modern Rural Sector

Between 1911 and 1965 the most striking increase in production took place in manufacturing. The farming industry grew at a somewhat slower rate; nevertheless, its expansion was phenomenal, given the extent of South Africa's rural problems. African reserves were – and, to a considerable extent, remain – ill-provided with marketing facilities. Their development was retarded by the absence of a large portion (up

Table 5.1: Gross Domestic Product by Kind of Economic Activity at Factor Cost, 1911-77 (R million)

Period	Agriculture, Forestry and Fishing	Mining and Quarrying	Manu- facturing	Construction	Electricity, Gas and Water	Transport- ation, Storage and Communication	Trade	Other	Total
1911	62	84	11	2	3	29	38	70	299
1915	56	67	17	3	3	29	38	91	304
1920	122	109	40	8	6	53	86	138	562
1925	107	85	41	9	7	58	79	145	531
1930	78	95	51	10	12	63	82	164	555
1935	93	133	73	14	15	73	92	188	681
1940	120	203	115	18	23	94	137	280	990
1945	179	199	227	26	29	140	205	491	1,496
1950	454	338	470	80	44	236	375	552	2,549
1955	578	470	780	109	83	373	583	843	3,819
1960	601	684	1,023	152	123	506	696	1,168	4,953
1965	760	947	1,745	299	181	710	1,055	1,733	7,430
1967	1,047	1,050	2,028	348	228	861	1,271	2,146	8,979
1970	1,021	1,236	2,828	507	307	1,074	1,655	3,029	11,647
1971	1,163	1,164	3,068	600	351	1,214	1,873	3,528	12,961
1972	1,316	1,513	3,314	680	407	1,269	2,080	2,965	14,544
1973	1,444	2,321	4,072	796	478	1,615	2,457	4,581	17,764
1974	1,894	3,193	4,699	943	549	1,799	2,868	5,304	21,249
1977[a]	2,502	3,991	7,051	1,359	1,116	3,489	4,108	7,837	31,453

Note: a. Preliminary figures.

Source: *South Africa: Official Yearbook, 1976* (Johannesburg, 1976), p. 369 and *Official Yearbook, 1978* (Johannesburg, 1978), p. 369.

to 50 per cent) of their able-bodied male labour force, and by the continued operation of farming systems requiring for their effective usage an almost unlimited supply of land. The white farmers were likewise in dire straits. The instability of agricultural prices in the 1920s and their rapid decline during the depression of the 1930s put a damper on improvements. White and black farming lands widely suffered from soil erosion and inadequate veld management. Experts pointed to the farmers' insufficient care in maintaining the humus and water content of the soil. Denudation of the plant cover protecting the soil had occasioned widespread erosion. The degradation of the soil was not necessarily the farmers' fault. All too often the vicissitudes of nature, droughts and other afflictions combined with a world-wide fall in prices to prevent farmers from improving or even maintaining the quality of their land. The average white agriculturist during the 1930s made but a pittance; his labourers received even less.

Nevertheless, the pace of agricultural innovation began to pick up at the time of World War One, and rapidly accelerated during and after World War Two. Between 1915 and 1960 the value of South Africa's gross domestic product produced by the agricultural sector increased more than tenfold. During the following fifteen years it once again trebled. This was a phenomenal advance, largely ignored abroad, achieved in the face of many obstacles: the unpredictability of its climate, the relative infertility of so much of South Africa's land mass, and the country's geographical structure, marked by the absence of great fertile river valleys comparable to the Nile of the Yellow River.

Innovation on the land was a complex process, intimately linked to the growth of mining, manufacturing and urban growth. The growing cities produced a rising demand for food; the expansion of chemical and metallurgical industries facilitated the application of industrial skills to farming. The mining industry indirectly assisted the farming industry through its ability to contribute to the public revenue, thus helping to finance a broad range of services and subsidies not directly related to the extraction of minerals. Between 1910 and 1960 the contribution made by the gold mining industry to the public coffers went up, in rand, from 2.8 million to 73 million. The development of service industries like insurance and mining provided the farmers with a variety of financial services. Luckily for the country's prosperity, South African farmers accumulated a considerable load of debt, amounting in 1958 to 431 million rand, as compared to the total value of all white farms of 3,087.4 million rand. These credits were used to improve the country's agricultural potential, and especially assisted in mechanising a substantial part of the South African farming industry.

Mechanisation began in a small way during the 1920s, and accelerated enormously during World War Two. Its impact was uneven. The presence of a large migratory black labour force inhibited the speed of mechanisation, as did some branches of the farming industry which could not easily be mechanised. Nevertheless, in the half-century between 1918 and 1957 the number of motor tractors operating on South African farms increased well over forty times. By 1963 about 65 per cent of all tractors on the African continent were operating on farms in South Africa. Between 1936 and 1965 the average cultivated area per tractor declined from 1,134 *morgen* (1 *morgen* equals 2.116 acres) per tractor to about 75 *morgen*. There was a remarkable rise in the value of the capital assets of all kinds of implements on white farms, from an estimated 10 million rand (at current prices) in 1909 to 250 million rand in 1965. Mechanisation in South Africa, as everywhere else, had far-reaching and universally beneficent consequences. By using high-speed tractors, farmers were able to complete their work faster than ever before. Rural entrepreneurs could plant their land more quickly after the rains had fallen; they were able to harvest crops at a considerable speed and at the desired moisture content. The demand for unskilled labourers — among the most poorly paid workers in the South African labour force — declined, as a combine harvester, serviced by a few semi-skilled men, could do the work of many unskilled hands. Yet there was no sharp increase of labourers on the farms. During the years from 1951 to 1961, the number of permanently employed male African workers on white farms actually went up from 592,000 to 630,000, as many new jobs needed to be done. Agricultural mechanisation created a new demand for African tractor drivers, machine operators and repairmen; agriculture also gave a boost to rural electrification, and to the development of new local industries turning out agricultural machines and implements.

Improvements in agriculture owed a good deal to agricultural research. This centred on the major universities and on the Department of Agriculture. In 1958 this body divided into the Department of Agricultural Technical Services to promote production by means of scientific investigations, training, information and control, and the Department of Agricultural Field Services, concerned with agricultural extension work, soil conservation, agricultural training outside the universities, veterinary field services and such activities. South African experts achieved enviable reputations in the study of soil fertility, the improvement of natural pastures, agronomical research and related subjects.

At the same time, South Africa began to take measures to protect its soil fertility. The passage of the Soil Conservation Act of 1946 marked a major advance. Ownership of the land ceased to confer upon the owner the right to abuse the soil. Ninety per cent of the white-owned farmland in South Africa by 1958 was embraced within conservation districts controlled by a National Soil Conservation Board. The quality of farming was bettered in a great variety of ways: through improvements in stock; scientific plant breeding designed to produce superior crops; the construction of cattle dips and dams; fencing; improved preparation and use of compost; the adoption of crop rotation, including soil-building and soil-binding crops such as the lucerne; contour farming and strip cropping on sloping ground to prevent erosion; tree planting to provide shelter; control of veld burning; and other agricultural developments. South Africa went through an agricultural revolution little known even to most of her own citizens. Between them, farmers, scientists, agricultural technicians and other experts changed the nature of the country's farming economy — and even the appearance of the countryside. South Africa's crops increased in quantity, quality and diversity. By 1960 South Africa had become a major producer, not merely of staples like corn and wool, but also of milk, cheese, fruit, meat, wheat and sugar.[9]

These changes went with a striking growth in state intervention in the marketing field. During the 1920s and 1930s, farmers never ceased to complain of fluctuating prices and inadequate profits. Unlike black farmers, white farmers had political pull, and the government tried to help white producers in a variety of ways through tariffs, subsidies and grants for capital works on farms. Above all, the government in 1937 set up a network of marketing boards, controlled in the main by producers, which wielded wide powers with regard to price fixing. By 1961 some 70 per cent of all agricultural produce was controlled by these boards. The effects of this supervision continue to be subject to dispute. During the early years of its operation, the marketing system set up through the Marketing Act of 1937 encouraged farmers to produce large surpluses that had to be exported at a loss. When local consumption of food increased during World War Two, controls pegged domestic prices at a level below the world prices, thereby reducing the farmers' hard-earned income. Advocates of the system point to the advantages of stabilising prices. Opponents argue — as we do — that the truly efficient producers do not need protection, and that price control interferes with the operation of the world market in a manner not anticipated by the planners. Nevertheless, South Africa's agricultural progress was astounding, all the more so because it had been little anticipated by the experts of the 1920s and 1930s.

South Africa essentially owed this advance to a relatively small group of white farmers, most of whom worked the land that they owned. By 1957 white agriculture centred on some 100,000 farms covering an area of about 103 million *morgen*. Of these farms, 75,000 were worked by their owners, 3 per cent by managers, and the rest were rented out or leased to sharecroppers. Standards of farming varied considerably, from poor to excellent. By and large, however, the less efficient farmers were increasingly squeezed out by rising costs and tough competition. Between 1960 and 1976, the value of South Africa's farm output rose in a striking fashion (from 808 to 2,938 million rand), whereas the number of farming units fell by a quarter.

The men who ran these farms have not, of late, enjoyed a good press. The old-style pioneer was gradually driven out of business. The best farmers were successful rural entrepreneurs, adept at modern management methods, skilled in using machinery, well qualified in agronomy, with a bachelor's degree or a diploma in subjects such as agriculture, commerce or engineering. Their way of life did not appeal to cultural conservatives apt both to misunderstand and to romanticise the peasant and his life-style. White farmers in South Africa were employers of African labour; they tended to vote for the National Party or for the conservative wing of the United Party; hence, they aroused the displeasure of South African liberals and socialists, most of them urban intellectuals. The modern farmer was neither picturesque in appearance, habits or speech. He made no appeal to literary artists, painters or movie-makers in search of subjects to excite the curiosity or compassion of a public fascinated by strange, outlandish or trendy subjects. But for all their real or alleged aesthetic and political deficiencies, the best of white farmers of Southern Africa formed a genuine economic elite. Between them, they added immeasurably to the production of food on a continent perennially short of victuals — no social class can make a prouder boast.

The Urban Sector

In 1941 C.W. de Kiewiet, a leading historian of South Africa, published a seminal work on the country's economic history. His book remains a classic. Yet, for all his analytical skill, he predicted mistakenly that manufacturing would develop but slowly in South Africa — this at the very moment when the country was poised for a major advance. De Kiewiet was not alone in his mistake. His pessimism was shared by most other experts who assumed that South Africa's general backwardness, the operation of the industrial colour bar, the persistence of the migrant labour system and the small size of South Africa's domestic capital would all help to impede the country's industrialisation. Three years after the appearance of de Kiewiet's book, for instance, S.H. Frankel, one of the greatest South African economists, proved to his own satisfaction that the South African manufacturing industries were, in a sense, parasitic on gold-mining, because the mines alone provided the foreign exchange that enabled factories to function in the first place.[10] The experts had the best of the argument. But, as happens so often in South Africa, the experts turned out to be wrong.

When South Africa entered World War One, the country's infant industries had already made a little progress. In doing so, they enjoyed a number of advantages. The country was amply supplied with raw materials of many different kinds. It was linked to an international network of banking and trade. A large part of South Africa's white population was relatively well educated; European immigrants, moreover, comprised many skilled men whose training had been paid for by their country of origin, much to South Africa's advantage. The country had an infrastructure of educational, technical and research institutes of a kind nowhere to be found elsewhere on the continent. The mining industry had created a reservoir of industrial and financial skills; the mines provided a local source of development capital that supplemented capital imports from abroad, especially from Great Britain. The mines had also helped to promote urban concentrations. By 1921 the majority of the country's white, Coloured and Indian people lived in cities; thereafter, the pace of African urbanisation also accelerated (see Table 4 in Part One, 'The Peoples of South Africa').

The development of cities was indispensable for industrial advance. Townsmen needed factory-made goods; they could no longer rely — like their forebears — on merchandise made on the farms: rough footwear, homespun clothing, home-made candles, etc. Romantics who deplore the decline of craft industries are apt to forget the disadvantages of pre-industrial life — the gruelling labour that goes into the production of home-made goods, the toil that goes into jobs like slaughtering pigs on the farm, washing clothes by hand, plucking geese, spinning cloth. The mass-produced shirt, bought in a department store serving a mass clientele, washed with mass-produced soap in a mass-produced washing machine, is an immeasurable blessing over a homespun garment,

The Economics of South Africa

mended many a time, hard to keep clean, reeking with sweat, expensive to produce and hard to replace. Mass-produced footwear is a boon compared with the down-at-heel *velskoen* (home-made shoes) worn by the pioneers when they did not go barefoot.

The South African manufacturing industries received their first boost during World War One when goods were hard to get from Great Britain, South Africa's accustomed supplier. After the end of hostilities, South Africa's economic infrastructure was strengthened by the formation, in 1920, of the South African Reserve Bank, the country's central credit institution. In the same year, the government set up the Board of Trade and Industries in order to encourage local industries by the imposition of import tariffs. The coalition between Nationalists and Labour Party supporters, formed in 1924, further supported protectionism, partly to promote economic nationalism, partly to find jobs for unemployed white countrymen who had drifted into the cities. Many of the new factories were designed to process agricultural commodities like cheese, bacon and tobacco. Others turned out consumer goods such as furniture and textiles. In addition, South Africa, from an early date onward, developed its own iron and steel industry, the first of its kind in Africa. Production was centralised through the South African Iron and Steel Corporation (ISCOR); its creation in 1928 as a public corporation was a milestone on the way to state enterprise operating alongside private enterprises within the framework of a mixed economy.

The world-wide depression of the early 1930s occasioned a slight fall in industrial production. The net output, in million rand, dropped from 68 to 61 between the years 1920-30, 1932 and 1933; but South Africa's economy in the long run turned out to be strikingly resilient, and received a boost when the country, in 1933, went off the gold standard. South Africa, in fact, weathered the storm more easily than almost any other country, a fact that may have contributed to the moderation of South African politics in an era that brought Hitler to power in Germany.

When World War Two broke out in 1939, South African prosperity once again seemed assured, as South African manufacturers once again were called upon to supply a great array of goods that could no longer be bought abroad. South African factories also participated in the war effort by turning out explosives, bullet-proof steel plates and many other war materials. At the same time, South Africans acquired many new industrial skills and displayed a considerable degree of initiative and ingenuity. Before the war, for instance, the skilled staff at ISCOR had almost entirely been Germans brought out on contract in order to train South Africans. The Germans were interned at the outbreak of the war, leaving as yet only under-trained South Africans to keep the works going. These workers, however, soon mastered their trade, and actually increased the country's iron output. In addition, many skilled workers joined the armed forces. The shortage became acute; Indian, Coloured and African labourers increasingly began to be recruited for semi-skilled and skilled jobs. This process continued after the end of the war, by which time Africans made up more than half of the work-force in industry. Africans in industry were among the best paid and the most highly skilled black workmen. Manufacturers had a material stake in a well trained and stable African labour force capable of providing a mass market for South African goods, and were therefore among the foremost advocates of reformist policies in the social sphere and among the foremost critics of the migrant labour system.

When the guns stopped firing, South Africa was all set for an African *Wirtschaftswunder*. The country's international prestige stood high; immigrants poured into the country, bringing with them a host of skills. Ironically, the Nationalist government, having come into power in 1948, did its level best to slow down the rate of white immigration so as to preserve the purity of Afrikanerdom. A host of potential citizens from Central, Southern and Eastern Europe were deflected from South Africa's shore, to the country's loss, and to the gain of countries like Australia, Canada and the United States. Nevertheless, the South African economy continued to grow at an extraordinary pace, having received a further unexpected boost by the discoveries of new and rich gold-fields in the Orange Free State and by the devaluation of the pound in 1949.

South Africa, unlike the rest of Africa, was able to supply the bulk of its investments from savings accumulated at home, though foreign investors played a valuable part in supplementing these funds and in assisting the country to acquire specialised technological enterprise (see Table 5.2). The country achieved remarkable advances in textile manufacturing, and also in metal and engineering industries, based on local supplies of iron and steel; liquid fuel and chemical industries gained a special advantage from the availability of locally mined coal. There was a striking improvement in the quality of South African-made goods and in their diversity. By 1945 manufacturing accounted for a larger portion of the gross national product than any other economic pursuit; twenty years later the share of manufacturing was larger than than of agriculture, forestry, fishing, mining and quarrying combined.

Table 5.2: Financing of Gross Domestic Investment, 1946-75

Period	Personal Saving	Corporate Saving	Current Surplus of General Government	Provision for Depreciation	Gross Domestic Savings	Net Capital Inflow from the Rest of the World	Change in Gold and Foreign Exchange Reserves[a]	Gross Domestic Investment
1946	95		23	100	218	80	87	385
1950	296		41	179	516	182	−143	555
1955	308	83	146	332	869	51	42	962
1960	289	194	222	482	1,187	−180	143	1,150
1965	571	316	296	719	1,902	255	41	2,198
1970	901	390	467	1,116	2,874	541	286	3,701
1971	1,176	447	316	1,268	3,207	764	239	4,210
1972	1,505	632	418	1,410	3,965	407	−396	3,976
1973[b]	1,116	1,352	964	1,578	5,010	−158	64	4,916
1974[b]	1,651	1,389	1,212	1,787	6,039	774	86	6,899
1975[b]	2,003	1,250	823	2,063	6,139	1,774	−158	7,755

Source: South African Reserve Bank.

Notes:
a. Increase −; decrease +.
b. Provisional.

162 *The Economics of South Africa*

The respective percentages were: agriculture and associated industries 10.2; mining and quarrying 12.7; manufacturing 23.3. South Africa had become the first industrial state on the African continent.

Recession and Recovery

In 1945 South Africa had been a respected member of the international community, a victor in World War Two, and a founding member of the United Nations. Fifteen years later this legitimacy had been lost. South Africa, the critics said, was nothing but a neocolonial dependency of Western capitalism. Alternatively, South Africa was being censored for being herself a colonial sovereign, lording it over her black subjects, and contemplating aggression beyond her borders. South Africa, like the European colonial empires in Africa, supposedly compared unfavourably with the Soviet Union as regards speed of economic development. At the same time, like the other Western colonial powers, South Africa was also reviled at times for 'overdevelopment', for promoting the real or supposed ills that go with the growth of towns and of urban industries, and with the disappearance of rural life-styles all over the world. South Africa, the critics said, was in the grip of a ruthless, well armed minority that kept its subjects helpless, starving and enslaved. Contrariwise, this oligarchy was also widely held to be weak and effete, facing rapid breakdown. The tide of decolonisation, Harold Macmillan, the British Prime Minister, announced at Cape Town, would not stop on South Africa's borders. The bloody rioting at Sharpeville in 1960 seemed to presage precisely such revolutionary change to come. Capital began to flee the country (see Table 5.2). The clock of history, the experts agreed, stood at five minutes before twelve. Soon the hour of midnight would strike for a doomed country.

Expectations of a rapid collapse were apparently shared both by CIA intelligence analysts, US State Department experts, and by most British and American academics. Far from being an engine for progress, the South African economy appeared to many of them to be decadent, subjects to structural 'dysfunctions' that would make the country's future questionable. As Pierre van den Berghe, a distinguished sociologist, put it, South Africa was busily digging its grave. The reasons for the country's impending demise were not far to seek. The key to South Africa's political economy was its ability to mobilise a great army of cheap black labour. The relative position of the blacks had, admittedly, improved a little in relation to the dominant whites during the late

1950s. But these marginal gains were quite inadequate to save the system. The availability of cheap — and therefore inefficient — labour had far-reaching economic consequences. Mechanisation would be impeded; the internal market for consumer goods would remain small owing to the workers' low purchasing power. Cheap labour, being poorly trained and underfed, was necessarily unproductive. The position was made by the maldistribution of the country's farming wealth. The rural masses, according to van den Berghe, were condemned to 'subsistence' starvation; the land would continue to deteriorate; hence the reserve army of black proletarians would forever be replenished and the migratory labour system would continue to operate with all its baneful consequences.

South Africa's systematic 'dysfunctions', the argument continued, were aggravated by an industrial colour bar that prevented the country from utilising the natural skills of the majority; whites continued to monopolise the skilled occupations, with the result that industrial progress was bound to lag. As van den Berghe put it, 'with no prospect of job improvement, non-Whites have little incentive to work better; on the other hand, the privileged, protected European worker likewise has little incentive to better his performance.'[11] The blacks thereby responded to discrimination with restrictions on output, passive resistance, minor sabotage and boycotts of shops and products. Productivity was bound to remain low. South African industry was condemned to remain inefficient. This disequilibrium could not last, and the system was bound for speedy breakdown. Van den Berghe's analysis and similar exercises were brilliant in terms of their logical construction and intellectual consistency. But they had little predictive value, being essentially morality plays cast into the language of economics and sociology.

The decade 1965 to 1975, in fact, saw a period of extraordinary economic expansion. Between 1965 and 1975 South Africa's gross domestic investment and the value of her gross domestic product more than trebled. The former went up from 2,198 million rand to 7,755 million rand; the latter increased from 7,932 million rand to 225,711 million rand (see Table 5.3). The country made some striking improvements in technology. The South African mines became major producers of base metals as well as of precious metals and diamonds. Agriculture continued to expand, so that South Africa remained one of the few countries in Africa able not only to feed herself, but also to export food on an extensive scale. South African manufacturers grew apace. The country developed modern chemical industries, and South African

164   The Economics of South Africa

Table 5.3: South African Gross Domestic Product, 1965-77 (at market prices)

Calendar Year	Gross Domestic Product (R millions)
1965	7,923
1966	8,591
1967	9,523
1968	10,255
1969	11,535
1970	12,724
1971	14,068
1972	15,749
1973	19,221
1974	23,379
1975	26,292
1977	33,820

Average Annual Growth Rate (per cent):
1965-75   12.5
1971-7   15.7
1976-7   14.2

Source: *South Africa: Official Yearbook, 1976*, p. 369; *Yearbook, 1978*, p. 371.

factories turned out an increasing number of capital goods characteristic of a highly developed economy: mining and agricultural machinery, cranes, ships, transport and electrical equipment.[12] Far from being totally inefficient and half-starved, the African labour force was becoming better educated,[13] and also somewhat better paid. The industrial colour bar weakened; by the early 1970s the shortage of skilled men and women had become so severe that the government began to set up technical training centres to supplement the efforts of private industry in training technically qualified Africans. Between 1970 and 1975 the Africans' disposable income doubled; hence, businessmen increasingly looked for profits to black and brown as well as to white customers. Disparities between white and black overall incomes remained acute. But South Africa was far from being the decadent caste society depicted in works such as van den Berghe's. The black industrial worker made very real progress. As Arnt Spandau, a well known Johannesburg economists, puts it:

> Compared with the average Russian income receiver, the Black South African machine operator earns a higher real income. For items such as bread, meat, apples, sugar, eggs, milk and soap, the Black machine operator spends only a fraction of the working hours required by his colleagues in Moscow [see Table 5.4]. With regard to durable consumer goods such as shoes and vehicles, the Witwatersrand Black also appears to be privileged compared with the Moscow worker. (In 1976, Blacks owned 370,000 of the motor vehicles in South Africa.)[14]

In comparative terms, black and brown South Africans had registered considerable advances. Black South African *per capita* income in the homelands exceeded the average income of numerous African countries, including Togo and Kenya, not to speak of poverty-stricken states like Lesotho and Niger. Urban Africans were doing better on average than the people of relatively advanced countries such as Ghana, Liberia and Senegal. Asian and Coloured South Africans had average incomes superior to those earned in Brazil, Chile and Turkey. A wide gap remained between Indian and Coloured South Africans on the one hand and white South Africans on the other. But widespread stereotypes to the contrary, the South African government had begun to make a genuine effort to close the wage gap between whites and blacks; whites, moreover, were far from enjoying the world's highest living standards; white South African average incomes were below those received by Americans, West Germans, Frenchmen and Australians (see Table 5.4).

During the mid-1970s some of this prosperity receded. South Africa had to face a host of troubles. But these were of a more prosaic kind than those anticipated by the radical critics of the late 1950s; South Africa experienced vicissitudes similar to those that beset the rest of the Western world. The country suddenly became enmeshed in a worldwide recession whose full effects had been delayed, owing to the cushioning effects of South African gold exports, massive borrowing abroad and heavy public expenditure. Recession abroad occasioned a decline of mineral exports. The long years of cheap oil for the Western world came to an end, and South Africa, like the other industrial countries, had to pay more for her oil imports.

Table 5.4: Approximate Work Time Required for Average Manufacturing Employees to Buy Selected Commodities in Retail Stores in Washington, DC and London, at State-fixed Prices in Moscow and Johannesburg during May 1976

Commodity	Washington	London	Moscow	Artisan (White)	South Africa: Witwatersrand Area Machine Operator (Black)	Labourer (Black)
White bread, 1 kg	21 min.	10 min.	20 min.	4 min.	12 min.	19 min.
Beef, 1 kg	34 min.	76 min.	3.5 hrs	52 min.	2.5 hrs	4 hrs
Pork sausages, 1 kg	71 min.	60 min.	2.6 hrs	36 min.	1.8 hrs	2.8 hrs
Potatoes, 1 kg	8 min.	23 min.	7 min.	6 min.	18 min.	28 min.
Apples, 1 kg	16 min.	24 min.	5.4 hrs	10 min.	30 min.	47 min.
Sugar, 1 kg	9 min.	15 min.	65 min.	4 min.	12 min.	19 min.
Milk, 1 litre	7 min.	11 min.	21 min.	5 min.	15 min.	23 min.
Eggs (10)	10 min.	13 min.	97 min.	8 min.	24 min.	37 min.
Vodka (0.7 litres)	67 min.	3.4 hrs	9.8 hrs	1.5 hrs	4.5 hrs	6.6 hrs
Cigarettes (20)	10 min.	27 min.	23 min.	8 min.	24 min.	37 min.
Soap, toilet, 150 gr	5 min.	10 min.	72 min.	8 min.	24 min.	37 min.
Lipstick	31 min.	54 min.	7.8 hrs	32 min.	1.5 hrs	2.5 hrs
Panty hose	17 min.	15 min.	9 hrs	15 min.	44 min.	70 min.
Men's shoes, leather	6.7 hrs	7.7 hrs	36 hrs	8.6 hrs	25.5 hrs	40.3 hrs
Men's business suit	25 hrs	40 hrs	106 hrs	34.6 hrs	102.6 hrs	162.1 hrs
Refrigerator, 150 ltr	47 hrs	50 hrs	168 hrs	79.3 hrs	235.1 hrs	371.5 hrs
Small car	6.9 months	11.1 months	3.1 years	6.5 months	1.7 years	2.6 years

Source: Arnt Spandau, *Economic Boycott against South Africa: Normative and Factual Issues* (University of the Witwatersrand, Labour Research Programme, Johannesburg, 1978), p. 83.

Above all, South Africa was hard hit by a temporary decline in gold prices: between 1974 and 1976 the price of gold dropped from about $195 an ounce to about $115 an ounce. South Africa devalued the rand first in 1971, then again in 1975. This devaluation demonstrated the country's continued dependence on gold, which earned some 43 per cent of the country's foreign exchange. Gold continued to play a crucial part in South Africa, especially in view of the country's large deficits on ordinary trading. Caught in a mood of excessive optimism, South Africa had heavily overspent. There had been a great deal of expenditure by public bodies — the central government, the provincial governments, the local authorities, the 'homelands'. Some of this money had been used unwisely or wasted, for the civil service was big and unwieldy, and the public corporations suffered from all the ills that traditionally beset bureaucracies. Public and private enterprise alike had embarked on huge capital projects, sound enough in themselves, but based on the assumption that the price of gold would continue to rise. When these expectations were not fulfilled, the economy suffered serious strains. In 1976 the real growth rate of the economy fell to 1.4 per cent, the lowest since 1945. Confidence among foreign investors declined — a serious matter for a country traditionally used to financing its trade deficits with long-term investments from overseas. By 1976, however, foreign bankers had become worried by the poor performance of South Africa's economy, the extent of her deficit, and her political and racial troubles. Foreign loans became increasingly hard to get. Since the country could not raise enough foreign funds to satisfy all her capital needs, she had to rely more heavily on borrowing from South African banks. South Africans were forced to embark on a programme of austerity, especially as the International Monetary Fund insisted on credit restrictions in the public sector.

These restraints, linked to more cautious fiscal and monetary policies, further impeded growth. The white and, to a lesser extent, the Indian community largely escaped the misery of unemployment, for their technical, commercial and managerial skills remained in demand. The black community suffered most heavily. No one knows how many Africans found themselves without a job — estimates varied from 800,000 to 2 million. The government's influx controls were designed as much to prevent unemployment in the cities as to keep the cities white. The South Africans, like Zambians, Russians and Chinese, enforced urban influx controls on the grounds that an underemployed labour force in the villages was easier to manage than an unemployed labour force in the towns.

168   The Economics of South Africa

Table 5.5: Per capita Gross Domestic Product at Market Prices, for Selected Countries; 1974, in US Dollars

United States of America	6,670
Germany, Federal Republic of	6,260
France	5,440
Australia	5,330
White South Africans	4,936
All South Africans (Average)	1,270
Asiatic South Africans	1,161
Coloured South Africans	988
Brazil	920
Chile	830
Turkey	750
Black South Africans (Soweto)	575
Black South Africans (Average)	451
Ghana	430
Morocco	430
Liberia	390
Senegal	330
Nigeria	280
Black South Africans (Homelands)	255
Togo	250
Uganda	240
Sudan	230
Kenya	200
Tanzania	160
Lesotho	140
Niger	120

Source: Spandau, *Economic Boycott*.

South Africa continued to struggle with its labour problems, as more than 250,000 new African workers continued to pour into the labour market. But South Africa's recession was nothing like as severe as the economic crisis that had struck Zaire or Zambia, both largely dependent on the price of a single commodity. The South African economy remained the most broadly based in Africa. There was no economic apocalyse, and in 1977 the country was set once more on the road to recovery. The physical volume of agricultural production in that year went up by an estimated 13 per cent. South Africa's record sharply contrasted with the miserable performance in socialist countries like Tanzania or Mozambique, enabling South Africa to feed herself, and to export agricultural products worth 1,159 million rand as well. Mines once more increased their production; businessmen had reduced their overgrown inventories; capital once more became available; the number of companies forced into liquidation dropped sharply.[15]

Recovery was encouraged by a programme of domestic austerity resulting in declining imports, with a substantial growth in exports. In 1970 South Africa cut its links with the dollar; Pretoria reduced the domestic money supply, reduced restrictions concerning the export of capital, and thereby diminished to some extent the threat of massive inflation. Moreover, the price of gold once more began to climb on the world's stock exchanges, and South Africa benefitted as the American dollar continued to erode in its purchasing power. African labour costs had risen on the mines, but the industry had begun to rationalise the use of manpower, to reduce the employment of poorly paid unskilled hands, to pay better wages, and to make plans for mechanisation. The government began to reconsider the problems of African labour and African entrepreneurship. Two government-sponsored bodies, the Wiehahn Commission and the Riekert Commission, made suggestions for far-reaching change that would push South Africa on the path of a more genuine economic liberty. (African trade unions, for instance, were to receive official recognition, and would be incorporated into the statutory framework of collective bargaining. Africans would be admitted to apprenticeship in 'white' areas; closed shop agreements preventing Africans from doing skilled jobs would no longer be permitted. Influx controls would be simplified and made less onerous. Entrepreneurs of all races would be allowed to do business anywhere.) Given a better use of its manpower, South Africa would surely become more 'crisis resistant' in an economic sense.

South Africa also enjoyed other advantages. The country had become a major producer of base metals. South Africa, for instance, capitalised on the production of chrome (indispensable to the Western countries for the making of stainless steel), of manganese (also essential to the steel industry) and vanadium. Foreign countries increased their dependence on South African uranium, and experts estimated that by the mid-1980s South Africa would probably replace Canada as the non-Communist world's second-largest producer of uranium. In an era increasingly concerned with energy shortages, South Africa had another trump card in its coal resources, and stepped up its coal exports.

170 *The Economics of South Africa*

Above all, South Africa's capital expansion projects were nearing completion; hence, the country's productive capacity was certain to be vastly enhanced by the 1980s. The newly constructed harbours at Richards Bay on the east coast and Saldanha Bay on the west coast would, by 1980, boost South Africa's export earnings of coal, phosphates, chromite, vanadium and steel alloys. The South African Coal, Oil and Gas Corporation (SASOL) will have vastly expanded its output of oil during the 1980s. The nuclear power station at Koeberg, planned under the auspices of the Nuclear Fuels Corporation of South Africa (NUCFOR, another state-owned giant), was expected to reach production in the early 1980s. South Africa's Atomic Energy Board (AEB) had successfully promoted research and developed a new uranium enrichment process that compared favourably with similar processes abroad. The Electricity Supply Commission (ESCOM) had planned a variety of new ventures, such as the Tugela-Vaal hydroelectric project, scheduled to come into operation in 1981. By the early 1980s ISCOR, another capital-hungry corporation, would have considerably added to the country's steel-making capacity. In addition, private industry had made enormous plans for the expansion of the chemical industries whose products included a vast range of goods — plastics, fibres, animal feeds, fertilisers, explosives, paints, soap and detergents, petrochemical goods, drugs, synthetic rubber and many other commodities. For all the strains in its economy, for all its social and racial tensions and its industrial inefficiencies, the South African economy was essentially sound. Pressure for divestment or withdrawal had little or no effect on US and European business investors.

Socialism: South African Style?

White South Africans take pride in depicting their country as a bastion of private enterprise. Left-wing critics, for their part, accuse South Africa of occupying a key position in what they regard as an interlocking system of global capitalism. But in practice, South Africa has developed a mixed economy and as in most other African countries, the state plays a vital part in the country's economic life. South African state enterprise owes nothing to Karl Marx, but a great deal to the British colonial tradition. British state enterprise was pioneered in the British African colonies. Outside the two Rhodesias, state enterprise was responsible for the creation of railways in the British colonies; the coal-mining industry in Nigeria was nationalised well before World War

One, at a time when public ownership of the mines in Great Britain seemed a socialist chimera.

In South Africa, the state intervened in economic life from the inception of the Union. The government assisted European agriculture in a variety of ways, making credit available for improvements, regulating the quality of wool, tobacco, butter and other farm products for export, making provision for good soil management, for agricultural co-operatives and irrigation, for the cure and prevention of disease, for marketing and such. Agricultural planning was largely financed from revenue derived from the gold-mines, and the indirect aid given to farming by the mining companies required an extensive degree of state intervention. The state played a major part in regulating safety on the mines, in imposing compulsory standards of feeding and housing for African mine-workers, and in protecting white mine-workers from being underbid by black competitors.

The state also entered the business of transport and production. The Act of Union (1910) made provision for a national railway system, and the South African Railways and Harbours came to dominate the country's entire transport system. Private corporations or municipal bodies pioneered the supply of electrical power before 1922; thereafter, ESCOM took over the bulk of these functions. In 1928 the government established the Iron and Steel Corporation (ISCOR, mentioned previously), and its operations were soon extended into manufacturing. ISCOR developed into a vast steel empire through controlling interests in a great variety of corporations. To all intents and purposes, the steel industry became virtually nationalised.

Under the impact of World War Two, South Africa in 1940 set up the Industrial Development Corporation (IDC), designed to promote the country's industrial development by giving assistance to private industries. The IDC's economic power expanded enormously thereafter; its authorised capital rose from 10 million rand to 350 million rand between 1940 and 1974 alone. Carrying out its stated task by aiding private industry, the IDC gradually set up great manufacturing complexes with interests in enterprises as varied as the manufacture of paper, lime, textiles, masonite, cellulose, wool products, leather, petrol products, transport, machinery and metal ware, and many others. The IDC collaborated for foreign concerns such as Rio Tinto in the Palabora complex and the Rossing uranium mine in Namibia. In 1960 the Corporation launched an Export Finance Scheme to promote trade and investment north of the Limpopo River, especially in Malawi, where the pattern of the IDC was followed by the Malawi Development Corporation. The

172 *The Economics of South Africa*

IDC and ESCOM also played a significant part in the Cunene project in Namibia and in the financing of the Cabora Bassa hydroelectric complex in Mozambique.

Above all, the IDC encouraged the creation of other state enterprises. In 1947 the IDC launched SASOL — like SOECOR (Southern Oil Exploration Corporation), designed to protect South Africa against an international oil boycott. SASOL (mentioned previously) operates the world's only viable oil-from-coal plant, and is greatly expanding its operations. The Armaments Development and Production Corporation (ARMSCOR, mentioned in the section on defence) develops and manufactures weapons; the National Defence Research Institute of the Council for Scientific and Industrial Research (CSIR) conducts military research in conjunction with the research departments run by ARMSCOR's subsidiaries. In South Africa, as elsewhere in the world, the Atomic Energy Board, founded in 1949, is a state corporation; so is the Nuclear Fuels Corporation. The state owns the Phosphate Development Corporation (FOSCOR, set up by the IDC in 1955), the Aluminium Corporation of South Africa (ALUSAF), and so forth.

The homelands development plans likewise depended to a large extent on state enterprise (see also the relevant section on the homelands). From 1959 the IDC set up new parastatal bodies — the Bantu Investment Corporation, the Xhosa Development Corporation, the Bantu Mining Corporation, the Coloured Development Corporation and the Rehoboth Development Corporation. The establishment of these and other bodies served many purposes.

This growth of government enterprise revolutionised South African investment policy. In 1950 private business invested a great deal more than did public authorities and public corporations. By 1971 public investments had almost caught up in size with those made by private corporations, and by 1976 private investment formed less than half of total investments (see Table 5.6).

In sociological terms, the parastatal bodies served many purposes. They helped to strengthen South Africa in the military sphere. They provided an outlet for the energies of public-spirited men, especially Afrikaners, who wished to 'improve' their country through planning in the moral, economic and social sense — there is more emotional affinity between Social Democratic planners in Sweden and Nationalist planners in South Africa than either would admit. As in Sweden, the state controls broadcasting and television in South Africa, and its programmes are inspired not merely to sustain the regime, but also to provide what the planners would take to be moral uplift.

The Economics of South Africa

Table 5.6: Gross Domestic Fixed Investment by Type of Organisation, 1950-76 (R million)

Year	Public Authorities	Public Corporations	Private Businesses	Total
1950	155	39	362	556
1955	264	51	554	869
1960	370	67	624	1,061
1965	699	156	1,122	1,977
1970	1,038	342	1,797	3,177
1975	2,629	1,346	3,823	7,798
1976	3,196	1,435	4,105	8,736

Sources: Nedbank Group, *South Africa: an Appraisal* (Johannesburg, 1977), pp. 97-8; J.A. Lombard (ed.), *Economic Policy in Southern Africa* (Citadel Press, Cape Town, 1974), p. 4.

The so-called parastatal organisations have played their part in weakening the hegemony of English-speaking South Africans in the financial sector — a major aim of the Nationalist government elected to office in 1948. Parastatal bodies assisted in the rise of independent Afrikaner businessmen through state patronage; they served instruments of separate development, thereby perpetuating the tradition of state enterprise in the homelands. Parastatal bodies also drew on South Africa's traditional mixture of supporting private enterprise through public expenditure in the field of African administration. White taxpayers, for instance, had traditionally made substantial contributions to provide subsidised housing for Africans in urban areas. Commerce and industry were enabled to reduce their wages because their workers were accommodated at public expense. Parastatal bodies, therefore, easily turned to the wider task of 'developing' the blacks in South Africa, an enterprise that might more easily have been left to the businessmen's private endeavours.

Altogether, the major state corporations became a great power in the land. Between 1946 and 1975 alone, the share of gross fixed investment held by these bodies rose from about 3 per cent to an estimated 17 per cent of the nation's total investments; their growth has shown no sign of diminishing (ISCOR's estimated expansion programme for 1975-84 alone will cost about 3,240 million rand). The state corporations accordingly have been important in what might be called the bureaucratisation of South Africa, especially of white South Africa. The work-force of the central government alone grew by 276 per cent between 1937 and 1966, against a total population growth of 87 per cent. By the early 1970s something like 30 per cent of all economically active whites were in the public sector, including 44 per cent of all whites with a university qualification.

The Growth of State Enterprise

What of the wider economic effects? Defenders of the state corporations point to their pioneering work in many industries. They argue that strategically vital functions, such as the development of nuclear industries, cannot safely be left to private enterprise; they consider that, in many sectors of the economy, social and political desiderata should take precedence over the private profit motive; they argue that the state sector of the economy has been reasonably efficient and free from graft, and that many private businessmen, in fact, want state intervention and look to the state for help. African nationalists, predictably, have not spoken out against state capitalism, any more than have Afrikaner nationalists of the traditional kind. Opposition to the power of the parastatal organisations derives from independent businessmen, including the new class of Afrikaans-speaking entrepreneurs.

In 1977 Dr Andreas Wassenaar published a remarkable little book in which he attacked the country's economic policy.[16] Wassenaar's attack carried weight, for he was an Afrikaner of Afrikaners, a man of practical experience, chairman of the great SANLAM insurance complex, chairman of the banking group BANKOR, director of the Volkskas (a big bank), director of the Federale Volksbeleggings (a great financial group), and of other enterprises. Wassenaar's work was moralistic, opinionated and full of purple prose, yet made some devastatingly accurate observations. South Africa suffered from a rampant bureaucracy and from profligate spending. According to Wassenaar, 'the public corporations in the RSA [Republic of South Africa] are part of a "creeping socialism" very similar to that in Britain'; they owe their existence to 'an almost inexplicable antipathy to the profit motive'; they are more inefficient than private firms, because civil servants do not operate under the same financial constraints as private entrepreneurs. The great complex of state enterprises, according to Wassenaar, have vastly complicated South Africa's financial problems by gambling on a sharp rise in gold prices, by running up huge debts, by adding to the country's bureaucratic maze. If unchecked, the present system will result in a state ascendancy that will benefit none but bureaucrats assisted by academic economists and sociologists, the new planning elite. The remedy lies in strengthening private enterprise, in reducing state regulation of industry, and in selling state corporations to private bidders.

Wassenaar's gravest offence in Nationalist eyes was perhaps to attack the South Africans' excessive respect for governmental authority, and to deplore the rulers' assumed spiritual sickness (*geesteskwaal*). Vorster attacked Wassenaar in Parliament in the most bitter terms, without, however, commenting on Wassenaar's critique of state enterprise. An evaluation of the parastatal bodies would take a book of its own. We shall limit ourselves to expressing our sympathy with many of Wassenaar's assumptions. Wassenaar could have strengthened his case by pointing to the Rhodesians' ability to withstand international sanctions with a degree of success that few outside observers had predicted. The Rhodesians' secret lay, to some extent, in their determination to move away from state enterprise (as represented by bodies like the Rhodesian Iron and Steel Commission, set up on the South African model in 1942).

Wassenaar did not go far enough. South Africa, as we see it, will not be able to use its enormous resources to the full until it has established a free market for land, a free market for labour and a free market for capital, cost-conscious and colour-blind. The alternative is likely to be an ethnic struggle for the control of public enterprise, a struggle superimposed on the battle for political control. The 'privatisation' of South African enterprise would entail a revolution more profound than an African take-over. But only the future can show whether South Africa will ever break the shackles of a state-dominated economy and of the regulating bureaucracy.

South Africa: the 1980s and Beyond

Whatever their political assumptions or their racial background, demographers are agreed on one prediction: South Africa by the year 2000 will have a population vastly greater than today's. This population will be heavily concentrated in existing urban areas; the Pretoria-Witwatersrand-Vereeniging complex alone may well become a gigantic conurbation containing nearly as many people as the whole of South Africa during the 1950s. There will be great new cities in places like Saldanha and Richards Bay. The proportion of whites to blacks will be somewhat reduced; nevertheless, every ethnic segment of the population will have

Table 5.7: Population Projections 1970-2000 Broken Down into Population Groups and Regions (figures in thousands)

Regions	Whites	Coloureds	1970 Asians	Blacks	Total	Whites	Coloureds	2000 Asians	Blacks[a]	Total[b]
Metropolitan Areas	2,453	1,050	544	3,362	7,409	5,120	3,227	1,340	8,113	17,800
Pretoria/Witwatersrand/Vereeniging	1,498	131	69	2,418	4,116	3,259	411	168	5,835	9,673
Cape Peninsula	452	738	12	133	1,335	807	2,204	18	322	3,351
Durban/Pinetown/Pietermaritzburg	345	59	458	570	1,432	763	231	1,148	1,375	3,517
Port Elizabeth/Uitenhage	158	122	5	241	526	291	381	6	581	1,259
Planned Metropolitan Areas	137	99	7	316	559	207	226	12	763	1,208
Saldanha (Region 3)	28	73	—	6	107	31	166	—	15	212
East London/King William's Town (Region 21)	92	24	2	228	346	113	57	3	550	723
Richards Bay (Region 34)	17	2	5	82	106	63	3	9	198	273
Planning Regions 1-38 (excluding Regions 3, 21, 34)	1,138	856	66	4,362	6,422	1,647	2,077	100	10,526	14,350
Black Homelands and Other	23	14	3	7,018	7,058	32	7	183	16,935	17,157
Total South Africa	3,751	2,019	620	15,058	21,448	7,006	5,537	1,635	36,337	50,515

Source: R.J. van der Wyk, *A Review of Some Long-term Trends in South Africa* (University of Stellenbosch, Stellenbosch, Bureau for Economic Research, 1976), p. 21.

Notes:
a. Not shown in NPDP, projected by the compiler.
b. Including projections of blacks.

grown extensively (see Table 5.7). The exact extent of this increase is hard to fathom. The tabulated figures represent no more than an estimate. The population might conceivably stabilise at a lower level, no matter what the experts say. On the other hand, the estimates exclude the population increase for Swaziland, Lesotho and Botswana, independent countries that yet form part of the greater Southern African complex. How, then, will they make a living? Much will depend on South Africa's foreign relations and on the nature of the domestic politics, all of them hard to predict.

We believe that there will not be war, revolution or peace. We assume, in perhaps an excessively hopeful fashion, that there will be no world war, that South Africa will not be plunged into a great external conflict. We take it that, for the time being, South Africa's neighbours — Namibia, Botswana, Zimbabwe and Mozambique — will remain economically and logistically too dependent on South Africa to engage in open hostilities. We hold, as we point out in Chapter 7, that there will be no armed revolution in South Africa — not, at any rate, in this century — but that South Africans will have to prepare for guerrilla actions and terrorist activities of a less dramatic kind.

We think it unlikely that the world will abandon gold as a means of international exchange. Gold, as we see it, will gain rather than lose in value, even if the Western countries should succeed in slowing down or arresting altogether their present rate of inflation. South Africa will have to continue coping with boycotts, with acts of sabotage and the like; a certain number of South Africans with marketable skills will emigrate. The country will suffer from a continuous shortage of technical and scientific skills, as well as a persistent shortage of capital. Nevertheless, South Africans will be in a far better position to cope with the brain drain than the remainder of sub-Saharan Africa, given the quality of South African technical education and research.

The shortage of foreign capital will certainly impede the country's growth, especially in the high-technology industries (these include the manufacture of computers for which the country at present relies on foreign suppliers, a dangerous form of dependence from the military standpoint). By and large, South Africa will probably generate enough domestic capital to meet its essential needs. Between 1964 and 1972 South Africa met 92 per cent of her capital requirements from domestic savings. Unlike many other Third World countries, South Africa has not confiscated foreign funds and has not defaulted on her debts. Therefore, the country will, in all probability, continue to attract some foreign funds for overt or covert investments.

178 *The Economics of South Africa*

Table 5.8: Production of and Demand for Minerals, 1974-2000

Minerals	1974 Production (metric tons)	1974 Demand (metric tons)	2000 Production (tons)	1974-2000 Production Growth Rate per annum (per cent)
Precious:				
Gold (kg)	759,000	–	818,600 kg	0.7
Silver (kg)	83,940	–	–	–
Diamonds (metric carats)	7,500,000	7,227,866	–	–
Metalliferous:				
Chrome	1,876,913	1,203,210	10 million	7.0
Copper	179,111	158,012[a]	–	–
Iron ore:				
haematite	8,647,709	7,692,396[a]	75 million	7.4
magnetite	2,905,188	1,772,331[a]		
Lead	3,316	–	500,000[b]	20.0
Manganese	4,757,088	3,304,779	20 million	6.0
Nickel	22,100	13,089[a]	120,000	7.0
Vanadium	14,551	–	42,500	6.5
Zinc (concentrate)	67,993	68,155	–	–
Non-metallic:				
Asbestos	333,272	274,458[a]	–	–
Coal:				
bituminous	64,620,678	63,013,477	230-250 million	5.5
anthracite	1,434,932	1,617,856		
Feldspar	39,540	43,333	–	–
Fluorspar	207,933	142,586	1.3 million	7.3
Iron pyrites	570,840	215,338	3,565,391	7.3
Lime and limestone	17,520,409	16,086,000	200 million	10.0
Magnesite	104,614	102,753	–	–
Phosphates	7,824,454	1,418,588	30 million	5.0
Vermiculite	182,613	155,426	–	–
Ornamental, building stone, sundry:				
Clays	673,278	619,573	–	–
Kaolin	48,844	61,531	–	–
Marble	18,120	9,090	–	–
Shale	516,747	481,095	–	–

Notes:
a. 1972 figures.
b. Projection for Southern Africa.

Source: Van der Wyk, *A Review of Some Long-term Trends*, p. 65.

Given these assumptions, South Africa's prospects for the 1980s seem quite good, especially for the mining industry.[17] The world as a whole has become increasingly concerned about the long-term provision of fuel and ores. South Africa is in the fortunate position of being less dependent on imported fuels than most other countries. Oil, in the mid-1970s, represented less than one-quarter of her energy consumption, compared with France or Japan (66 and 73 per cent respectively). South Africa relies on domestically mined coal for about three-quarters of her energy needs. If the experts are to be trusted, coal production will expand in a phenomenal fashion and will reach 230 to 250 million tons per annum by the year 2000, as against 62 million tons produced in 1973. Economists also foresee a tremendous increase in the production of other base minerals such as chrome, iron ore, manganese, vanadium, asbestos, fluorspar and phosphates (see Table 5.8).

South Africa is also rich in uranium. In terms of the technology of the 1970s, thermal nuclear reactors used no more than 2 per cent of the uranium potential; users of nuclear energy, therefore, had to husband their resources, and South Africa occupied a strong position as a uranium producer, possessing something like a quarter of the world's uranium resources as known at the time. South Africa has made considerable advances in nuclear technology; a 5,000-ton uranium enrichment plant is due to be commissioned in 1984, so that the energy picture seems reasonably hopeful.

The relative importance of the gold industry, on the other hand, is likely to decline. The downward trend may well be delayed by a long-term rise in gold prices. But given the importance of gold in South Africa's export economy, South Africans will have to make major readjustments by investing in alternative export industries as the country's auriferous resources become exhausted. In 1974 the value of South Africa's gold production amounted to 81 per cent of its merchandise exports. Table 5.8 provides an intelligent estimate of future possibilities. It can do no more. South Africa's overall mineral production might be restricted by lack of capital and, above all, by the pervasive lack of highly trained manpower. Alternatively, the assumed global shortage of raw materials might turn out to be a chimera, as investors might discover substitutes as yet unimagined, and as mining of the ocean floors may become a commercial possibility in the 1990s, rendering the US self-sufficient in the production of nickel, copper or cobalt by the next century. We can only consider possibilities, and in these South Africa remains rich.

The country's agricultural future is even harder to delineate. The experts agree that the country will continue to produce more food, and for the time being South Africans will have enough to eat. It is possible that African farming methods might improve through increased mechanisation, through improved planning and fertilisation methods and better seeds on larger units. But again, the fate of agriculture will depend on the fate of the cities. The homelands cannot reform their agricultural methods unless industries can create more jobs in the cities and the new homeland towns, for there is no point in pushing cultivators off the land when there are no jobs for them in the urban areas.

The ultimate constraints on agricultural production are, however, of an ecological kind, and these are as yet inadequately understood. South Africans may in the future be faced with a severe energy shortage, though the experts are by no means agreed on the future.[18] South Africa might also be faced with a severe shortage of water, assuming that existing catchment, storage and transportation techniques will not much alter, that rainfall is the major water source, and that subterranean water is relatively insignificant. In 1974 South Africa had more water than it needed. By 2000 the country may experience a deficit amounting to 30 per cent of the demand (see Table 5.9). If the water deficit cannot be met, South Africa will become unable to supply all her own victuals. Both cereal and oil crops may run up deficits of about 20 per cent by 1985, and around 50 per cent by the year 2000. All these calculations, however, are highly speculative.

For all their difficulties, South Africans, a generation hence, will produce vastly more than at present. Manufacturing will make great advances; the importance of service industries is likely to increase. If the experts are to be trusted, private consumption by all races will increase; the gap between white and black living standards will somewhat diminish; African consumption expenditure by 2000 will more than double European expenditure in 1970 (see Table 5.10).

South Africa is certain to continue influencing the economics of countries like Botswana, Lesotho, Swaziland, Mozambique, Zimbabwe, even Zambia and Malawi, that rely on South Africa as a market for their goods, as a place of employment for surplus labour, and as a source of supply. The landlocked inland territories rely to a considerable extent on South African transport facilities; this dependence may diminish in the future, but is unlikely to disappear.[19] The importance of South Africa's trade with black Africa as a whole has been widely overestimated. South Africans have a natural advantage in, say, supplying Zambia with mining machinery, or Mozambique with equipment

The Economics of South Africa 181

Table 5.9: Availability of and Demand for Water in South Africa: Projections for the Period 1974-2000[a]

	1974 Milliard Cubic Metres per annum	2000 Milliard Cubic Metres per annum
Water available according to present supply techniques	21	21
Demand for water according to present consumption practices	11	30
Shortfall (—) or surplus (+)	+ 10	—9
As percentage of demand	(+ 91%)	(—30%)

Note: a. Projections based on existing techniques of supply and current consumption practices.
Source: Van der Wyk, *A Review of Some Long-term Trends*, p. 47.

for harbour works. But even if South Africa were to become politically acceptable as an African trading partner, South Africans would enjoy no special advantage over foreign competitors in distant countries like Zaire or Ghana. In 1955, before South Africa had been subjected to an African boycott, her exports within Africa amounted to just 19.4 per cent of her total exports; by 1974 this figure had diminished to 13.6 per cent. But South Africa will surely remain the economic giant of the continent.

How will the giant use his strength? The 'black African' option at the moment seems to be foreclosed. Western Europe, especially Great Britain, has remained South Africa's major trading partner and her major source of foreign capital (see Tables 5.11 and 5.12).

But given its growing isolation, South Africa may increasingly be called a member of what might be called the international outcasts' league, comprising also Israel, South Korea, Taiwan — and possibly Brazil. All these countries have vigorous economies that have advanced at an unprecedented pace; the first four are physically threatened from without, and are exceptionally strong militarily in relation to their size. Their respective regimes have widely lost international legitimacy. Israel, South Korea and Taiwan are also physically threatened in their very existence as independent states.[20] These countries have no common borders, and they are not troubled by quarrels with one another. There are indications that they might become increasingly linked in a variety

Table 5.10: Projection of Total Private Consumption Expenditure for Various Racial Groups, 1970-2000 (1975 prices)

Racial Group	1970		1980		1990		2000	
	R million	Per cent	R million	Per cent	R million	Per cent	R million	Per cent
Whites	8,284	69.0	13,235	64.4	20,757	59.6	32,920	55.0
Coloureds	815	6.8	1,619	7.9	3,294	9.5	6,603	11.0
Asians	263	2.2	491	2.4	858	2.4	1,439	2.4
Blacks	2,642	22.0	5,200	25.3	9,876	28.4	18,942	31.6
Total	12,004	100.0	20,545	100.0	34,785	100.0	59,904	100.0

Source: Van der Wyk, *A Review of Some Long-term Trends*, p. 37.

Table 5.11: Imports and Exports to and from Major Trading Partners 1969-76 (R million)

Source and Destination	1969	1970	1971	1972	1973	1974	1975	1976 Eleven Months	Percentage Contribution
Imports from:									
United States	370.5	423.4	469.7	459.9	529.8	811.5	985.0	1,174.1	21.4
West Germany	292.9	374.0	408.9	411.1	606.8	925.0	1,033.9	993.2	18.1
United Kingdom	499.6	561.2	670.6	586.8	629.9	823.1	1,097.3	974.0	17.8
Japan	188.4	220.8	292.1	265.8	381.2	600.4	612.0	563.3	10.3
France	61.2	88.1	104.7	96.7	125.3	196.9	244.8	222.3	4.1
Italy	84.9	104.3	105.2	94.4	120.9	204.0	203.4	200.1	3.7
Other countries	639.7	775.3	833.5	912.0	888.4	1,355.1	1,392.1	1,352.9	24.6
Total imports	2,137.2	2,547.1	2,884.7	2,826.7	3,282.3	4,916.0	5,568.5	5,479.9	100.0
Exports to:									
United Kingdom	510.3	446.4	418.8	531.3	699.7	793.7	903.7	908.8	22.1
Japan	151.8	180.6	182.9	259.3	246.4	429.3	487.3	459.0	11.0
United States	110.0	129.3	121.1	147.0	163.7	429.7	429.7	420.4	10.2
West Germany	102.2	109.1	110.3	132.5	189.7	426.8	426.8	440.2	10.7
Belgium	63.2	55.7	56.9	81.6	120.7	137.1	137.1	176.7	4.3
Switzerland	3.2	5.2	8.4	15.5	31.1	170.6	170.6	149.0	3.6
Other countries	591.9	616.6	670.4	876.9	975.5	1,351.7	1,351.7	1,564.9	38.1
Total exports	1,532.6	1,542.9	1,568.8	2,044.1	2,426.8	3,738.9	3,906.9	4,119.0	100.0

Source: Dan Prinsloo, *United States Policy and the Republic of South Africa* (Foreign Affairs Association, Pretoria, 1978), p. 52.

Table 5.12: Foreign Investment in South Africa Distinguished by Region (R million)

	1973	1974	1975
Total Foreign liabilities to:			
EEC	6,698	7,945	9,851
Rest of Europe	956	1,147	1,690
Americas	1,776	2,557	3,566
Africa	375	447	498
Asia	216	279	348
Oceania	78	84	85
International Organisations and Other	281	298	412
Total	10,380	12,757	16,450

Source: Prinsloo, *United States Policy*, p. 54.

of ways through trade, weapons development, or even nuclear engineering and weaponry. South Africa, for instance, can supply its partners with a wealth of raw materials, including enriched uranium; Israel is rich in technical know-how for peaceful and warlike purposes alike; Iran has oil to sell in exchange for modern technology; Taiwan and South Korea are developing into modern states whose manufacturing industries are growing at a pace unsurpassed in the economic history of the world. Leagued for their common survival, the countries of the 'Fifth World' might conceivably become a new factor in world history.

Notes

1. See S. Daniel Neumark, *Foreign Trade and Economic Development of Africa: a Historical Perspective* (Stanford University, Food Research Institute, Stanford, 1964), especially pp. 44-9.
2. A.J. Boeseken, *Slaves and Free Blacks at the Cape, 1658-1700* (Tafelberg Publishers, Cape Town, 1977), *passim*.
3. Union of South Africa, *Report of the Economic Commission*, UG No. 12 (Pretoria, 1914), p. 35, cited by L.C.A. and C.M. Knowles, *The Economic Development of the British Overseas Empire* (Routledge and Son, London, 1930), p. 320.
4. Great Britain, Parliamentary Paper Cd. 2842 of 1905, p. 331, cited by Knowles and Knowles, *The Economic Development of the British Overseas Empire*, p. 319.

The Economics of South Africa 185

5. Irving Howe, *World of Our Fathers: the Journey of the East European Jews to America and the Life They Found and Made* (Simon and Schuster, New York, 1976), p. 116.
6. See, for instance, Oscar Handlin, *Boston's Immigrants 1790-1880* (Atheneum, New York, 1965), *passim*.
7. By 1912 South Africa had a population of 5,973,394 people, including 1,276,242 whites, slightly more than New Zealand's. South Africa's exports amounted to £62,974,219; her imports stood at £38,833,960. The comparative figures for the Gold Coast were £4,307,802 and £4,023,322 respectively.
8. S. Herbert Frankel, *Investment and the Return to Equity Capital in the South African Gold Mining Industry, 1887-1965* (Harvard University Press, Cambridge, Mass., 1967), p. 27.
9. See D. Hobart Houghton, *The South African Economy* (Oxford University Press, Cape Town, 1964), *passim*, a book on which we have drawn heavily.
10. C.W. de Kiewiet, *A History of South Africa: Social and Economic* (Clarendon Press, Oxford, 1941), especially the last chapter, and H.S. Frankel, 'An Analysis of the Growth of National Income of the Union in the Period of Prosperity before the War', *South African Journal of Economics* (June 1955). See also Frankel's brilliant study, 'The Tyranny of Economic Paternalism', supplement to *Optima* (1960), and his classic work *Capital Investment in Africa* (Oxford University Press, London, 1938).
11. See Pierre van den Berghe, *South Africa: a Study in Conflict* (University of California Press, Berkeley, 1967), *passim*, especially p. 199.
12. The literature on labour utilisation is extensive, ranging from Sheila Van der Horst's pioneering work *Native Labour in South Africa* (Oxford University Press, London, 1942) to W.J. de Villiers, *The Effective Utilisation of Human Resources in the Republic of South Africa* (General Mining and Finance Corporation, Johannesburg, 1974).
13. Between 1965 and 1975 the number of African pupils in secondary schools increased from 66,568 to 318,568; the number of pupils in all schools increased from 1,957,836 to 3,731,455; the percentage of the black population at school rose from 14.12 to 21.07, the highest in sub-Saharan Africa.
14. See Arnt Spandau, *Economic Boycott against South Africa: Normative and Factual Issues* (University of Witwatersrand, Labour Research Programme, Johannesburg, 1978), p. 83.
15. See *Standard Bank Review* (Johannesburg, September 1977) for an analysis.
16. A.D. Wassenaar, *Assault on Private Enterprise: the Freeway to Communism* (Tafelberg Publishers, Cape Town, 1977), especially pp. 144-5, 148. For a critique of Wassenaar's views from the private enterprise standpoint, see for instance Brian Kantor, 'On Freedom and Private Enterprise in South Africa', *Social Dynamics* (Cape Town), vol. 3, no. 1 (1977), pp. 26-34.
17. See L.G. Abrahamse, 'South Africa, 1976-1990' in E.A. Kraayenbrink (ed.), *South Africa, the Next Fifteen Years: a Microcosm of World Problems* (South African Institute of Race Relations, Johannesburg, 1976), pp. 9-18.
18. The case for the pessimists is put by Dr D.J. Kotze, Director of Energy in the Department of Planning and Environment. Dr Kotze stresses the following five points regarding South Africa's future: its great energy source: coal will be unable to meet demands within fifteen years; its huge uranium deposits, in reality only one-fifth as large as its coal resources, cannot serve as an alternative for very long; no economically exploited oil or gas resources have yet been discovered in South Africa – hydro-electric power can play only a small role due to the country's water shortage; sun, wind and tide power will not be able to play any significant role soon enough; the immediate crisis – the day when the demand for

oil will exceed the supply — is expected in 1985. But all such predictions are speculative.

19. See D.S. Prinsloo, *Revolutions and Railways in Southern Africa* (Foreign Affairs Association, Pretoria, 1978), *passim*. For a detailed study, see Julian Burgess, *Interdependence in Southern Africa* (Economist Intelligence Unit, London, 1976), and J.A. Lombard, J.J. Stadler and P.J. van der Merwe, *The Concept of Cooperation in Southern Africa* (Econbureau, Pretoria, 1968).

20. We are indebted to Martin C. Spring for showing us his manuscript on the subject.

6 SOUTH AFRICA: STRATEGIC AND DEFENCE POTENTIAL

Cape Town was known to the early mariners as the Tavern of the Seas. It is one of the strategic prizes of the world. European settlement in Southern African began in 1652 with the arrival of Jan van Riebeeck, who had been sent out by the Dutch East India Company to establish a station on Table Bay, a port of call where Dutch ships might obtain fresh water and provisions on the long route to the East Indies. During the French Revolution and the Napoleonic Wars, the Cape of Good Hope passed into the hands of Great Britain and became a cornerstone in the development of British sea power. Without command of th sea-lanes around the Cape, the British position in the South Atlantic and the Indian Ocean would have been untenable, and the makers of British strategy knew this. Again in World War Two, Great Britain could hardly have sustained hostilities against the Axis powers in the Middle East without command of the Cape route. When the Mediterranean was closed by the Germans, the Cape played an equally important part in the defence of Allied shipping; experts have estimated that out of five convoys of 1 million tons each approaching Europe in wartime, four had to round the Cape. Had German U-boats denied the use of the Cape route to Allied ships, Great Britain would certainly have been hard pressed and Nazi Germany might well have won the war. The importance of the Cape route has continued to grow since World War Two.

South Africa in World Strategy

Control of the Cape route remains a major asset to the West. An average of 6,800 ships called at South African ports each year between 1957 and 1966. The number almost doubled when the Suez Canal was closed as a result of the Arab-Israeli conflict. It reached a yearly average of about 12,000 for the period 1967 to 1972. A total of 950 ships passed the Cape route in one month of 1974 alone. By 1975 some 24,000 ocean-going vessels passed this particular 'choke point' every year — about 66 a day (see Table 6.1). Of those 24,000 vessels, 9,476 docked in South African ports, including 1,600 or so from the United Kingdom,

188 *South Africa: Strategic and Defence Potential*

Table 6.1: Ships Passing the Cape of Good Hope in One Month (February 1974)

Flag	Freighters	Tankers	Total Ships	Percentage of Grand Total
United Kingdom	118	69	187	19.20
Liberian	45	84	129	13.00
Norwegian	27	45	72	7.43
Greek	61	12	73	7.53
Communist nations	105	7	112	11.55
Dutch	30	15	45	4.64
French	17	17	34	3.50
West German	37	6	43	4.43
Italian	20	10	30	3.09
United States	16	2	18	1.86
South African	–	23	23	2.37
Japanese	24	9	33	3.40
Indian	23	1	24	2.47
Spanish	1	3	4	0.41
Portuguese	9	2	11	1.13
Panamanian	19	8	27	2.78
Danish	14	5	19	1.96
Swedish	8	7	15	1.55
Miscellaneous	63	8	71	7.32
Totals	637	333	970	100.00
Daily Averages	22.75	11.89	36.64	

Source: South African Defence Department.

1,375 from Greece, 1,064 from Liberia, 590 from the Netherlands and 382 from the United States.

The Cape is particularly important to oil tankers, whose former route to and from the Mediterranean took them through the Suez Canal. Most of these ships are now too large to go through the canal, so more than half of Europe's oil supplies – and a quarter of its food – passes round the Cape of Good Hope. Moreover, the increasing dependence of the United States on imported Middle Eastern oil has further increased the American stake in the Cape route — already the world's most crowded shipping lane; by the 1980s, according to some estimates, 60 per cent of US oil imports may have to be supplied via the Cape. Additionally, the United States has defence treaties with 43 countries, 41 of which lie overseas. Ninety-nine per cent (by volume) of its overseas trade is transported by ship. Any threat to the world's sea-lanes consequently jeopardises American national security.

In years to come, Western Europe and Japan will probably become even more dependent on Middle Eastern oil rather than less so, as Table 6.2 shows. Seventy per cent of Western Europe's strategic materials already must come round the Cape. Since the bulk of this traffic must skirt the coasts of Africa, its steady flow depends to some extent on South Africa and South African ports (see Figure 6.1). The Cape route is not likely to lose its present importance in relation to the Suez Canal. According to Dr Alvin J. Cottrell, several factors work against such a shift. The repair facilities of South Africa are growing in importance. The existing glut on the world's tanker market and the use of tankers for storage purposes subtract from the marginal time savings that may be attained by using the shorter Suez route. The development of South African resources and industries has changed former patterns of trade, and more shipping now goes to South Africa rather than around it. South African-European trade links are being tightened by advances made in containerisation, a process that will add to the size of cargo ships and present them with problems similar to those already faced by supertankers.

A key position is now held by the VLCCs (very large crude carriers — of 160,000 tons or more). These ships require costly facilities for refuelling and enormous dry docks for repair. The new large port of Saldanha Bay, about a hundred miles north of Cape Town, was specifically planned to accommodate tanker traffic and to provide dry-dock facilities. Another major project is Richards Bay harbour, which is linked to the development of the Sishen-Saldanha iron-ore export scheme. The deep-water port at Richards Bay is designed to accommodate vessels displacing up to 152,000 tons and, eventually, those displacing 254,000 tons. As part of a major development project, the harbour is being equipped to handle bulk cargoes such as bituminous coal and anthracite. Between them, the new ports will supplement the trade of the existing ports as they are listed, in order of importance, in Table 6.3.

By the end of 1978 about 70 per cent of South African imports were containerised, and with the new ports in operation, the present

190 *South Africa: Strategic and Defence Potential*

Table 6.2: Estimated Demand for Middle Eastern Oil (mbd)

Year	United States	Europe	Japan
1973	3.30	12.80	4.20
1980	14.00	19.00	9.00
1985	18.00	24.00	12.00

Source: Patrick Wall (ed.), *The Indian Ocean and the Threat to the West* (Stacey International, London, 1975), p. 184.

Figure 6.1: Main Oil Movements by Sea, 1973

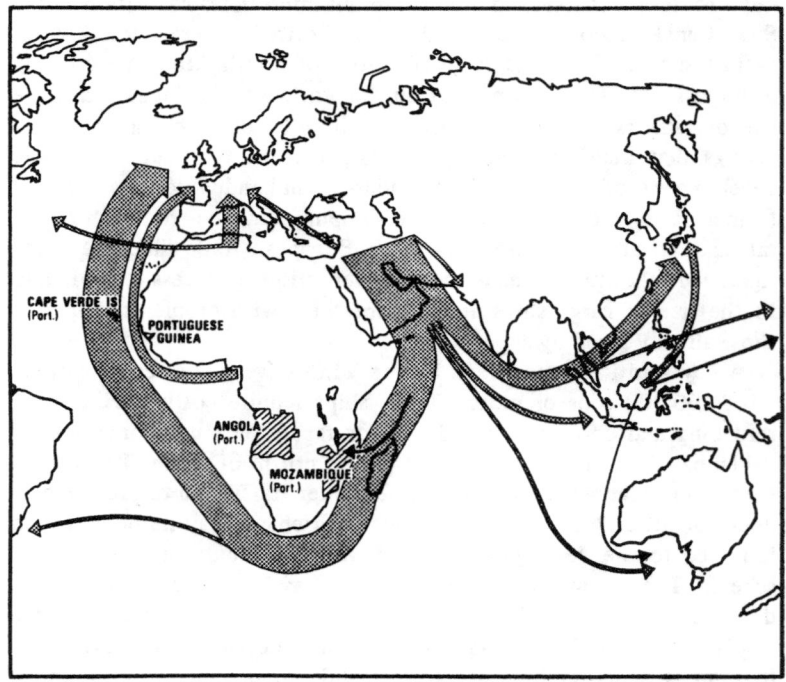

Source: Institute for the Study of Conflict, *The Security of the Cape Oil Route* (ISC Special Report, London, 1974), p. 43.

South Africa: Strategic and Defence Potential

Table 6.3: The Trade of South Africa's Ports, 1977-8 (million tons)

Port	
Richards Bay	13.09
Durban	35.43
East London	3.54
Port Elizabeth	7.34
Mossel Bay	0.26
Table Bay	9.44
Saldanha Bay	11.68
Total	63.22

Source: *Official Yearbook of South Africa*, 1978, p. 414.

congestion of South Africa's harbours should come to an end. The country will then be in a position to dispense with the use of Maputo in Mozambique, and even to handle traffic from its various neighbours, including Swaziland, Botswana and Rhodesia. It can also provide more technical advantages to shipping. South African engineers have developed remarkable skill in dealing with VLCCs both inside and outside harbours. Minor repairs can be made under way without slowing a vessel's speed; technicians and spare parts are transferred to and from a ship several hours' steaming time before the vessel has rounded the Cape and seven hours after. Helicopters capable of lifting several tons can supply ships with mail, fresh food, medical help and such. Although the VLCCs do not touch land, they depend on this umbilical cord, which can only function with a stable land base. Smaller tankers are able to use the dry docks at Durban harbour, and the deep berths in the harbours at Durban and Cape Town. At the time of writing, these ports were swamped with traffic, and lines of tankers waited to be served.

Port facilities are presently being extended to handle the oil trade and the increasing traffic in minerals and raw materials required by the West and by South Africa's expanding industrial economy. The rapidly growing demand for harbour-service vessels such as tugs, dredges, floating cranes, pilot boats, shipping craft and naval ships has contributed to the growth of an active shipbuilding industry, fostered since 1967 by government subsidies. In 1977 South African shipyards turned out cargo vessels of a substantial size — all of direct or indirect strategic significance. These defence capabilities are augmented by a network of

192 South Africa: Strategic and Defence Potential

Table 6.4: Mineral Potential of the Republic of South Africa

Mineral	South African Production and Reserves	Western Use
Gold	The Republic of South Africa (RSA) produces more than 70% of the world's gold, and has the world's greatest reserves	World's monetary system
Diamonds	50% of the world's gem diamonds are mined in the RSA and Namibia; RSA has 50% of world's reserves and 60% of Western reserves	Gem and industrial diamonds
Coal	RSA has 2% of world's known coal reserves — 12,000 million tons — and 5% of Western reserves	
Uranium	RSA produces 16% of the free world's uranium and has 25% of world's reserves and 30% of Western reserves	Nuclear power
Iron ore	RSA has vast high-quality resources; RSA possesses 6% — 5,000 million tons — of known world reserves of iron ore containing 60% iron, and 8% of Western reserves	
Vanadium	RSA has world's largest known source	High-grade steel
Manganese	RSA is world's second-largest producer after USSR, has world's largest reserves of very high-quality manganese, and exports 15% of world production	Manufacture of ferro-alloys
Asbestos	RSA is sole source of crocidolite asbestos and amosite asbestos; it has 14% of world's proven reserves and 16% of Western reserves, and produces 10% of world supplies	Asbestos cement products
Chrome	RSA's production is second only to that of USSR; RSA has 25% of world's reserves	Manufacture of steel
Platinum	RSA is world's largest producer and exporter; has 83% of world's reserves	Car exhaust systems, fertilisers, jewellery
Copper	RSA has one of the world's highest-producing mines in Phalaborwa; holds 2% of world's and 4% of the West's reserves	Electrical and other copper products
Fluorspar	RSA has world's largest deposits; 34.6% of world's reserves	Steel production
Vermiculite	RSA has second-largest known best-quality reserves and second-highest production — 39.4% — in the world	Heat and sound insulation

South Africa: Strategic and Defence Potential

Table 6.4: continued

Mineral	South African Production and Reserves	Western Use
Titanium	RSA has very large deposits; impact expected soon on world markets	Manufacture of aircraft engines and fuselages
Nickel	RSA has largest African deposits, and ranks sixth in world's reserves	Steel production
Baddeleyite (Zirconium and hafnium oxide)	Strategic mineral, at present commercially available only from RSA	Atomic reactors and special steel
Ferrochrome	RSA is largest producer in world — 12.5% world production; expected to increase	Stainless steel
Phosphate	RSA is only large producer in world, and will soon become major exporter of phosphoric acid; enormous reserves of highest quality	
Tin	RSA production is small — twelfth in a total list of 40 world producers, but major tin reserves ate either in Communist countries or in areas of relative political instability	
Lead and zinc	Recent discoveries in NW Cape could make RSA one of great Western producers	
Other	RSA: barytes, bentonite, beryllium, bismuth, calcite, corundum, feldspar, fireclay, flint clay, fluorite, fuller's earth, graphite, gypsum, kaolin, kieselguhr, lead, limestone, magnesite, mica, mineral pigment, pyrite, pyrophyllite, salt, silica, sillmanite, talc, tantalite-columbite, tantalum, tiger's eye	
All minerals	1974 total production reached record level of 3,928 rand, including a gold production of 2,533 rand	

Source: South Africa, *White Paper on Defence, 1977* (Pretoria, 1977), pp. 38-9. See also Peter Vannemann and Martin James, 'The Soviet Intervention in Angola: Intentions and Implications', *Strategic Review* (Summer 1976), p. 96.
Note: Like all government estimates, these figures are approximative and subject to error.

airfields, by a growing aircraft industry established in 1964 with the creation of the Atlas Aircraft Corporation of South Africa, and by the development of such bodies as the Council of Scientific and Industrial Research, whose Aeronautical Research Unit is concerned with high-speed aerodynamics, structures, propulsion and aircraft operation.

As a source of strategic raw materials, South Africa is of vast importance to the Western world, as shown by Tables 6.4 and 6.5. Whether in peace or in war, such supplies would be hard to replace were they denied to the West, or if they came under Soviet influence. A left-wing revolutionary government in South Africa might, of course, in its own economic interest, continue to sell raw materials and to furnish maritime facilities to members of the North Atlantic Treaty Organization (NATO), but such a prospect would be problematical.

South Africa also forms the corner-stone of a wider system of Southern African states. Southern African railways, harbours and airports play a key role in the commerce of Namibia (South-West Africa), Zimbabwe, Botswana, Swaziland and Lesotho. (Except for Namibia these are all landlocked countries that are wholly dependent on the South African communications network. Namibia alone has access to the coast, but Walvis Bay, its main port, belongs to South Africa.) South Africa's neighbours rely to a considerable extent on its capital, know-how and technical services; they cannot do without its imports and markets. South Africa's economic influence extends even to African countries outside this state system — countries that take a militantly anti-South African stand in world diplomacy. (Zambia, for instance, has paid a heavy price for boycotting Rhodesia, yet increasing its reliance on South African supplies.)

Namibia would perish without its connection with South Africa, which supplies it with certain export markets, easy marketing facilities, price stability and relatively high quality and low prices in imports. The South Africans also furnish Namibia with skilled manpower and a great variety of specialised services, as well as food and machinery — indeed the bulk of the country's consumer goods and physical capital. Because of its enormous natural handicaps, Namibia faces great difficulties that a poor country cannot solve on its own. It contains large areas of wasteland, its internal market is small, and its vast size makes provision of an adequate transport system expensive. All the requirements of a modern economy — cement, machinery, building materials, even food — have to be imported. Droughts are an ever-present threat. Primary industries such as agriculture, fishing and mining — the country's basic pursuits — are vulnerable to great fluctuations in demand and

South Africa: Strategic and Defence Potential

Table 6.5: Combined South African and USSR Percentages of World's Reserves of Selected Mineral Commodities

Commodity	South Africa's Percentage of World's Reserves	USSR's Percentage of World's Reserves	Combined South African and USSR Percentage
1. Platinum Group Metals	86	13	99
2. Vanadium	64	33	97
3. Manganese Ore	48	45	93[a]
4. Chrome Ore	83	1	84[b]
5. Gold	49	19	68
6. Fluorspar	46	4	50
7. Iron Ore	4	42	46
8. Asbestos	10	25	35
9. Uranium	17	13	30
10. Titanium	5	16	21
11. Nickel	10	7	17[c]
12. Zinc	9	8	17
13. Lead	4	13	17

Notes:
a. Apart from Austrialia, negligible reserves in Western World.
b. Most of the remaining reserves are in Rhodesia.
c. Conservative estimate.

Source: W.C.J. van Rensburg and A.D. Pretorius, *South Africa's Strategic Minerals – Pieces on the Continental Chessboard* (Johannesburg, 1977), p. 136.

to the perils posed by an unfriendly nature. South Africa, on the other hand, exports not merely machinery, but also food; its government-sponsored development schemes have started a great array of new enterprises in Namibia: bakeries, slaughterhouses, filling stations and factories. The assistance supplied by South Africa to Namibia through the so-called Bantu Investment Corporation has been much more successful than similar foreign-aid programmes mounted in Africa by Western European countries or the United States. Namibia, or for that matter Lesotho, Botswana or the Transkei, would be ill advised to snap the South African link. Even Mozambique needs South African help in a variety of fields, especially in selling its electric power and in port and railway development, as we noted earlier. South Africa attracts labour migrants from far beyond its borders, and sends capital and managers and technicians beyond its boundaries. South Africa's neighbours, then, are involved in its economic fortunes to an intimate degree. If the South African economy were to collapse as a result of internal unrest or foreign wars, the adjoining countries would suffer in equal measure, a subject to which we shall return.

South Africa's economic power beyond her borders is parallelled by its political influence. Countries like Swaziland and Lesotho cannot afford to alienate the South African giant. South Africa has, and for a long time will continue to have, an immense impact on the politics of Zimbabwe and Namibia, no matter who rules in Salisbury or in Windhoek. Any efforts made by the West to bring peace and to liberalise the regimes of Zimbabwe or Namibia will require a large measure of South African goodwill.

Conventional defence planning in the West has traditionally stressed the danger of a Soviet land assault on Western Europe. Given the weakness of the Soviet navy in the years following World War Two, Western strategists were inclined to take almost for granted the existing superiority of NATO in the oceans of the world. The Suez crisis of 1956 probably helped to convince Moscow that the Soviet Union had to acquire sufficient naval strength to challenge the United States in distant parts of the globe, and the Cuban missile crisis of 1962 certainly strengthened the Kremlin's determination to turn the Soviet Union into a great maritime power. Under the brilliant leadership of Admiral Sergei Georgeievich Gorshkov, who was appointed Commander-in-Chief in 1962, the Soviet navy rapidly expanded. By 1976 the USSR possessed a nuclear-powered, submarine-launched, ballistic missile force — including submarines under construction — superior to the combined US, British and French naval forces. The Strategic Arms Limitation Talks (SALT) agreement stabilised the inferiority of the United States by setting a lower ceiling for US nuclear submarines than for the Soviet ones, an arrangement that would have been inconceivable at the time of the Cuban crisis.[1]

The Soviet Union's naval forces include missile cruisers, missile-firing patrol boats, destroyers, a powerful air arm, an amphibious force and a logistics support force of tankers and supply ships that lessens the navy's dependence on foreign bases. In addition, the USSR has a great merchant fleet (which is expected to reach 27 million tons in 1980), the world's largest fishing fleet (approximately 4,000 vessels in 1976), and a flotilla of hydrographic survey ships that provide detailed military intelligence. Unlike Western merchant fleets, these ships are centrally controlled from Moscow; their personnel are interchangeable, and naval and civilian ships are designed for mutual support.

The goal of US designers is to produce ships that are fit to exercise control of the seas over long periods — navy vessels characterised by endurance, survivability and habitability — while Soviet planners have a different object. They stress lightweight construction permitting a high degree of manoeuvrability and great offensive firepower — qualities needed for a fleet whose mission is to deny control of the seas to an enemy. Soviet naval strategy in the 1970s, unlike that of the first half of the twentieth century, which was designed to defend the homeland, is geared to isolate the United States by cutting the sea lines of communication that connect the United States with its allies and its source of raw material, and to enable the Soviet military to support 'wars of liberation' around the world. This strategy was demonstrated in a world-wide context by the great 'Okean '75' exercises. More than a hundred ships were deployed in co-ordinated operations in the North Atlantic, the Mediterranean, the western Pacific and the Indian Ocean; Soviet aircraft operated from facilities in Cuba and Guinea among other locations.[2]

In this ongoing struggle against the West, Soviet strategists place much emphasis on the strategic importance of Africa. The 'liberation' of South Africa would strengthen the military position of the Soviet Union in the world at large. 'Liberation' would also put the USSR and its future allies in a position to deny vital raw materials to the Western world whenever the political situation demanded such a course. The Soviet navy would play a major part in this process. In peacetime, Soviet warships would provide backing to Soviet diplomacy. In wartime, as Admiral Gorshkov puts it, the fleet would assure 'the disruption of the ocean lines of communication, the special arteries that feed [the enemy's] military and economic potentials'.[3]

The power of the Soviet Union and its allies on land and in the air make the capabilities of its navy seem even more impressive; they also make direct numerical comparisons between US and Soviet naval forces somewhat misleading. The transoceanic trade of the Soviet Union is small. Soviet fleets are not needed to protect Soviet shipping on the high seas. These naval forces are only justified by Soviet planning for war — to deny oceanic transit to the Western world, thereby crippling NATO, starving Europe and Japan into surrender, and isolating the United States. True naval parity therefore requires NATO forces not only to be stronger than those of the Warsaw Pact, but also to be well supplied with overseas bases at a time when the menace of Soviet submarines is infinitely greater than the threat of German U-boats was in two world wars.

Between 1969 and 1973 alone, the number of 'shipdays' of Soviet warships and auxiliaries, excluding submarines, increased from 1,400 to 7,250. The strengthening of the Soviet fleet was not parallelled by a comparable Western effort. Given the vital dependence of the NATO powers on the availability of Middle Eastern oil, the South Atlantic and the Indian Ocean play a particularly important part in Soviet calculations. Since 1968 Soviet naval vessels have maintained a permanent presence in the Indian Ocean, while the NATO alliance has not been operating there or in the South Atlantic. The USSR, moreover, gained a variety of naval and air facilities in diverse locations.

These strongholds are not necessarily secure. During the Somali-Ethiopian war that started in 1977, the Soviets lost their Somali facilities, having shifted their support to Ethiopia. With Soviet and Cuban help Somalia has been defeated. If Ethiopia should succeed in restoring its power in the rebellious province of Eritrea, the Soviet position might be enormously strengthened. As a reward for the services rendered to Ethiopia by Cuban troops and Soviet advisers, the Soviet Union might acquire a naval base at Massawa. This port may be valuable not merely as a threat to Western communications, but also as a means whereby the Soviet Union could help to safeguard its own maritime route to the Soviet Far East.

The United States, which has also sent task forces to the Indian Ocean, would like to freeze both its own naval presence in the Indian Ocean and that of the Soviet Union at their present levels. President Carter made the demilitarisation of the Indian Ocean a campaign issue in 1976. Agreement is not likely to be reached, however, given the extent of Soviet reservations. The Soviets, moreover, continue their support to 'wars of national liberation' both in Namibia and South Africa that are directed against Western interests, while insisting on the universal illegitimacy of Western support for all anti-Communist movements. The Soviets have begun a military build-up in Mozambique and are stockpiling supplies. By April 1978, 250 tanks and 35 MIG-21 fighters and SAM missiles were spotted at Maputo. Whatever happens, the Soviet Union's use of its political influence, naval power and intelligence skills, adding to its existing and potential facilities for naval deployment, continue to make the USSR a powerful force in the Indian Ocean.

The Kremlin's position in South Africa has been further strengthened by the Soviet-Cuban conquest of Angola and by Soviet support for

Mozambique; both of these nations are self-proclaimed Marxist-Leninist republics. In the past the maritime facilities in Portuguese Africa were open to the United States. Thus, when the Suez Canal was closed as a result of the Arab-Israeli war of 1967, Luanda in Angola and Lourenço Marques (now Maputo) in Mozambique became key ports in relation to US naval deployment in the South Atlantic. In rotating ships of the US Middle East force 'homeported' at Bahrein in the Persian Gulf, for example, an American destroyer had to sail from its naval base on the east coast of the United States back across the Atlantic to Monrovia in Liberia, where it replenished and then proceeded to Luanda for new supplies. From there the destroyer had to embark on the longest, most treacherous part of its journey — 2,800 miles around the Cape of Good Hope to Maputo. This long trip was necessary because, for political reasons, the US navy is unable to use any of the excellent ports available in South Africa (see Figure 6.2).

The trip was dangerous for a destroyer; by the time the vessel had reached Maputo it was well below 25 per cent of its fuel capacity. A vessel low on fuel is less stable than one that is fully loaded, and bad weather encountered on rounding the Cape endangers crew and ship. Today the ports of Angola and Mozambique are no longer available to the US navy. The US installations on the island of Diego Garcia in the Indian Ocean are much further to the north and east, but Diego Garcia is not suited to be a major naval base.

Nuclear-powered vessels, of course, are much less dependent on foreign bases than are conventionally powered ships, but a substantial portion of the US fleet continues to require conventional fuels. Non-nuclear attack carriers of the 70,000- to 80,000-ton class, such as the John F. Kennedy, must still round the Cape, and they require replenishment at sea from supply ships and oilers at planned intervals along the route.[4] In fact, the US navy's capability to replenish its ships at sea gives it a mobility and endurance for sustained operation the Soviet navy cannot yet match.

America's loss has been Russia's gain. At the time of writing, Mozambique still enjoyed some degree of independence from its Soviet and Cuban allies, but Soviet influence there was on the increase. East Germans supposedly controlled the country's vast security apparatus, which was designed to cope with widespread internal protest against the despotic rule of the National Front for the Liberation of Mozambique (FRELIMO). Soviet and Cuban advisers trained the country's armed forces. Above all, the Soviets were reported to be turning the deep-water port of Nacala into a naval base to give themselves a major

200 South Africa: Strategic and Defence Potential

Figure 6.2: The Naval Balance, United States-USSR, 1977

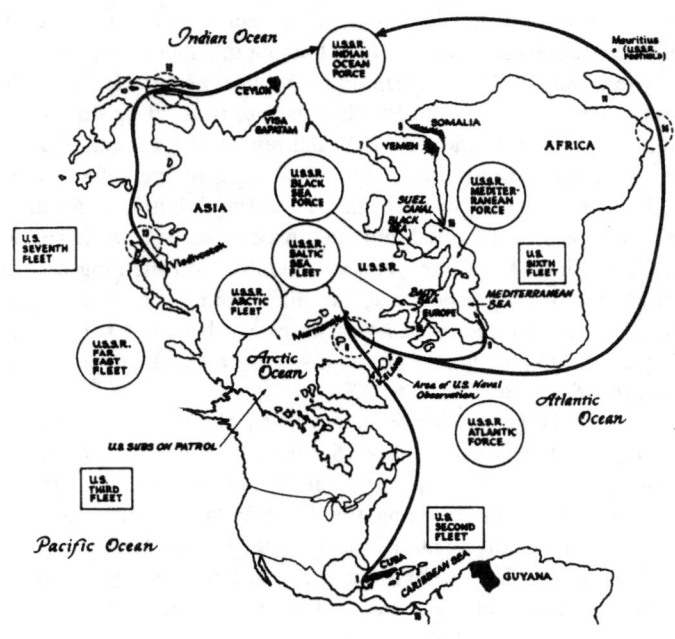

World's maritime choke points

1. Straits of Florida
2. Windward Passage
3. Mona Passage
4. Iceland Strait
5. Iceland Strait
6. Barents Strait
7. Persian Gulf
8. Red Sea
9. Strait of Gibraltar
10. Danish Straits

11. Mozambique Channel
12. Strait of Malacca
13. Tsushima (Korea) Strait
14. Cape of Good Hope
15. Suez Canal
16. Panama Canal

Shaded areas on figure above are Soviet footholds.

The naval balance

Units	United States	USSR
Major Combat Ships	177	200
Submarines	117	380
Carriers	13	2

Source: Reprinted with permission from Captain Paul B. Ryan, USN Retired, 'Canal Diplomacy and US Strategic Interests', *Naval Institute Proceedings* (January 1977).

South Africa: Strategic and Defence Potential

stronghold in the southern part of the Indian Ocean.[5]

The Popular Movement for the Liberation of Angola (MPLA) regime in Angola, for its part, depended on Cuba and the Soviet Union for its very existence. Cubans controlled the administration and the secret police. An estimated army of more than 20,000 Cuban soldiers helped the government forces to cope with widespread resistance on the part of guerrillas operating in both northern and southern Angola. The Cuban ambassador, Oscar Oramas, one of the architects of Cuba's invasion of Angola and a senior figure in the Cuban Communist Party, was a key operative of the DGI (the Cuban Intelligence service), which in turn is supervised by the KGB. The Soviet Union has made no attempt to secure naval bases in Angola, but this position could well change. It is possible that the USSR – or other Warsaw Pact powers like East Germany – would seek strategic gains by developing facilities in the deep-water ports of Lobito Bay and Luanda. Baia dos Tigres in Southern Angola has a superb deep-water anchorage that, if properly developed, would provide an excellent harbour for Soviet submarines preying in wartime upon the busy maritime African coast. Modern airfields at Luanda and Lobito, and at Henrique de Carvalho in Central Angola, could be enlarged to accommodate long-range aircraft.[6] Should Cuban and Soviet forces therefore strengthen their foothold in Angola and Mozambique, the position of the Western nations would further deteriorate.

The South African naval and air forces are in no position to deal with the Soviet menace on their own. Still, they are technically proficient, and their potential is being augmented. South Africa's most important naval base, situated in Simonstown, one of the most important naval positions in the southern hemisphere, is being expanded at a cost of 15 million rand. When planned operations are completed – possibly by 1981 – Simonstown will accommodate between 40 and 50 additional naval vessels, and will have tripled its 1977 capacity. The South African navy commands additional bases at Walvis Bay in Namibia and at Durban. Naval and air reconnaissance are centred on Silver Mine in the Cape Peninsula in bombproof underground installations that have been deeply tunnelled into rock, and naval headquarters were shifted in 1977 from Silver Mine to Pretoria, where they co-ordinate closely with the army and airforce commands. Silver Mine provides central direction for detailed surveillance of the maritime routes of the southern hemisphere. If South Africa were to form alliances with other nations, Silver Mine would be capable of accommodating representatives of their naval forces.

202 South Africa: Strategic and Defence Potential

The South African navy itself is primarily designed to cope with danger from submarines and mines, and to provide coastal defence (see Table 6.6). The South African naval forces were designed for co-operating with Western navies in safeguarding the Cape route. The imposition of a Western arms boycott has since prevented South Africans from purchasing additional warships in the West. They now concentrate on short defence and emphasise the construction of home-built, missile-carrying speed boats. The South African navy patrols the littoral and the local approaches of the Republic and of Namibia. Continuous daily air reconnaissance provides essential information concerning shipping — including Soviet shipping — round the Cape, while helicopters provide South African frigates with a stand-off weapons delivery system. The South Africans could, therefore, give valuable support to any Western force operating in the Indian Ocean. Above all, Simonstown offers a complex overhaul, repair, dry-dock and storage capability that is unequalled elsewhere in the Indian Ocean and comparable in sophistication only to Singapore. Diego Garcia, which is being developed as a permanent support base to provide logistic assistance to US carrier forces, will be only a fuelling station with a modest replenishment capability. As noted previously, for political reasons the United States has abstained from the use of South African naval facilities and from co-operation with the South African naval command.[7]

From the military standpoint, America's self-denying ordinance concerning South Africa was all the more serious, given the limitations concerning air bases and air space facing the US with respect to overseas deployment by air. In 1958 the US had available for its use 26 major air bases outside the NATO area and Korea; twenty years later their number had shrunk to ten — none of them in Africa, South America or the Middle East.[8] Given the growing power of the Soviet Union, and its formidable ability to transport vast numbers of Cuban and other allied forces, complete with tanks and other heavy equipment, to the remotest parts of Africa, the time had come to re-evaluate American political strategy concerning South Africa.

The Defence Infrastructure

With the publication in 1947 of *When Smuts Goes*, which outlined South Africa's impending breakdown, Arthur Keppel-Jones started a new genre of futurology. Many scholars and journalists over the last

South Africa: Strategic and Defence Potential

Table 6.6: South African Navy and Air Force, 1978

Branch	Strength and Equipment
Navy:	5,500 (1,400 conscripts) 3 Daphne-class submarines 1 destroyer (ex-British 'W'-class) with 2 Wasp ASW hel 3 ASW frigates (each with 1 Wasp hel) 3 Reshef-class FPBG with Gabriel SSM 1 escort minesweeper (training ship) 10 coastal minesweepers (ex-British Ton-class) 5 large patrol craft (ex-British Ford-class) (3 Reshef-class FPBG on order)
Reserves:	10,500 Citizen Force
Air Force:	10,000 (4,500 conscripts); 345 combat aircraft (incl 70 with Citizen Force and operational trainers) 2 lt bbr sqns: 1 with 6 Canberra B (1) 12, 3 T4; 1 with 9 Buccaneer S50 1 FGA sqn with 32 Mirage F-1AZ 1 fighter/recce sqn with 36 Mirage IIICZ/EZ/RZ/R2Z 1 interceptor sqn with 16 Mirage F-1CZ 2 MR sqns with 7 Shackleton MR3, 18 Piaggio P166S 3 tpt sqns with 7 C-130B, 9 Transall C-160Z, 28 C-47, 5 DC-4, 1 Viscount 781, 4 HS-125, 7 Swearingen Merlin IVA 4 hel sqns: 2 with 40 Alouette III, 1 with 19 SA-330 Puma, 1 with 14 SA-321 L Super Frelon 1 flt of 11 Wasp with AS.11 (naval assigned), 2 Alouette II Other hels incl 17 Alouette III, 40 SA-330 Puma 4 comms and liaison sqns (army assigned) with 20 Cessna 185A/D/E, 36 AM-3C Bosbok, 20 C-4M Kudu Operational trainers incl 16 Mirage IIIBZ/DZ/D2Z, 12 F-86, 120 MB-326 M/K Impala I/II, other trg ac incl 110 Harvard (some armed), 5 C-47 ac, 10 Alouette III hel R.530, R.550 magic aam; AS 20/30 asm
Reserves:	25,000 Active Citizen Force 5 COIN/trg sqns with 60 Impala I/II, 10 Harvard
Paramilitary forces:	110,000 Commandos (in inf bn-type units grouped in formations of 5 or more with local industrial and rural protection duties). Members do 24 months basic training, followed by reserve training. There are 13 Air Cdo sqns with private aircraft, 35,500 South African Police (SAP) (19,500 whites, 16,000 non-whites), 20,000 Police Reserves

two decades have predicted the collapse of white-controlled South Africa by internal revolution, external intervention or a combination of the two. These assumptions require a reassessment based on military and economic facts, taking into account South Africa's strong economic and political position. It is the only sub-Saharan state with an industrial and logistic infrastructure strong enough to enable it to maintain by itself a reasonably up-to-date system of land, air and sea defences. South Africa, on its own, can field a balance force, with a modern navy, an air arm and an army complete with armoured formations.

The country's military policy is based on the assumptions that threats to South Africa are not merely local, that a bipolar conflict continues in the world, and that the Kremlin will continue to proclaim the need for intensifying the international class struggle between 'socialism' and 'capitalism'. The nuclear balance of terror has made the threat of conventional war greater rather than smaller. Peace is indivisible because every local conflict affects to some degree the global balance of power. South Africa's military preparations aim, therefore, at providing for counter-insurgency warfare of short and long duration, and for conventional war-making ability. The country's striking power is based on part-time forces, with specialist leadership provided by a strong permanent nucleus.[9] Strategic doctrine stresses the need for effective intelligence, the ability of the defence force to support the civilian administration at a moment's notice, the maintenance of a mobile force available for immediate duty, and the need for decisive action and for 'total defence' that embraces every aspect of national power.

South Africa's President, who is elected by a bicameral Parliament, is nominally Commander-in-Chief of the South African Defence Force (SADF). Effective power is vested in the Prime Minister who, to all intents and purposes, controls the defence forces through the Ministry of Defence. In addition, the Ministry of Justice, Police and Prisons (set up in 1966 as the Ministry of Police) has functions linked to internal defence. South Africa reputedly maintains an extensive internal and external intelligence network that has sources not merely within South Africa, but also apparently within states of the Organization of African Unity (OAU), the Warsaw Pact and Western Europe. Intelligence data are collected and evaluated by the Bureau for State Security (reorganised since the time of writing). This body serves to advise the Prime Minister on questions affecting internal and external security. National security is co-ordinated by a State Security Council (SSC), which advises the Prime Minister on the formulation of national strategy, including its political, economic, psychological and military aspects. All of these intelligence groups are dynamic and interacting.

South Africa, as we have indicated, is the industrial giant of the African continent, the only African country with a major iron and steel industry and with petrochemical and advanced engineering plants. The Republic's military power is thus enhanced by a substantial industrial and logistic infrastructure on a scale that has been attained nowhere else in Africa. The defence establishment is linked to great quasi-governmental bodies such as the South African Iron and Steel Industrial Organisation (ISCOR, created in 1928), the Nuclear Fuels Corporation, the Uranium Corporation, and the South African Coal, Oil and Gas Corporation (SASOL, set up in 1957). The country produces iron, steel, chemicals and a broad range of high-grade engineering goods, all of which have military significance. Its nuclear technology is of a high order, and South African scientists have developed their own method of enriching uranium that will multiply the nation's earnings from foreign trade. South Africa expects to become a larger exporter of uranium within about ten years. This may bring it increasing political influence, as experts expect serious world-wide shortages of both raw and enriched uranium during that period.

South Africa also has the technology required to build nuclear weapons.[10] Until now it has abstained from testing nuclear bombs, but it has not signed the nuclear non-proliferation treaty. This places US diplomats in a difficult position. The United States has continually urged South Africa to sign the treaty. According to Joseph Nye, Jr., a Deputy Undersecretary of State and architect of President Carter's nuclear policy, the United States would be willing to sign security agreements with future signatories of the non-proliferation treaty, offering US nuclear guarantees as a substitute for nuclear weapons, in addition to the benefits of nuclear co-operation in the civil sphere. Since South Africa already possesses its own nuclear energy, and since the Carter administration could not possibly offer a military guarantee to South Africa, the benefits of signing the nuclear non-proliferation treaty are by no means apparent to South Africans. Their nation, already one of the world's nuclear powers, will certainly further strengthen its international position in that field.

The defence complex, including ARMSCOR (which was created in 1976 through a merger of the Armaments Board and the Armaments Development and Production Corporation of South Africa) with its subsidiary arms factories, is one of the country's most advanced technical

206 *South Africa: Strategic and Defence Potential*

organisations, one that is engaged in manufacturing, operating and maintaining a wide range of highly sophisticated equipment. About 45 per cent of defence expenditures goes to internal development, providing private industry with a considerable work-load and spreading technical know-how to the entire labour market, particularly to the engineering profession.

A major effort has been made to maintain adequate oil reserves. The extent of these is not known, but by 1977 the country was reputed to have stored a two- to five-year oil supply in abandoned mine shafts. Coal liquefaction has been perfected through SASOL for the purpose of producing fuels, petrochemicals, fertilisers and tar products. South African coal liquefaction technology holds a leading position in the world. (At the time of writing, the Americans were negotiating to obtain from South Africa the improved Fischer-Tropsch technique to make oil from coal.) When present plans are completed South Africa will produce 36 per cent or more of its fuel needs from domestic sources.[11] The bulk of South Africa's oil imports at the time of writing came from Iran. At the end of 1978 the new Iranian government announced that it would no longer supply oil to South Africa. But given South Africa's ability to pay for oil imports with gold, and given the existence of great international trade networks skilled in dealing 'under the counter', South Africa was not likely to run out of fuel. Sanctions were certain to raise the cost of imports, and thereby slow down industrial development. South Africa, on the other hand, was in a strong position owing to the extent of its coal resources. (By 1979, the country produced about 90,000,000 tons of coal a year, of which 15,000,000 tons were being exported. By the end of the century, South Africa's estimated coal production will amount to 200,000,000 tons, thereby giving the country a good deal of leverage in the international energy field.)

Defence and defence-related industries thus have considerable impact on the South African economy (see Table 6.7). Defence expenditures have risen considerably during the past seven years — from about 2.3 per cent of the GNP in 1969-70 to an estimated 5.3 per cent in 1977-8.[12] Despite the increase, South Africa's expenditures have not been excessive in comparison with those of countries like the United States, Nigeria or the USSR. Though they are a burden on the economy, defence expenditures do not cause a major political or economic strain, given the extent of the country's resources.

South Africa's industrial infrastructure enabled the country to emphasise self-sufficiency in arms production and improvement in its

South Africa: Strategic and Defence Potential

Table 6.7: South African Defence Expenditures, 1975-8 (R million)

Expense	1975/6	1976/7	1977/8
Command and control			
Operating costs	76.6	92.9	112.8
Capital costs	23.7	32.1	62.2
Total	100.3	125.0	175.0
Landward defence			
Operating costs	223.3	283.3	424.9
Capital costs	238.6	361.7	482.2
Total	461.9	645.0	907.1
Air defence			
Operating costs	20.5	25.5	79.6
Capital costs	42.5	46.3	46.1
Total	63.0	71.8	125.7
Maritime defence			
Operating costs	26.3	31.5	33.3
Capital costs	59.6	130.7	198.8
Total	85.9	162.2	232.1
General training			
Operating costs	53.1	43.0	61.9
Capital costs	11.3	28.8	6.3
Total	64.4	71.8	68.2
Logistic support			
Operating costs	154.5	218.7	250.8
Capital costs	83.6	78.3	137.5
Total	238.1	297.0	388.3
Personnel support			
Operating costs	11.5	10.9	16.7
Capital costs	15.7	20.2	22.7
Total	27.2	31.1	39.4
General SADF support			
Operating costs	2.7	3.7	4.6
Total defence requirements			
Operating costs	568.5	709.5	984.6
Capital costs	475.0	698.1	955.8
Total	1,043.5	1,407.6	1,940.4
Cash voted (all departments)	1,043.5	1,407.6	1,711.7
Estimated percentage of state expenditures	15.0	17.0	19.0
Estimated percentage of GNP	4.1	4.9	5.1

Source: South Africa, *White Paper on Defence, 1977* (Pretoria, 1977).

ability to withstand foreign economic pressure, especially pressure applied through an oil boycott. Arms production has recently been centralised through ARMSCOR. According to a Ministerial statement issued in 1977, South Africa supplied 75 per cent of its arms requirements, excluding naval craft, from domestic sources. By 1979 weapons manufactured at home included missiles, electronic equipment, motorised equipment like the Ratel infantry combat vehicle, small arms, maritime assault vessels, naval frigates and ordnance, including a new 35 mm field gun. Before joining the international arms embargo, France had supplied the country with submarines and other naval craft. Jordan, oddly enough, had furnished it with tanks, and Israel had sold it naval craft and expertise. A variety of aircraft was being produced under French and Italian licences, including Mirage fighters, the SA 330 Puma helicopter, and the MB-326M Impala light-strike aircraft.[13] The key nation involved in building up the South African arms-manufacturing potential was France: Panhard provided licences for armoured cars; the Société Nationale Industrielle Aerospatiale and its subsidiary, SUD Aviation, helped to provide equipment to manufacture the Mirage; and French firms sold helicopters and submarines and other military hardware to South Africa (see Table 6.8).

According to expert testimony introduced by Sean Gervasi to the Subcommittee on Africa of the US House Committee on International Relations, the South African arms build-up is considerably greater than has been indicated by conventional sources such as the London International Institute of Strategic Studies or the *Defense and Foreign Affairs Handbook* (see Table 6.9). Thus South Africa is in a position to deploy substantial armoured forces supported by a modern and well trained air force. The South Africans have not as yet tested nuclear weapons, but they have the industrial capacity, the technical knowledge and the raw materials required to construct a substantial nuclear arsenal and a tactical delivery system. The country's military power is therefore greater than at any other time in history.

South Africa's defensive capability is likely to be affected to some degree by the international arms boycott that was recently imposed on the country by the UN. The national produces all the *matériel* required for counter-insurgency warfare, but it still requires foreign skills in complex forms of military engineering connected with rocketry, computers and nuclear arms. The decision made by the French government at the end of 1977 to halt the construction and trial run of the *Good Hope*, a warship being built for South Africa, was an ill omen, but the South Africans will certainly surmount the boycott, just as the

Table 6.8: Deliveries of Weapons Systems Known to be in Service with the South African Defence Forces (by the end of 1976)

Item	Manufactured/ Licensed by	Delivered
Mirage III fighter/bomber trainer/recce	France	95 +
Mirage F-1 all-weather multipurpose fighter	France	48 +
Aermacchi MB-326M Impala I strike/trainer	SA/Italy	300
Aermacchi MB-326K Impala II strike	SA/Italy	100
Lockheed F-104G Starfighter/bomber	US ex-Luftwaffe	40
North American F-51D Cavalier c. insurgency strike	US	50
Aerospatiale Alouette III armed attack helicopter	France	115 +
Aerospatiale/Westland 330 Puma assault helicopter	France/UK	40 +
Aerospatiale/Westland 341 Gazelle general-purpose helicopter	France/UK	2 (?)
Agusta-Bell 205A Iroquois utility/s.r. helicopter	US	25
Lockheed P-2 Neptune antisubmarine patrol	US	12
Centurion Mk 10 heavy tank	UK	240
Centurion Mk 7 heavy tank	UK	150
M-47 Patton main battle tank	US/Italy	100
M-41 Walker Bulldog light tank	US	100
AMK-13 light tank	France	80
M-113A1 armoured personnel carrier	US/Italy	(400)[a]
Commando V-150 armoured personnel carrier	US/Portugal	(300)
Piranha armoured personnel carrier	Switzerland	(100)
Daimler Ferret MK 2 scout car/antitank armoured car	UK	450
M-3A1 White armoured personnel carrier	US	400
Saracen FV603 and FV610 armoured personnel carrier	UK	700
T-17 El Staghound armoured car	US	450
Shorland Mk 3 armoured car	UK	(200)
Short SB 301 armoured personnel carrier[b]	UK	(300)
Sexton 25 pdr self-propelled gun	Canada	200
M-7 105 mm self-propelled gun	US	200
M-109 155 mm self-propelled gun	US/Italy	(50)

Notes: South African defence authorities, when asked to comment, would not commit themselves to details, but stated categorically that the South Africans have never had Starfighters.
  a. Figures in parentheses indicate orders on which delivery continues.
  b. In service with the South African police.

Source: Sean Gervasi, 'The Breakdown of the Arms Embargo against South Africa', testimony to US Congress, House Committee on International Relations, Subcommittee on Africa, 14 July 1977.

210   *South Africa: Strategic and Defence Potential*

Table 6.9: Arms Inventory: South African Defence Forces (by the end of 1976)

Item	IISS[a]	Currently in Service
Combat aircraft	113	625
Helicopters	92	215
Tanks	161	535
Armoured cars	1,050	1,430
Armoured personnel carriers	250	960
Self-propelled guns	n.a.[b]	294
Medium and light artillery	n.a.	380

Notes:
 a. International Institute for Strategic Studies, *The Military Balance, 1976-1977* (IISS, London, 1976).
 b. Not available.

Source: Sean Gervasi, 'The Breakdown of the Arms Embargo against South Africa'.

Rhodesians did with far fewer resources. South Africa's industrial strength, its ability to pay for imports in gold, and the nature of international trading 'leaks' have rendered the country largely immune to formal boycotts. It is difficult, therefore, to dissent from the considered opinion of the *Washington Post* that the arms boycott has come to late:

> Compared to any of the Black African countries on or near its borders, South Africa has a huge arsenal and a military expertise that is far superior to any of them now or in the near future. The Soviet Union is involved in arming Angola and Mozambique, but neither is likely to pose even a potential threat to the South Africans for years, and probably decades.[14]

The Defence Force of South Africa

The Defence Force of South Africa operates as an integrated organisation under the Chief of the Defence Forces, assisted by the respective Chiefs of Staff of the army, navy and air force. The Defence Planning Committee consists of the combat force commanders, the senior federal manager of ARMSCOR and a number of special members appointed by the Minister. The Defence Staff contains divisions for operations, personnel, intelligence, logistics and management service. Further modifications of the army structure have been made to assure rapid local control of counter-insurgency operations, and the Defence Force has completed a number of major telecommunications projects that are regarded as its nerve centre.

During his term of office as Minister of Defence, P.W. Botha, now the South African Prime Minister, turned the army into a formidable military instrument. The army's peacetime strength was officially estimated at 50,000 men, including 43,000 conscripts. There were 10,000 men in the air force, 5,500 in the navy and 138,000 in the Active Reserve (Citizen Force). The so-called commandos operated as a paramilitary force designed for local defence and counter-insurgency operations. The number of soldiers actually mobilised in 1977 may have been considerably larger — some observers place their full strength at about 130,000 men. If necessary, South Africa could mobilise 250,000 members of the Citizen Force and, by calling up all reserves, between 400,000 and 450,000 men. The backbone of the Defence Force is the Permanent Force of professional cadres; its flesh and bones, so to speak, are the reservists of the Citizen Force, who provide the bulk of the combat and administrative units that would be deployed in the field if the Republic were at war. Like the commandos, reservists serve for a year and are then called up annually for short training periods during the subsequent five years. They can be quickly mobilised for service and, after a brief and intensive period of retraining, can be committed to full-scale operations. Their morale is high, and postings to the border areas of Zimbabwe, Angola and Mozambique sharpen their training through experience in field operations.

There are eleven territorial commands in the armed forces, each with its own training units and full-time force units. Similar Citizen Force units are readily available to combine with Permanent Force units into brigades and task forces. (By 1978 these were officially listed as an armoured and two mechanised brigades (with Centurion tanks), four motorised infantry brigades, three parachute battalions and twenty artillery and anti-aircraft artillery regiments, along with engineer, signal and other specialist troops.) According to Gervasi's testimony before the House Subcommittee, the South Africans have accumulated armoured vehicles and personnel carriers of many different designs, and an impressive force of helicopters (see Tables 6.8 and 6.9).

The land forces are supported by a balanced air force consisting of a strike force, a maritime command, an air transport command and a light-aircraft command that includes helicopters and light fixed-wing aircraft (see Table 6.9). The need is emphasised for mobility, decentralised control, close co-operation between land, sea and air forces, co-operation with the civilian population, and close acquaintance with local terrain — both in conventional and in counter-insurgency warfare. Air defence is strengthened by static and mobile radar units, coupled with modern interceptors and backed by surface-to-air missiles. The Defence Force resembles that of Israel in that its strength depends essentially on the reservists.[15]

The career cadres of the Defence Force, the Permanent Force, make up only 7 per cent of the entire defence establishment and less than 3 per cent of the land forces. The Permanent Force is small in relation to the tasks assigned it, and South African military experts constantly complain of personnel shortages. The Defence Force has no trouble attracting recruits; its difficulty lies in keeping trained men. The steady turnover works against the cost-effective deployment of experienced manpower. The services of these highly trained men are not entirely lost, however, as they automatically join the reserves and can be called up by the Defence Force in case of need.

The Permanent Force, which was once mainly a preserve of English-speakers, is now primarily officered by Afrikaners. According to figures published in the *Johannesburg Star* on 13 December 1974, some 85 per cent of the Permanent Force staff in the army and 75 per cent of the corresponding staff in the air force consisted of Afrikaners. The South African navy is no longer jokingly referred to as the 'Royal South African Navy'.[16] Promotion in the military goes by merit rather than by linguistic affinity, although Afrikaans dominates the officers' mess. The officer corps does not form a separate caste; its ethos is technocratic, as befits a cohesive white society devoid of feudal traditions. Its members are better educated than they were in the nineteenth century, when locally raised units were comprised of a large number of frontiersmen trained in the bush rather than at school. Today officer candidates are required to pass the matriculation examination, and subsequently receive an advanced military education. Possibly one-third of all officers are former sergeants. The creation of the Military Academy of the South African Defence Force in 1950 further contributed to military professionalisation in an army whose officers rarely had degrees. Today the officer corps is one of the country's many professional groups; it is not a military caste but an integral part of the professional middle class.

The architects of the military academy wanted to place officers' training on an equal footing with the training of professional men in civilian jobs in order to raise South African military standards to those attained overseas by equipping officers to cope with an increasingly complicated defence structure, to service sophisticated weapons, and to carry out military and related research. The academy was originally affiliated with the University of Stellenbosch; later its staff became the faculty of military science, military history, geography and such, but also taught subjects like mathematics, political science, public administration, aeronautics, nautical science, accountancy, computer science and physics. Graduates initially advanced into the lower and middle echelons of the Defence Force; by the 1970s they were being promoted into top-ranking posts.

The South African Defence Force reflects the strengths and weaknesses of the country's white society at large. It contains a high proportion of men with developed technical skills. South Africans can thus maintain and deploy sophisticated modern equipment much more easily than can most of the black African forces whose recruits are drawn mainly from the villages. The army is essentially the white electorate in arms, so the country does not face military *coups d'état* of the black African and Latin American varieties. The armed forces face a limited emigration of well educated young whites, mainly English-speaking South Africans, who prefer to leave their country rather than serve in what they regard as an Afrikaner-run apartheid state. But from the rulers' standpoint, this exodus merely removes the discontented from white society; the rate of departure is not sufficiently high to make a serious impact on the armed forces. The army is highly motivated, and is integrated into European society. Desertion and major infractions of discipline are not great problems. 'Fragging' is unknown. South Africa is exempt from the class conflict that divided America during the Vietnam War, when a large stratum of college students — mainly of middle-class origin, exempt from the draft, and often guilt-ridden about their status in society — were arrayed against resentful blue-collar workers who were being conscripted into the army. The common military experience by whites of all social ranks and language groups strengthens cohesion in a country where white reservists feel that they are defending their own homes rather than some distant colony.

The armed forces are non-political in the sense that their members are not expected to belong to a particular party. If they have any political leanings, they tend to be more pragmatic about them than the older Afrikaner Establishment and the police; the latter are regarded by critics as the 'mailed fist of apartheid'. The army has rarely been used for police duty, and it enjoys greater popularity than the police. The public appeal of the fighting services is enhanced by their excellent record in combat. South African troops did well in the two world wars, and also in recent operations in Angola where — contrary to Cuban propaganda — they more than held their own against Cuban troops. South Africa's withdrawal from Angola was caused by logistic and supply problems and by the lack of US support; it was not caused by Cuban forces.

The army, like major industries, is also more pragmatic in racial affairs than the older South African establishment. Admiral H.H. Bierman, Chief of the South African Defence Force until 1976, felt convinced that South Africa must be able to call on all races for defence if it were to be able to resist the potential Soviet threat in the South Atlantic. His successor, General M.A. de M. Malan, shares Bierman's view. The South African navy recruits Coloured and Indian as well as white sailors. In 1975 the Defence Force began to accept recruits for a recently created Cape Corps Service Battalion composed of Coloured citizen soldiers; they are eligible to join the Permanent Force at the expiration of their twelve-month training period. In the same year, for the first time in the history of the South African Defence Force, Coloured soldiers received commissions, part of Botha's policy of strengthening the country's defensive potential by making some concessions to Coloureds as well as Indians.

In addition, the South Africans began to recruit a limited number of Africans; by the time of writing, the first black battalion was being constituted, and plans were under way for providing the black homelands with small force of their own. Judging by the Rhodesian precedent, South Africans seem likely in the future to rely more extensively on African and Coloured fighting men, a development fraught with wider social consequences.

The Role of the Police

For purposes of 'internal defence', South Africa places considerable trust in its police force, which was established in 1913 by amalgamating the four provincial forces. Unlike the British or American police, that of South Africa is a national force. It is a semi-military body, and is regarded as the 'first line of defence in the event of internal unrest'; its members receive a thorough training in infantry drill, infantry combat and more conventional police skills. Its administrator, known as the Commissioner of the South Africa Police, is responsible to the

South Africa: Strategic and Defence Potential

Minister of Police. (The Commissioner's duties are extensive, since in addition to conventional defence and police responsibilities, policemen are expected to undertake inquiries on behalf of government departments; in the more remote country areas they also act as assistant clerks and court messengers, and as immigration officers, wardens, revenue and census officers, health inspectors, inspectors of vehicles, postal agents, meteorological observers, mortuary attendants and more.)

By 1975 the police included about 54,000 men; 68 per cent of these were white (mostly Afrikaners), about 28 per cent were Africans, and the balance consisted of Indians and Coloureds.[17] The official goal is to permit each segment of the population to be policed by members of its own community. Contrary to the prevailing stereotype, South Africa is not a 'police state' in the sense that the streets are full of policemen on the beat. The total number of policemen per thousand people stood at 1.43 in 1912; sixty years later the figure is almost the same − 1.48. The proportion of policemen to civilians in South Africa is smaller than it is in the United States; moreover, public order has been maintained in South Africa with relatively little violence. Albie Sachs, a bitter critic of apartheid, has estimated that between 1917 and 1973 South African policemen have opened fire on rioting crowds on roughly thirty occasions (including Sharpeville in 1960), killing 500 Africans in all. He considers that his estimate may be on the low side; another 3,000 Africans may have lost their lives during the same period when individual policemen opened fire − allegedly while hunting suspects or in self-defence.

For Sachs, these figures indicate a long-continued reign of white terror. Certainly, 3,500 people slain are 3,500 too many, but in comparison with European countries like Germany and Russia over a sixty-year period, or with many African countries that have attained independence since World War Two, South Africa has been extremely pacific. Zambia, for instance, has in many ways been a model African state − a country that has avoided savage civil war of the Nigerian kind, or ethnic mass slaughter of the sort that decimated post-independence Burundi. Yet in Zambia, more than 700 people were killed in one year alone − 1964 − when the Zambian government smashed the so-called Lumpa Church, a dissident ecclesiastical organisation.[18]

The practice of measuring South Africa with a different set of weights derives not from the real nature of South Africa's misdeeds but from the country's relative liberality. In South Africa, foreign journalists and foreign academicians can move about the country and report with much greater freedom than they can in, say, Mozambique or Angola.

Police brutality is all too common and needs to be eliminated, even if only in the interests of efficiency and the rulers' enlightened self-interest. Government-appointed commissions of inquiry (such as the so-called Theron Commission appointed in 1973 to investigate the condition of the Coloureds) provide evidence of abuses at public expense. Such facilities do not exist in Marxist-Leninist republics like Angola or Mozambique, or even in so-called bourgeois states like Zaire. South Africa thereby gets a disproportionate amount of unfavourable publicity of a kind that reflects the easy accessibility of the evidence more than its nature.

Contrary to a widespread stereotype, the average white South African policeman is not necessarily brutal, ill educated or inefficient. European recruits must have at least a 'junior school certificate', and must be fully bilingual; special training is available at police training colleges — one for each major racial grouping — with advanced courses at the University of South Africa for officers who seek academic qualifications (including a B.Pol. degree).

Nevertheless the police force has many weaknesses. Policemen are poorly paid. And, as Jordan K. Ngubane, a South African writer, explained in his testimony given before the US Senate, the bulk of the police are compelled to perform a great deal of unproductive labour. Much of their work deals with the enforcement of apartheid legislation, giving them the kind of unpopularity the armed forces have avoided. African policemen are more poorly educated than whites; black recruits are accepted with a 'standard 6' — i.e. an elementary-school background. Black South Africa is actually underpoliced; 15,000 black police are too few to enforce the law among a population of some 19 million black people in an area larger than Western Europe.

There is a serious crime problem in major cities like Cape Town and Johannesburg. Nevertheless, the police should not be underestimated. Life and property are safer in the white areas in South African cities than in most American urban communities of comparable size; the police can take some credit for this accomplishment in a racially diverse country that is riddled by differences of class and income. With the support of an extensive intelligence network, and with the supervisory power entailed in the various pass laws and in anti-terrorist and anti-Communist legislation, the police form a vital component of South Africa's internal defence. They are trained to act in co-operation with the armed services and the civil administration, and are well equipped for the task of counter-insurgency. No revolutionary breakdown could occur without being preceded by an effective disruption of the police establishment.

Notes

1. In 1977 the Soviet strategic nuclear-submarine forces consisted of 78 submarines with 845 missiles; the US strategic submarine forces consisted of 41 submarines with 656 missiles.
2. J. William Middendorf, 'American Maritime Strategy and Soviet Naval Expansion', *Strategic Review* (Winter 1976), pp. 16-25.
3. Cited in David Rees, 'Soviet Strategic Penetration in Africa', *Conflict Studies*, vol. 77 (November 1976), p. 4.
4. Alvin Cottrell, 'Strategic Routes, Key Passages and Choke Points in and around Southern Africa: Threats Posed to Them by Hostile Local or External Forces' in Roger Pearson (ed.), *Sino-Soviet Intervention in Africa* (Council on American Affairs, Washington, DC, 1977), pp. 46-7.
5. Robert Moss, 'Fellow-Traveling in Mozambique', *National Review*, vol. 23 (December 1977).
6. Peter Vanneman and Martin James, 'The Soviet Intervention in Angola: Intentions and Implications', *Strategic Review* (Summer 1976), pp. 92-103.
7. See William H. Lewis, 'How a Defense Planner Looks at Africa' in Helen Kitchen (ed.), *Africa: From Mystery to Maze*, Vol. 12 of *Critical Choices for America* (D.C. Heath and Co., Lexington, Mass., 1976), pp. 277-309; by way of contrast, see Wolfgang Reith, 'Die Bedeutung Südafrikas für die Verteidigung der westlichen Welt', *Europäische Wehrkunde*, vol. 26 (June 1977), pp. 275-80.
8. Bruce Palmer, Jr., 'U.S. Security Interests and Africa South of the Sahara', *AEI Defense Review*, vol. 2, no. 26 (1978), p. 40.
9. See South Africa, *White Paper on Defence, 1977* (Pretoria, 1977), p. 9. For Soviet military doctrines, see, for instance, Philip A. Karber, 'Die taktische Revolution in der sowjetischen Militardoktrin', *Europäische Wehrkunde*, vol. 26 (June 1977), pp. 265-74. For Soviet strategic concepts see, for instance, Richard Pipes, 'Why the Soviet Union Thinks It Could Fight and Win a Nuclear War', *Commentary*, vol. 64, no. 1 (July 1977), pp. 21-34.
10. In 1977 the South African government publicly promised that South Africa would use nuclear energy for peaceful purposes only, and would abstain from testing nuclear bombs. The South African Minister of Finance, Owen P.F. Harwood, on the other hand, indicated that his country would exert the right to use its nuclear potential in any manner it thought fit.
11. South Africa maintains virtually complete secrecy on its trade and consumption of oil. According to the Economist Intelligence Unit, *Interdependence in Southern Africa: Trade and Transport Links in South, Central and East Africa* (July 1976), p. 17, South Africa relies on oil for less than 25 per cent of its energy requirements. This is expected to decrease to 20 per cent by 1980. Of the existing energy requirements, 5 per cent is supposedly produced by the oil-from-coal plant. The main suppliers were Iran (no longer a supplier since the Iranian revolution), Saudi Arabia, Iraq, Qatar and Abu Dhabi, in that order. The oil embargo adopted by the General Assembly of the UN in 1962 has had no serious effect on the country. Jonathan Baker, 'Oil and African Development', *Journal of Modern African Studies*, vol. 15, no. 2 (1977), pp. 175-212, provides detailed information regarding the oil potential of South Africa and of the continent as a whole, as well as South Africa's ability to withstand an oil boycott.
12. Estimated expenditures for the year 1977-8 will be 1,711.7 million rand;

this is 19.1 per cent of all state expenditures and 5.1 per cent of the GNP, compared with 5.3 per cent of East Germany's expenditures, 5.4 per cent of United States', 7.9 per cent of Nigeria's, and 12 per cent of the USSR's. Increases were as follows (in million rand):

	1975–6	1976–7	1977–8
Total expenditures	1,043.5	1,407.6	1,711.7
Estimated percentage of state expenditures	15.0	17.0	19.0
Estimated percentage of GNP	4.1	4.9	5.1

Source: *White Paper on Defence* (Pretoria, 1977), pp. 12, 14.

13. For weapons sold to South Africa from abroad, see the Stockholm Institute of Peace Research. For a list of major South African armament firms, shipbuilding firms and aerospace systems, as well as weapons and organisation, see *Defense and Foreign Affairs Handbook, 1976–1977* (Copley Associates, San Francisco, 1977), pp. 413–15.

14. 'Arms Embargo Comes Too Late to Affect South Africa', *Washington Post*, 28 October 1977.

15. In 1977, 7 per cent of the full-time men were members of the Permanent Force, 6.6 per cent belonged to the National Service, and 3.1 per cent were civilians. Of the part-time men, 54.9 per cent were Citizen Force members and 28.3 per cent were commandos, for a total of 83.2 per cent.

16. According to the *Johannesburg Star*, 28 December 1974 (cited by Jordan K. Ngubane before the US Congress, Senate Subcommittee on Africa, 94th Cong., 1st sess., June 1975, p. 417), in 1974 85 per cent of the Permanent Force staff spoke Afrikaans and 15 per cent spoke English. Among the generals and admirals, the proportions were 70 per cent and 30 per cent, respectively; in the air force 75 per cent spoke Afrikaans and 25 per cent spoke English; the navy contained equal numbers of Afrikaans-speakers and English-speakers.

17. Cynthia M. Enloe, 'Ethnic Factors in the Evolution of the South African Military', *Issue*, vol. 5, no. 4 (Winter 1975), pp. 21–8.

18. See Albie Sachs, 'The Machinery of White Domination in South Africa' in Leonard Thompson and Jeffrey Butler (eds.), *Change in Contemporary South Africa* (University of California Press, Berkeley, 1975), pp. 223–49, for figures. For the Lumpa Church, see Andrew Roberts, *A History of Zambia* (Heinemann, London, 1976).

7 SOUTH AFRICA: A REVOLUTIONARY SITUATION?

How stable, then, is this establishment? To what degree is it subject to revolutionary change? Can the system be overthrown by military action or by naval blockade? Alternatively, will the South African establishment succumb to revolution from within, to guerrilla warfare, to urban terror, or to more peaceful movements such as demonstrations and strikes that could culminate in the break-up of authority?

Conventional War against South Africa

War games are an exercise in futurology, and like all futurological exercises they usually bear little resemblance to what actually happens. The number of variables is too large and the field of knowledge is too small to make accurate predictions possible. Military planners, like their colleagues in the social sciences, can only make educated guesses, but some guesses are more accurate than others. We believe that a number of possible scenarios may, without question, be discarded from the start.

Combined action on the part of the Organization of African Unity may be excluded. On paper, the independent black states of Africa can raise considerable forces. In 1977 the Nigerian armed forces amounted to some 221,000 men, organised in four infantry divisions, twelve independent regiments and supporting units; the army of Zaire, organised into thirty battalions, numbered 34,400 men. The members of the OAU, however, lack a common military organisation, military doctrine, leadership, training methods, deployment plan and general staff. Armies like those of Zaire, for logistic reasons, cannot operate in strength outside their own borders, and they have yet to prove that they can fight a modern, Western-style army.

The value of possible future support to African insurgents from the OAU states, however, is admittedly not to be discounted.[1] These nations could supply weapons, training and military bases on the borders of South Africa. But the African states could hardly send their own armies against South Africa. Such an operation would endanger the stability of army-centred states such as Zaire or Nigeria, whose armed forces are essential in the strength of the existing governments. The Zambian army is small; it includes some 5,000 men organised into four infantry battalions with their supporting units. Angola is unusual among the African states in seeking to build a people's army based on conscription, but it has been ravaged by civil war, and its equilibrium depends on the presence of foreign troops.[2] Mozambique offers no offensive threat to South Africa other than that of harbouring guerrillas, although a recent Soviet weapons build-up should be noted.

Intervention by means of conventional forces thus would have to be carried out with troops drawn from outside Africa, possibly with 'proxy armies' supported by the Soviet Union. Their employment is not inconceivable. Soviet and also East German theoreticians defend the despatch of Cuban soldiers to Angola as a new form of 'international working-class solidarity'. The Cuban example might well be followed by others. Cuba itself is not in a position to launch yet another large military campaign overseas; its total armed strength in 1978 was only 189,000 men and more than a fifth of them were heavily engaged in Africa. Even a more powerful state like East Germany, whose armed peacetime forces number 201,000 men including security units, could not contemplate a major effort outside Europe (although minor ventures might be possible).

Assuming that members of the Warsaw Pact were willing to risk armed action in South Africa, and assuming that they were able to overcome the political obstacles in their way, they would still face extraordinary difficulties. An army determined to invade South Africa by land would lack suitable bases. In 1978 Mozambique could hardly have served as an advance base for a great army because of the country's economic dependence on South Africa. Cuban and Soviet advisers have come to Mozambique in substantial numbers. Despite FRELIMO's socialist and anti-South African rhetoric, however, Mozambique miners continued to work on the Rand, hydro-electric power from Mozambique was still sold to South African industries, and South Africans were running the port of Maputo. Mozambique, moreover, is deficient in communications, especially in traffic links from north to south. Only one bridge crosses the Zambezi; all other crossings are by ferry. Mozambique harbours are inadequate, with Beira poorly dredged and available only for coastal shipping, while the larger port of Maputo — like Beira — has a channel approach. In 1978 the Soviet navy used the port of Nacala, which is too distant from South Africa to form as yet a serious threat.

Angola is even less likely than Mozambique to menace South Africa.

South Africa: A Revolutionary Situation?

The country was in a perilous condition by 1979. European settlers had departed, leaving the country without most of its managerial and technical skill; the coffee crops had largely failed; UNITA, a dissident southern group, remained active; traffic had not been restored on the Benguela railway; and in many parts of Angola the Cubans and MPLA government forces controlled only the towns. North-south communications were totally inadequate. The logistic problems alone eliminated Angola as a possible base for an army operating against South Africa. Namibia is equally ill suited to become a base for hostile action, even if it were to become an independent country beyond South African control. Its coastline is desolate and poorly supplied with ports. The terrain is mostly inhospitable; the distances are vast. South African armoured forces could easily strike at the flanks and rear of invading units as they advanced inland.

Zimbabwe would be better suited as a land base, should the country move firmly into the Communist orbit. It is well supplied with roads, airfields and railway communications, and it has substantial industries that would afford supply and repair facilities to an enemy army. An invading force striking southward from Zimbabwe, however, would still encounter enormous obstacles. Inland communications routes are long; the Limpopo River is a natural barrier, and the bridges across it could easily be knocked out. In any case, the Soviet Union would be hard pressed to provide the transport required for building up a land-borne invasion force that would have to operate against a strong enemy on the other side of the world. This opponent, moreover, would enjoy all the advantages of internal lines of communication and mobile defence, resting on a powerful industrial infrastructure. The sheer extent of South Africa's territory (471,000 square miles) would enable it to rely on defence in depth.

The defending armies might well be hampered by guerrilla operations (as we show in the following section), but partisan operations in South Africa have so far been negligible. Even were they to increase in extent, they could not be mounted on a scale that would prevent South African forces from operating effectively. Comparable situations are numerous. During World War Two Soviet partisan formations rendered superb service. They functioned in a country where Nazis had alienated most of the population by insane atrocities. Swamps, forests and sometimes mountainous country offered excellent hideouts. Considerable stocks of weapons were available; so was assistance from the Soviet High Command. Yet the ability of the guerrillas to interfere with German military operations still remained strictly limited. They could never prevent the German army from striking where it wished. The position of potential guerrilla forces in South Africa would be much more difficult; such forces would be in no position to equal — much less improve on — the past performances of Soviet guerrillas.

A seaborne invasion might be considered as an alternative to an assault by land, always assuming that the South Africans had no nuclear weapons to prevent such a venture from the start. In 1965 the Carnegie Endowment for International Peace prepared a contingency plan. Its report, entitled *Apartheid and United Nations Collective Measures*, envisaged naval and air operations that might ultimately culminate in a full-scale invasion of South Africa — a venture that would require at least 100,000 UN soldiers and would entail casualties ranging from 19,000 to 38,000 men. As fighting continued, the blacks in South Africa would step up their own campaign of violence and terror, the South African Defence Force would lose control over the internal situation, and the regime would collapse. The South African army is now a great deal stronger than it was in 1965, however. An invading force of 100,000 men would surely be inadequate today. Even if the political difficulties preventing UN action could be solved, the black resistance groups would lack both the arms and the organisation to play the part assigned to them by the Carnegie Endowment planners.

A South African 'D Day' would be a more difficult undertaking under present circumstances than the series of landings in North Africa and even in Normandy in World War Two. An invading force capable of quickly smashing South African resistance would require considerable numerical superiority over the defenders; no less, perhaps, than three armoured divisions, three mechanised divisions and two airborne divisions, with extensive technical and logistic support and decisive air superiority, would be required. The effort to maintain such a force would be staggering. South Africa has a limited number of ports, and they are relatively easy to defend. An invader would have no adequate bases — with harbour, supply and repair facilities — available within several thousand miles of the Cape. A seaborne force would have to be marshalled in distance cities like Rio de Janeiro or Dakar, with an advance base in Luanda. An invading force would also have to reckon with the possibility that South Africa, in desperation, might employ a few nuclear weapons on the battlefield; their employment would probably make a 'D Day' landing of the kind practised in Normandy in 1944 as obsolete as a charge of armoured knights at the battle of Agincourt.

The invaders would also have to overcome logistic difficulties. An

South Africa: A Revolutionary Situation? 223

allied army landing at Cape Town would still be a long way from the Pretoria-Johannesburg complex, South Africa's industrial heartland. Landing at Durban would add to the length of seaborne supply lines. The Durban harbour could be blocked without difficulty, and the heavy surf on the beaches south of Durban would make the use of landing craft particularly perilous. Having occupied South Africa, the victor would presumably have to administer and feed a disorganised civilian population whose supply system would probably have broken down. The political consequences of an invasion would be hard to predict. Only one thing can be said with certainty: a defeated and disorganised South Africa would not be governed by a liberal and democratic regime of the kind favoured by liberal academicians responsible for the Carnegie war plan. Defeat in war, unless it is followed by a long and effective military occupation, is apt to produce chaos or armed dictatorship. The chances of establishing a liberal, pro-Western regime in South Africa as a result of armed intervention are nil. The chaos and bloodshed of Angola are a more likely result.

The project would also encounter extraordinary political difficulties. The airlift, amphibious and engineering capabilities, together with the tremendous concentration of power needed to execute such an operation, are presently commanded only by the United States. The South Africans are convinced that the Americans will not wage such a war in Southern Africa; from the standpoint of US political, strategic and economic interests such an enterprise would indeed be sheer lunacy.

A naval blockade of South Africa might be considered a less bloody way of forcing the country to its knees. Conceivably, the UN might — at some future date — call upon the Soviet Union and its allies to blockade South African ports until South Africa agreed to dismantle its political system. The Soviet Union might perhaps accept such an assignment, given the right political atmosphere. The Soviets might even offer to work in collaboration with US naval forces as part of an international campaign against 'racism' — a campaign that would revert to the principles of the Popular Front on a global basis. International intervention could even draw on past precedents, such as the actions taken by the Great Powers against the 'Unspeakable Turk' in the nineteenth century or by the British African Squadron against slave traders.

A blockade would also entail intervention on the part of nuclear-powered vessels that were not dependent on local supplies of fuel. A blockade of South Africa would hardly affect the economy of the Warsaw Pact states; the West would be injured much more severely and Western Europe, especially Great Britain, would be affected much more seriously than the United States. A blockade would interfere with facilities for the vital tanker traffic around the Cape, and would deprive the Western nations of their commerce and their returns from South African investments.[3] The countries most seriously affected by a blockade would be backward, vulnerable states, like Mozambique, Malawi, Zambia, Lesotho, Botswana and Swaziland, that have economic ties with South Africa.

South Africa would also suffer severely. Fuel consumption would be drastically cut. Industrial production would diminish. Farming would suffer. Unemployment would increase. Living standards would fall, particularly among the Africans, who would be less able to defend their economic interests than the whites. A blockade would not by itself, however, bring about the overthrow of the regime. The country would be reduced to a siege economy that could strengthen the existing state machinery by extending its armoury of economic controls (such as rationing). South Africa is sufficiently well supplied with raw materials and industrial and scientific resources to withstand a siege. The country's only major deficiency is oil, but its dependence on imports of such essential materials is being curtailed through oil hoarding on a huge scale and through the expansion of its coal-to-oil production. In some respects South Africa might even benefit from the challenge of a blockade by being compelled to further diversify its economic production.[4] For Western interests as a whole, however, a blockade of South Africa would constitute yet another political and military defeat.

Prospects for a Violent Revolution

South Africa has a revolutionary tradition, albeit one that is very different from the left-wing stereotype. In 1914 an Afrikaner minority that was opposed to South Africa's entry into World War One took up arms. Eight years later the country was once more in the throes of an attempted revolution; white miners on the Witwatersrand went into battle in an uprising designed to protect white living standards. Their slogan, 'Workers of the world unite for a white South Africa', strangely blended racist with Communist sentiments. The rebels were organised into well armed commandos. They enjoyed a certain measure of sympathy from Afrikaner reservists in the Union Defence Force who were drawn — like the strikers — from the ranks of poverty-stricken white countrymen. According to a secret report issued by the South African

Defence Headquarters at the time, the rising was extremely dangerous and might well have overpowered Union forces had similar insurrections broken out in other urban centres.

The movement failed, but the skilled European workers were henceforth accepted into a political partnership with the ruling establishment; as a result, the promised South African revolution receded into the future. The insurrectionary forces had failed because they had not been able to secure substantial white support. They had been denied the backing of white skilled workers, technicians, foremen and industrial supervisors — a group indispensable to the success of a city-born revolutionary movement. From a national perspective, the Afrikaner people — once a semi-proletarian community containing most of South Africa's 'poor whites' — ceased to be a revolutionary element. The European working class made its peace with the establishment in return for substantial economic concessions. By World War Two the 'poor whites' had largely been absorbed into industry and service occupations. Unemployment, once the bane of white workers, ceased to be a major problem for the European workers.

The long-promised 'coming revolution' will have to depend primarily on people of African, Coloured and Indian origin. But, as we have indicated, these groups are split along ethnic and cultural lines. The Indians have little or nothing to gain from an African victory; it would place them in the same exposed position as their fellows in East Africa, where Indians have been expelled or have suffered racial discrimination. Militant intellectuals apart, Indians, Coloureds and Africans do not identify strongly with one another. The theoreticians of Black Consciousness look to a united anti-white front of all oppressed, whether they are brown or black; but studies on social attitudes between the races have provided little evidence for the growth of a collective antiwhite consciousness among educated Coloureds and Africans.[5]

The leadership of the militant opposition has suffered from serious structural weaknesses that in turn reflect the country's social structure. Political leadership has traditionally depended on white intellectuals and professional people. (According to a widespread stereotype, these have been either Jews or British South Africans, with an occasional Afrikaner thrown in, but actually Afrikaners have played a major role in the opposition — for instance 'Bram' Fischer, a leading Communist; Piet Beyleveld, an advocate of Coloured rights; and Jan Steytler, a distinguished Progressive.) The opposition, however, has failed to recruit Afrikaners into the revolutionary ranks, and this has been a serious disability in a country where previous attempts at both armed insurrection (in 1914 and 1922) and extended guerrilla war (during the South African war, 1899-1902) depended on Afrikaners. African, Indian and Coloured leadership has lacked a strong industrial base; the militant cadres have derived mainly from the ranks of clerks, teachers, lawyers, clergymen and journalists, and some from the industrial periphery — men ill suited either to run or to wreck an industrial economy.[6]

Recent changes in the composition of the industrial labour force have somewhat improved the position of the revolutionaries. Africans now occupy an increasing number of skilled and even submanagerial positions. Nevertheless, the Establishment remains strong. Managerial positions in industry have not been infiltrated, nor have leading posts in the civil service, the fighting forces and the police. Revolutionaries cannot aspire gradually to occupy leadership posts within the arms industry, the petrochemical industry, the iron and steel industries, telecommunications, aviation, the merchant marine and other such enterprises. Therefore they cannot easily disrupt the country's essential industries or take over the economy in the event of a successful revolution.

The opposition is divided and poorly organised, a subject to which we shall return. The most far-reaching claims for the allegiance of all South African revolutionaries come from the Communist Party of South Africa (SACP), founded in 1921, and the oldest Marxist-Leninist party on the African continent. It also has links with SWAPO. These bodies, like FRELIMO and MPLA, describe themselves as 'movements' or 'fronts'; in other words, they do not claim to be disciplined parties, but profess to unite 'the masses' under Marxist leadership.

A number of advantages accrue to SACP. More than any other Marxist-Leninist party in Africa, it draws support from gifted intellectuals, most of them exiled; many of these people (such as Ruth First and Brian Bunting) have become prominent in academia and have had their works published overseas. SACP and its allies also draw organisational and financial support from the Eastern Bloc. Through their publications SACP and the ANC can thus create abroad an image of great strength that is not warranted by their real numbers and influence. The *African Communist*, a quarterly published by SACP in London and printed in East Germany, holds an important position ideologically. The party is linked to a network of overseas anti-apartheid organisations — not necessarily Marxist — that are supported by liberals, humanitarians, moderate socialists and Communists who collaborate in the tradition of the Popular Front against what they regard as a Fascist and racist

South Africa: A Revolutionary Situation? 227

regime. SACP exercises varying degrees of influence in some of these organisations through the classic method of getting party members into key positions. (The Anti-Apartheid Movement in Great Britain seldom diverges from established SACP orthodoxies, while the ANC closely co-operates with the World Peace Council, a Soviet front organisation.)

The exiles' morale has gained vastly from the success of Mozambique and Angola in attaining independence, from the growing respectability accorded to Marxist-Leninist revolutionaries in the West, and from optimistic expectations concerning the future of Rhodesia and Namibia. Nevertheless, the opposition suffers from serious problems. The exiles are often out of touch with their own country; they are subject to severe internal quarrels; they (rightly) fear the activities of South African agents in their midst; and they are excessively optimistic about the chances of a quick change in their political fortunes. These are weaknesses that have been common to exiles throughout the ages. The opposition also has other deficiencies. Formal leadership within the SACP has fallen to elderly people — to men like Moses Kotane, an African veteran and the SACP Secretary-General, and Dr Yusuf M. Dadoo, the party's Indian Chairman and the successor to J.B. Marks, who died at an advanced age in 1971. The party does not publish details concerning its middle-level leadership. It relies heavily, however, on a group of men and women now in their early fifties who live abroad. (Prominent left-wing militants include Lionel and Hilda Bernstein, Brian Bunting, Fred Carneson, Joe Slovo, Ruth First (Slovo) and others.) From the African standpoint, the SACP suffers from a major deficiency: the leading expatriates are mainly white intellectuals in an army of officers without soldiers. The SACP has not tried to maintain a united front with other exiled groups, such as the Unity Movement of South Africa. The latter condemns SACP on the grounds that 'its preponderant element . . . is drawn from the White petty bourgeois intellectual section' who have 'their own Herrenvolk prejudices'.[7] Another dissident body that is at odds with SACP is the PAC (Pan-Africanist Congress of Azania [South Africa]), which was founded in 1959 by P. Leballo and the late R. Sobukwe as a breakaway movement from the ANC. The PAC censures the ANC, and also SACP, for their reliance on white leadership, their links with Moscow and their divorce from the African masses. It, too, was banned in 1960. The PAC admires the People's Republic of China, while SACP takes the Soviet Union for its model.

On the question of how revolution is to be accomplished, the resistance movements are equally divided. The PAC has an almost anarcho-syndicalist vision of a spontaneous rising in which the masses will take to arms and sweep away an important white regime. Inspired by Chinese example, the congress looks towards insurrections in the cities that will pin down the enemy's forces from the outset. These risings, supported by widespread African strikes, will in turn provide the opportunity for guerrilla warfare in the countryside. The African struggle will be prolonged. Still the insurgents will have to rely on their own efforts alone, not on UN intervention.[8]

For its part, SACP considers that the coming guerrilla struggle must be initiated in the rural areas, and must be co-ordinated with armed efforts in the cities. Armed combat, while necessary, should not be considered purely from the military standpoint, but must be conducted by 'political cadres, subordinate to the political movement', with operations 'planned to arouse and organize the masses'.[9] SACP does not view the impending confrontation as merely a local matter. South Africa occupies a key position within the world-wide capitalist system. The victories of the MPLA and FRELIMO in the former Portuguese colonies have opened a new chapter in the history of revolution. To use the party's jargon, they have introduced 'a truly qualitative change' and opened up gigantic new perspectives, 'the possibilities of which are breathtaking'.[10] Nevertheless, SACP argues, the revolution will not arrive at the tip of Russian or Cuban bayonets, but only by a united effort of all vanguard movements. The party thus looks to united action with bodies such as the South African Student Organisation (SASO) and the Black People's Convention (BCP, now also banned). SACP welcomes the growth of the Black Consciousness movement, while criticising the 'go it alone' philosophy of young black militants who are suspicious of white and Indian allies. It remains opposed both to exclusive forms of black nationalism and to 'separate development'. In SACP's view, the African 'homelands' have no future. Their inhabitants can never be more than white puppets. In practice, therefore, SACP ignores their very existence, thereby forgetting the Leninist principle that revolutionaries should operate through any institution that actually commands some degree of power.

SACP and its allies, in other words, wield little real power. Their importance has been vastly exaggerated by a curious conjunction of forces — the propaganda of SACP and its Soviet and pro-Soviet backers abroad, and the publicity given to the party by the South African government at home. The party and the South African government, each for its own purposes, have a vested interest in magnifying SACP's assumed influence, but the party's real revolutionary potential is negligible at present. The tales spread by white propagandists and red agitprops alike concerning an impending Marxist revolution in South Africa should be consigned to the realm of political fable, where they belong.

Non-violent and Semi-violent Ways to Revolution

There are many ways to start a revolution. Not all of them require mounting the barricades. Some theoreticians believe that a regime weakened from within and lacking support from the people at large might succumb to a combination of civil disobedience and strikes. In theory, the notion sounds attractive; in practice, the aim is hard to achieve in a country whose governing cadres are quite solid. In South Africa the theory was first tested during the 1950s, when the ANC launched a series of passive-resistance campaigns. The ANC hoped that these campaigns would gather irresistible momentum and would overstrain the resources of the government; hence the government would be forced to surrender. South Africa's resources, however, proved vastly superior to those available to the ANC. In the end, 'the structure of Congress and its inability to create a firm communications network capable of learning by its errors served to make Congress action self-defeating, despite its great potential of support among Africans in South Africa.'[11]

Civil disobedience has been tried in other ways. Africans have attempted at various times to oppose the government by tearing up their passes, burning down the huts of 'collaborators' in rural areas, and boycotting buses. Failures have been universally rationalised on the grounds that such campaigns helped to 'educate the masses'. In fact, such ventures have never had any lasting impact on the power structure except in the imaginations of their planners.

Industrial strikes have also been widely considered as a political weapon. Their use is by no means new in South Africa. In 1920, for instance, some 40,000 African mine-workers went on strike in an industrial disturbance that was much more extensive than those that affected South Africa during the 1960s. The strike weapon was blunted to some extent by South Africa's reliance on migrant labour (which is hard to organise) and by the influx of labour from abroad — from countries such as Mozambique, Botswana and Transkei, where wage rates are lower than they are in South Africa. Industrial action would become more effective if South Africa were to be denied the services of these labour migrants. The mine industry cannot easily do without foreign labour; only a minority (albeit an increasing one) of South African mine-workers come from within the borders of the Republic. The majority are from Lesotho and the Transkei; some also come in from Botswana and Mozambique. The coal-mining industry could exist without outside labour, but the gold-mines could hardly function, since they cannot be mechanised as easily as open-cast mining.

Industrial action in South Africa, however, faces formidable obstacles. Even if the Transkei were to develop sufficiently to be able to stop exporting its labour, Lesotho would continue to send its sons abroad. The South African labour force is ethnically split. Whites and blacks do not co-operate easily; neither do the Zulu, the Sotho, the Tswana and other black ethnic groups. There are striking contrasts between skilled and unskilled, between white-collar and blue-collar workers, and above all between workers with jobs and the unemployed.[12] These conflicts do not make the strike weapon irrelevant, however. More Africans are entering the industrial labour force. More Africans are gaining skilled and responsible positions. There are now many opportunities for successful strikes that aim at improving the workers' income and conditions. Black trade unions, which are legal, though they are denied official recognition at present, are certain to increase their bargaining power in the future.

Industrial action, however, cannot easily be turned into an insurrectionary weapon. At present the black labour force in South Africa is too isolated politically, too heterogeneous in character, too poorly organised and too unstable occupationally to stage the equivalent of, for example, the British general strike of 1926. The former British High Commission Territories, the countries along the South Africa's northern rim and the Bantustans within the country's own borders presently provide the country with a great reserve army of migrant labour. Until this army has been 'demobilised', the strike organiser's task will remain immensely difficult. Even if these obstacles were to be surmounted, strikes could hardly be used as a means of overthrowing the government. Foreign precedents for the use of strikes as a means of political warfare, compared with economic pressure, have not been encouraging. The British general strike of 1926 was a failure. The millions of foreign workers employed in Nazi Germany during World War Two could never even attempt to disorganise the German war machine.

The same objections apply to the use of riots and sabotage. Soweto,

South Africa: A Revolutionary Situation? 231

the huge black suburb serving Johannesburg, was shaken by bitter riots in June 1976, and by more violence throughout 1977. Some 600 people were killed in the 1976 riots. Rioters burned and looted in protest against government policies. The riots made effective administration of the huge township, with its 1.2 million people, infinitely difficult, and worsened relations between the government and the population. Militant students managed to persuade or coerce nearly 200,000 students in Soweto schools to boycott classes and the idea caught on; but school boycotts, however impressive, do not affect the basic power structure. In the long run, they merely limit the education obtained by the students, thus making their struggle for a good job even harder than it was in the first place. Since Soweto is more than 15 miles outside Johannesburg, its riots had little direct impact on the whites, and threatened neither projects nor businesses.

The riots threw into sharp relief the internal conflicts between young people and their elders, between men with jobs and the unemployed, between workers and students. They also gave expression to widespread African discontent.[13] Resentment is prevalent against the government's pass laws, against control of entry into the cities, against the operation of the colour bar, against a multitude of restrictions great and small, against discriminatory forms of education, against the police, and against an ever-expanding bureaucracy. The riots led to a number of administrative reforms. For instance, the South African authorities promised that Soweto would be granted full autonomy in local government. The riots, however, did not succeed in setting off a serious urban insurrection comparable to the white miners' rising in 1922; hence the country's basic structure was left unaltered.

Many of South Africa's critics simply refused to accept the inability of the rioters to change the basic structure of government. The riots supposedly expressed a new Black Consciousness that was bound to transform South Africa. Sooner or later, these critics believed, white morale would crack and South Africa would become ungovernable. They seemed to be oblivious to the fact that similar predictions had been made for a generation; every riot, every commotion had, at the time, supposedly presaged similar consequences. Over the last generation, the oppositional literature in South Africa has built up a dream world of its own, a world where time was forever 'running out', where the clock perpetually marked 'five minutes before midnight', where the consciousness of the oppressed eternally experienced new changes of a qualitative kind.

Nevertheless, the realities of power were very different. Even the

SACP, though convinced that the riots marked a new revolutionary chapter, was cautious in its analysis:

a. Despite the difficulties experienced by the enemy's law enforcement agencies in a few of the townships, the enemy and the organs of the state power were not in such a state of collapse or disruption that the capacity of the ruling class to act cohesively and to contain military actions, had been broken. The actions of a revolutionary movement, however well-organized, are not sufficient on their own to create a classical revolutionary situation. This, as Lenin has said, comes about through the maturing of special objective and subjective factors.
b. The actions themselves although widely spread were neither altogether nation-wide in character nor did they involve the mass of the rural people. In two of the major urban centres, those around Johannesburg and Cape Town, the workers responded in large numbers, but primarily as an act of solidarity, without raising any independent demands on the issue of the state power. The relatively weak response from the countryside reflects a very low level of rural liberation organization. In the towns, too, the limited response in many areas (Natal, Eastern Cape and the OFS [Orange Free State] were relatively quiet) suggests an urgent need to improve levels of political and economic organization, and of mobilization, especially at the point of production.
c. The people remain unarmed, and this fact obviously reduces the possibility of transforming the demonstration into an effective assault on state power.
d. The political general strike has a prime place in our revolutionary tactics. It is, however, fallacious to believe that, in the absence of general insurrectionary conditions, the working class can be expected to 'starve' the ruling class into political submission by protracted withdrawal of labour. We remain convinced that in the appropriate conditions, generalized industrial action will be one of the most decisive factors in the struggle for people's power.[14]

This caution was well justified. As Engels remarked of European cities at the end of the last century, conditions for urban insurrection have become militarily less favourable than they were in the past. Since the Nationalist government took over in 1948, South Africa has seen the

South Africa: A Revolutionary Situation? 233

greatest slum-clearance programme in his history. Slums like Sophiatown have disappeared. Black townships are physically segregated; they are located miles away from white cities, and government forces can regulate their access routes, electricity and water supplies. The slum-clearance projects have not only improved housing conditions, but have also given a military advantage to government forces. Most of the African population lives in small houses laid out along straight roads that can be controlled by armoured cars and helicopters, and there are few urban jungles such as those of Algeria, where guerrillas can seek hideouts in a maze of alleys, backyards and winding lanes. A huge urban aggregation like Soweto provides some cover, but not a secure one. Soweto provides an excellent setting for the urban riot, which has traditionally been the weapon of the unemployed, the uprooted, the unpolitical looter and the politicised young. Historically, however, riots alone have not proved to be effective means of crushing a determined government. Unarmed or poorly armed rioters cannot seize the means of production or of governance, as the widespread but wholly unsuccessful outbreaks in 1953 in East Germany showed. The police in South Africa are permitted to use firearms in case of need, and they do so. The white population at large is plentifully supplied with weapons; hence riots cannot easily spill from the black into the white areas. The courts, the legislature and the mass media do not provide convenient sounding boards for violent protests.

Violent outbreaks may in fact strengthen government control by cementing white unity across class lines. Commotions that are confined to the African townships are likely to destroy only public facilities set aside for the use of Africans; hence violence may have the unanticipated result of opening new rifts within the black population. The aftermath of new riots may create a mood of despondency once the initial euphoria has passed and the government has had yet another opportunity to display its might. The government crackdown after Sharpeville in 1960 largely broke overt African opposition to the regime. This time Black Consciousness and the discontent of the youth may sustain the opposition; far more blacks are in school now than in 1961, and a mood of political activity may well follow in 1979. But reports from South Africa show that overt resistance has stopped in Soweto — the students are back in school.

Most important, the blacks lack a united political leadership. There is, indeed, a good deal of discontent. Many urban Africans are restless and insecure. Crime is rife in the black townships. Jobs are hard to get and to keep. The cost of living, moreover, keeps rising, and inflation always strikes hardest at the poor. Militants cannot easily get arms, however, and the masses are unwilling to rise at the sound of the clarion, for the price of failure is too high and the chance of success too small. As urban African leaders emerge they are arrested, detained, banned or driven into exile and their movements suppressed. No single African, Indian or Coloured leader or group has been able seriously to challenge the government and survive to operate internally. Through its use of preventive arrests and police informers the government has been able to remove or to neutralise every opposition movement to date. Youth leaders since 1976 have faced the same problem. There can be no growth of leadership if it is constantly changing. The government's pass system puts enormous obstacles in the way of organising a national movement, and there are no signs that these difficulies are close to resolution.

The Future of Guerrilla Warfare

According to would-be revolutionaries, the surest way to victory in South Africa is through guerrilla warfare. Guerrilla warfare has become a subject of popular debate. Many revolutionary intellectuals now look to this kind of combat as the answer to all revolutionary problems — as a means of radicalising the masses. Guerrilla warfare has acquired an aura of romance that once was reserved for the exploits of cowboys in the Far West. Yet the annals of guerrilla warfare are full of failures as well as successes. It is neither a romantic nor a new tactic, nor is it an infallible recipe for success.[15]

There are a number of well defined routes that guerrillas have successfully taken in the past. The incumbent power, weakened by war and disillusioned in its mission, may battle for possession of a transmaritime province and finally give up, unwilling to face continued internal opposition, foreign disapproval and vast expenditures. Such was the case of Great Britain in Ireland after World War One, and of France in Indo-China and Algeria after World War Two. In both cases, public opinion in the metropole proved decisive in creating a climate for withdrawal. Progressives now believe that London and New York can somehow be transformed into South Africa's metropole — a metropole that can secure the surrender of its colonial or neocolonial 'possession' by financial, diplomatic or military pressure on its satraps in Pretoria. This model, however, has no application to South Africa — hence the progressives' baffled indignation and their suspicion that a good cause is being betrayed by evil men. Alternatively, guerrillas can win if they are supported by an effective regular army. Wellington's British army in Spain rendered indispensable assistance to Spanish guerrillas fighting the armies of Napoleon. The Red Army liberated Belgrade in World War Two, thereby helping Tito's forces to win. North Vietnamese regular forces redeemed the weaknesses of Communist guerrilla fighters in South Vietnam and finally won the war. In South Africa, however, the guerrillas cannot mobilise regular forces of the kind that Mao Tse-tung considered indispensable to victory in guerrilla warfare.

The Portuguese experience was rather different. In Portuguese Africa the government forces were themselves radicalised by the experience of the guerrilla war. The Portuguese colonial empire collapsed — not because the army was defeated, but because its Portuguese officer corps became disillusioned with the war, overthrew the Lisbon government, and, in the case of Mozambique, actually helped to install a FRELIMO government against the efforts of FRELIMO's local white and black opponents. The South African army, however, does not suffer from the class and status divisions that plagued the Portuguese army; the South African armed forces are local bodies, not metropolitan ones. South Africans would be fighting at home, not overseas, and for their own survival, not for other people's property. Their armed forces represent the more youthful part of the white electorate; they may well act as a liberalising element within the body politic, but hardly as a means of overthrowing the government.

The chances for guerrilla warfare are equally good in a society whose ruling class is divided, dispirited or corrupt, as was apparently the case in Vietnam. From the partisans' standpoint, the ruling class should be incapable of further developing the country's resources; political institutions that sustain the government should have degenerated to such an extent that they serve as brakes on economic expansion. The coercive machinery of the state — the army and the police — should be easily penetrable by the revolutionaries; better still, the military forces should have suffered crushing defeat in a foreign war. The opposition should be united, and be guided by a determined and cohesive party.

None of these conditions exists in South Africa. The most radical European dissidents are to be found in the churches and universities; their professional aspirations and styles of life in themselves prevent them from penetrating the army, the administration and the police. The state machinery is efficient. The ruling groups are confident. Part of this confidence derives from the extraordinary growth in the country's economic potential, as we have noted elsewhere. Above all, the revolutionaries have no working model of an African society that is capable of appealing even to a powerful minority within the European community. Neither in civil liberties nor in economic development have the records of independent African countries like Equatorial Guinea, Uganda, Zaire, Mozambique or Angola been such as to inspire confidence among the whites.

Guerrilla organisers in South Africa presently face a vast array of administrative obstacles. The security forces are watchful and reasonably well informed. The police force, with its intelligence network, is more efficient and better remunerated than its opposite number in pre-revolutionary societies such as late-nineteenth-century Russia. The government exercises numerous administrative restraints upon any revolutionary body; for instance, both pass legislation and the registration book that must be carried by all Africans make it difficult for them to move around the country and to organise the masses. Revolutionaries have no means of disrupting the army, either by military defeat or by subverting its morale; yet this task is one they must carry out if they are to be guided by history. It was military defeat or demoralisation that provided the impetus for the English revolution of 1640, the Russian revolution of 1917, the German revolution of 1918 and the Portuguese revolution of 1974. The revolutionaries in South Africa do not understand how to weaken the white civilian cadres. Neither black militants nor their white allies in churches and universities know how to speak the language of white workers, farmers or businessmen. Members of the left-wing intelligentsia, commonly a diploma-bearing salariat dependent on public employment, are apt to treat workers and businessmen with the snobbish disdain that Jane Austen's gentlemen and gentlewomen once felt for persons engaged in 'trade'. In practice, the intellectuals' assumptions and terminology may unwittingly service a counter-revolutionary purpose in South Africa.

South African revolutionaries have taken heart from the guerrilla victory in Zimbabwe. But Zimbabwe cannot easily serve as a revolutionary paradigm. The 250,000 Rhodesian whites were but a fraction of South Africa's. Rhodesia's GNP and defence budget were puny when compared with South Africa's. (The respective figures in 1978 were: $3.1 billion and $442 million as against $43.8 billion and $2.6 billion.) Nevertheless, the guerrilla threat needs to be taken seriously. The ANC remains allied to SWAPO. The USSR is their chief arms supplier. Arms used in Zimbabwe included the AK 47 assault rifle, the Tokarov pistol, the DSHK M 38/46 multipurpose heavy machine gun, the RPG antitank bazooka and the PMD land mine. Zimbabwe forms an exposed salient; its defenders have to guard a huge border that skirts Mozambique, Botswana and Zambia. The northern border of Namibia is also long, but is patrolled more easily than that of Zimbabwe. South Africa, on the other hand, has so far largely been shielded from assault. A guerrilla attack in strength against South Africa would face a host of technical problems.

Guerrillas have tried to prenetrate South Africa through Botswana, with the Zambezi crossing point to Kazungula serving as a 'freedom ferry'. Botswana, however, is itself in an exposed position. Economically dependent on South Africa, geographically enfolded by Zimbabwe, South Africa and Namibia, Botswana has to tread carefully. The South Africans have strengthened frontier-control checkpoints, tightened the laws on travel documentation, increased border patrols, and assigned a fleet of motor boats to operate on the Zambezi along the Caprivi strip. Partisans who are under the command of SWAPO and depend heavily on Ovambo support are in action on the northern border of Namibia, but their military impact has been small. The level of 'incidents' declined sharply during 1977; most casualties were caused by mines rather than small-arms fire. At the time of writing, SWAPO was reported to have only a few hundred men in the field; it depended on bases in Angola, where although its relations with the MPLA were cordial, the rulers could give it little help. SWAPO was hardly in a position to make serious headway against the powerful concentration of South African troops in the northern part of Namibia. Even if those troops were to surrender their present position there, topographical factors alone would render a large-scale partisan assault on South Africa from that location extremely difficult.

Similar considerations apply to partisan attacks from Mozambique. A large part of the border is covered by Kruger National Park, a vast depopulated area that provides South Africa with a buffer zone. The most vulnerable section of the border lies in the area that abuts on Swaziland and Natal. Guerrillas would surely try to use these regions as 'ports of entry' into South Africa, preventing government forces from sealing off all borders. The country's physical size, however, would pose enormous logistic problems for the guerrillas, while government forces could rely on an excellent system of roads and airfields. Furthermore, the border with Mozambique has been cleared of trees and shrubs to the depth of a mile, and this cleared area has been mined, lighted and patrolled. Guerrillas might conceivably try to counter some of these obstacles by sending sabotage teams into South Africa as labour migrants. Infiltration, however, must overcome the ever-present threat from informers, and the fact that registration books and pass laws greatly restrict the ability of underground fighters to move around inside the country.

Future guerrilla attacks against South Africa are certain to be accompanied by urban terrorism. Attempts will be made to assassinate policemen and to attack Europeans at random by setting off bombs in restaurants, supermarkets, cinemas and oil refineries. Sporadic attempts at sabotage, begun in the 1960s, may well be stepped up in order to weaken white resolve, disrupt industrial production, and interfere with the operation of essential services. This type of warfare, however, is subject to severe limitations, even if revolutionaries were able to solve the difficult technical problems involved in starting such a campaign under South African conditions. The civilian population, including the African people, are likely to be alienated by the disruption of essential services and indiscriminate killing. Hungry and homeless people, moreover, become more dependent on government relief, not less so.

A modern industrial economy can easily be hampered by sabotage, but it can only be put out of action by air power applied on a gigantic scale. (Well trained German saboteurs aided by widespread civilian resistance could not prevent French occupation of the Ruhr in 1923, and neither the German blitz nor 'V' weapons — to give a more spectacular example — could knock out Great Britain in World War Two, despite all pre-war predictions.) Thus the ability of saboteurs to damage the South African economy is puny.

Some theoreticians believe that a well planned campaign of urban terror might destroy the present mood of confidence among the whites. Even though physical damage might be kept within tolerable bounds, it is argued that European morale would disintegrate if enough bombs were set off in supermarkets and cinemas. Past experience in Kenya, wartime experience in occupied Europe or present-day occurrences in Ulster, Lebanon or Israel, however, suggest that terror only pays temporary dividends, and that ordinary men and women can adjust to perils with astonishing resilience.

Alternatively, urban guerrillas might concentrate on murdering police officers and their families. According to theoreticians of terrorism like Carlos Marighella, the police would thus be provoked into taking repressive measures that, in turn, would cause the police to be more hated by the people and would thereby accelerate a breakdown of police morale. Irish guerrillas adopted this strategy during the Anglo-Irish hostilities of 1919-21, with the result that the Royal Irish Constabulary simply collapsed. The Irish precedent, however, cannot easily be reproduced in South Africa. The morale of the Irish police had already been weakened by a government policy of financial stringency, by government insistence on submitting all security work to the test of political expediency, and by the hostility to which the police had been exposed in the press, in Parliament, and in many courts and juries. The South African Establishment is better organised, more cohesive and more efficient than the former British 'ascendancy' in Ireland. The tasks of breaking down police morale and establishing 'no-go' areas in South African towns would be infinitely more difficult than they were then in Ireland.

In the future, guerrillas may well prove to be a serious nuisance to South Africans.[16] Partisans may be expected to increase small-scale attacks as well as to create a certain amount of urban terrorism, possibly supplemented by 'external efforts' such as attacks on South African consulates and the overseas headquarters of South African firms. Guerrillas may also attempt to hijack South African planes or to sabotage South African ships. They will intensify their attacks in the future. One day South Africa may have to face convergent raids from Mozambique, Zimbabwe, Botswana and Namibia, with foreign military formations – Cuban, Nigerian and such – stationed on the Republic's doorstep. The effectiveness of guerrilla raids, however, is strictly limited, as the Israeli example has shown. South Africa probably has contingency plans for strikes against neighbouring bases in the event of all-out war, or even the kind of war that gets into the headlines in the Middle East. South African resources are much greater than Israel's, and its geographical size is almost sixty times greater; hence South Africans can rely upon defence in a manner unthinkable to the Israelis. Partisans, however well organised, cannot paralyse the economy, the armed forces or the state. Theoreticians of guerrilla warfare argue that South Africa cannot possibly wage an anti-insurgency campaign while at the same time maintaining a sophisticated industrial economy, given the relative paucity of the country's white population. This argument, however, ignores the experience of Rhodesia, which – contrary to the forecasts made by most of the real or assumed experts – managed for fourteen years to resist an international boycott and the assaults of partisans from abroad, strengthen its armed forces, and at the same time expand and diversify its economy, even though the proportion of whites to blacks in Rhodesia was much smaller (1:24) than it is in

240 *South Africa: A Revolutionary Situation?*

South Africa (1:5).

Given the present conditions, hopes for a violent overthrow of the South African system — either by a foreign invasion or by internal or external guerrilla assaults — belong in the realm of military fantasy.

Notes

1. In August 1977 General Ignatius Acheampong promised increased training facilities in Ghana to SWAPO. Brigadier Shehu Musa Yar Adua, the Nigerian chief of staff, promised additional backing to the Southern African liberation movements in the form of financial, moral and diplomatic support, as well as of military training. He also promised that the Nigerian army would intervene if any independent African state were to be attacked by a Southern African regime. He added that much as the Nigerian armed forces would like to fight alongside the liberation forces, the latter had not requested any such help. FBIS-SSA 77-148 (2 August 1977), p.D1.
2. According to recent estimates, by 1978 these comprised 20,000-22,000 Cubans. The Angolan army proper was estimated at about 32,000 men.
3. According to a study completed by the British Association of Industries in 1977, a boycott of South Africa would increase British unemployment by 70,000, as one of her most prosperous overseas markets (£600 million a year) would have to be sacrificed. South Africa would be most seriously affected in terms of fuel consumption, but even so, it is not as vulnerable as many observers think. South Africa does not run on oil. Of the country's energy needs, only one-quarter is based on oil; the remaining three-quarters are based on coal.
4. Rhodesia thus diversified her economic production in two world wars, when supplies from Great Britain became scanty. In a little-known ersatz industries venture, German East Africa created a whole range of small-scale substitute manufactures during World War One when the infant colony was totally cut off from the Reich and yet managed to carry on with the help of local resources for about two years.
5. See Tables 3.9, 3.10 and 3.11 in Chapter 3.
6. Anthony Sampson, *The Treason Cage: the Opposition Trial in South Africa* (Heinemann, London, 1958), includes an appendix listing the social background of 156 leaders accused in the treason trial that lasted from 1956 to 1961. Full statistical accuracy is not possible on the basis of the information given, but certain features clearly emerge. The oppositional leadership came almost entirely from the towns; only three of the men in the dock made their living by farming. The largest professional group was made up of clerks, who numbered at least 35 out of the original 156, and probably more. There was a large group of professionals — about 36 persons — composed almost entirely of physicians, clergymen, teachers and journalists. Leadership in modern industry was represented by a solitary industrial chemist. Altogether, the white-collar occupations accounted for at least 93 out of the original 156, including the great majority of the leaders. The working-class element may have included about 28 persons, 9 of whom appear to have been unskilled and 14 factory workers or truck drivers; only 5 people would be ranked as highly skilled, and they were employed mainly in jobs on the industrial periphery, such as cabinet-making, dressmaking and photography. The 'strategic' industries were not significantly represented. There were also some 29 people variously described as 'veteran campaigners', organisers, or just plain 'agitators' whose incomes probably derived wholly or in part from the

organisations they helped to lead.

7. See I.B. Tabata, *The Awakening of the People* (Spokesman Books, London, 1974), and idem, *Imperialist Conspiracy* (Prometheus Publishing Company, Lusaka, 1974).

8. For an account favourable to the PAC, see Richard Gibson, *African Liberation Movements: Contemporary Struggles against White Minority Rule* (Oxford University Press, Oxford, 1972). A more recent study is R.W. Johnson, *How Long Will South Africa Survive?* (Macmillan, London, 1977).

9. *The African Communist*, vol. 43 (1973), pp. 60-1.

10. Ibid., vol. 64 (1976), pp. 30-1.

11. Edward Feit, *African Opposition in South Africa: the Failure of Passive Resistance* (Hoover Institution Press, Stanford, 1967), p. 193. The standard history of the ANC is Peter Walshe, *The Rise of African Nationalism in South Africa: the African National Congress, 1912-1952* (University of California Press, Berkeley, 1971).

12. Figures on the extent of African unemployment vary greatly; so does the definition of 'unemployment'. Estimates ranges from 900,000 to 2 million unemployed. The lower figure seems more acceptable but still high. On the other hand, unemployment among Europeans has not assumed major proportions. This disparity between employment figures for whites and blacks — and the disparity in skills and in economic resources available to white and black workers — remain great. Hence outside economic pressure on South Africa, even if it were successful, would hit black workers, the weaker partners in the labour force, with greater severity than Europeans.

Inside South Africa foreign investment has become basically a class issue among blacks, Coloureds and Indians. Workers, businessmen and other people who earn their money in the private sector want continued foreign investment. Academics, ministers, welfare workers and teachers oppose new investments and some even call for divestment. Black trade unionists such as Lucy Mvubelo of the National Union of Clothing Workers call for more investments because that will mean more jobs for blacks. Chief Gatsha Buthelezi, leader of the Zulus, changed his mind last year about new investments; he now wants economic sanctions to be imposed on South Africa because of the Biko incident, but he is not advocating the withdrawal of companies.

13. See Tables 3.9, 3.10 and 3.11 in Chapter 3.

14. 'The Way Forward from Soweto: Political Report Adopted by the Plenary Session of the Central Committee of the South African Communist Party, April 1977', *The African Communist*, vol. 70 (Third Quarter, 1977), pp. 31-2.

15. See L.H. Gann, *Guerrillas in History* (Hoover Institution Press, Stanford, 1971).

16. According to a statement made by Major General W. Black, head of general operations in the South African Defence Force, South Africa has initially entered the stage of classical insurgency war through internal subversion, sabotage and terrorism. The enemy will attempt to widen the scope of guerrilla operations with the object of overextending the security forces to such an extent that certain areas could be taken over by the partisans. These regions would then serve as bases to spread the war.

For other studies attempting to assess the direction of South Africa's drift, see, for instance, Leonard Thompson and Jeffrey Butler (eds.), *Change in Contemporary South Africa* (University of California Press, Berkeley, 1975); Johnson, *How Long will South Africa Survive?*; and Ian Robertson and Philipp Whitten (eds.), *Race and Politics in South Africa* (Transaction Books, New Brunswick, NJ, 1978).

PART THREE:

SOUTH AFRICA AND THE WORLD

8 SOUTH AFRICA AND THE WEST

A World War Two cartoon by David Low shows Hitler listening to a famous speech by General Smuts broadcast over the BBC in support of the British. Looking at Smuts's picture, the Führer muses, 'How they must have tortured the poor man!' Low's cartoon represented both British hatred of Hitler and British admiration for the Premier of South Africa.

Smuts was indeed a popular man in London. The former Boer guerrilla leader had become a British field marshal; he held a high place in British war councils; he later became a founder of the United Nations. His country's reputation stood equally high in the Western world. South Africa's allegiance to the Western powers in World War Two was much more important than it had been in World War One. During the desperate years, 1939-41, South Africa stood by the British in the war against Nazi Germany when both the Soviet Union and the United States were neutral. South Africans distinguished themselves in many theatres of war. Without South African port facilities, Great Britain could hardly have continued to fight in the Middle East. South African gold resources were important in maintaining British financial stability during World War Two and its aftermath.

South African Economic Links to the West

Great Britain's South African connection is of old standing. Modern South Africa, as we have seen, is in many ways a British imperial creation. The Union of South Africa was originally a prototype of what modern Marxists would call a neocolonial dependency. The Union of South Africa initially depended on Great Britain for most of its imported capital, for foreign markets, advanced technological and scientific skills, for its diplomatic representation abroad and its naval protection from foreign enemies. South Africa thus was a British economic dependency. South African mining magnates like Cecil Rhodes and Alfred Beit supported British scholarship connected with South Africa; the dignified architecture of Rhodes House in Oxford still serves as a visual reminder of a chapter in Anglo-South African history that has long since passed.

During and after World War Two, South Africa increasingly emancipated itself from British economic tutelage; the British share in the South African economy steadily declined. Yet the British stake in South Africa remains far from insignificant. South Africa is an important purchaser of British merchandise and a major source of supply for British imports. (In 1977 the value of Britain's South African commerce was worth several times her trade with the Argentine. South African imports from the United Kingdom amounted to £581,063,000; exports to the United Kingdom stood at £879,724,000. The corresponding figures for the Argentine were £130,271,000 and £120,040,000, respectively. The sterling area, moreover, still accounted for the largest share of South Africa's foreign investments, about 58 per cent in 1978.) After a remarkable growth of some 700 per cent during the 1960s, however, the proportion of British investments began to decline relative to that of Continental Europe — about 24 per cent at the time of writing — and the dollar area, now about 18 per cent.

Nevertheless, the British stake in South Africa is still of considerable importance, vastly more important to the British domestic economy than the corresponding American or West German shares are to the economies of their respective countries. South Africa accounts for about 9 per cent of Britain's total foreign lendings and 14 per cent of Britain's overseas earnings. The loss of Britain's South African holdings, whether brought about through outright confiscation or the effects of an economic blockade, would be an economic disaster for the British.[1]

Western Europeans also have a considerable economic interest in South Africa. A study by the policy planning division of the German Foreign Office showed that 48 minerals essential to Germany industry were imported from South Africa. Seven of these minerals were considered critical. In the case of manganese, Germany's dependence on South Africa is so great that a 30 per cent cutback in supplies would cause a quarter of all German factories to close their doors within three months; the number of unemployed might rise to 7 million.[2] France likewise has a considerable economic stake in South Africa, a major customer for French arms. France herself has no oil and little coal, and therefore invests heavily in nuclear power, so that the South African connection remains a valuable economic asset. Despite left-wing efforts to turn the South African question into a major political affair, South Africa remains a side issue in French politics.

In economic terms, the American connection is not as important to South Africa as the link to Western Europe. But given US political power, South African foreign policy must hinge for the time being on maintaining at least tolerable relations with the transatlantic giant. American contacts with Southern Africa are of long standing. American trading vessels and whalers were a common sight in Cape Town from the end of the eighteenth century. During the nineteenth century, American missionaries — including black missionaries from the African Methodist Episcopal Church — helped to spread a knowledge of the Gospel among the blacks, along with literacy and a variety of industrial and agricultural skills. As the frontier closed in the West, American scouts, hunters and soldiers of fortune drifted to the edge of the Southern African frontier.

Americans took a particularly important part in the development of South Africa's mining industry. By the 1870s and 1880s the United States was the world's foremost mineral producer. Americans, more than members of any other nation, probably had more engineers. geologists, mine operators and other experts within their borders, and hundreds of these experts ended up working the gold and diamond fields of South Africa. Even though most of the capital in the South African mines derived from overseas British or local South African sources, the United States exported a variety of people, technical skills and capital goods. Americans had much success, for instance, in selling ox wagons at the Cape. They were active in agricultural improvements. The South African citrus and wine industries and the Rhodesian tobacco industry owed a great debt to US pioneers. American missionaries helped to introduce the cultivation of rice, cotton and cane sugar to South African blacks.[3] Americans also made their names as veterinary surgeons and agricultural scientists, as well as in many other fields.

Americans even took some part in South African military affairs. South Africa was remote from the United States, but Americans were stirred by the South African War of 1899-1902. As volunteers, they fought on both sides (Irish-Americans tended to fight alongside the Boers) and took part in the post-war reconstruction. General W.C. Gorgas of Panama fame, for instance, reorganised the health services of the Rand mines. Teachers from the United States played their part in the development of South Africa's academic life. Industrial training for blacks owed much to Booker T. Washington and to Tuscaloosa and Tuskegee. American industrialists had a share in South Africa's incipient industrial revolution. American capital, at Herbert Hoover's suggestion, helped set off industrial development in the 1920s and 1930s; the influx of American manufacturing skill began in 1924 when Ford opened its first South African automobile assembly plant.

After World War Two there was a striking increase in American investments, and by the mid-1970s American funds placed in South Africa amounted to an estimated 17 per cent of all foreign holdings in that area (see Table 8.1). At the same time, there was a considerable increase in South African-US trade, and by 1975 the United States had acquired a fairly substantial share in South Africa's foreign commerce (see Table 8.2). These figures have to be kept in perspective, however. In terms of total US foreign trade and investment, the South African connection amounts to little, as indicated by Table 8.3.

Nevertheless, the number of American firms operating in South Africa is considerable (about 350 in 1979), although most US investment in South Africa (book value about $1.6 billion) derives from a relatively small number of companies.[4] Major corporations include Union Carbide (a great chrome producer), Newmont Mining, Kennecott Copper Corporation, Phelps Dodge, United States Steel, American Metal Climax and others; these have played valuable parts in the transfer of capital and new technologies to South Africa. The manufacturing component of American investment is particularly important. In 1970 more than 50 per cent of those funds were placed in manufacturing industries, 10 per cent in mining and 25 per cent in petroleum. Americans are particularly important in the development of advanced technology. Ford and General Motors hold about a third of the automobile market. American firms dominate the market for computers which, at the present time, are still being imported from abroad. Caltex, Mobil and Exxon have a 40 per cent share in South Africa's market for petroleum products. US firms have helped to build up South Africa's refining capacity and thus they contribute to supplying South Africa with energy, about a quarter of which derives from petroleum. US capital has been invested in the mining of gold, diamonds and various base metals. In addition, Americans are deeply involved in heavy engineering, in the manufacture of agricultural, mining and construction equipment, in the rubber industry and in electronics. Their interests are concerned with a wide variety of services, including banking, shipping and insurance.

How are these investments to be evaluated? Opinion in the United States is bitterly divided. The National Association for the Advancement of Colored People (NAACP), hardening its stand, now calls for total withdrawal of American firms from South Africa. Some universities, church groups and foundations have decided to sell their stock holdings in South African firms. According to a senior General Electric executive quoted in *Time*, 'no responsible firm today could ignore the concerns of large blocks of shareholders in the churches and universities'.[5]

Table 8.1: Total Foreign Liabilities in South Africa, 1975 (R million)

Region	Amount
European Economic Community	9,851
Other European nations	1,690
Americas[a]	3,566
Africa	498
Asia	348
Oceania	85
International organisations and other sources	412
Total	16,450

Note: a. Capital derived from the Americas comes mainly from the United States. Investments from Canada are often made by companies that are wholly or partly owned by Americans.

Source: Nedbank Group, *South Africa: an Appraisal* (Johannesburg, 1977), p. 225.

Table 8.2: Exports and Imports to and from Major Trade Partners, 1975 (R million)

Country	Amount	Percentage
Exports		
United Kingdom	903.7	
Japan	487.3	
United States	429.7	
West Germany	426.8	
Belgium	137.1	
Switzerland	170.6	
Other countries	1,351.7	
Total	3,906.9	
Imports		
United States	985.0	21.4
West Germany	1,033.9	18.1
United Kingdom	1,097.3	17.8
Japan	612.0	10.3
France	244.8	4.1
Italy	203.4	3.7
Other countries	1,392.1	24.6
Total	5,568.5	100.0

Source: Nedbank Group, *South Africa: an Appraisal*, pp. 204, 214.

Table 8.3: American-South African Trade in the US Context, 1977 (R million)

	Amount
Gross national product	1,899,600.00
Gross domestic investment	195,500.00
Exports: to all foreign countries	120,163.20
to South Africa	1,054.40
Imports: from all foreign countries	146,816.70
from South Africa	1,268.80

Source: US Department of Commerce, *Survey of Current Business* (July 1978).

Advocates of reform — such as the Reverend Leon Sullivan, a black minister from Phildelphia and a director of General Motors — demand that South Africa must be changed from within. Apartheid is to be overcome through a strict code of business conduct outlawing racial discrimination, assisting the technical training and the promotion of blacks, and encouraging the formation of trade unions. In 1977 more than a hundred American firms signed the Sullivan Code, drawn up by the Reverend Sullivan. The code states that eating facilities and toilets must be desegregated; it demands equal employment opportunities, equal pay for equal work, apprenticeship and management trainee programmes for blacks and browns as well as whites, improvements in living conditions for non-whites, support for unionisation, and promotion of non-whites to higher posts.

The makers of the Sullivan Code assume, as do the radicals, that American capitalists have the power to change Third World countries by manipulating their power structure through economic pressure. This assumption is a dubious one. The advancement of Africans and Coloureds in industry did not start with the Sullivan Code, and is linked to wider structural changes in the South African economy. (The wage differential between whites and blacks is smallest in the most advanced industries, in services like insurance and banking and — the academic stereotype notwithstanding — in the central government.) The impact of the Sullivan Code can, at best, be marginal. The same applies to American industrial investments in general. The industrial revolution was not brought about by American enterprise in South Africa. American firms merely strengthened an existing trend. In our opinion, the development of manufacturing industries is wholly beneficial. Industries develop new skills; these skills, in the long run, benefit the entire labour force. Manufacturing industries, on the whole, pay higher wages than extractive industries, and the benefits of these wages have percolated downwards, albeit slowly. Lastly, the development of manufacturing has encouraged the development of an internal market. Blacks and Coloureds are now being valued not merely as hands, but also as customers — perhaps the most far-reaching departure in the social history of South Africa.

Pro-South African Lobbies in the West

Given the importance of Great Britain's economic stake in South Africa, given also a long history of Anglo-South African co-operation, pro-South African feelings might be expected to be strong in Great Britain. The opposite is the case, even though many British firms have a stake in the area. (British and South African multinational corporations are closely interlocked. The Anglo-American Corporation of South Africa, for instance, one of South Africa's greatest mining corporations, is linked to such British firms as Johnson Matthey, the Selection Trust, Chartered Consolidated, and to numerous enterprises in countries as far afield as the United States, Canada, Indonesia, Brazil, Zambia, Austrialia and Ireland.) British firms with South African links, however, do not act as a concerted pro-South African lobby. Their political influence in no wise corresponds to their economic importance. Their economic interests do not necessarily converge; they do not form a united bloc; their power does not measure up to that of a liberal-minded bureaucracy; they cannot rely on a great body of pro-South African opinion.

Since World War Two South Africa has attracted British emigrants in large numbers (see Chapter 1). But the emigrants' friends and relatives are too diverse, too scattered and too unorganised to affect British thinking about South Africa. The prosperity, real or supposed, of the emigrants in the Antipodes is as likely to arouse envy as it is to produce sympathy for expatriate kinsmen overseas. The British Tory Party was friendlier in its attitude towards South Africa than was Labour. The Tories had traditionally supported conservative white South African leaders like Smuts in Pretoria and Lord Malvern in Salisbury, whom the Tories regarded more or less as men like themselves. But the advent of the National Party in 1948 and the elevation of Ian Smith to the Southern Rhodesian Prime Minister's office in 1964 appeared to many old-fashioned Tories almost as an impious reversal of the natural order — victories gained by small-town politicians over their social betters. Right-wing Tories might continue to back South Africa for economic or strategic motives, but never for emotional reasons. The Labour Party, widely pro-Boer during the South African War, later transferred its sympathies for the underdog from Afrikaners to Africans. Right-wing radical movements such as the National Front wield no real power in British politics, and their racially inspired support for the Pretoria regime tarnishes rather than brightens South Africa's image overseas.

European Continental powers are less affected by the conscience vote than are English-speaking countries. The German Federal Republic has often expressed its opposition to all forms of racial discrimination. But Germany, alone among the world powers, has openly criticised the Anti-Apartheid Movement for its ulterior motives. Stung by repeated criticism concerning the alleged nuclear axis between Bonn and Pretoria, the German Federal Press and Information Office issued a document that identified the ANC and the German division of the Anti-Apartheid Movement as responsible for the campaign. According to the Germans, the primary objective of the instigators was not to end apartheid but to lower the international standing and credibility of the German Federal Republic, thereby striking at the West as a whole and strengthening the position of the Soviet Union in international affairs. The French, like the Germans, are inclined to be fairly pragmatic in their dealings with South Africa. French skill and French capital have played a major part, for instance, in building up the South African armament industry, yet Paris has managed to maintain good relations with most countries of black Africa.

In terms of world politics, however, the American connection matters more to Pretoria than do its links with London, Paris and Bonn. The task of maintaining these links will not be easy. To the great majority of Americans, South Africa is a remote land about whose affairs they know little and care less. Most of them would have trouble locating the Transvaal on the map. Its political and racial problems are far removed from the ordinary life of the people in the United States whose thoughts are preoccupied with domestic and local affairs. The debate concerning South Africa, bitter and strident as it may be, concerns only a minority who as often as not are quite unaware of their countrymen's lack of concern.

Party politics plays but a limited part in the US debate concerning

South Africa. During the last two decades or so, American political parties have provided less patronage than they did in the past. The party structure has weakened. The all-embracing division between liberals and conservatives cuts across both parties. American political parties today must deal with electors who are more free than their ancestors from ties of acknowledged class affiliation, ethnic affinity and regional loyalties. Within Congress, power has become more diffuse. In the House of Representatives alone there are now more than 140 subcommittees, some of them wielding a great deal of influence. Congressmen thus have grown more responsible to 'single-issue' pressure groups organised into lobbies or political action groups. The special interest groups have to work through their allies in Congress, in the congressional staff, and in those agencies of the bureaucracy that regard particular interest groups as their constituencies.

White South Africa has no ethnic lobby of its own in the United States. There is no Afrikaner, no British South African vote of the kind that can be mobilised, for example, on behalf of Israel, Greece or Ireland. White 'Middle America' commonly has a vague feeling of sympathy for the whites in Southern Africa, sometimes because of — and sometimes in spite of — the white Africans' racial outlook. But the sentiment of racial kinship is too little focused to be mobilised for political purposes. Sentiments of racial kinship would only become a force in America if racial hostilities within the United States were to be violently exacerbated, or — more likely — if 'Middle America' should become much more exasperated than at present with the conscience vote and its good causes.

American corporations with holdings in South Africa do not supply the equivalent of an ethnic lobby. Business lobbies are only really effective where specific, narrowly defined issues are concerned that are of direct financial importance to particular firms. But American entrepreneurs, for the most part, are not interested in the collective — as opposed to the sectional — interests of capitalism. Gulf Oil does business in the Marxist People's Republic of Angola where its installations are protected by Cuban troops.

Overall, US businessmen tend to be defensive rather than aggressive, especially on questions of 'social responsibility' — including apartheid — issues of particular concern to South Africa. The stakes held by American firms in South Africa are not of sufficient importance to their world-wide interests to justify serious public relations risks. Contrary to widespread assumptions, the rate of profits earned on American investments in South Africa is actually lower than in the rest of Africa.[6] US firms with financial stakes in South Africa are unlikely to play a major part in a political confrontation, unless they are forced to disinvest in a manner that would cost them a great deal of money. Otherwise they are likely to go along with piecemeal reforms under the Sullivan Code, which American managers tend to approve on economic as well as moral grounds.

The closest thing to a pro-South African lobby is found in some conservative groups within the United States. These groups sympathise with South Africa as a Christian country, an anti-Communist bastion, a strategic asset, a bulwark of white supremacy, or a defender of capitalism. White South Africa receives a good deal of sympathy among members of the American gun lobby and among former Green Berets who regard South Africa as a stronghold of the West. South Africa often enjoys high regard among evangelical Christians, respectful of a country that bans pornographic literature. But the defenders of South Africa, like its opponents, think primarily in American domestic terms; they are apt to project domestic American concerns on the African screen. African issues on their own cut no ice in American politics. Senator Dick Clark, a militant liberal and head of the influential Subcommittee on African Affairs of the Senate Committee on Foreign Affairs, failed to be re-elected in 1978; his defeat owed only a little to his African policies — his opponent called him 'the Senator from Africa' — but derived more from internal American issues such as the taxpayers' revolt, discontent with the performance of public services, and, above all, the 'right to life' question.

Among the most powerful of South Africa's friends is the American Legion, a moderately conservative ex-servicemen's organisation with about 4 million members. Its national executive agreed in 1977 to promote an 'urgent nation-wide educational program on the increasing importance of the economic, political and military significance of the Republic of South Africa and the national interests of the US'. Pro-South African views are widely shared in the armed services and among reserve officers. These groups are represented in Congress by a body of conservative senators and members of the House of Representatives that can be mobilised over certain issues, such as the Byrd Amendment to let Rhodesian chrome be purchased in spite of the UN boycott.[7]

The federal bureaucracy has been far from united over South Africa. Its divisions have tended to reflect those within American academia, with the technically oriented departments more inclined towards a policy of neutrality than the politically oriented bureaux such as the State Department or the US Delegation to the United

Nations, who take an anti-South African stance. The Department of Defense has understood the value of co-operation with South Africa for purely military reasons; up to 1975 the National Aeronautics and Space Administration (NASA) had benefitted from co-operating with South Africa concerning tracking stations. The Department of Commerce has evinced no desire to threaten American investments in − or trade with − South Africa. The Treasury has shared the Commerce Department's concern about America's balance of payments position at a time of rising inflation. The Treasury has also been anxious to prevent damage to South African−American relations that might interfere with South Africa's role as a supplier of gold to the international money market.

The United States does not have a domestic propaganda department. The US Information Agency does not operate within the borders of its own country. But foreign countries, including the Soviet Union, Cuba, China, the smaller Eastern European countries, the African nations, the UN and its various agencies, deploy, between them, vast funds to put the case against South Africa, either directly or indirectly, through organisations subsidised from abroad. South African official propaganda is puny by comparison. According to Martin C. Spring, the American churches alone spent at least $ 5 million a year on the anti-South African campaign − several times the amount devoted by South Africa to its information service in the United States.[8] The South African Department of Foreign Affairs maintains an embassy in Washington and a number of consulates in major cities; the South African Department of Information (in process of reorganisation at the time of writing) maintained offices in some large American cities. South Africa also employs three accredited lobbyists in Washington. In addition, the South Africa Foundation, financed mainly by businessmen, tries to promote the case for South Africa, though not necessarily on lines approved of by the South African government or welcomed by it.[9]

The pro-South African lobbies, moreover, face a difficult choice. South African officials are determined to steer away from right-wing militants; South Africa does not wish to be associated with American anti-Semites, Negrophobes or anti-Communists of the ultra-rightist kind. The South Africans prefer to concentrate their efforts on the middle-of-the-roaders, mainly businessmen. Moderate businessmen, however, are hard to mobilise in a crisis. They do not take part in demonstrations; they are not visible; they make no impact on academia and in the prestige media where the South African case goes largely, though by no means entirely, by default. The pro-South African lobbies are strong enough, for the moment, to act as a veto group. They are able to prevent dramatic forms of intervention such as a general trade embargo, a naval blockade or American military intervention. But unless white/ black relations should sharply deteriorate in the United States, South Africa will never again command the friendly respect which it enjoyed in this country when Smuts was at the helm in Pretoria.

The Development of Anti-South African Opinion

The Boers (Afrikaners) have never had a good press. The majority, though by no means all, of the British missionaries in nineteenth-century South Africa regarded the Boers with considerable hostility, as did most humanitarian imperialists in secular fields. The Boers were enemies alike of the black man and the Queen. They stood in the way of Africa's salvation. They also spoke a barbarous patois; they were sunk in sloth. Their racial prejudice and their addiction to semi-servile forms of employment hindered the free flow of labour, acted in restraint of trade, and thereby impeded the creation of a free-market economy in South Africa.

During the Boer War the image of the Boer briefly improved among humanitarians and Little Englanders. The Boers were seen for a time as members of a small nation rightly struggling to be free, victims of a war provoked by imperial proconsuls and mining magnates. After the creation of the South African 'Pact government' in 1924, reconciling Nationalists and white labour, the reputation of the Afrikaners once more declined among British liberals; so did the good name of the British settlers in Africa whom the Victorians and Edwardians had widely regarded as culture heroes, representatives of white middle-class values in 'Darkest Africa'.

During World War Two and its immediate aftermath, white South Africans temporarily redeemed their reputation through the military and economic support supplied to Great Britain, but after the victory of the Nationalist Party in 1948 the South Africans' reputation never recovered. There was a similar swing in American opinion. Few Americans had concerned themselves with South Africa before World War Two. Most of those who did saw nothing wrong with white minority rule. European colonial empires were expected to last for a long time, and South African whites were identified with the pioneers who had opened America's own frontiers. Missionaries might sympathise with black Africans, but anti-black discrimination in South Africa was not troublesome to a white American society that excluded blacks from nearly all senior posts in the armed services, the bureaucracy, the great universities and the major corporations.

American opinion began to change during and after World War Two. The defeat of Nazi Germany was a defeat for racialism. In the fight against Nazism, black American soldiers had gained distinction on the battlefield; black workers for the first time had made an acknowledged major contribution to manufacturing industries. The American civil rights struggles of the 1950s and the 1960s made a deep impression on white Americans, as did the break-up of the white colonial empires in Africa. At the same time, the white settlers' stock in Africa began to fall. White colonists were looked upon during the Victorian era as culture heroes, as archetypal representatives of bourgeois values who carried civilisation to darkest Africa. Black Africans, on the other hand, were widely — and mistakenly — identified with the slum-dwellers of Pittsburgh and Manchester, proletarians who should be uplifted by their betters.

There was a swing in public opinion during the 1950s and 1960s, not merely in the United States and Great Britain but even among educated South Africans. The white settler widely ceased to be admired — as he had been in Victorian popular literature — as a clean-cut, lantern-jawed pioneer; he became instead, for many Western intellectuals, the Philistine *par excellence*, a 'bounder' and a parasite, an attitude pungently expressed, for instance, in a South African *avant garde* poem concerning emigrants on the boat to Cape Town:

> The Pilgrim Poppa grilling manly torso
> Sprawls on the deck in Port Said purchased hat.
> Here, by the floating Serpentine (but more so),
> The Pilgrim Momma chides her Pilgrim brat.
>
> They talk to Wogs and niggers, trash and treasure,
> And bargaining. The urgent wail of sex
> And Tin Pan Alley stirs in strident measure
> The unfulfilment of our lower decks.[10]

Novelists like Nadine Gordimer and Doris Lessing no longer valued their former countrymen's productive skills. The literary elite came to depict white Rhodesians or white South Africans primarily in terms of social oppression or psychological deviance in a world of bleak despair. As a modern literary critic put it, 'Lessing's message is ... complete moral and social bankruptcy.'[11] Even Afrikaans-speaking writers like Andre Brink took a similar line: Martin Mynhardt, the villain of Brink's novel *Rumours of Rain*, is a successful entrepreneur, but callous, insensitive, a moral eunuch who exploits his wife, his mistress and his African employees; by contrast, Bernard Franken, a lawyer — a professional man — leads a life of virtue that takes him into the revolutionary underground and prison.

The pictorial arts echo the same message. Films like 'Last Grave to Dimbaza', 'Soweto' or 'Afrikaners' depict the Afrikaners as grim, heavy-jowled churchgoers with never a smile on their faces. Townships such as Soweto or Dimbaza are represented through images of broken bottles and dustbins; children peer sadly through barbed wire. Academic publications likewise concentrate on the negative aspects of South African society without giving equal coverage to the more displeasing aspects of black rule in independent Africa. *Issue*, for instance, the organ of the African Studies Association, featured in its first five issues two special numbers and forty additional articles dealing with white minority regimes in Southern Africa and their civil rights violations. By contrast, only one issue was devoted to Burundi, where the Tutsi had subjected the Hutu to genocidal terror unequalled in the modern history of Africa.[12]

The reasons for this state of affairs are complex. For one thing, relevant data are much harder to secure in countries like Guinea or Burundi than in a relatively open society like South Africa. Scholars, journalists and pastors can travel about South Africa more easily than they can through most African countries. But, above all, the Western social reformer can identify much more easily with white South Africans than with Tutsi or Bemba; he thus feels a vicarious sense of guilt regarding South Africa which he does not experience regarding atrocities committed in Zambia or Burundi. It is not, therefore, surprising that many Africanists accept a double standard where South Africa is concerned. The ASA (the African Studies Association in the US) as a body does not object to official control of research in independent black Africa; yet these self-same scholars would protest furiously if South Africa — or, for that matter, West Germany or the United States — were to impose similar restrictions on American scholars working in those respective countries.

The media also give disproportionate weight to the evils, as compared to the benefits, of white rule in South Africa, and to the lack of civil rights for Africans in South Africa as against civil rights violations

South Africa and the West

in the rest of Africa. Contrary to conservative white South African stereotypes, American newspapers are by no means all hostile to South Africa. Conservative journals like the *National Review*, business-oriented publications such as the *U.S. News and World Report*, dailies like the *Washington Star* generally take up a moderately pro-South African position. But even conservative pressmen usually look on South Africa through the mirror of the South African English-language press, the only vigorous opposition press to be found on the African continent and one which is hostile to the Afrikaner government.¹³ In any case, the wider impact of an occasional pro-South African article in the United States in no wise compares with that of great liberal dailies like the *New York Times* or the *Washington Post*, periodicals such as the *New Republic*, or of magazines like *Time, Look* or *Saturday Evening Post*, all critical of South Africa. *Reader's Digest*, alone among the popular magazines, generally adheres to a pro-South African line.

The anti-South African bias of the liberal media is emphasised by the extraordinary selectivity that distinguishes their reporting. In November 1977 'Accuracy in Media', a Washington-based organisation, published a survey of the coverage given by the *New York Times*, the *Washington Post* and the three major television networks – CBS, NBC and ABC – on human rights in five selected countries under authoritarian rule. They found that in 1976 1 story about human rights was published on North Korea, a hard-line Stalinist country; 7 about human rights in Cuba, despite Cuba's thousands of political prisoners and its proximity to the United States; 16 stories about human rights in Cambodia, where the Cambodian government had been slaughtering hundreds of thousands of people. Against this there were 90 columns, stories and editorials published on South Korea, and 137 on Chile, both pro-Western countries. During the same year the South Africa Foundation calculated that the *New York Times* and the *Washington Post* alone had published 513 stories, editorials and columns about civil rights in South Africa, hardly a contender for the crown of brutality when compared with Cambodia, North Korea or – for that matter – Uganda or Burundi.¹⁴

No one knows for sure how far public opinion is shaped by the media, or how far the media merely mirror public opinion. Whatever their influence, the liberal media do reflect the views held by a great number of men and women engaged in a variety of progressive causes – pro-abortion and anti-capital punishment, pro-Cuba and anti-Chile, pro-student and anti-police, pro-wild life protection and anti-nuclear power, pro-pacifist and anti-military. These causes have no intrinsic connection with South Africa, yet their supporters can usually be relied upon to take an anti-South African stance. This new class of educated men and women employed in teaching, public administration and other professions, are like the conservatives of old; they project domestic preoccupations on the world overseas. They look upon white South African farmers or white entrepreneurs with the disdain reserved for 'Middle America' at home. Similarly, they identify black South Africans with the poor blacks at home. The problems of South Africa, like those of the world at large, are interpreted in terms of America's own. Since the Vietnam War, the impact of the new class on US foreign policy has grown and has increasingly influenced American policy regarding South Africa.

Anti-South African Lobbies in the West

By the late 1960s educated opinion in the West had become overwhelmingly anti-South African. The anti-South African alliance has certain characteristics in common. It is a loose coalition that depends for its cohesion upon certain common assumptions rather than being a tight organisational network. It derives its support primarily from intellectuals and professional people rather than from workers or the lower middle class. It comprises a wide spectrum. In Great Britain, for instance, Liberals, Labour Party supporters, Communists, backers of the New Left in all its various shades and even some Tories take pride in their anti-South African stand. The Popular Front may have died in Spain, but it has revived to operate against South Africa on the grounds that the Pretoria regime represents the world's last Fascist holdout, the last country on earth where Communists, Liberals and progressive Conservatives may justly co-operate against the common foe.

The anti-South African lobbies in Great Britain generally maintain a high academic standard, drawing support from the British and from a substantial group of outstanding South African *émigrés* whose attainments have greatly enriched anthropology, African economics and related studies in Great Britain. Geographically, the movement mainly centres on London where the exiled South African Communist Party and the African National Congress have established their headquarters. Organisationally, the anti-South African movement depends on a number of 'action' groups connected through linked memberships and directorates. They make up for small membership and low budgets through their ability, their drive and their connections with the publishing industry, the world of politics, the bureaucracy, and with leading journals such as the *New Statesman* or the *Guardian*, and the BBC. Ronald Segal, for instance, a South African *émigré* and an editor, was an influential member of the Defence and Aid Fund of Christian Action and of the Movement for Colonial Freedom, Honorary Secretary of the South African Freedom Association, Convenor of the International Sanctions Conference of the Anti-Apartheid Movement, as well as editorial adviser to Penguin Books, whose African Library became a favourite vehicle for *émigré* South African Communist authors such as Ruth First and Brian Bunting, as well as for 'bourgeois' liberal scholars.[15]

Along with Great Britain's decline as a world power, these British movements declined in international importance compared with their American counterparts. American support for black South Africans nowadays comes from radical organisations, unions, black Americans, the liberal media, the Establishment churches, academia, and what might be called the Afrophile segment of the federal bureaucracy. The weakest of these, for the time being, is the black ethnic lobby. On the face of it, this should not be so. Black Americans form more than 12 per cent of the American population; black Americans are more numerous, respectively, than Jewish, Irish or Polish Americans, all of whom have exercised considerable influence in bringing about the independence of their particular homelands. But black Americans have not, up to now, been able to mobilise their strength to anything like its full potential. The politics of ethnic influence in the United States require a lobbying apparatus, the ability to mobilise an electoral threat, and a successful appeal to the symbols of American nationhood.[16] Black Americans have acquired considerable influence in domestic politics, especially those in the big city. But as yet they lack the cohesion and the organisation required to make their weight felt effectively concerning such foreign issues as South Africa. Most Black Americans in the past have never been much interested in Africa. 'Back to Africa' movements have attracted but a small number of blacks, and few black Americans today take an active interest in African affairs.

The reasons for this are not hard to explain. The blacks were the last group in America to attain full equality. Racial segregation in US schools was only outlawed in 1954, six years after Malan had entered the Prime Minister's office in South Africa. Black leaders during the 1950s were preoccupied mainly with domestic problems concerning civil rights, education, poverty and unemployment. There were few blacks in the higher levels of the US bureaucracy, business or politics, and those blacks who were influential concerned themselves more with the American South than with South Africa.

Black politics in America only became militant for a time during the 1960s, when there were widespread race riots; there was also the Vietnam War. Many black activists turned from the struggle for civil rights to revolutionary socialism and Third World solidarity. The strategy of militancy gave blacks increased visibility on the campuses. But the revolutionary line entailed many practical disadvantages. When Irishmen, Poles, Czechs or Jews had organised to bend US foreign policy in favour of specific 'ethnic' causes — the independence of Ireland, Poland, Czechoslovakia or Israel — they had appealed to sentiments with a wide popular appeal in America. Polish and Czech nationalists during World War One had played the anti-monarchist card, and after World War Two they had made use of anti-Communism in America. Irish nationalists had appealed to long-standing American hostility to British imperialism. Zionists had American sympathies for the persecuted and American respect for the people of the Old Covenant; none of these issues were in conflict with the sentiments of the American majority.

By contrast, black revolutionary socialism or self-identification with the Third World peoples made little appeal beyond the world of the campuses. Middle America was alienated by the call for revolutionary violence, and by the would-be revolutionaries' obscure or scabrous terminology. American revolutionaries consistently supported African exile movements. But these were often split among themselves; hence, their US supporters were apt to become involved in the domestic issues of foreign states without relevance to American issues. Black radicals identified with the newly independent countries of black Africa, and gained a new feeling of dignity from the influence of the African bloc at the UN. But publicity concerning Africa was by no means an unmixed blessing for black Americans; black prestige also suffered sometimes, as black Americans were unfairly identified with the turbulence and bloodshed that has characterised so many of the post-colonial regimes in Africa.

The black ethnic cause suffers from other disabilities. Blacks traditionally vote for the Democratic Party. Democratic politicians, therefore, are not afraid of black mass desertions to the Republican Party when Democrats offend black voters over a 'black' issue. Blacks at the moment do not have an effective lobbying apparatus within the Democratic Party; hence, they cannot easily make electoral threats. The traditional liberal alliance between Jews and blacks has weakened, partly over the issue of Israel, partly over domestic problems like busing, quotas and competition for public service posts. The American black community remains heterogeneous in character, and hard to mobilise. Black Americans will not readily rally over South Africa, a country with which they have no religious, linguistic or cultural links comparable to those that may tie, say, an Italian American to the Italy of his forebears. Moreover, to help the revolution abroad, black Americans first have to join the Establishment at home — all the more so at a time when the radicalism of the 1960s is on the wane and a cautious conservatism is in the ascendant.

The history of black American involvement in South Africa hinges on a number of minor lobbies. During the 1950s black Americans placed special emphasis on cultural ties with Africa. But the American Society of African Culture (AMSAC), founded in 1957, played an active political part through holding conferences in its New York City headquarters, and also in co-operation with black American colleges. AMSAC invited prominent African leaders like Agostinho Neto (MPLA, Angola), Sam Nujoma (SWAPO, South Africa) and intellectuals such as Bloke Modisane and Lewis Nkosi to discuss cultural and political topics.

Equally important was the American Committee on Africa (ACOA), founded in 1953 by civil rights activists for the purpose of sustaining African independence movements and advocating an American boycott of South Africa. ACOA, headed by George Houser, a white liberal, co-operated with other liberal bodies such as Operation Crossroads Africa and helped to form the American Negro Leadership Conference in Africa (ANLC), initiated in 1962 at Columbia University, a liberal stronghold. ANLC co-operated with movements like the NAACP, CORE, the Urban League, the National Conference of Negro Women; it achieved minor successes through lobbying with the State Department — for instance, over the visit of a US aircraft carrier to Cape Town. But ANLC was unable to mobilise mass support among black Americans. By the late 1960s, moreover, ANIC came under fire from militant left-wingers like John Henrik Clarke, a founder of the African Heritage Society of America (AHSA), and from the radical black caucus within the African Studies Associations (ASA). ANLC ceased to be effective and was replaced by a variety of new lobbies including Transafrica, headed by Randall Robinson. Transafrica enjoys excellent relations with the OAU delegation in New York and with the State Department but, given the divisive nature of black American society, Transafrica's effective influence also remains limited.

Following Andrew Young's resignation from his post as US Ambassador to the United Nations, black Americans made more concerted efforts to influence US foreign policy. In 1979 leading black American politicians, representatives from the NAACP, the National Urban League and the Southern Christian Leadership Conference (SCLC) met in Washington to call for a black role in foreign affairs. But the Middle Eastern issue made a poor battleground from the blacks' point of view. The Southern Christian Leadership Conference's new commitment to the Palestine Liberation Organization helped to isolate blacks from their erstwhile Jewish allies, who might have been willing to go along with blacks over South Africa but who would not countenance negotiations with the avowed enemies of Israel. In all probability, therefore, the black Americans' bargaining position over South Africa thereby diminished rather than increased.

Academic and clerical organisations supported and financed mainly by liberal whites are of greater political account than the black organisations, even than the powerful NAACP. American churchmen have played a long and honourable part in the evangelisation of Southern Africa; missionary links with South Africa remain strong, and South African social problems continue to be interpreted widely in missionary terms. Clerical bodies with a special stake in South Africa include the World Council of Churches and its American affiliate, the National Council of Churches (NCC), which has some thirty member churches, including the United Methodist Church, the United Presbyterian Church, the Episcopal Church, the Church of Christ and other denominations.

The NCC unites within its ranks the Protestant Establishment but excludes evangelical sects as well as such vigorous new bodies as the Church of Scientology. It stresses social responsibility rather than personal salvation; the council funds such organisations as the Interfaith Center on Corporate Responsibility. The NCC actively sympathises with what it considers to be the black freedom struggle in South Africa, and church funds have passed into the coffers of African guerrilla organisations — ostensibly for humanitarian purposes. Establishment churches have also taken an active part in calling for disinvestment from South Africa as part of a campaign that churchmen widely regard as comparable to the anti-slavery struggle during the nineteenth century.

Academics today are probably more important in fashioning public opinion than are clergymen. Professors are more numerous than pastors and in a secularised society like that of modern America their views may carry greater weight than those of the preachers. Conservative academic opinion, however, has little chance of influencing American policy. Grouped in the American African Affairs Association, conservative Africanists form a negligible minority compared with the 1,350 members of the African Studies Association. Up to now, the views of conservative Africanists have carried no weight in Washington; indeed, they are seldom even called on to advise or to testify. Liberal academicians, on the other hand, play an important part in such lobbies as ACOA, which publish newsletters, background papers, and research memoranda; they call upon congressmen and senior officials in the administration; they secure a good deal of coverage for their activities in liberal newspapers like the *New York Times*; they send speakers to college campuses, to church-related gatherings and seminars. Their involvement with ACOA probably also exerted some influence on the anti-apartheid policy pursued by the United Automobile Workers (UAW). The UAW aversion to apartheid was shared, in turn, by the AFL-CIO as well as by bodies like the International Defense and Aid Fund for South Africa, the African News Service, and so forth.

The influence on US foreign policy of these and kindred lobbies can easily be exaggerated. Lobbyists come and lobbyists go. They speak with conflicting voices. They cannot impose their views on the country's foreign policy unless they find powerful allies within the ranks of the legislature and the bureaucracy, which exercise a considerable influence by reason of their financial expenditure in Africa alone. Estimated fiscal assistance to Africa for 1978 amounted to $544 million, including $476 million for economic aid and $68 million for military aid. Among these agencies, bodies like Health, Education, and Welfare (HEW) or the Agency for International Development (AID), concerned with giving aid to less developed countries, naturally sympathise with the newly independent black countries rather than with South Africa which receives no development aid, no 'soft' loans, and does not rank as a financial client.

Bureaucratic involvement in Africa is extensive. By 1978 a total of 29 US government departments, agencies and permanent commissions were concerned with African affairs in some form. These range from major bodies like the departments of the Interior, Defense, Agriculture, Housing and Urban Development, HEW, to the National Aeronautics and Space Administration (NASA), the Export-Import Bank of the United States, the Agency for Volunteer Services (Peace Corps), and the National Endowment for the Humanities.[17] Between them, these new technical departments have deprived the Department of State of an ever-increasing number of functions. To give just a few examples, the Department of State has lost operational responsibilities for intelligence to the CIA, foreign assistance to AID, and information to the International Communication Agency. Other departments have developed their own 'mini-State Departments'; for example, the Defense Department has its own Office of International Security Affairs. The State Department has further lost in influence, as heads of state can now communicate by telephone or travel by jet aircraft without paying much heed to the advice of locally accredited ambassadors.

Nevertheless, the most important American government agency concerned with American/South African relations is still the Department of State. Before World War Two the State Department, like the Foreign Office in Great Britain, drew most of its personnel from the Establishment, more so than any other governmental agency. There was some truth to the stereotype of the State Department official drawn from 'old' Anglo-Saxon stock, educated in Eastern Ivy League schools, Anglophile in orientation, and English in manners. After World War Two, the State Department began to broaden the social and geographical basis of recruitment, and the men recruited in the 1950s and the early 1960s were beginning to move into senior positions by the late 1970s. The new men included black Americans like Ambassador Donald McHenry, who had joined the State Department in 1963 as a Foreign Service Officer and later helped to represent the United States at the United Nations. Others were liberal intellectuals like Anthony Lake, a Harvard graduate and a Princeton PhD, appointed Foreign Service Officer in 1962, later a Democratic Party campaigner, a Carter supporter, and subsequently Director of the Policy Planning Staff under the Carter administration.

Within the State Department, power is far from centralised and decision-making is widely dispersed. By and large, the State Department takes an anti-South Africa line, both for reasons of ideological conviction and from the standpoint of America's real or supposed national interests. The Bureau of African Affairs is primarily concerned with strengthening US ties to the new African countries; the Bureau of International Organization Affairs and the US Mission to the United Nations are preoccupied with America's international position within the UN; the Bureau of Intelligence and Research shares the preconceptions of liberal academia. The State Department's anti-South Africa policy was actually justified as the only way to keep Soviet influence from growing. Unless we support liberation movements in Southern Africa, went the argument, these bodies would turn to the Cubans and the Soviets. The United States then would not only lose its moderating

South Africa and the West 267

influence, but would have to stand by and see violence rule the arena. By not supporting the moderates, however, the United States made certain that the issue could only be settled by war.

Notes

1. Reiner Lock, 'Foreign Investments in South Africa' in Ian Robertson and Philip Whitten (eds.), *Race and Politics in South Africa* (Transaction Books, New Brunswick, NJ, 1978), pp. 188-9.
2. Basil Hersov, 'Demands of a New Era', *South Africa International*, vol. 9, no. 4 (April 1979), pp. 169-85.
3. See Clarence Clendenen, Robert Collins and Peter Duignan, *Americans in Africa, 1865-1900* (Hoover Institution, Stanford, 1966); Clarence Clendenen and Peter Duignan, *Americans in Black Africa up to 1865* (Hoover Institution, Stanford, 1964).
4. The replacement value of these investments is two to three times higher than the book value.
5. 'America's South African Dilemma', *Time* (September 1978).
6. According to the computations of Ann Seidmann (*Issue*, vol. 1, no. 3 (Fall 1974), p. 71), the rate of profits in US investments in South Africa for the years 1968, 1970 and 1973 respectively stood at 17.3, 16.3 and 18.8, as against the rest of Africa: 27.8, 26.9 and 21.8.
7. The Byrd Amendment (section 503 of the Military Procurement Act of 1972, PL 92-156) for a time enabled the United States to break international sanctions against Rhodesia in so far as strategic minerals like chrome were concerned. Private lobbies in favour of the amendment included the American Iron and Steel Institute, a number of mining companies and the Tool and Stainless Steel Industry Committee. See Anthony Lake, *The 'Tar Baby Option': American Policy toward Southern Rhodesia* (Columbia University Press, New York, 1977), pp. 226-31. For a contrasting view, see Western Massachusetts Association of Concerned African Scholars (eds.), *U.S. Military Involvement in Southern Africa* (South End Press, Boston, 1978).
8. Martin C. Spring, *Confrontation: the Approaching Crisis between the United States and South Africa* (Valiant Publishers, Sandton, Cape Town, 1977), *passim*.
9. According to Barbara Rogers's critical account of South African propaganda, entitled 'Sunny South Africa' (*Africa Report* (September-October 1977), pp. 2-8), the combined budget of all South African 'propaganda agencies' in the United States, including such non-governmental agencies as the South Africa Foundation, amounted to $ 1,301,465. Judged by the standards of American academia, this is an insignificant amount, scarcely more than 1 per cent of the annual operating budget of a major private university such as Stanford ($ 118.652 million in 1979).
10. Excerpt from R. Reynold, 'The Emigrant Ship', *Africa South*, vol. 3 (July-September 1959), p. 12.
11. Rosemary Dinnage, 'Before her Time: Doris Lessing', *New York Review of Books* (26 September 1978), p. 12.
12. David B. Abernethy, 'Assessing Human Rights Violations: a Comparison of the Contemporary South African and Ugandan Regimes', paper prepared for the Conference on Human Rights and Educational Responsibility, Pomona College, Claremont, 18 November 1978, and made available to us by the author.
13. According to Freedom House, an American civil rights organisation, only

five countries in Africa in 1977 complied with most of the criteria of a free press: Botswana, Gambia, Morocco, South Africa and Rhodesia. Only six countries in Africa had newspapers that were not government-owned or -controlled; Gambia, Kenya, Liberia, Morocco, South Africa and Rhodesia. Three countries – South Africa, Rhodesia and Morocco – had national news agencies that functioned independently of the government. South Africa alone had a vigorous opposition press. *African Freedom Annual* (Sandton, Cape Town, 1978), pp. 47-8.

14. John Chettle, 'Solzhenitsyn, South Africa, and the Fashions of the Day', paper prepared for the Confederation of Church and Business People in Toronto, Ontario, Canada, 29 June 1978, and kindly made available to us by the author.

15. For a more detailed breakdown, see Harold Sore and Ian Greig, *The Puppeteers*... (Tandem Books, London, 1965) and Ronald Segal, *Political Africa*... (Praeger, New York, 1961). In West Germany, the Anti-Apartheid-Bewegung in der BRD und West Berlin publishes *Informationsdienst Südliches Afrika* which likewise mingles factual information with anti-Western propaganda.

16. Martin Weil, 'Can the Blacks do for Africa what the Jews did for Israel?' in Réné Lemarchand (ed.), *American Policy in Southern Africa: the Stakes and the Stance* (University Press of America, New York, 1978), pp. 313-22.

17. For a survey of the US government departments concerned with African affairs, see *Issue*, vol. 7, nos. 2-3 (Summer/Fall 1978).

9 THE WEST, THE SOVIET UNION, AND SOUTH AFRICA

South Africans like to see their country as the centre of world interest; they share this characteristic with the nationals of many other small countries. However, the average American high-school graduate and many a college-trained American would be hard put to identify South Africa's chief cities on the map or to give an intelligent account of its government. For the West as a whole, South Africa has long been a backwater. But as the nation emerged from a state of political obscurity, its reputation continuously declined and relations with the Western world tended to worsen.

Western Estrangement from South Africa

British alienation from South Africa began in 1948 when Smuts fell from office. Old-fashioned Tories resented the Afrikaners' seizure of power and their 'disloyalty' to the Empire. (The ill-fated Federation of Rhodesia and Nyasaland, lasting from 1953 to 1964, was in fact intended to be a British bastion against Afrikaner as well as African nationalism.) Adherents of the Labour Party, having improved Britain, increasingly became convinced that Britain's new proletariat was to be found in Africa. Humanitarians derided the Afrikaners' racial practices. Egalitarians had contempt for a country where all Africans were supposedly living in misery and all whites (including working-class British emigrants to South Africa) supposedly lazed around in the sun, happy owners of two cars and a swimming pool.

The South African contribution to the Allied cause in World War Two arouses no interest within a new generation for whom the war against Hitler and Mussolini is a remote memory. Within the British bureaucracy, the political influence of the Treasury and the service departments has declined, much to South Africa's disadvantage. The decay of British naval strength is particularly relevant to the South African situation. As long as the British continued to play a role 'east of Suez', the South African card seemed of considerable value. The Royal Navy had used the port of Simonstown, and the British were South Africa's major suppliers of arms. But when the Labour government of

269

Harold Wilson came into power in 1964, London suspended arms sales in accordance with a United Nations embargo on arms to South Africa. Labour, for the time being, did not prohibit the continuing export of spare parts for weapons, ships and planes already supplied, so that South Africa continued to remain an important market for British arms manufacturers. During the 1970s Great Britain ceased to supply arms to South Africa, even though the Cape route continued to remain vital to British overseas commerce.

The widening split between Washington and Pretoria began in the late 1950s. During World War Two the United States and South Africa had been allies. Washington, disliking the notion that the British Empire might develop into a unified trading bloc, had welcomed the independence of the dominions within the British Empire and had seen nothing wrong with Pretoria's economic nationalism. The Sixth South African Armored Division had served in Italy in the Fifth US Army under General Mark W. Clark, who had a high opinion of the South Africans under his command. South Africa was equally acceptable in the political sphere. A liberal American Democrat, used to collaborating with white 'Dixiecrats' within his own party, might have objected to South African racial policies, but he certainly did not look upon South Africa as a Fascist menace of international proportions.

South Africa would have liked to solidify into a formal alliance its relations with the United States and NATO.[1] South African diplomacy never reached this goal, but *de facto* co-operation between Washington and Pretoria remained close. In 1951 the two governments signed an agreement for reimbursable military assistance under the US Mutual Defense Assistance Act. Great Britain transferred the Simonstown naval base to South Africa in 1955, with the provision that the British and their allies could use the base in wartime, even if South Africa were not a belligerent. US naval vessels made regular use of South African ports for supplies and repair. US scientists and engineers co-operated with their South African colleagues in a space-tracking programme in South Africa (beginning 1957) and in the construction of space-tracking stations (begun 1960). At the same time, the two countries closely co-operated in the field of nuclear development. In 1957 Washington and Pretoria signed a ten-year agreement relating to the industrial use of atomic energy (renewed in 1967).

Washington's estrangement from South Africa can be dated from 1958 when the United States for the first time voted in favour of a UN resolution expressing concern over South Africa's racial policies instead of abstaining on such a resolution. During the Kennedy era (1961-3)

South African/American relations worsened, although South African politics had not noticeably changed. Not even Verwoerd's most bitter critics considered him more reactionary than his predecessors, Malan and Strijdom. No new quarrels disturbed relations between Pretoria and Washington. The tensions between the two countries derived solely from ideological differences between them and from changes within US society and US politics.

The Kennedy administration went further than any previous American administration in its attacks on South Africa. Kennedy did not confine his opposition to verbal condemnation, but announced that the United States would cease selling arms to South Africa after 1963. Senior officials like Chester Bowles, Adlai Stevenson, W. Averell Harriman, G. Mennen Williams were all strongly pro-African, and the ambassadors appointed by Kennedy to African diplomatic posts were liberal American intellectuals.[2] The Johnson administration followed the precedents set by Kennedy, and in some ways went even beyond them. In 1964, for instance, the United States voted for a UN Security Council resolution to study the feasibility of sanctions against South Africa.

In practical terms, this growing American hostility to South Africa as yet did not mean a great deal to Pretoria. No matter what the politicians might say, trade between the two countries grew in a striking fashion, leaving the United States with an increasingly favourable trade balance. Between 1960 and 1976 US exports to South Africa grew from $288 million to $1,350 million; imports from South Africa rose from $108 million to $927 million; South Africa's American trade deficit went up from $180 million to $432 million. American investors lent more money to South Africa. Between 1963 and 1970 the book value of US investments in South Africa more than doubled, from $411 million to $868 million. American reliance on South African minerals increased. As early as 1968-9 the United States depended primarily on South Africa for 85 per cent of its antimony, 38 per cent of its chrome, and more than 33 per cent of the metals deriving from the platinum group.[3]

Moscow, for the time being, showed but little interest in Africa south of the equator. Soviet trade in the region was negligible. Soviet strategists looked to land power in Europe for its strength rather than to naval power overseas. The orthodox Communist parties counted for little in Africa and, initially, received but scanty support from the Soviet Union. During World War Two Stalin had made no attempts to embarrass his Western allies in Africa. After hostilities ended, his interest in 'black' Africa remained small. A hard-liner at home, he believed that 'bourgeois' nationalists like Kwame Nkrumah of Ghana were imperialist lackeys who represented only the comprador class, the African agents of white colonialism in Africa. Leadership of the future revolution, Stalin believed, must fall to the nascent African proletariat.

Stalin's death in 1953 brought about major changes in Soviet African policies, and from the mid-1950s the Communists re-evaluated their African stance in the light of policy changes at home. In 1956 the Congress of the Communist Party of the Soviet Union (CPSU) admitted that national independence in Africa might be won under African 'bourgeois' leadership. The small Communist parties in Nigeria, Senegal and South Africa all stressed the need for a broad-based alliance that would include the 'national bourgeoisie' as well as the peasants, the petty bourgeoisie and the working class in the struggle for 'national democratic revolutions' as stepping stones to socialism. The new policy was much more realistic than Stalin's narrow orthodoxy. Communists in sub-Saharan African concentrated on infiltrating trade unions, African nationalist movements, on building up networks of agents and supporters through local 'peace movements', cultural fronts, youth leagues, women's associations, scholarship programmes for study in the Soviet Union and similar measures. Communists of the pro-Soviet (as opposed to the Sinophile) persuasion played down the need for armed struggles, except in the Portuguese colonies, Rhodesia and South Africa. But in practical terms, these efforts as yet did not amount to a great deal. American policy-makers shouldered little risk by attacking Portuguese colonialism or South African racialism at a time when the Soviet Union and its allies seemed ill prepared to intervene.[4]

From the South African viewpoint, the Soviet Union was a remote enemy, not an immediate threat. South Africa continued to be protected for the time by a series of foreign bastions beyond its borders. The Portuguese showed unexpected resilience in resisting the African guerrillas who, from 1961 onward, had taken up the struggle against Lisbon's rule. Rhodesia, having published its Unilateral Declaration of Independence (UDI) from Great Britain in 1965, defied the experts by successfully resisting Great Britain, the United Nations and the African states until 1979.

During the Nixon era, US official disapproval of South Africa relented slightly. Whereas the Africanists in the State Department looked to increased pressure on the 'white minority regimes' in Southern Africa, the National Security Council and the Defense Department argued in favour of a cautious South African-American *rapprochement*.

The new policy, expressed in an National Security Study Memorandum (NSSM 39, 1970), derived from four assumptions. The whites in Southern Africa would retain power for a considerable time, especially in South Africa, where military power could easily curtail internal or external African opposition to white rule. Increasing industrialisation in South Africa would improve the condition of the blacks, thereby leading to greater internal stability. The United States was likely to effect internal reforms in South Africa by maintaining friendly relations with Pretoria rather than by issuing empty threats that would merely make the whites more obdurate. The Nixon administration could not afford to penalise American businessmen in the name of a policy that was not working in the first place.[5]

Nevertheless, Nixon was far from being a traditional conservative. While pledging himself not to interfere in the 'internal affairs' of any African nation, the President in 1970 committed himself to outspoken censure of South Africa and Rhodesia in a manner inconceivable thirty years earlier, and in a fashion applied to no other government:

> There is no question of the United States condoning, or acquiescing in, the racial policies of the white-ruled regimes. For moral as well as historical reasons, the United States stands firmly for the principles of racial equality and self determination.[6]

The United States, according to the President, believed in peaceful rather than warlike change. But the United States abhorred 'the racial policies of the white regimes'; the real issue was to find a means of changing them without drifting into the vortex of violence and counter-violence.

In formulating their policy regarding South Africa, Nixon and Secretary of State Kissinger believed themselves to be acting from a position of relative strength. But the Communist victories in Vietnam, Cambodia and Laos, the shift in the world-wide military balance of power in favour of the Soviet Union, the international energy crisis following an unprecedented increase in the price of Arab oil, President Nixon's resignation after the Watergate scandal and the overthrow of the Portuguese dictatorship in Lisbon by the Portuguese army all brought about far-reaching changes in the international scene and in Africa. Portugal decided to grant independence to its colonial possessions. At the tail end of the war in Mozambique, Portuguese troops actually helped to install a Marxist regime headed by FRELIMO, against opposition from local white settlers and from various African ethnic groups such as the

Nkonde. In Angola, pro-Communist officials, backed by the then influential Portuguese Communist Party, gave support to the MPLA in its struggles against its rivals, and in July 1975 the MPLA expelled the other liberation movements from the capital.

The Soviet Union's New African Strategy and the Western Liberal Response

The 1970s were a revolutionary decade. They witnessed a dramatic change in the form taken by Soviet intervention in Africa. Until 1975 the Soviet Union and its allies had confined themselves to training guerrillas, subsidising pro-Soviet organisations, thereby encouraging liberation wars by indirect means. From 1975 onward the Soviet bloc began to interfere directly through Cuban ground troops and East German and Soviet supporting staff. In September 1975 strong Cuban forces disembarked in Luanda, thereby initiating a new phase in Soviet foreign policy designed to spread Communism and to compensate for weaknesses at home by military victories abroad. The United States would not respond to the new challenge directly, but confined itself to supplying small amounts of arms and cash to the anti-MPLA forces. The United States, as well as African states like Zambia, also gave covert encouragement to South Africa which, in October, sent a small fighting force across the Angolan border to give assistance to UNITA. The South Africans and their Angolan allies nearly succeeded; but in December 1975 the US Senate, by an overwhelming majority, imposed a ban on all further assistance, overt or covert, to the anti-Communist forces in Angola. At a crucial point in their advance, the South Africans were suddenly bereft of further American support. Afraid to face the Communist bloc at such a distance from their own borders, the South Africans — despite their excellent military performance against the Cubans — pulled back. Guerrilla warfare continued in Angola, but the way was open for the seizure of power throughout the greater part of Angola by MPLA and Cuban forces.

The new strategy of direct intervention, carried out under the banner of 'proletarian internationalism', had far-reaching consequences. This formula was applied with much success to Ethiopia, where the Soviet Union and Cuba airlifted large numbers of troops and heavy supplies over great distances in an impressive display of military strength, thereby enabling the Ethiopians to defeat a Somali invasion and largely suppress a widespread rebellion in Eritrea. Impressed by real or imagined analogies between the fall of the 'feudal' monarchies in Ethiopia and Tsarist Russia, the Soviets became convinced that Ethiopia was one of the keys to Africa. Ethiopia became to the Soviets a testing ground for the ability of a Marxist-Leninist revolution to survive in a hostile world, a test for the efficacy of proletarian internationalism as a revolutionary instrument in backward society; a strategic bastion in the Horn of Africa; and a potential manpower reservoir for military operations in other parts of Africa. Only the future would show whether their assessment was correct.

By the end of the 1970s Marxism-Leninism had made considerable gains. The new regimes of Angola, Mozambique, Ethiopia, the People's Republic of the Congo and Benin all claimed to be based on Marxist-Leninist principles. In practice, these regimes varied widely. Benin and the People's Republic of the Congo practised Marxism-Leninism of a largely rhetorical kind. Even the remaining three states were not ruled, for the time being, by orthodox Communist parties. Their systems of government might rather be described as 'Afro-Marxist'.

The Afro-Marxist organisations, of course, shared many of their characteristics with non-Marxist parties in Africa, so that the distinction between them was not always easy to draw. The Afro-Marxist organisations, moreover, were not carbon copies of the Communist Party of the Soviet Union, as were the Communist parties of Eastern Europe. In Angola, for instance, the MPLA transformed itself at the end of 1977 from a mere 'movement' to a Marxist-Leninist party (MPLA-PT or MPLA Party of Labor). The MPLA operated as a self-styled 'vanguard of the proletariat', uniting workers, peasants and intellectuals within its ranks, this in a country overwhelmingly dependent on backward cultivators. The party depended to a considerable extent on support among the *mestiços* (persons of mixed Afro-European ancestry, among the best-educated people in the country). On the other hand, the party's influence was weak among dissident ethnic communities such as the KiKongo people in the north and the Ovimbundu in the south. About half of the Central Committee's members came from the military.

The MPLA stressed the virtues of 'scientific socialism'. Religion was considered as no more than 'a distorted reflection . . . of reality that is basically determined by the living conditions of men'.[7] In foreign policy, Angola supported the Soviet Union, while domestically the Marxist-Leninist government relied heavily for much of its revenue on Gulf Oil Company. The MPLA's regime for the moment depended on Cuban — and to a lesser extent on East German and Soviet — military assistance against popular guerrilla movements. Mozambique managed to steer a somewhat more independent line. FRELIMO, the Marxist-Leninist ruling party, looked to Chinese as well as to Soviet models, having placed special emphasis on the construction of communal villages.

Nevertheless, the emergence of Afro-Marxist parties helped to shift the ideological balance of power in that they generally accepted the Soviet Union as a desirable model to imitate. More important, Cuban military intervention shifted the strategic balance of power on the continent. Proletarian internationalism introduced a new division of labour in the international sphere. Cuba mainly furnished ground troops and instructors for countries as far afield as Angola, Ethiopia and the People's Republic of the Congo. East Germany provided specialists and instructors, especially for the purpose of training police and secret police units. The Soviet Union, in addition to making available weaponry and training facilities, sent out senior staff officers to handle military planning. Politically weak regimes like those of Cuba and East Germany gained in prestige and in Third World legitimacy. Guerrilla warfare in Rhodesia and South-West Africa was stepped up, and South Africa herself appeared increasingly threatened.

The Americans responded in an ambiguous fashion. They tried to change the internal balance of political power in South Africa by forcing her government into making political concessions to blacks. At the same time, the Americans put pressure on South Africa to facilitate the creation of black regimes in Namibia and Rhodesia. In 1976 Ian Smith, under joint pressure from South Africa and the United States, reluctantly conceded the principle of 'black majority rule' with safeguards for whites, a decision that had the unintended result of starting Rhodesia on the road to Marxism.

When President Carter took office, he selected a new team to take charge of African policy in the State Department. The new appointees largely represented the views of the McGovernite minority within the Democratic Party, to the exclusion of those in the centre and right associated with the liberal anti-Communism of Senators Jackson and Moynihan.[8] For instance, Vice-President Mondale played a special role in formulating general policy; Andrew Young became Ambassador to the United Nations; Richard M. Moose was made Assistant Secretary for African Affairs; Anthony Lake took charge as Director of the Policy Planning Staff. Their views corresponded to those of the President who, before the election, actually had been questioned in a *Playboy* interview whether he should not rather be leading a crusade for the liberation of blacks in South Africa.

The new administration repudiated the agreement concluded between Kissinger and Smith over Rhodesia, and refused to accord recognition to a moderate and racially mixed government in Salisbury. The Carter team used harsh language in condemning South Africa. Above all, the administration took it for granted that the United States had the right to interfere in South Africa's affairs, and that black political rights within the Republic of South Africa could only be satisfied within the framework of a unitary state through the institution of a universal franchise, defined by Vice-President Mondale as 'one man, one vote, with each vote equally weighted'.

The liberal members of the Carter administration, however, laboured under severe constraints in that American (and also British) public opinion would not back a tough line against South Africa.[9] The Foreign Policy Association, an influential American group primarily composed of liberals, completed an opinion study of its members and found that 51 per cent of them wanted to work closely with South Africa to maintain stability; only 10 per cent wanted to sever ties with Pretoria if the South Africans were to continue with their policy of apartheid. A nation-wide Harris poll proved even more discouraging from the liberal standpoint. While the majority of Americans disapproved of South African policies, more than 76 per cent of the respondents considered that Americans had no more right to interfere in their internal affairs than had South Africans the right to impose their views on Americans.

The 1978 elections strengthened conservatives within both the Democratic and the Republican parties, leaving American liberals on the defensive over domestic and foreign matters. The Carter administration became increasingly convinced that the United States required South African co-operation in dealing with the Namibian and Rhodesian questions. Increased pressure on South Africa would strengthen the *verkramptes* within the National Party as against the *verligtes*; it was argued that Americans would gain more concessions from the Afrikaners by using the carrot rather than the stick. The administration began to use more diplomatic language in dealing with the South Africans. No attempt was made to suspend US trade with South Africa. For all practical purposes, the policies pursued by Carter and his predecessors came to differ more on matters of emphasis than of substance. As Ambassador Young put it in a Senate hearing, 'there is really no clear break [with the Kissinger policy] . . . It is more an evolution from that policy.'[10] But whatever Carter's tactical shifts, the President continued to uphold the cause of human rights as 'the soul of our foreign policy . . . the very soul of our nationhood'.[11]

Because of Cuban/Soviet intervention in Southern Africa, the debate concerns issues much wider than those relating to South Africa alone. For civil rights advocates like Andrew Young and adherents of the 'New Politics', South Africa is a microcosm of the Western world in its relations to the Third World, a country where a white minority oppresses a black majority. In the past, Young believes, the United States has consistently sided with the world's tyrants. This evil must be righted by applying the principles of the American civil rights movement to US foreign policy. According to Young, the civil rights movement has played a crucial part in the modern world; during the Vietnam War the civil rights cause developed into the anti-war movement; the anti-war movement in turn created a wholly new approach to world problems.

The civil rights issue transcends the hostility between the Soviet Union and the Western alliance. Hopefully, the 'black diaspora' in the West will now take a prominent part in the struggle for black liberation in the remaining bastions of white rule in Southern Africa.[12] The Soviet Union, for all its deficiencies, has always been at least a decade ahead of the United States in understanding the forces at work in the Third World, and therefore deserves a better press than it gets from reactionaries.

As the advocates of the New Politics see it, the Soviet Union and Cuba do not pose a military threat to the United States in Africa. In the words of Anthony Lewis, a distinguished liberal journalist, we must not 'exaggerate the impact of distant events' like the Angolan struggle on the fortunes of the United States.[13] The United States must not counter force with force in Africa; a military response would only compound the problem of violence and would, in any case, be ineffective, given Soviet determination and given the sympathies of the African peoples.

Most American liberals do not take as friendly a view towards the Soviet Union and its East German and Cuban allies in Africa as do the proponents of the New Politics. However, they do argue that the United States, in its own self-interest, cannot afford to side with losers like the played-out regime in Pretoria. The needs of *Realpolitik* and of morality alike call for American support to African revolutionaries like the MPLA in Angola, the Patriotic Front in Zimbabwe and the African National Congress (ANC) in South Africa. These organisations are not Soviet puppets; their ties to the Soviet Union depend far more on instrumental than on ideological considerations. Sudan, Egypt and

Somalia broke their links to the Soviet Union when these became inconvenient; Angola and Mozambique may be expected to do the same, provided the United States does not spoil its case by siding with white racists.

Realpolitik, the liberals continue, makes nonsense of the economic arguments put forward by the pro-South African lobby in this country.[14] American trade and investment in South Africa form but a negligible percentage of America's GNP; the loss of the US economic stake in South Africa would not have serious consequences for American capitalism, much less for America at large. In any case, even a Marxist-Leninist regime in Pretoria would still wish to trade with the United States. Gulf Oil is doing well in Angola; General Motors might operate just as successfully under the auspices of a black socialist government in South Africa determined to raise popular living standards by gaining wider access to foreign capital, foreign technology and foreign markets.

Liberals are unimpressed by strategic arguments that stress the importance to the West of the Cape route and of South African raw materials. Even if a black-ruled South Africa were to be allied to the Soviet Union, the Soviets could not use their position to interfere with Western oil supplies without risking general war. Either the ensuing military conflict would quickly be settled by negotiation, in which case existing stocks would enable the West to continue for the time being or the conflict would turn into a nuclear Armageddon, making the oil issue irrelevant. Regardless, the Soviets have more effective means of stopping Western oil supplies shipped from the Middle East than by mounting a naval blockade from the Horn of Africa or around the Cape. An air assault on the Middle Eastern oil fields, a military occupation of the oil-producing countries, a naval attack on Western maritime communications in the North Atlantic, are all preferable on a cost/benefit basis. The Soviet intervention in the Indian Ocean must be seen more in defensive terms, as a means of protecting Soviet maritime traffic from the European parts of the USSR to its Far Eastern portions and as a means of countering Western submarine or carrier-borne nuclear attacks on the Soviet heartland from the Indian Ocean.

Admittedly, Soviet access to the ports of Southern Africa would strengthen the Soviet image as a global power; but Soviet intervention would not seriously affect America's strategic position. In any case, the importance of foreign bases can easily be exaggerated. In 1976 the Soviets were able to ferry men and *matériel* to Angola without access to permanent bases in the area. The strategic future of the United

States depends on its own productive power and national resolve — not on ties with faraway countries of which it knows little and which it should trust even less.

The Implications of Soviet Strategy

We ourselves remain unconvinced by the liberal case. The Soviets and their allies see the world in a very different light from that used by Andrew Young and his supporters or by political scientists like William Foltz or Robert Price. The military, naval and air power of the Soviet Union and its allies has grown apace. Their military doctrine stresses not defence, but the merits of a sustained and unrelenting offensive. Soviet military might, in turn, strengthens the revolutionary forces throughout the Third World.[15] Soviet strategic calculations concerning the shift in the global correlation of forces go with renewed emphasis on the 'two camps' doctrine that underlines the 'insoluble contradictions' between the capitalist and the socialist worlds.

In its struggle against the West, the Soviet Union places special importance on proletarian internationalism, a prominent concept in Soviet thought since 1975. Proletarian internationalism stresses the solidarity of the world Communist movement and the various 'liberation' groups, the primacy of the USSR and of the CPSU within this global movement, and the manner in which the interests of local Communist parties and individual Communist countries converge in the greater cause of world revolution. Proletarian internationalism provides a rationale for direct military assistance to liberation movements in other parts of the world throughout Soviet proxies like Cuba and East Germany, thereby opening 'vast new revolutionary vistas'. This is made easier now that the Soviet navy has the capability of assisting wars of liberation.

In formulating their plans, Soviet experts allot particular importance to Africa, and especially to its southern portion. They regard Southern Africa as strategically important. They also stress the increasing dependency of the United States and its allies on imported raw materials at a time when Western capitalism is going through a crisis which, according to Soviet experts, cannot be resolved within a capitalist framework. Revolutionaries must strive to intensify this crisis by tying the emergent countries of the Third World to the Soviet bloc, by 'Finlandising' the states of Western Europe, by controlling the West's access to raw materials — all this designed to isolate the United States. Socialist revolutions in Africa will play a valuable part in weakening world capitalism by making it more dependent on imports that it can no longer control. The expansion of Soviet military power will make this objective more easily attainable.

> At the present state, the historical function of the Soviet Armed Forces is not restricted merely to their function of defending the Motherland and the other socialist countries. In its foreign activity, the Soviet state actively and purposefully . . . supports the national liberation struggle, and resolutely resists imperialist aggression in whatever distant region of our planet it may appear.[16]

Marshal Grechko does not make idle boasts, but prefers judicious understatements. Despite the vast superiority of the United States in technological skill and national wealth, the Soviet Union now enjoys a numerical and qualitative superiority over the West in nuclear weapons, strategic aviation, most kinds of naval vessels, armoured fighting vehicles and artillery. Far from diminishing, this superiority seems to grow apace. At this time, the USSR can mobilise more men than can the United States, Great Britain, France and Western Germany combined, though these Western countries far outnumber the Soviet Union both in an industrial and a demographic sense. To support its overseas adventures, the Soviet Union can rely on the army of Cuba — militarily the most powerful state in Latin America; in addition, the Soviet Union at this moment is able to airlift about six of its own elite divisions, complete with tanks and artillery, over thousands of miles within less than 72 hours. It is a formidable, world-wide threat — more powerful even than Hitler's Germany, untroubled by Hitler's racial paranoia, but just as determined on global supremacy.

The Soviet Union uses national liberation movements as one of many politico-military devices to advance its cause. These movements have gained widespread sympathy from Western liberals on the grounds that they represent the cause of social justice, a more egalitarian social order, a more progressive form of economic organisation, and a society more in keeping with Western notions of civil rights than the regimes displaced by the revolutionaries.

Unfortunately, however, liberal hopes have been disappointed everywhere. Far from promoting economic progress, the new regimes in Angola, Mozambique and Ethiopia now find themselves in a much worse economic state than their predecessors. Power in the Marxist-Leninist republics remains concentrated in the hands of a 'new class' of party functionaries, soldiers, bureaucrats and ideologues — a salaried elite whose power rests on effective control over the means of production and distribution, and on coercion. The new oligarchies operate without restraints of the kind found even in South Africa — a relatively free press, an independent and self-respecting judicature, an autonomous electorate, however restricted in numbers, and other restraints on government.

The Marxist-Leninist republics have not surmounted the problems of ethnicity. Ethiopia remains an Amharic state; the MPLA has failed to make itself popular among the KiKongo or the Ovimbundu; FRELIMO has few supporters among the Nkonde people. The opposition in the Marxist-Leninist states is being repressed with a brutality that makes South Africa a model of liberal democracy. Forced labour camps, political re-education centres and political prisons coerce all opponents of the regimes. Since 1974 the revolutionary government of Ethiopia has supposedly murdered about 30,000 people; thousands more are held — according to Amnesty International — in miserable prison camps where they are exposed to torture and terror. Bombing and napalming scar tribal villages in the south of Angola. The 'counter-revolutionary' methods practised by Cubans and MPLA forces against UNITA insurgents make Sharpeville look insignificant.

Events in Angola in 1974-5 destabilised the whole of Southern Africa. The Russians learned from the Angolan episode that wars by proxy pay off. The Soviets used the same tactics in Ethiopia and will be strongly tempted to use them in other places — possibly in the assault on South-West Africa (Namibia) and finally against South Africa. The Cubans have become Moscow's all-purpose mercenaries in Africa. At the time of writing, as many as 20,000 Cubans have been deployed in Angola and another 20,000 in Ethiopia. Thousands of Cubans were stationed in other African countries like Mozambique, Guinea and the People's Republic of the Congo. East Germany supposedly maintained another 17,000 military and other specialists, far more soldiers than had been stationed in the Kaiser's colonies before World War One. The Soviet Union bore a major share of the cost; the Russians subsidised the Cuban economy to the tune of $2 million a day. They invested over $500 million in the Angolan campaign, and they have spent over $1 billion there since 1975 and perhaps $2 billion in Ethiopia.

The strategic effect of Cuba's Angolan venture is well appreciated by the Russians, who call it a revolutionary event for Southern Africa. Clearly, the US senators who voted to cut off all aid to anti-

The West, the Soviet Union, and South Africa 283

Communist movements in Angola did not understand what was happening. They kept talking about another Vietnam — ignoring the fact that two-thirds of the people and two-thirds of the political movements were opposed to the MPLA. Clark, McGovern and Tunney argued that the MPLA were only radical nationalists who would resist a Russian take-over. UNITA, in the centre and south of the country, continues to fight. UNITA bands widely confine the Cubans to the cities and prevent the Benguela railway from operating. Cuba has suffered about 5,000 casualties and some defections. FLEC fights on in Cabinda. Neither group is supported by the West, though conceivably they could win and could deny Angola to the Russians.

Cubans and Russians are busy turning Angola into a pro-Communist state with close ties to the Soviet Union. Top Soviet and Cuban officials train the secret police and the information bureaux. All important government Ministries are run by Cubans, and the Cuban army enforces obedience. Angolan refugees keep making their escape to Zambia, Zaire, and especially to South-West Africa.

Mozambique is also being Sovietised. Podgorny visited Maputo and announced close ties between the two nations. Samora Machel has nationalised many enterprises, has established political re-education centres and forced labour camps, and the government regulates all aspects of its citizens' lives. Many are fleeing from harsh communisation, arbitrary arrests, detentions and executions, and mass punishments of villages. Yet no Western press campaigns attack these brutalities.

Can Zimbabwe provide a different model? In 1976 Ian Smith, pressured alike by South Africa and the United States, concluded the so-called Kissinger Agreement that obligated his government to submit at long last to black rule. Zimbabweans of all colours elected a moderate government in 1979 headed by Bishop Abel Muzorewa. The bishop, however, failed to secure an end to the war. International sanctions against Zimbabwe continued, and so did the international diplomatic boycott. Zimbabwe remained an unrecognised republic. After lengthy negotiations, Zimbabwe returned to an interim government presided over by a British governor in the last exercise of British sovereignty over an African colony. The guerrilla forces obtained official legitimacy; guerrilla leaders returned to the villages, and Zimbabwe once more prepared for elections in a general atmosphere of fear and intimidation.

The new elections, held in early 1980, gave a decisive victory to Robert Mugabe, head of the Zimbabwe African National Union (ZANU), a Marxist-Leninist body allied for the time being with its rival, the pro-Moscow Zimbabwe African People's Union (ZAPU) in the so-called Patriotic Front. Mugabe fought his campaign on a platform of extreme moderation. Upon winning, he displayed an apparent degree of magnanimity rarely equalled in the modern history of Africa. His new government included members of the white minority (at present entitled to twenty parliamentary seats). Mugabe also gave Ministerial appointments to supporters of ZAPU, now the principal opposition, that derives its main strength from the Ndebele people, a black ethnic minority in a country whose inhabitants mainly speak the Shona group of languages. Mugabe vowed to co-operate with white officials and white military officers. 'Whether you are white or black,' he concluded, 'forget the grim past.'

Mugabe's new line represented apparently an astonishing reversal of everything he had ever believed in. Less than a year ago his party's journal, *Zimbabwe News*, had bitterly denounced the white officials who had 'oppressed, discriminated [against], jailed, raped, murdered and massacred' the common people. Forgotten was the promise that ZANU would continue the battle 'as long as the capitalists and racists continue to own our land, factories, and mills, and as long as their greed for profits and corrupt luxury keeps our society in wage slavery and poverty'.

Can Mugabe stick to his moderation? The optimists believe that he will and that Zimbabwe might provide a future model for South Africa. Unfortunately, however, the Patriotic Front is not a united body. There are divisions of personality and ethnic splits, as Shona supporters of ZANU clash with Ndebele backers of ZAPU. In the past, guerrilla warfare set brother against brother, clan against clan, village against village; the legacy of hatred remains hard to extirpate. The countryside has suffered severely. The country's industrial equipment, once modern, is now widely outdated or worn out. Yet at a time when the economy has begun to falter Mugabe is suddenly expected to produce rabbits out of his hat. Years of Marxist propaganda have produced vast expectations among his followers. The revolution was expected to bring prosperity to all, but prosperity lies far beyond the horizon. Mugabe's own guerrillas, tough men inured to violence, especially expect to be rewarded for years of hardship in the bush. So do the ZAPU partisans who make up for lack of numbers by strict organisation and Soviet weaponry. For years on end, the revolutionary cadres have called for the seizure of white farms, factories, workshops and stores. How can Mugabe suddenly reverse the party line without incurring censure from his own militants as a 'Tshombe', as a traitor and as a 'sell-out'?

If Mugabe should yield to the militants and turn against the whites, how can he prevent the rapid emigration of skilled whites, followed by the kind of economic chaos that earlier struck Mozambique under similar circumstances?

Moderates have other reasons for concern. Marxist-Leninists are past masters at the art of camouflage. In Eastern Europe, for example, every single Communist party that attained power after 1945 originally set out on a moderate programme. The Popular Front approach invariably found wide acceptance among liberal intellectuals in the West. Czechoslovakia, liberal academicians kept assuring us during the intermediate aftermath of World War Two, would never go Communist — until the Prague *coup* of 1948 put an end to the hopes for a National Front. The Chinese Communists during the late 1940s successfully advertised themselves as 'agrarian reformers' and 'Jeffersonian democrats'. Castro for a time was supposedly but a Cuban nationalist.

Can Mugabe go along a different route? If he should succeed in doing so, he may become known to history as an African Bismarck. Mugabe, however, may not be able to control the forces that he helped to set in motion. His country might well slither into economic chaos and end as a Soviet ally, dependent on military and economic support provided by Moscow, Havana, and perhaps by East Berlin.

No matter what American liberals believe, Soviet strategists believe in gaining control over global 'chokepoints'. Why do the Soviets want to control the Horn of Africa, if not for strategic reasons? Why support and fight for control of Ethiopia and South Yemen when these countries have neither minerals or wealth? Why endanger *détente* by supporting revolution in Africa and invading Afghanistan? The answer is clear: the Soviets have a plan, and they work to implement it.

The Soviets have moved — and will continue to move — to control strategic areas. With the West so dependent on African minerals and Middle East oil, the Soviets have a major advantage. In contrast, the Soviet Union at present is scarcely dependent on Middle East oil, for the Soviets are the world's largest single producer of oil. The bulk of the West's oil comes through the Strait of Hormuz separating Iran from the Arabian Peninsula. Soviet activity in the Persian Gulf has increased enormously. The take-over of Afghanistan dealt a severe blow to Western strategic interests. Since the Soviets already control the entrance to the Red Sea and the Suez Canal, any further extension of Soviet influence would be detrimental to US interests and those of its allies, be it in the Strait, around the Cape, or off the coast of Angola. Prudence and a respect for history suggest we prevent the further spread of

Soviet influence anywhere in the world where we have major interests. Furthermore, we should not count on regimes established by Cubans and Russians to become independent or to sell us their minerals in time of stress or conflict.

The United States has a major stake in South Africa's minerals. US long-term vulnerability in four strategic minerals — chromite, manganese, vanadium and platinum — may be greater than in petroleum. Southern Africa has become 'the Persian Gulf of minerals', and South Africa a supplier of minerals as important as Saudi Arabia is in oil. With South Africa out of the market, the Soviet Union would become the major supplier of these four important minerals. But in twenty years the Soviets may have exhausted many of their deposits, and most of the world's known supplies of chrome will be in South Africa and Zimbabwe. At present the USA buys most of its chrome from the Soviets — a not too pleasant dependence, since tank and ship armour need chrome.

Cut-offs of chrome, cobalt, manganese or the platinum group of minerals would be disastrous. Any interruptions in supplies would produce price increases and add to inflation. While the United States has stockpiles, Western Europe and Japan have none. Alternative supplies from black Africa are not dependable, as supplies may be interrupted through civil strife. For example, chrome production in Zaire's Shaba (Katanga) province were interrupted when ex-Katangan policemen, training in Angola, attacked the mining centres. The Soviets and East Germans profited from their foreknowledge by buying up supplies several months before the planned assault.

The United States then faces a difficult choice — how to balance its strategic and economic requirements with its desire for political reform and stability in the area. The West must find a solution or suffer what may be irreparable loss.

Notes

1. See Daan Prinsloo, *United States Foreign Policy and the Republic of South Africa* (Foreign Affairs Association, Pretoria, 1978), *passim*.
2. Anthony Lake, *The 'Tar Baby' Option: American Policy toward Southern Rhodesia* (Columbia University Press, New York, 1977), p. 74.
3. Figures from Prinsloo, *United States Foreign Policy*, pp. 64-7; see also preceding section on trade.
4. For the Soviet involvement in Africa, see Helen Desfosses Cohn, *Soviet Policy toward Black Africa: the Focus on National Integration* (Praeger, New York, 1972); Peter Duignan, 'Sub-Saharan Africa' in Witold S. Sworakowski (ed.), *World Communism: a Handbook, 1918-1965* (Hoover Institution Press,

Stanford, 1973), pp. 402-11; Grayson Kirk and Nils H. Wessell (eds.), 'The Soviet Threat: Myths and Realities', *Proceedings of the Academy of Political Science*, vol. 33, no. 1 (1978).

5. See Prinsloo, *United States Foreign Policy*, pp. 48-50; Lake, *The 'Tar Baby' Option*, pp. 122-34.

6. *US Foreign Policy for the 1970s: a New Strategy for Peace*, a report to the Congress of the United States by Richard Nixon, President of the United States, 18 February 1970 (US Stationery Office, Washington, DC, 1970), p. 89.

7. See text of the Central Committee Report to the First MPLA Congress in Angola, *Granma* (14-15 December 1977).

8. Basil Hersov, 'Opportunity and Responsibility', *South Africa International*, vol. 8, no. 4 (April 1978), pp. 173-96.

9. A Gallup poll conducted in Great Britain in October 1978 showed that the government's policy regarding Rhodesia did not meet with widespread popular approval: 45 per cent of the respondents wanted sanctions to be stopped as against only 24 per cent who considered that the trade embargo should be continued; 71 per cent opposed British financial support of the activities of the Patriotic Front operating against the Smith government. See *Daily Telegraph* (London), 7 November 1978.

10. Subcommittee on African Affairs, Senate Committee on Foreign Relations (US Congress, Session), *Hearings* (6 June 1977), p. 14. On the rightward drift of US policy, see also Daniel Sutherland, 'US Southern African Policy', *Christian Science Monitor*, 22 November 1978; John F. Burns, 'US Testing Policy on Africa', *New York Times*, 3 December 1978.

11. Carter's speech at a White House conference, *San Francisco Chronicle*, 7 December 1978.

12. See, for instance, Ali Mazrui, *Africa's International Relations: the Diplomacy of Dependency and Change* (Heinemann, London, 1978).

13. For an excellent attack on this misconception from the standpoint of a liberal writer, see Colin Legum, 'A Letter on Angola to American Liberals', *New Republic*, vol. 174 (31 January 1976), pp. 15-19.

14. An excellent presentation of the liberal argument is made by Robert Price, *US Foreign Policy in Sub-Saharan Africa: National Interest and Global Strategy* (Institute of International Studies, Berkeley, 1978). For a statement of opposing viewpoints, see Kenneth Adelman and Gerald J. Bender, 'Conflict in Southern Africa: a Debate', *International Security*, vol. 3, no. 2 (Fall 1978), pp. 67-122.

15. R. Judson Mitchell, 'Union of Soviet Socialist Republics' in Richard R. Starr (ed.), *Yearbook on International Communist Affairs, 1978* (Hoover Institution, Stanford, 1978), p. 87. For more explicit Soviet statements, see Walter F. Hahn and Alvin J. Cottrell, *Soviet Shadow over Africa* (University of Miami, Center of Advanced International Studies, Miami, 1976), pp. 14-22.

16. Marshal A.A. Grechko, 'The Leading Role of the CPSU in Building the Army of a Developed Socialist Society', *Voprosy Istorii KPSS*, no. 5 (May 1974), as translated in *USA/FN Soviet press translations*, no. 74-7 (31 July 1974), cited in Hahn and Cottrell, *Soviet Shadow*, p. 22.

10 WHY SOUTH AFRICA WILL SURVIVE

Few countries are as unpopular as South Africa today. The Pretoria regime has become for British and American progressives what the 'Unspeakable Turk' was to the British conscience vote in the nineteenth century — the acme of oppression. According to its critics, the Pretoria regime is run by a reactionary clique wedded to a policy of rigid *immobilisme*. South Africa represents the worst aspects of Western civilisation: white racism, capitalist exploitation and the ruthless domination of the 'Third World' by the 'First World'. South Africa's system of government is not merely a standing insult to the dignity of man. It is threatened by an impending revolution that must lead either to the surrender of the white minority or to a racial bloodbath. The black insurgents are bound to win; justice, the force of numbers and the power of world opinion are on their side. The tide of history is bound to sweep the white oppressor into oblivion. Hence the Western powers, especially the United States, should use their influence — diplomatic, economic, moral, and perhaps even military — to break the fetters that weigh down the black and brown peoples of South Africa.

No Revolution around the Corner

We ourselves dissent from the orthodoxy of the lectern and the pulpit. Unlike a truly decadent ruling class, South African whites are willing to tax themselves heavily and to conscript their sons. Most white South Africans do not live in idle luxury; neither are they the archetypal representatives of the global bourgeoisie. We pointed out previously that more than 80 per cent of South African whites depend for their livelihood on wages and salaries; the average income per head of the population is less than that of Frenchmen or Australians. The whites perform essential economic functions; for the time being the greater part of South Africa's administrative, entrepreneurial and technical skills are drawn from Europeans, though this position will certainly change in the future.

In economic terms, South Africa's history has been an extraordinary success story. Sixty years ago the nation was a poverty-stricken land dependent, like so many Third World countries today, on the export of raw materials. Today it is the economic giant of the continent. Its GNP is more than ten times that of Kenya and more than twenty times that of Ethiopia. It is a major producer and exporter, and the only sub-Saharan country capable of producing the most sophisticated manufacturing products — from mining machinery to computers. Its industrial growth rate has, in fact, been astounding. Between 1916 and 1970 its manufacturing output alone increased in value from R27,908,000 to R3,101,892,000. It is the wealthiest, fastest growing, most powerful state of Africa, with a growth rate since World War Two second only to that of Japan.

South Africa faces difficult economic problems, especially widespread African unemployment. Though the economy will continue to expand, South Africa will find ever-increasing difficulties in providing enough jobs for black school drop-outs. Compared with the majority of Third World countries, however, South Africa's economic future looks hopeful. At a time of world-wide inflation, Pretoria stands to gain from sharply rising gold prices (these increased from about $150 per ounce to about $680 early in 1980). Above all, South Africa — alone in sub-Saharan Africa — has built up a reasonably balanced economy complete with modern manufactures, extensive mining industries and an advanced agricultural sector.

South Africa's dynamic qualities sharply distinguish it from many African countries — Marxist and non-Marxist alike — nations that never tire of criticising Pretoria, but that have permitted their economies to deteriorate and that must cope with the problems of political disintegration. In the late 1950s and the early 1960s the bulk of Western academicians and policy-makers concerned with Africa assumed as a matter of faith that independence would usher in a new era of 'nation-building', 'mobilisation', economic growth and peaceful development. Some African states — Kenya and the Ivory Coast, for example — have indeed done well since the departure of their former imperial masters. Many other countries, however, such as Angola, Mozambique, Zaire and Equatorial Guinea, have had to pay a heavy price for liberation. In many cases independence has entailed the rise of a new parasitic class of party functionaries, bureaucrats and ideologues whose ill-considered interference has brought about economic decline. Peasants are reluctant to grow cash crops if they can only sell them at prices pegged below market value. Investors hesitate to risk their savings if they are subject to sudden expropriation or to confiscatory bribes and taxation. The exodus of former 'colonialists' from Zaire, Angola and Mozambique has deprived these countries of technicians, specialists and entrepreneurs whose skills are now badly missed.

South Africa has maintained a reasonable degree of internal stability, unlike countries as diverse in their respective political philosophies as Zaire and Mozambique which have to cope with widespread lawlessness, banditry and loss of worker morale. The breakdown of law and order is apt to have consequences that are often poorly understood by academicians working in the safety of Western University campuses or habituated to doing field-work in the security of the bygone imperial era. The very disparity in the documentation available for, say, Zaire on the one hand and South Africa on the other has indeed created distortions. Academicians interested in South Africa are able to draw on a great wealth of government reports, sociological surveys and official inquiries that reveal the country's ills; journalists can travel about South Africa in relative security. Corresponding material does not exist in anything like comparable quantities for Angola and Zaire; anthropologists and journalists do not readily take trips into the outlying parts of Zaire or, for that matter, into Burundi or Equatorial Guinea. The very availability of information concerning South Africa thus creates informational distortions.

In military terms, South Africa is well equipped. It is a match for any conventional opponent except a superpower. South Africa is equally prepared to deal with guerrilla incursions. It is true that Portugal, after a ten-year conflict, was forced to shed its colonial empire after the military revolted. It is equally true that Rhodesia, after 14 years of UDI, was forced to negotiate for a black majority government. But South Africa's position is different in both a qualitative and a quantitative sense. South Africa, for one thing, is vastly stronger militarily and economically than either Portugal or Rhodesia. (South Africa's GNP in 1977 stood at $44.8 billion in 1977 compared to Portugal's $16.4 billion and Rhodesia's $3.1 billion.) Rhodesia's white population amounted to no more than a quarter of a million people; contrary to all expert predictions, this small group managed to hold out for 14 years after Ian Smith's declaration of unilateral independence. Within the next decade South Africa's white population will probably exceed 5 million, and she will find herself in an infinitely stronger position for a prolonged struggle than was Rhodesia.

South Africa, like Israel, will certainly face long-drawn-out partisan operations. Guerrillas now attempt to hide arms and supplies in prepared caches; they will attempt to build an underground organisation and start their campaign with attacks against police stations, army posts and similar targets. But as we pointed out in the section on defence, the guerrillas will meet with extraordinary difficulties. Partisan operations on their own will not suffice to bring down the regime in the foreseeable future. It is true that South Africa will be ringed by hostile states for the first time — Mozambique, Zimbabwe and possibly in the future Botswana and Namibia. But, as pointed out in previous chapters, Mozambique, Zimbabwe and Namibia all depend on South Africa economically. South Africans for the time being continue to run Mozambique's railway and principal port. The South Africans exercise an even greater stranglehold over Zimbabweans through South Africa's control of Zimbabwe's southward communications by road, air and rail, and through Zimbabwe's continued reliance on South Africa as a source of capital, skilled labour and services, and as a market. Zimbabwe cannot function, much less rebuild its war-torn economy, without South African assistance. Hence, just as Israel has managed to hold out, South Africans should be able to contain the effect of partisan operations.

Defence is not cheap. But there is no likelihood that South Africa is about to collapse under the weight of heavy military investment. South Africa's defence expenditure accounts for a smaller percentage of the GNP than that of the United States, not to speak of Nigeria or the Soviet Union — 5.1, as opposed to 5.4, 7.9 or 12.0 respectively. South Africa is the military and industrial giant of the African continent; her economy should therefore be capable of coping with the military expenditure that the country must now shoulder.

Critics of South Africa make much of the many economic, social and political disabilities that now face black and brown South Africans alike. The censors have an excellent case. Nevertheless, as indicated previously, the benefits of economic development have begun to trickle down to all racial groups, albeit in uneven measure. Black South Africans — despite their disabilities — are among the best-paid, best-educated, most urbanised blacks in Africa. Instead of emigrating to 'free' Africa, blacks vote with their feet to go to South Africa. Black South Africans have a higher life expectancy than West Africans (50.0 years as opposed to 39.2 years). Black wages have gone up steadily; the industrial colour bar has recently been eliminated; social and educational services available to black South Africans compare favourably with the best available to Africans in any part of black Africa. UN propaganda notwithstanding, there are now substantial numbers of black South Africans who have a great deal more to lose than their chains.

South Africa's apartheid measures seem insignificant in comparison with enforced population movements within the Soviet Union which were huge in scale, yet we have normal relations with the Soviet government that was responsible for that systematic discrimination and those mass expulsions. We seek to deal with Communist regimes; we even work towards a *détente* with them. Churchmen no longer lead protest movements against 'Godless Communism'; few leftist students or university teachers cry out for the protection of human rights in the Soviet Union, let alone in North Korea, East Germany or Vietnam. The liberal left argues that we should 'understand' the Communists, that we should not 'provoke' them, and that we should try to soften their regimes by promoting trade and cultural relations, by extending loans on easy terms. In our dealings with South Africa, on the other hand, the international conscience vote adopts a standard or morality regretfully different.

The Importance of South Africa to the West

Soviet and Western strategists both agree that South Africa occupies an important position on the chessboard of international power. South Africa presently controls the Cape route — a major consideration at a time when Soviet naval power has become influential in the western part of the Indian Ocean — and it is the only African country capable during wartime of supplying its allies in the western part of the Indian Ocean with a vast industrial infrastructure. It plays a major role in the global economy as the world's greatest producer of gold and as a major exporter of uranium, diamonds, chrome, manganese and other minerals. The West cannot afford to abandon South Africa. The West would be ill served if we should help to turn South Africa into yet another Angola — from which the whites fled or were expelled, and where a civil war continues to rage — at a time when Soviet strategists are rightly convinced that the military balance of power, once so unfavourable to them, has swung their way. South Africa's policy may offend the governments of countries like Guinea and Rwanda, which, between them, wield two paper votes at the United Nations. But the real power — as opposed to the voting power — of all African countries is small, and the Western nations cannot afford to buy their capricious favour by concessions that would further weaken the West itself.

Moreover, the West has a particular interest in a secure passage around the Cape of Good Hope and in access to the mineral wealth of Southern Africa for itself and its allies. Western (including US) reliance on imported minerals is on the increase. It is, of course, perfectly true that up to now Communist and pro-Communist powers have made no attempt to halt the supply of strategic raw materials to the Western powers in pursuance of political objectives. In the long run, however, the danger to the West of a growing dependence on raw materials that are controlled by hostile powers is very real, given the Communists' assumption that trade, like cultural contacts and conventional diplomacy, is a legitimate weapon in 'the intensification of the international class struggle' against the so-called 'forces of imperialism'.

As regards naval and military strategy, the development of nuclear weapons has not rendered conventional notions irrelevant. A pro-Communist South African government would be perfectly within its rights to prohibit to Western oil tankers the use of South African repair facilities or transit rights through South African territorial waters, which might be expanded to a 200-mile zone. The development of nuclear weapons has not stopped the outbreak of conventional wars, as seen in the three decades since the end of World War Two; major wars have since taken place in the Middle East, India, Korea and South Vietnam, all fought with non-nuclear weapons. As the Russians see it, Soviet strategic advances tend to be incremental; each tactical victory in turn begets new victories. The loss of Western control over the Cape sea route and over the raw materials of Southern Africa would, in turn, vastly assist in the Finlandisation of Western Europe. The United States ought therefore to extend the boundaries of the NATO alliance beyond the Tropic of Cancer — an arbitrary boundary that makes no sense in the light of Soviet naval strategy — and to associate South Africa with the Western system of defence.

The Carter administration rejects this policy because it believes that any form of co-operation with South Africa would jeopardise US relations with the independent black states of Africa, and indeed with all the nations of the Third World. It makes no sense, this argument states, to endanger, say, our growing trade with Nigeria — a country important for its oil — for the sake of propping up an endangered white regime in Pretoria. From 1973 onward, US trade with Nigeria began to exceed American–South African commerce in value. Nigeria is now a major foreign supplier of oil; the United States would be ill advised to forgo her 'black' African trade for the sake of her somewhat smaller traffic with white South Africa. America's South African investments are an insignificant part of the total US foreign investments abroad (1.12 per cent in 1973, yielding no more than 1 per cent of US foreign earnings). The United States could easily write off this revenue in the interests of international morality.[1] Admittedly, disinvestment would not by itself wreck the South African economy. But, the liberal argument continues, the withdrawal of foreign capital would slow down economic growth, retard the development of the country's high technology, and, by occasioning unemployment, raise revolutionary consciousness among the black masses. At the very least, disinvestment is a symbolic act, a moral gesture that will impress the Western 'conscience' vote and the Third World nations abroad as an example of disinterested morality.

The anti-South African campaign has made steady progress in the United States where pension funds play a major part in the investment market and where churches, trade unions and universities hold a substantial amount of stock in major companies. American economic disengagement from South Africa, however, would have little impact. American investments are dwarfed by the 57 per cent stake held by Great Britain. Most of South Africa's investment capital is now generated at home, not abroad. South Africa, moreover, is far from defenceless in an economic sense. Thanks to its powerful position as a producer of gold, platinum, chrome and uranium, the country would be in a strong position to retaliate if the United States or other Western nations were to embark on economic sanctions. Without South African platinum for catalytic converters, for instance, the United States would probably have to call off the entire automobile emission-control programme.[2] The West is increasingly dependent on South African chrome, which is vital in the production of stainless steel and superalloys used in tanks and cars. In some ways, liberals in the West in fact give a boost to the South African gold industry by advocating inflationary policies that have the unintended effect of driving up gold prices. As long as the Western currencies deteriorate, South African gold in the long run is certain to gain rather than diminish in importance.

Advocates of disinvestment in South Africa talk of 'pulling out'. But they do not indicate how this could be done effectually. American firms cannot simply dismantle their plants in South Africa and ship back the parts to the United States. Most of the personnel employed in South Africa — even the highly placed managers and technicians — are South Africans who would stay in the country of their birth. South African exchange control regulations would, in case of need, prevent the repatriation of foreign capital. If the present investors were to sell their existing holdings in South Africa, such sales simply would benefit the new purchasers — South African, American or European — who would be able to acquire stock at artificially depressed prices. The physical plant, the technology and the personnel would all remain in

South Africa. Only the ownership would change hands.

South Africa certainly looks to foreign credits. But it is not sufficiently dependent on imported capital to be vulnerable to ultimata from the outside world. Between 1976 and 1977 the foreign capital inflow declined from R989 million to R211 million. Yet at the same time the government managed to turn a balance-of-payments deficit running at R2,592 million to a surplus of R1,277 million.

A complete world embargo on South African trade is hard to enforce, as we pointed out in our section on defence. But even if the world community were willing to cut all its ties, South Africa would not be the greatest loser. David Owen, the former British Foreign Secretary, has indicated that Great Britain's extensive South African portfolio — worth more than $5 billion and amounting to about 9 per cent of all British investments abroad — makes his country vulnerable on the South African connection. South Africa's African neighbours — Lesotho, Botswana, Swaziland, Zimbabwe, Mozambique, and to some extent even Zambia — all rely heavily on the South African link and could hardly survive economically if they were cut off from world trade through an economic blockade of South Africa.

Sanctions can work, in the sense that they can do considerable damage to an economy. Rhodesia survived fourteen years of world sanctions, but at a heavy price. The problem is that although sanctions can bring economic suffering to a country, it cannot produce political reform. South Africa can survive an oil and arms boycott. Oil provides only 25 per cent of the country's energy needs, and the government has stockpiled two to five years' reserve supply. South Africa has become almost self-sufficient in weapons. South Africa has also begun to draw closer to other 'pariah states' such as Taiwan. (Early in 1980, South Africa agreed to supply uranium to Taiwan, as well as scientific and technical information.) A ban on imports to South Africa would force South Africa into a neutralist position, but would not bring down the whites. It would, ironically, produce an economic boom through import substitution, as shown by a study of the Federated Chamber of Industries and the Afrikaanse Handelinstituut: South Africa can buy R1,000 million's worth of goods domestically produced rather than imported. Still the South Africans would suffer severely if the world were to boycott their exports. A South African economist, Arnt Spandau, has estimated that a 20 per cent reduction in exports could cause unemployment in South Africa (of whites 90,000, of blacks 340,000); incomes would drop greatly (whites by R520 million, blacks by R471 million). Furthermore, unemployment and income decline would hit all the states of Southern Africa. The questions to be answered, then: Is the cost worth the objectives to be gained? Would the objectives be gained even after all this suffering?

What is to be Done?

In our view, advocates of domestic reforms in South Africa should welcome rather than deplore South Africa's commercial connections with the wider world. The rise of her manufacturing industries has created new jobs for blacks as well as for brown and white people. To some extent, industrial growth has also brought about a reallocation of income between the various racial groups. Between 1970 and 1977 the white share of the total income declined by 1 per cent a year, while that of the blacks grew by that same percentage. According to Erich Leistner, a South African economist, the consumption by blacks at the end of the century will be twice the size of South Africa's total consumer market at present. The development of manufacturing, therefore, has proved a blessing to South African blacks, whose industrial wages are higher than comparative wages in countries as far afield as Kenya, Nigeria, the Philippines and India.[3]

The importation of private capital has other, more far-reaching advantages. Private investments will strengthen the private sector in South Africa as against that of the state. Such a shift in the economic balance of power will displease advocates of a socialist solution in South Africa. We ourselves, however, regard capitalism rather than socialism as the world's most revolutionary force. Contrary to socialist theory, the free enterprise system has, throughout the world, been economically more successful than has socialism. East Germany's economic performance compares poorly with West Germany's; North Korea does not stand comparison with South Korea, any more than development in the People's Republic of China measures up to development in Taiwan, Hong Kong or Singapore; in Africa, the Ivory Coast is more prosperous than Guinea or Angola. 'The bourgeoisie', as Marx and Engels pointed out with such eloquence in their *Communist Manifesto*, 'has created more massive and productive forces than have all the preceding generations together.' The capitalist system is subversive of all traditional restraints, 'all fixed, fast-frozen relations with their train of ancient and venerable prejudices are swept away, all newly formed ones become antiquated before they can ossify.'[4] A truly free market in land and labour would have far more revolutionary consequences for South Africa than a socialist take-over there that would, in the first place, simply replace Afrikaner by African bureaucrats. As we see it, South Africa stands in need of a fully fledged capitalist transformation that will slowly but deliberately dismantle the vast machinery of state control that prevents South Africans of all colours from selling their goods, their land and their labour to their own best advantage, from moving where they want to more, from dwelling where they want to dwell.

These notions are not popular amongst Western liberals today. According to our critics, racialism is inherent in South African capitalism, an indispensable source of its superprofits. A substantial group of scholars argue that apartheid, far from impeding industrialisation, has actually made industrialisation more profitable. The migrant labour system and the colour bar have, in their view, provided the whites with a means of holding down the wages of African workers, thereby generating a surplus to sustain economic expansion and to provide a high standard of living for the whites. The price, however, is high; it includes low labour productivity, a restricted internal market, a widespread shortage of skilled labour and low wages for the majority of the labour force.[5]

In our opinion, these critiques take inadequate account of the qualitative changes in South African capitalism and of its dynamic qualities compared with the economic systems — both socialist and non-socialist — in many parts of black Africa. The weaknesses ascribed to South African capitalism, the prevalence of migrant labour, the restricted nature of the internal market, the shortages of skilled labour, the inefficient use of manpower — all, of course, are almost universal to the economies in sub-Saharan Africa.

The radicals fail to allow for the anti-apartheid stand of South Africa's own capitalists — magnates like Harry Oppenheimer — who presumably understand their own economic interests better than professors overseas. As regards the moral case against investment in South Africa, we see little merit in critics who decry the $1.7 billion or so invested by Americans in South Africa but who accept without questioning the $60 billion lent by Americans to the Soviet Union and its allies in the Warsaw Pact. South Africa — the point bears repeating — is infinitely less tyrannical than the USSR. Apartheid at its worst is incomparably more humane than the system of mass liquidations and mass deportations by which socialism has been built in the Soviet Union.[6] South Africa, unlike the Soviet Union, does not regard its social system as a model for the entire world to follow; neither do

South Africa's armed forces constitute a mortal military threat to the West.

What are the whites' options? For the moment, defeat by African revolution or by armed invasion can be excluded. Whites will not capitulate and they cannot be defeated. The nation is not a police state or even a garrison state. There are relatively few political prisoners, and people not actively opposing the regime have relative freedom and a high standard of living by Third World standards. Repression is harsh against specific activists, but not against the general population. This situation could change if Afrikaners felt threatened and isolated. The Afrikaner is a pragmatist and enjoys his privileged position, so he is willing to make concessions and to avoid a totally repressive state.

The Canadian scholar Heribert Adam rejects most options for the whites: power-sharing, emigration, partition, modified apartheid.[7] At present, power-sharing would involve no more than consulting with blacks while offering political power to Indians and Coloureds. The whites will not make major concessions, or share a common franchise, or establish a federal system for the present. They see no way to stop further concessions once they adopt a one-man/one-vote system, for they would be in the minority. Migration is not a practical policy for most of them; only highly skilled professional people can pack up and leave. In any case, most whites feel they are Africans and do not want to leave.

Schemes for partitioning South Africa are being put forward in various forms. We discuss Ngubane's plan for a multistate system below (p. 303), and some Natalians advocate a free Natal. But the truth is that no one can agree on a just partition of South Africa, and partition clearly makes no sense in an economically integrated industrial society. To gain support for a modified form of apartheid seems to be the policy at present. This programme will cost a great deal if the Bantustans are to be built up and made viable and attractive. More land and resources will have to be assigned to blacks. Meanwhile, some concessions to urban blacks, Indians and Coloureds are being made to get them to acquiesce to a modified apartheid system. This is not, however, likely to satisfy Africans in the long run.

A liberal democratic solution is not on the cards. One-man/one-vote is not a realistic goal; to solve ethnic conflicts, South Africa will have to institutionalise group rights. While democracies can allow power to pass from party to party, ethnically and racially diverse societies cannot do so. When a party loses power in a democracy, it does not have its basic rights endangered, whereas ethnic groups that lose political power often lose everything else as well. Historically, ethnic politics have been harsh, and they usually entail the dominance of one group over the others. Hence, Vorster told Bantustan leaders that the Nationalist Party would not allow power to slip from its hand. White leaders in South Africa will continue to decide unilaterally how much to concede to black demands. This is not because they are evil men or even racists, but because of South African history and the multiracial structure of its society.⁸

The whites have too long dominated the blacks, and they have benefitted too much from this dominance to give up power. Ethnic cleavages are deep between whites, blacks, Indians and Coloureds, and the apartheid system has allowed few opportunities for the development of associations and alliances that transcend ethnicity. In any election based on a one-man/one-vote principle, the white minority would lose. Whites naturally, therefore, resist this procedure. Adam correctly concludes that, given the inequalities that separate the groups, no Western democratic political system can be built until these equalities can be reduced.⁹

South Africa continues to be torn by racial dispute, and an interracial consensus cannot be achieved in South Africa's multiracial, multiethnic society at this time. Ethnic complexities are further complicated by struggles between classes that are divided along colour lines. Whites, who own most of the land and control most of the economy, fear that any political surrender will lead to the loss of their economic control and their culture. They cannot agree among themselves, much less with any other social faction. Ethnic polarisation is increasing. Anti-white feelings are strong and have recently led to a coalition between the Coloured Labour Party, the Indian Reform Party and the Zulu Inkatha movement designed to draw up a new constitution for a 'non-racist' society. For a consensus to be reached, individuals in the various racial, economic and political groups would have to stand apart from those groups on important issues in order to act for the benefit of the larger unit of South Africa.

To attain a consensus society, the various groups would have to develop a higher level of agreement among the competing ethnic, racial, economic and political groups. They would have to share a common political culture and value system. It is hard to imagine Afrikaners thinking of themselves as citizens of a multi-South African nation rather than as members of their ethnic group, but if they fail to transcend those narrower loyalties, South Africa's future may be bleak. Because conflict will not resolve the country's problems and consensus may be impossible to achieve, a third way should be tried — a consociational system.

Consociation implies continued social and ethnic diversity based on a policy of pragmatism and tempered by co-operation between the elites in each social group. These elites could act as brokers to limit conflict and to reach accommodation and a balance of power between their conflicting interests. The consociational state would require the exercise of a joint veto and local autonomy for each group along with proportional representation. Such a solution would, however, face great difficulties. The whites would hold disproportionate influence, since they command so much of the country's property and so much of its managerial and technical skills. Blacks could thus argue that even this moderate solution would be merely white supremacy in disguise. Calls for a class or race war would be hard to ignore.

Can a peaceful South Africa be created in the future? We believe it can, but it will be a difficult task. A successful regime will have to recognise the diversity of South Africa's ethnic, political and economic groups, and will have to mediate between them. The striking differences in status and material wealth between blacks, browns and whites will gradually have to be reduced. Political power cannot be restricted to whites and to traditional tribal rulers; leadership roles must be shared among all group elites. South Africa will have to accept a federal system, but not one based only on the homelands (Bantustans) concept. All racially discriminatory legislation and practices will have to be ended. Some progress has already been made towards the last goal. For example, segregation has ended in some hotels, bars and restaurants. Legislation such as the Group Areas Act and the Mixed Marriages and Immorality Acts, however, must also be repealed. In short, apartheid will have to be dismantled. Strong efforts need to be made to build a South African consciousness and to stress nationalism based on equality before the law and on human rights.

Police brutality must end. Job reservations and other restrictions on black, Indian and Coloured businessmen must be abolished. There should be more education and greater opportunities for blacks and Coloureds. Urban blacks should be given more self-government, and political power should be shared in some measure by the whites with all the peoples of South Africa. (At the time of writing, reforms along these lines were being suggested by the Wiehahn and Riekert commissions, government-appointed bodies.) African administration needs to be reformed. The government has to stop suppressing moderate opposition leaders and start to communicate with them. The inane South

African censorship system should also be changed. Censorship in South Africa is neither rational nor consistent. Nadine Gordimer's *A World of Strangers* is banned in paperback but not in hardback; all Mphahlele's books are banned, yet copies of his *Down Second Avenue* can be bought in Cape Town bookshops. The Publications Act of 1974 makes the possession of any 'undesirable material' an offence liable to fine or imprisonment, yet literate white households have copies of many banned books. Government enforces the law only selectively — when it wants to get someone. There is an *Index of Objectionable Literature in South Africa*.

This complicated, delicate process of accommodation, power-sharing and leveling can only succeed if all groups agree to co-operate. Such co-operation will not be easy in a multiracial, ethnically diverse society — a society that has long been dominated by whites and is under attack by the SACP, the ANC and the PAC, as well as many radical states and the United Nations. Nevertheless, there are some grounds for hope.

Reform in South Africa will come from within. It will derive from the ruling Nationalist Party rather than from a divided opposition. As we have pointed out before, the National Party is not a monolithic bloc run, like a Communist party, on the rigid principles of 'democratic centralism'. The party is being transformed by those social and economic forces that shape and reshape South African society as a whole.

Half a century ago the Afrikaners were mainly rural people. The average Nationalist voter was an indigent farmer, a white workman often without a job, an employee, a teacher or a rural clergyman. In certain respects, the National Party resembled a pre-World War Two peasant party in Eastern Europe — anti-capitalist, anti-urban, ethnocentric and anti-Semitic. Since then the Afrikaners have moved into the towns; they have risen in the social sphere; the 'poor white', fearful of African competition and Negrophobe in outlook, has largely disappeared.

The National Party today is a coalition that contains bankers, factory owners and professional men along with white workers and farmers. The conservative wing remains strong in the caucus, the cultural organisations, the civil service and the police; it is supported by white workers, employees and small farmers. But there is now a substantial reformist group made up of businessmen and professional people, technicians and specialists in both the public and private sectors, clergymen and senior members of the defence establishment anxious to strengthen the country's industrial power and determined to create a wider social consensus. The National Party no longer speaks of combating the Jews or repatriating the Indians. Whatever the party's failings, it has done more in the fields of African slum clearance, the expansion of social services for Africans, Indians and Coloureds, and the economic development of the rural African areas than all its supposedly more liberal predecessors. Within the party, moreover, the reformers are gaining strength over the conservatives. (A poll taken early in 1980 by the *Sunday Times*, a Johannesburg paper, concluded that 85.5 per cent of registered National Party members supported Botha; only 6.4 per cent backed Andries Treurnicht, the right-wing leader of the party's Transvaal wing.)

South Africa, in other words, is no longer committed to a policy of rigid conservatism. In recent years, white South African politicians have begun to search for alternatives to their present Westminster system where whites rule by parliamentary democracy — for whites only. Cabinet Minister Koornhof has pushed for a Swiss-canton system. Vorster wanted a strong presidential system and a series of parliaments based on race. Others, like C.P. Mulder, outline a policy of breaking up South Africa into ethnic homelands for each of the races and ethnic groups.

The new Botha plan for sharing power envisages three separate parliaments — for whites, Coloureds and Indians respectively — who will look out for their own people. The blacks are not to have their own Parliament. The country's affairs are to be run by a Cabinet Council of seven whites, four Coloureds and three Asians under the chairmanship of the Executive State President. The President, who will be elected by a multiracial assembly of 50 whites, 25 Coloureds and 14 Asians, would have the deciding vote in the Cabinet Council. There will also be a special multiracial President's Advisory Council. Opponents have attacked the plan as unwieldy; the three Parliaments could make different laws for each racial group. Critics also fear that the President will have too much power. At least the plan shows that the white leaders recognise the problem and accept the fact that they cannot rule alone.

Another solution to the deeply divided society of South Africa would be to break up the Republic even more by adding to the independent Transkei another state, Natal. At one stroke the Afrikaners would rid themselves of one of the largest black ethnic groups — the Zulus (2,867,177) — and the majority of English-speaking whites. When they made the Transkei independent, the Afrikaners removed the Xhosas, one of the largest ethnic groups in the country (3,044,634) and the natural leaders of African nationalism in South Africa. The Xhosas have traditionally been the best educated, most vocal of African nationalists, and have provided all but two of the leaders of African nationalism since 1912. Were Natal to be made a second independent state, the Zulus and most English-speaking whites would no longer form part of the African state. The Afrikaners could deal more easily with the remaining 8 to 9 million blacks in the other three provinces. Under this solution, a federal union would allow each state or unit to pursue separate policies.

The most original proposal was drawn up by Jordan K. Ngubane, a black South African who set out a blueprint for the new South Africa fifteen years ago in his book, *An African Explains Apartheid*. He proposed a Swiss cantonal federation which would have four types of states: African, Afrikaner, English and non-racial. These ethnic states would, in part, be based on traditional living areas. Ngubane recognised the conflicting interests of each racial group, and therefore sought a democratic framework which would guarantee that no one group would dominate the others. It satisfies those who want black majority rule but who would protect legitimate white interests. Unfortunately, few people have read Ngubane's book. Fewer still espouse his ideas.

Rapid change, then, is unlikely in South Africa. Blacks cannot put much pressure on he government; outside forces are too weak to bring about revolutionary change. P.W. Botha would probably like to make some concessions, but he may find them hard to grant due to the election of the hard-liner (*verkrampte*) Andries P. Treurnicht as head of the Transvaal branch of the National Party, a key position. Botha now faces a strong Nationalist leader on his right. Treurnicht, a Dutch Reformed minister, is one of the National Party's leading conservative intellectuals, an eloquent speaker and former editor of an influential Afrikaner newspaper. He controls a powerful section of the National Party in Parliament, and he is therefore the second most powerful politician in South Africa. Only the Prime Minister, who is the national leader, outranks him. Treurnicht and his supporters have opposed almost all racial reforms or deviations from apartheid in recent years. As number-two man in the former Bantu Affairs department, he had control over the nation's 18.5 million blacks. A paternalist and racist, he opposed efforts to remove petty apartheid regulations, arguing that this would endanger the whole structure.[10] The Muldergate scandal further strengthened Treurnicht — a strict Calvinist — while discrediting *verligtes* involved in the affair. The National Party is not likely to embark on a programme of genuine change unless the party either wins over or breaks with its right wing and the moderates take over.

As we see it, the West should endeavour to promote a policy of reform by supporting the *verligtes* within the National Party rather than the South African opposition, whether liberal or revolutionary. In practice, the United States has done the opposite. It has weakened reform-minded nationalists by an ineffective combination of sermons and insults that merely serve to consolidate white power. The National Party wields effective power in South Africa. Effective change within the country then is likely to come from that party within the system rather than from forces outside it.

We realise that our position is hardly popular. Liberal academicians will argue that the right-wingers are bound to win, that even the *verligtes* cannot be trusted to grant justice to the blacks, and that any concessions made by the *verligtes* will count for little and come too late. We are also aware that economic advancement for black and brown South Africans will not necessarily lead to a political transformation of the country. Change will be slow and its pace will be uncertain.[11]

Nevertheless, we are convinced that our policy provides the best hope for South Africa. We cannot, moreover, see any objections on moral grounds. As we stated before, South Africa is not the world's most oppressive country. Even militant African nationalists are willing to co-operate with South Africa on pragmatic grounds. Mugabe is willing to deal with South African businessmen. South African technicians help to keep Mozambique running. Machel's government even sends African labour migrants to the mines of the Witwatersrand and sells to South Africa electric power from the Cabora Bassa complex that South Africa helped to build and finance. Zambia is another opponent of apartheid; but South Africa is one of its premier trading partners, a source of much-needed mining machinery and other supplies. If radical states can be pragmatic about South Africa, why not the West? The alternatives are worse. Neither the United States nor Western Europe have any interest in promoting strife and civil disorders in South Africa, much less in supporting movements that will look to the Soviet Union for support or in establishing bloodstained tyrannies of the kind now in power in Ethiopia and Angola. Both in our own interest and in South Africa's, we should recast Lenin's slogan and call for 'all power to the moderates'.

Notes

1. William Foltz, 'US Policy toward Southern Africa: Economic and Strategic Constraints' in Réné Lemárchand (ed.), *American Policy in Southern Africa: the Stakes and the Stance* (University Press of America, Washington, DC, 1976), pp. 247-73, argues that there are no serious strategic or economic constraints on American policy towards South Africa and that the United States has no vital stake in South Africa.
2. Herman Nickel, *The Case for Doing Business in South Africa* (Georgetown University, Ethics and Policy Center, Washington, DC, 1978).
3. See United Nations, *Statistical Yearbook, 1976-77* (United Nations, New York, 1977), pp. 620-3, Table 179; also Department of Statistics, *Quarterly Bulletin of Statistics* (Pretoria), vol. 12, no. 1 (March 1978).
4. Karl Marx and Friedrich Engels, *The Communist Manifesto* (Charles Scribner, Chicago, 1965), pp. 21-2, 23.
5. See, for instance, Giovanni Arrighi and John S. Saul, 'Nationalism and Revolution in Sub-Saharan Africa' in G. Arrighi and J.S. Saul (eds.), *Essays on the Political Economy of Africa* (Monthly Review Press, New York, 1973); Frederick A. Johnstone, *Class, Race, and Gold* (Routledge and Kegan Paul, London, 1976); Martin Legassick, 'Capital Accumulation and Violence in South Africa', *Economy and Society*, vol. 3, no. 3 (1974), pp. 253-91; Harold Jack Simons, *Class and Colour in South Africa, 1850-1950* (Penguin Books, Harmondsworth, 1969).
6. For comparative purposes, see, for instance, Aleksandr Nekrich, *The Punished Peoples: the Deportation and Tragic Fate of Soviet Authorities at the End of World War II* (Norton, New York, 1978).
7. Heribert Adam, 'When the Chips are Down: Confrontation and Accommodation in South Africa', *Contemporary Crisis* (1977), p. 4.
8. Ibid., p. 432.
9. Ibid., p. 433.
10. Andries P. Treurnicht, *Credo Van'N Afrikaner* (Tafelberg, Cape Town, 1977).
11. For a contrasting interpretation, see Colin Legum, *Southern Africa: the Year of the Whirlwind* (Greenwood Press, Westport, Conn., 1977).

INDEX

Adam, H. 298
Afghanistan 285
African National Congress (ANC)
    alliance with Communists 127-8, 227, 252, 260
    alliance with Indians 138-9 and USA 278
    Freedom Charter 126
    leadership 123, 126, 240n5
    organisation 123-4, 127, 140n9
    origins 55, 57, 122-3
    programme 124-7
African politics 122-36
    see also under specific organisations
Africans
    agriculture *see* agriculture, African
    education *see* education, Africans
    ethics 46-7, 63
    franchise 54-5
    in Defence Force 214
    land ownership 57-9, 65, 76
    migrant labour 56-60, 63-6, 78-9, 146-50, 160-4, 230
    reserves 55-9, *see also* homelands
    resistance to conquest 49-53, *see also* homelands, race relations
    skilled labour 59
    trade unions 230, 300
    traditional society 44-9, 64
    urban *see* urban Africans
Afrikaanse Studentebond 120-2
Afrikaner Party 108, 110
Afrikaners
    British attitudes toward 256
    economic control 109
    origins 5-8, 22
    political role 19-24, 225-6, 301, *see also* National Party
    religion *see* Dutch Reformed Church
Afro-Marxism 275-6
agriculture
    African 46-7, 57
    European 5-6, 18, 150, 152-7, 171
    future prospects 180
    marketing 156-7

    mechanisation 155
    research 155-6
    soil conservation 154-6, 180, 185n18
Anglo-American Corporation 251
Angola 113, 117, 274-6, 279, 281-2, 285, 289, 304
Anti-Apartheid Movement 227, 252, 261
apartheid *see* race relations, apartheid legislation
Armaments Development and Production Corporation (ARMSCOR) 172, 205-6, 210
Asians *see* Indians
Atomic Energy Board (AEB) 170

banking 143
Bantu Investment Corporation 100n, 172
Bantu Mining Corporation 100n
Basuto *see* Sotho
Basutoland *see* Lesotho
Biko, S. 130
Black Consciousness 41, 87, 130-1, 134, 225
Black Peoples' Convention (BPC) 130-1, 139, 228
Boer War *see* South African War of 1899-1902
BophuthaTswana 66
Botha, L. 15, 20, 57, 124
Botha, P. W. 97-8, 112, 135, 211, 214, 302
Botha, R. F. 97, 121
Botswana 56, 180, 194, 230, 237
Broederbond 20, 116, 119, 121
Bunting, B. 226-7, 261
Bureau of State Security (BOSS) 204
Buthelezi, G. 75, 133-4
Byrd Amendment 254, 267n7

Cabinet 96, 302
Cachet, Lion 26
Cape route 187-91, 270, 279, 285, 292-3
Cape Town 8, 223
Carnegie Endowment for

307

International Peace 222
Carter, J. 276-7, 280
Catholics 132
censorship 301
chiefs 45-6, 57, 75-6, 124
choke points 200
churches
  race relations 132-3
civil disobedience 229
Coloured Development Corporation 172
Coloured Labour Party 41, 133-4, 138, 299
Coloured National People's Union 137
Coloured People's Party 138
Coloured Representative Council 130, 134, 137
Coloureds 33-8
  church 10-11
  demography 34
  education 37
  housing 37-8
  illegitimacy rate 35
  in Defence Force 214
  labour 30, 34, 42
  language 35
  origins 33
  politics 36, 115, 130, 136-7
  religion 10-11, 35, 42
  social condition 34-5, 37-40
Communist Party of South Africa see South African Communist Party
Congress of Democrats (COD) 125
consociation system 299-300
conventional war against South Africa 219-23
courts 96, 102-3
Cuba 197-9, 220, 239, 240n2, 274, 278, 280, 282

Dadoo, Y. 126, 227
demography
  common features of racial groups 1-4
  homelands 64
  population growth 2-3, 24, 48, 90n1, 175-6, 185n7
  urban 4, 67, 86
Diego Garcia 199, 202
Dube, J. 57, 124
Durban 77, 79
Dutch Reformed Church 19-20, 120, 130, 132
  see also under individual churches

ecology see agriculture, soil conservation
economy
  development 1867 to 1914 142-52
  development 1914 to 1945 152-62
  development 1945 to 1980 162-70
  future prospects 175-84
  gross domestic product 151, 161, 164, 168, 290
  incomes of racial groups 31
  labour statistics 30
  see also agriculture, banking, industry, mining, shipping
education
  Africans 54, 79, 185n13
  Coloureds 37-8
  universities 17, 37, 143-4
  whites 18, 25
Electricity Supply Commission (ESCOM) 170
embargoes see strategy, blockade
English-speaking South Africans
  economic rate 8-9, 24
  education 25
  origins 8-9
  politics 27-8, see also Progressive Party, South African Party, United Party
  race attitudes toward 25-6
  settlers 8-9
  urban 9
Episcopalians 132
Ethiopia 274-5, 281-2, 304

Federasie van Afrikaanse Kultuurvereniginge (FAK) 120-1
Federation of Rhodesia and Nyasaland 269
First, R. 126, 226-7, 261
Fischer, A. 126, 225
France 208-9
Freedom Charter 126, 139, 140n8
Frente de Libertação de Moçambique (FRELIMO) 127, 199

Gandhi, M. K. 41
Genootskap van Regte Afrikaners 10
Gereformeerde Kerk 11, 19n, 120
Germany 246, 252, 296
gold standard 106, 159
Gordimer, N. 29, 257, 301
Graaf, D. P. de V. 110

Index

Great Britain
  anti-South African lobbies 260-1
  policy toward South Africa 269-70
  pro-South African lobbies 251-2
  see also investments, Great Britain, trade, Great Britain
Great Trek 10-11
Group Areas Act 37, 90n8, 102n, 125, 138, 300
guerrilla war 221-2, 234-40, 241n16

health
  mines 150
Herstigte Nasionale Party (NHP) 105, 109, 113-14
Hertzog, A. 121
Hertzog, J. B. M. 15, 106, 119
homelands 60-77, 300
  agriculture, 64, 66, 68-9
  area 60-2
  bureaucracy 66
  communications 62
  Communist views 228
  criticism of 56-8, 65-6, 68-9, 73-7
  industries 68, 70-1
  international recognition 74, 77
  investments 68, 71-2
  land claims 75
  minerals 66, 72-3
  national income 72-3
  population 64, 67

Hottentots see Khoikoi
Huggins, G. M. (Lord Malvern) 135

immigration, white 3, 24-5, 32, 144, 251
Immorality Act 36, 300
Indian Ocean 197, 202
Indian Reform Party 41, 133, 299
Indians
  crime 39
  entrepreneurs 40
  labour 37-40
  languages 37
  politics 39, 41, 115, 130, see also Gandhi, M. K., Indian Reform Party
  social conditions 39-40
  urban population 40
Industrial Development Corporation (IDC) 100
industry

employment 29
  origins 17, 157-8
  Pretoria-Witwatersrand complex 2, see also investments, state corporations
  social effects 163-5, 296
  USA share 248
  World War II 159, 171
inflation 169, 233-4, 294
Inkatha Yen-kululeko Yesiwe 41, 133, 299
intellectuals
  views on South Africa 256-60
investments
  African attitudes toward 241n12
  decline in 1976 167
  growth 1965 to 1975 163
  state corporations 170-3
  statistics 161, 173, 184
  USA 247-9, 253-4, 271, 293-4, 297
ISCOR see South African Iron and Steel Corporation
Israel 27, 181, 184, 239

Javabu, T. 57
Jeugbond 119
Jews 25-9
Johannesburg 2, 79
  see also Pretoria-Witwatersrand complex, Soweto

Kaffir wars 50
Kaunda, K. 112
Kennedy, J. F. 270-1
Kenya 28, 165, 289
Khoikoi (Hottentots) 8
Kimberley 77
Kissinger, H. 273, 277
Koornhof, P. W. 98, 302
Kotane, M. 126, 227
Kubicek, R. V. 14

Labour Party (South African Labour Party) 108
Land and Agricultural Bank of South Africa 102
Leballo, P. K. 129, 227
Lesotho 52-3, 56, 180, 194-5, 230
Lessing, D. 29, 257
Lovedale 54
Lutuli (Luthuli), A. 125, 134

Malan, D. F. 21, 261
Malan, M. 97, 214

310 Index

Malawi 126
Mandela, N. 125, 134
manufacturing see industries
Maputo 220
Marks, S. 14
Matanzima, Kaiser D. 75
media attitudes on South Africa 258-9
Methodists 132
migrant labour see Africans, migrant labour
Milner, A. 12
minerals
  potential 178, 192-3
  world reserves 192-3, 195
Mines and Works Act of 1911 59
mining
  base minerals 169, 178-9, 192-3, 286
  coal 169, 178, 192, 230
  diamonds 11, 144-5, 178, 192
  gold 145-8, 152, 167, 177-9, 192, 230
  part of GDP 152
  profits 152
  role in South African war 14-15
  socioeconomic effects 149-52, 154-5
  uranium 179
Mixed Marriage Act 36, 300
Mosheshwe (Moshesh) 52-3
Movimento Popular de Libertação de Angola (MPLA) 127, 201, 221, 237, 274-5, 278
Mozambique 113, 127, 180, 195, 199, 220, 237, 279, 281, 283, 289, 304
Mugabe, R. G. 283-4, 304
Mulder, C. P. 28, 97
'Muldergate' scandal 98, 122, 303
municipal government 104

Namibia 28, 112, 115, 127, 194-5, 283
Natal 28, 298, 302-3
Natal Indian Congress 139
Natal Indian Council (NIC) 138
Natal Indian Organisation 138
National Association for the Advancement of Coloured People (NAACP) 248, 263-4
National Party
  and Afrikaners 19-21
  associated bodies 119-20
  development 1977 to 1979 110-14
  dissensions 121-2, 301-2
  in World War II 108
  organisation 118-19
  origins 20
  philosophy 116-17
  programme 22, 36, 109, 114-15, 118, 121-2
  social composition 20-2, 106, 110, 117-18, 301-2
  verkramptes 23, 110, 112, 120, 277, 303
  verligtes 23, 110, 112, 115, 119-20, 277
National Union of South African Students (NUSAS) 130
Native Land Act, 1913 57
Nederduitsch Hervormde Kerk 19n, 120
Nederduitse Gereformeerde Kerk 19n, 120
neocolonialism 151, 162
New Republic Party 111, 113-14
Ngubane, J. K. 298, 303
Nigeria 113, 219, 240n1
Nixon, R. 272-3
Non-European Unity Movement 137
Nuclear Fuels Corporation of South Africa (NUCFOR) 170
nuclear power 170, 179, 217n10

oil supplies 188-91, 206, 217n11, 279, 285, 295
Oppenheimer, H., 116, 297
Organisation of African Unity (OAU) 126, 130

Pan Africanist Congress (PAC) 127, 129, 134, 227-8
Parliament 95-6
Paton, A. 29
platinum 66
police 214-17, 233, 235-6, 238-9, 300
population see demography
Population Registration Act 36
port facilities 187, 189
Portugal 272-5
press, 25, 259, 267-8n13
Pretoria-Witwatersrand complex, Soweto 2, 175, 223
Prime Minister
  functions 96-7, 204-5
Progressive Party
  composition 27, 110
  elections 1961 to 1974 111

Index

official opposition 1977 113
  programme 114
provincial governments 103
public enterprise *see* state
  corporations
public services 99-100, 109

race relations
  African attitudes 87-9, 131-2
  apartheid legislation 35-8, 81, 87,
    90n8, 102n, 231, 298, 300,
    304, *see also under individual
    laws*
  churches 132-3
  cities 18-19, 47-149, 233, *see also*
    Soweto, urban Africans
  Coloureds 10-11, 25, 35-6, 38,
    87, 132-3, 187
  consociation 299-300
  early black/white contacts 7-9,
    13, 52-3
  Indians 25, 40-1, 139-40
  industries 16, 22, 59, 162, 165,173
  land segregation 55-9, 298-300,
    see also homelands
  literature 29
  mining 10-11, 106, 146-7, 149
  religion 10-11
  slavery 60, 142-3
  USA and South Africa compared
    7, 13, 33, 55-6, 60, 87, 143,
    149
  white attitudes 121-2
railways 150, 171
Reserve Bank of South Africa 102,
  159
reserves *see* homelands
revolution
  prospects for 224-34, 288, 290-1
Retief, P. 9
Rhodes, C. J. 14, 135
Rhodesia *see* Zimbabwe
Richards Bay 170, 175

Saldanha Bay 170, 175
Sempala, S. 83-4
Separate Amenities Act 37
Separate Representation of Voters
  Act 37
Shaka 50-1
Sharpeville rioting 162, 233
shipping 187-91
Simonstown 201, 269-70
slavery 8, 60, 142-3
Smith, I. 283

Smuts, J. C. 15, 106, 116, 137, 269
Sobukwe, R. 227
soil conservation *see* agriculture, soil
  conservation
Sotho 51-3
South Africa Foundation 115, 255
South African Black Alliance (SABA)
  133-4
South African Bureau of Race Affairs
  112
South African Christian Leadership
  Conference 121
South African Coal, Oil and Gas
  Corporation (SASOL) 102, 170,
  172
South African Communist Party
  (SACP) 125-6, 226-9, 260
South African Congress Alliance 125
South African Congress of Trade
  Unions (SACTU) 128
South African Defence Force 97
  air arm 208-9
  army 211-14, 222
  equipment 209-10
  expenditure 207
  navy 101-3
  officers 212-13
  organisation 210-14, 235
South African Indian Congress
  (SAIC) 125
South African Indian Council 139
South African Iron and Steel
  Corporation (ISCOR) 100, 102,
  106, 159-60, 170
South African Party 110, 113
South African Students' Organisation
  (SASO) 130, 139, 228
South African War of 1899-1902
  13-15, 54
South-West Africa *see* Namibia
South-West African Peoples'
  Organisation (SWAPO) 127
Soweto 79, 81-7
  rioting 230-3
state corporations 100-3, 170-5
  employment 101
  expenditure 101
State Security Council 204-5
strategy
  blockade 223, 240n3, 295
  South African role 187-202, 204,
    292-3
  see also conventional war,
    guerrilla war
Strijdom, J. G. 119

312 Index

strikes and revolution 229-30
Sullivan Code 250
Supreme Court 103n
Swaziland 56, 180, 194

Tambo, O. R. 125, 128
Tanzania 113
Theron Commission 36
trade
  and trekker economy 7, 49-50
  foreign 183, 191, 246, 249-50
  Germany 246
  Great Britain 246
  USA 249-50, 271
Transkei 60-2, 73, 230, 302
Transkei Development Corporation 71-2
trekboer 6-7, 49-50
Treurnicht, A. P. 98, 302-3
tribalism 47n

Umkhonto we Sizwe 127
União Nacional para a Independência Total de Angola (UNITA) 221, 274
Union of South Africa
  formation 15, 95
United Party
  composition 20-1, 118
  election 1910 to 1974 111
  programme 107
Unity Movement of South Africa (UMSA) 130
urban Africans
  age and sex distribution 85-6
  crime 77, 88
  grievances 88-9, 131-2
  health 87
  housing 78, 80-3, 173
  occupations 86
  origins 77-80
  population 4, 67
  unemployment 167, 241n12, 289, 295
  wages 84-5, 90n13, 165-6, 168, 250, 291, 296
Urban Foundation 80
urban terrorism 238-9
USA
  academics' views on South Africa 264-5
  anti-South African lobbies 261-7
  black views on South Africa 262-3
  Department of State 265-7, 272
  navy 197-200, 217n1, 220

  policy toward South Africa 270-1, 276-80, 286, 304
  pro-South African lobbies 253-6, *see also* investments, USA, trade, USA
  South African propaganda in 267n9
USSR
  armed forces 28
  navy 196-8, 200, 217n1
  policy in Africa 271-2, 274-5, 280-1
  world strategy 196-9, 285-6, 293

van den Berghe, P. 162-3
Verwoerd, H. F. 117, 119
Viljoen, G. 121
voortrekkers see Great Trek, *trekboer*
Vorster, B. J. 97-8, 112, 115, 122

Warneck, G. 11
Washington, B. T. 247
Wassenaar, A. 174-5
water supplies 180-1, 185
whites
  English-speakers 24-31
  historical background 5-11
  illegitimacy rate 35
  impact of Boer War 13-16
  in modern times 16-19, *see also* Afrikaners, English-speakers, Jews
  urban population 4
Wiehahn Commission 169, 300
Witwatersrand 12
  rising 1922 105-6, 224-5
  see also Pretoria-Johannesburg complex
World Council of Churches 129, 264
World War II
  South Africa 187, 222, 257

Xhosa 22, 122, 302

Young, A. 276-7, 280

Zaïre 219, 289-90
Zambia 126, 180, 258, 304
Zimbabwe 112, 180, 194, 221, 236, 239, 240n4
Zimbabwe African National Union (ZANU) 236, 283-4
Zimbabwe African Peoples' Union (ZAPU) 127, 284
Zionism 27
Zulu 22, 122, 302
  military organisation 50-1
  see also Inkatha movement

For Product Safety Concerns and Information please contact our EU
representative GPSR@taylorandfrancis.com
Taylor & Francis Verlag GmbH, Kaufingerstraße 24, 80331 München, Germany

www.ingramcontent.com/pod-product-compliance
Lightning Source LLC
Chambersburg PA
CBHW071801300426
44116CB00009B/1170